D1566196

"Tell Mother Not to Worry"

Soldier Stories From Gettysburg's George Spangler Farm

Ronald D. Kirkwood

SB

Savas Beatie
California

First edition, first printing

ISBN-13: 978-1-61121-706-3 (hardcover)
ISBN-13: 978-1-61121-707-0 (ebook)

Library of Congress Cataloging-in-Publication Data

Names: Kirkwood, Ronald D., 1955- author.
Title: "Tell Mother Not to Worry": Soldier Stories From Gettysburg's
    George Spangler Farm / by Ronald D. Kirkwood.
Other titles: Soldier stories from Gettysburg's George Spangler farm
Description: El Dorado Hills, CA : Savas Beatie, 2024. | Includes
    bibliographical references and index. | Summary: "The George Spangler
    farm in Gettysburg is a place of reverence. This book profiles scores of
    additional soldiers and offers new information on events and experiences
    at the farm. While also completing the story of George and Elizabeth
    Spangler's historic farm, it provides a deeper and richer understanding
    of what these men and women endured-suffering that often lingered for
    the rest of their lives"-- Provided by publisher.
Identifiers: LCCN 2024000164 | ISBN 9781611217063 (hardcover) | ISBN
    9781611217070 (ebook)
Subjects: LCSH: Gettysburg, Battle of, Gettysburg, Pa., 1863. | United
    States--History--Civil War, 1861-1865--Hospitals. | George Spangler Farm
    & Field Hospital (Gettysburg, Pa.) | Gettysburg, Battle of, Gettysburg,
    Pa., 1863--Personal narratives. | Soldiers--United States--Biography. |
    United States. Army of the Potomac. Corps, 11th. | United
    States--History--Civil War, 1861-1865--Medical care. | Military
    hospitals--Pennsylvania--Gettysburg Region--History--19th century. |
    Farms--Pennsylvania--Gettysburg Region--History--19th century. |
    Spangler family.
Classification: LCC E475.53 .K573 2024 | DDC 973.7/81--dc23/eng/20240228
LC record available at https://lccn.loc.gov/2024000164

SB
Savas Beatie
989 Governor Drive, Suite 102
El Dorado Hills, CA 95762
916-941-6896 / sales@savasbeatie.com / www.savasbeatie.com

All of our titles are available at special discount rates for bulk purchases in the United States. Contact us for information.

Maps by Derek Wachter

Printed and bound in the United Kingdom

For Barb.

"The amputation work under an open shed presented the most ghastly sights that could be witnessed."

— *XI Corps hospital worker William R. Kiefer, 153rd Pennsylvania*

George and Elizabeth Spangler had this photo taken in 1862 or 1863 at the studio of portrait photographer John S. Speights on West Middle Street in Gettysburg. The photo was provided by their 2X great-grandson Maurice Spangler. Maurice is a native of Kansas and a great-grandson of George and Elizabeth's son Daniel, who had prints of the photo made in the 1890s by photographer A. M. Hartung in Enterprise, Kansas.

Table of Contents

Table of Contents (continued)

Maps, photos, and illustrations have been interspersed throughout
the manuscript for the convenience of the reader.

Foreword

The George Spangler land is tucked into its own unique corner of the sprawling Gettysburg landscape. Most battlefield visitors have never heard of the farm, let alone seen it. And that's a shame, because it is not only one of the most fascinating places on the entire field, but a haunting one. To know its history is to know its pain.

The fact that it exists today for us to see and ponder is the result of the tireless work of many people and organizations who toiled for years to save the farm, its dilapidated buildings, and its history, including the late Gettysburg hospital expert Gregory Coco and historians Kathleen Georg Harrison and Wayne Motts. In 2008, the Gettysburg Foundation bought 80 acres of this precious land within the wide V formed by Granite Schoolhouse Lane and Blacksmith Shop Road. The National Park Service, Adams County Historical Society, Keystone Preservation Group Inc., and LSC Design Inc. stepped in to help by preserving and interpreting the Spangler experience.

Author Ronald Kirkwood stands on their shoulders. After years of volunteer work at the site followed by the lonely work of researching and writing, he offered forth *"Too Much for Human Endurance": The George Spangler Farm Hospitals and the Battle of Gettysburg* (Savas Beatie, 2019). Its release added color and texture to the entire Spangler landscape by introducing untold numbers of people to what happened there. Ron based his study on a stunning collection of primary source accounts. This archival jigsaw puzzle put together, piece by painstaking piece, the story of the XI Corps field hospital complex and the mélange of people who suffered in horrific agony there, comforted by those who did all they could to alleviate the anguish of the unfortunate.

The character cast is indelible. War found George and Elizabeth Spangler and their four children when a Union officer decided their land was needed for the Army of the Potomac's Artillery Reserve. Its 106 guns, supported by hundreds of wagons and more than 2,000 men and as many horses inundated the once-tranquil landscape. The family remained on the farm throughout the fighting and thereafter, an experience that remained with them for the rest of their lives.

Among the Union wounded was a 42-year-old private named George Nixon III, whose descendant would one day become president of the United States. George was mortally wounded on the evening of July 2 with two rounds in his right side. He died days later on the Spangler farm, leaving a widow and nine children behind.

The most famous of the Confederates treated at the XI Corps hospital was Brig. Gen. Lewis Armistead, who with his hat on his sword tip crossed the stone wall into the Angle during "Pickett's Charge" before being hit. His curious death, explored in fascinating detail in *"Too Much for Human Endurance,"* warrants a second look within these pages with additional information undiscovered when the first book went to press.

One of the leading roles was played by Dr. James A. Armstrong of the 75th Pennsylvania, who served as the hospital's surgeon-in-chief. The man and hour met on those bloody acres. Armstrong treated hundreds of maimed men, authorized the Christian Commission permission to scrounge the town for lumber to keep the Spangler patients out of the mud, detailed a Buckeye musician to bury the dead and record their names, and ultimately signed off on whether an injured soldier was sufficiently fit to return to duty.

Rebecca Price was an unworldly 25-year-old when she stepped out of her normal life and into that slice of Hell. She served as a nurse to hundreds of young men clinging to life, writing their letters, bathing their faces, and holding their hands as they died. She could still see their faces and hear their voices more than a quarter-century later when she confided to her children, "Why even now . . . it makes me heart-sick to think of it."

"Too Much for Human Endurance" is one of those rare publications that reaches into the past to resurrect a cast of characters long gone, and into the present with a fresh set of actors, most of whom had no idea they were part of the Spangler story. Ron's dive into the family's genealogy uncovered scores of descendants—so many with so much interest that they even held their own Descendants Day gathering on the old Spangler farm. It is rare events like these that make writing a book worthwhile. The whole is greater than the sum of the parts.

Each page of Ron's first book drove home the devastation wrought by lead and iron, the agony suffered on those acres, and the lives forever changed and lost there. To read his book is to see Gettysburg in an entirely different light. He thought he was finished with the Spangler saga—"One and done," as he often explained. But the pull of history wasn't finished with him yet.

"Tell Mother Not to Worry": Soldier Stories From Gettysburg's George Spangler Farm continues where *"Too Much for Human Endurance"* left off, while also doubling back on itself. Readers will delight in being introduced to soldiers and medical personnel whose stories were not shared in the first book. Other chapters circle around to flesh out added details (like those surrounding General Armistead) and add fresh stories and personalities that, so to speak, ended up on the cutting room floor during Round One.

If I shared much more, I would need to post a "spoiler alert." Turn the pages and enjoy.

*   *   *

I accepted Ron's first book, collaborated with him on its edits, and published it to strong success all without ever having met him. In fact, several years passed before I was able to shake his hand, a wonderful event that transpired on the Spangler property within the shadow of the old stone house. It was there Ron told me, mostly in passing, that he was "thinking of a follow-up book." I assured him that I was interested. Months passed without anything more, and I thought it was something he had put to the side.

I was wrong, and happily so.

Theodore P. Savas
Publisher

Introduction

I either planned nor considered a second book on the George Spangler farm. This was going to be one and done.

After *"Too Much for Human Endurance"* was published in May 2019 I spent two years writing magazine stories and giving talks on a variety of topics related to the farm: an overview presentation, Civil War-era medicine, the women who came to the rescue at Spangler, Granite Schoolhouse, and the military importance of the farm. Even during the height of the pandemic, I put on a mask and flew as far as Texas and Wisconsin and drove from Pennsylvania to Chicago, Fort Wayne, upstate New York, and Michigan for socially distanced talks. Counting pandemic-required Zoom presentations, interest in this special farm was such that Book 1 kept me busy throughout 14 states.

Then there were the Spangler descendants. I often wondered while writing *"Too Much for Human Endurance"* who was out there and what they knew. Did Spangler descendants know they were connected to this place? So I spent several months doing Spangler genealogy and found more than 100 of them, and it turns out about 95 percent of them had no idea they were descended from this historic farm, including those who grew up just down the road from it. But once they were informed, they became enormously proud. We held a Descendants Day gathering at the farm in 2022 with 65 direct descendants of George and Elizabeth Spangler in attendance, from nearby Adams County but also as far away as California, Vermont, Illinois, Kansas, and South Carolina. Today, they are fully invested, dedicated descendants.

Descendants ended up playing a key role in this sequel and the story of the farm, particularly descendants of George and Elizabeth's son Daniel, who moved away to Kansas and built his life on the frontier. Daniel's grandson, Norman

Spangler of Kansas, told me stories that were passed down to him through his father, George (Gettysburg George's grandson), some of which I use in the Spangler family chapter of this book. Daniel's great-grandson, Maurice Spangler of Kansas and now South Carolina, knew I was searching for a photo of George and Elizabeth and walked up to me at Descendants Day and handed me a photo of them and calmly asked if that's what I was looking for. I gasped and gave him a big, tight hug. We now all know exactly what George and Elizabeth looked like thanks to their 2X great-grandson Maurice. And once I tracked down where Daniel lived in a sod dugout in western Kansas before moving east to the town of Enterprise, Kansas, Maurice's brother, Calvin Spangler, drove across the state and met with the current landowner and took photos of the site. Calvin now travels from Kansas to Gettysburg and his family's farm once a year, bringing his son, Duncan, the 3X great-grandson of George and Elizabeth.

So I was plenty busy and grateful. And then Christopher Philip DiElsi of Ridgefield, CT, and author and historian Carolyn Ivanoff of Gettysburg and Seymour, CT, told me about Spangler hospital worker Pvt. James R. Middlebrook of the 17th Connecticut, whose story I didn't have in Book 1. That prompted two days of research at the Connecticut Historical Society in Hartford, and now an entire chapter in this book focuses on Middlebrook.

And then George Spangler Farm & Field Hospital guide and researcher extraordinaire Jim Fielden of Cleveland gently nudged me by sending medical records and pensions of some of the XI Corps hospital patients that he found interesting, prompting 17 days of research at the National Archives and Records Administration in Washington, D.C., to go through pension files, Volunteer Carded Medical Records, Compiled Military Service Records, registers with wounded lists, and surgeon folders.

I was fully invested in the need for a Spangler sequel at this point with the encouragement and patient nudging of Christopher, Carolyn, and Jim. Mixed in with the 17 days in D.C. were seven days of research at the U.S. Army Heritage & Education Center in Carlisle, PA, five days at the Gettysburg National Military Park archives, three days each at the beautiful new Adams County Historical Society building, the New York Public Library, and the National Museum of Civil War Medicine in Frederick, MD, plus single days at Notre Dame Hesburgh Libraries in South Bend, Landis Valley Village & Farm Museum in Lancaster County, PA, the Historical Society of Pennsylvania in Philadelphia, New York State Library Archives in Albany, Easton (PA) Public Library, and the Gettysburg Foundation's Finfrock Cottage library. Electronic research took me virtually to Kansas for the Spangler chapter, Missouri for the chapter on Confederate Brig. Gen. Lewis Armistead, and all over the country on the ever-handy Internet.

In addition, publisher Ted Savas used to jokingly/not jokingly threaten to break my first book into two if I kept sending him material, so I had good stuff left over that either got cut or abbreviated in *"Too Much for Human Endurance"* because of space concerns. For example, the stories of eight men from the 154th New York in one tent at Spangler—five of whom died—got squished into two paragraphs in Book 1. In Book 2, this tent of suffering has three chapters devoted to it. Now I can tell their dramatic stories in detail. This book gives me room to run. Now I can focus on the stories of the ordinary soldiers at Spangler.

For me, one of the most important parts of this book is not only the stories of the wounded and dying men at Spangler but also the suffering of mothers, wives, and children left behind. Just about everything that happened at Spangler impacted a loved one back home. Many stories of loved ones are told here along with the soldiers' stories after they left Spangler. An amputation might have saved a soldier's life, but it didn't end his suffering. That lasted until he died. Many of these men weren't well when they arrived in Gettysburg anyway, with often-deadly chronic diarrhea inflicted by the Army lifestyle and poor diet being the main complaint. Reading their pension files at the Archives in their own words opens your eyes to suffering that often lasted decades. Reading the pension applications of someone left destitute by the death of their son or husband at Spangler, one can only feel compassion and sympathy as they beg for and sometimes demand financial assistance from the government to ease their pain. These soldiers and their family members lived through a kind of suffering and debilitation that most of us today can never imagine or understand, and hopefully this book adequately describes their burden.

This book also continues to describe sad and gory scenes and smells at the XI Corps and 1st Division, II Corps hospitals on Spangler land. One soldier who had an arm amputated before arriving at Spangler describes what it felt like to wake up during that amputation when the chloroform wore off. New information is added to familiar faces such as Armistead, Capt. Fred Stowe, Henry Van Aernam, Marilla Hovey, and the men of the Artillery Reserve. Dozens of new stories retell both the suffering and the courage of surgeons, chaplains, ambulance drivers, the wounded, the dying, and the Spanglers themselves. Two chapters reveal the seemingly always-ignored Granite Schoolhouse hospital and a chapter is devoted to events on the Spanglers' Powers Hill, another location that usually receives little attention. More wounded and dead have been added to the XI Corps hospital's count and there's a partial wounded list for the First Division of the II Corps in this book. I'm particularly pleased that the last chapter of the book is devoted to George and Elizabeth's descendants, whom I happily now claim as friends. Deliberately, little was repeated from the first book in this one, other than to extend or continue the original story.

This book is aided greatly by the contributions of experts from across the country. If there was a medical condition that I didn't understand or if I felt the reader would benefit from a more detailed look at something, such as the hay trolley in the Spanglers' barn, then I asked for professional help, and in every single case I received that help in a timely, friendly, and encouraging manner.

Little did I know after writing *"Too Much for Human Endurance"* that there was still so much more to tell about what happened at George Spangler's farm. Little did I know that I still had so much more to learn. Research for this book has taught me that. I do know, though, that we'll never get the full story of this farm. We'll never know it all. But this book gets us closer to that elusive full picture. And by telling the stories of this place and its soldiers and their family members during and after the battle, we also are telling the stories of what happened at other hospitals throughout the Civil War.

My Spangler infatuation started in 2013 in my early days as a Gettysburg Foundation volunteer when Volunteer Coordinator Ray Matlock told me that the Foundation was opening the George Spangler farm to the public and he asked if I would be interested in being a guide out there. I said sure, but what's the George Spangler farm? I was hooked quickly once I got out there, and that beginning with Ray—as inauspicious as it was—led me to begin research on the farm in 2016 with the full intent of writing a book. Since then, George and Elizabeth and their farm have become my full-time job in retirement. If I'm not researching it I'm writing about it or I'm telling stories about it or leading tours there. It's a part of me now, a labor of love, and for that I couldn't be more grateful. It's been a wonderful adventure and a high privilege. And really, I have Ray Matlock to thank for that.

Barring a dramatic discovery of some kind, this book ends my eight years of George Spangler farm research and book work. But I'm glad now that I decided to do a second book and that the story is being continued. And I'm grateful to Christopher, Carolyn, and Jim for planting the seeds. I'm glad now that it didn't turn out to be one and done after all.

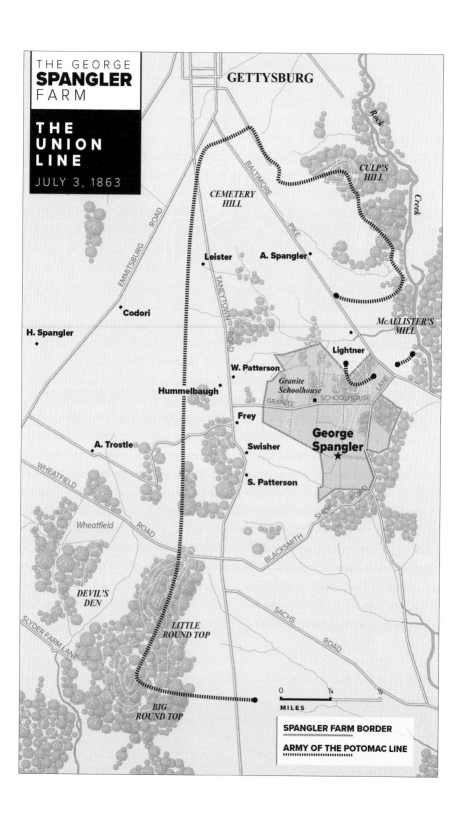

THE GEORGE
SPANGLER
FARM

**THE
UNION
LINE**

JULY 3, 1863

GETTYSBURG

CULP'S
HILL

Rock

Creek

BALTIMORE

PIKE

CEMETERY
HILL

EMMITSBURG ROAD

TANEYTOWN ROAD

Leister

A. Spangler

Codori

H. Spangler

McALLISTER'S
MILL

Lightner

W. Patterson

Granite
Schoolhouse

GRANITE

SCHOOLHOUSE

LANE

Hummelbaugh

Frey

George
Spangler
★

A. Trostle

Swisher

S. Patterson

SHOP ROAD

WHEATFIELD

Wheatfield

ROAD

BLACKSMITH

DEVIL'S
DEN

SACHS

ROAD

SLYDER FARM LANE

LITTLE
ROUND TOP

BIG
ROUND TOP

0   ¼   ½

MILES

SPANGLER FARM BORDER

ARMY OF THE POTOMAC LINE

Chapter 1

Was Armistead Treated
Unkindly at Spangler?

"[Armistead] often begged that he might be moved from the door but was not."

— *First Lieutenant Thomas C. Holland, 28th Virginia, on Confederate Brig. Gen. Lewis Armistead's placement in George and Elizabeth Spangler's summer kitchen*

A step into the Spanglers' summer kitchen is a step back in time. The white plaster walls with the black soot are original and attest to the smokiness of 19th-century cooking. The fireplace stone is original as installed by George and Elizabeth Spangler, as is the severely charred wood immediately outside the fireplace, which becomes less charred the farther you step away from the intensity of another era's fires. More than 90 percent of the sturdy, well-made window panes in the summer kitchen have stood the test of time, and the wood ceiling is original. Only the floor is new because it was collapsing, but the Gettysburg Foundation used a similar color to the original when rehabbing the building.

Those sooted walls, that fireplace, that charred wood, that ceiling, and those marked window panes have all borne witness to the XI Corps hospital that occupied this property from July 1 to August 6, 1863. They were there when Confederate Brig. Gen. Lewis Armistead and Army of the Potomac Capt. Frederick Stowe occupied that little room. Today, thanks to the Gettysburg Foundation's rehabilitation of the farm and these features' survival through many generations and many farm owners since the Spanglers, we can see what Armistead and Stowe saw as they lay in there. It seems it really is possible to go back in time in this summer kitchen.

And now, thanks to new research relating to Armistead, we can even see his approximate view in the building because we now know that his place of death on July 5, 1863, was on the floor directly in front of the door inside the summer kitchen.

Confederate Brig. Gen. Lewis A. Armistead
Gettysburg National Military Park

The house served as the VIP wing for the XI Corps hospital and there wasn't much room. Only Union officers with the rank of colonel or above were treated in the small two-bedroom, two-story house, and the Spangler family of six occupied one of those bedrooms. That left the little summer kitchen for those considered the next most important wounded, which would be Armistead and Stowe, the son of well-known abolitionist author Harriet Beecher Stowe of *Uncle Tom's Cabin* fame. Armistead was placed in the summer kitchen because of the hospital staff's respect for him and his rank, even though he fought for the enemy. Combined with Stowe, that 12-foot by 17-foot space hosted two of the best-known names in the hospital.

Stowe arrived before Armistead on July 3 and likely was placed along the north wall inside the summer kitchen beneath the two windows and in front of the Spanglers' large fireplace. Anything of the Spanglers' worth eating or using would have by then been removed from the kitchen by the food- and supply-starved hospital staff and replaced by hospital goods. Protected storage space was hard to come by. That meant there would not have been much space for Armistead, which is why he was placed literally in front of the door on the kitchen's south side opposite Stowe.

Estimates on what time Armistead arrived at Spangler vary. Dr. Daniel G. Brinton said 4 p.m. and Dr. Henry Van Aernam said dusk (about 8 p.m. in 1863 in the era before daylight saving time). Both surgeons said they were among Armistead's two or three primary caregivers. First Lieutenant Thomas C. Holland of the 28th Virginia, Brig. Gen. Richard B. Garnett's brigade, was one of the few Confederates still standing and fighting who followed Armistead across the stone wall at the end of Pickett's Charge on the afternoon of July 3. Like Armistead, the 23-year-old Holland was struck down, taking a Minie ball that entered his left cheek and exited through the back of his neck. Also like Armistead, he was taken to Spangler. "I was a little to his [Armistead's] left and had passed only a few

The Spanglers' summer kitchen today. *Ron Kirkwood*

paces when I fell, unconscious as to what was going on," he recalled later. "During that afternoon General Armistead and myself, and quite a number of officers were removed to the temporary hospital over beyond Cemetery Heights." Holland said his ambulance was directed to Spangler by an ambulance officer or surgeon.[1]

The solid wood summer kitchen door probably was taken down soon after the Spanglers' farm was seized for the hospital on July 1 because it was the perfect size and weight for an operating table. If not an operating table, there were plenty of other uses for that door in that hospital, even if only for firewood. Armistead's head and upper body lay close to or in front of where the wood door once stood, meaning he possibly had a view of the Spanglers' front yard and access to fresh air. But this also meant every single hospital staffer entering the little room had to step over him. Holland paid particular attention to the eminent Confederate officer.

"I have omitted one cruel act done by the Enemy and it's almost too sad to dwell on at all," Holland wrote in his journal after the war. "Brig. Gen. Armistead was badly wounded in arm & leg about the same time I was and taken to the 11th

---

1 Interview of Van Aernam, Aug. 4, 1890, Edwin Dwight Northrup Papers, Box 35, Carl A. Kroch Library, Cornell University; David L. Ladd and Audrey J. Ladd, *The Bachelder Papers: Gettysburg in Their Own Words, Jan. 5, 1863 to July 27, 1880*, Vol. 1 (Dayton, OH, 1994), 358. Brinton told Bingham, "I am obliged to depend on my memory, as I kept no notes of the wounded I treated"; Holland, "With Armistead at Gettysburg," *Confederate Veteran Magazine* 29 (February 1921): 62.

Corps Hospital where he laid across a door that every person had to step over. Being exposed in this way & an excitable man besides he was so distressed & so uneasy that he finally died. He often begged that he might be moved from the door but was not."[2]

Holland remembered Armistead telling XI Corps doctors and staff to "please don't step so close to me" as he lay on a cot in the shade of Spangler trees after his arrival, but it seems logical with this new information about Armistead's placement and discomfort by the summer kitchen door that he could have said it there.[3]

Holland said he witnessed Armistead's burial at Spangler and provided his rank for the inscription on the piece of wood used to mark his grave. He said Armistead's remains were placed "in a rough box" and buried. A Philadelphia embalmer had Armistead's body exhumed within a month of his burial, embalmed him, had him reburied, and notified Armistead's relatives in Baltimore that they could have his body for $125, or about $3,000 today. Included for the $125 was a "common outside case" with "a zinc coffin sealed" inside. The zinc blocked air flow and greatly reduced the speed of decomposition. Armistead's relatives paid up and had his body exhumed again and shipped to Baltimore in October 1863, where he now rests downtown in Old St. Paul's Cemetery on busy Martin Luther King Jr. Boulevard, only five or six blocks from modern-day Oriole Park at Camden Yards.[4]

Holland's criticism of the treatment of someone at Spangler who would evolve after death into a beloved Confederate symbol is understandable but perhaps not entirely fair. Armistead was given special treatment befitting his rank with placement in the summer kitchen and was cared for by multiple XI Corps surgeons. While most wounded at the farm on July 3 suffered in the filthy and cramped barn or in open fields without tents when the thunderstorms hit, Armistead remained dry, closely monitored, and enjoyed the respect of his attending doctors and nurses.

What absolutely cannot be disputed is the importance of Holland's observations of Armistead's placement and treatment at Spangler and their discovery in 2022 in relation to Spangler nearly 160 years after the battle. For that, we owe much gratitude to Thomas C. Holland. His story prior to his arrival at Spangler, at Spangler, and for years afterward is also worthy of note, and part of it was even honored for decades with a marker on the Gettysburg battlefield.

---

2 Journal of Thomas C. Holland, provided by the Kingdom of Callaway Historical Society in Fulton, MO. Journal provided by the Gary Altheiser family.

3 Holland, "With Armistead at Gettysburg," *Confederate Veteran* 29, 62.

4 Journal of Thomas C. Holland; www.in2013dollars.com/1860-dollars-in-2017?amount=125, accessed March 7, 2023; Gettysburg Field Hospital Research #5, Surgeons, US and CS, Surgeons, Civilian, Box B72-2, Folder B-72-2-250 Dr. J. W. C. O'Neal, Gregory A. Coco Collection, Gettysburg National Military Park Archives (hereafter "GNMP").

Confederate 1st Lt. Thomas C. Holland
"The Hollands and Their Kin: History and Heritage,"
by Isham C. Holland, and Kingdom of Callaway
Historical Society (Fulton, MO)

Holland was shot through both thighs at Gaines Mill on June 27, 1862, and left on the field presumed dead for a day. He was eventually picked up and recuperated for four months before returning to his unit in time for the fight at Gettysburg.[5]

Of Gettysburg and Pickett's Charge, he remembered, "I advanced about 10 paces farther" than Armistead after crossing the stone wall on July 3 until being knocked out by a Minie ball that entered his left cheek, broke his jaw, and exited the right side of the back of his neck. He was taken to the Army of the Potomac XI Corps hospital, where he was treated during his entire stay at Spangler by 54th New York surgeon Charles W. Hagen. Holland said, "I was treated kindly by him as long as I remained at Gettysburg."[6]

Holland called his wound "a very bad one and in a very dangerous place [face & neck]" but in typical minimizing fashion it was called a "flesh wound" with treatment by "water dressing," as noted in the XI Corps hospital register.[7]

Holland was transferred from Spangler to Baltimore on July 12 and was also treated and held in Philadelphia, Davids Island in Long Island Sound outside of New York City, and Johnson's Island in Lake Erie near Sandusky, Ohio, before being exchanged in March 1865. A part of his jawbone was cut out and buried at Davids Island. After the war he moved from Lynchburg, Virginia, to Callaway County, Missouri, where he went to college, taught school, ran a successful business, and raised a family.[8]

5 From a family history written by the Rev. I. C. Holland, the grandson of T. C. Holland, provided by the Kingdom of Callaway Historical Society in Missouri (hereafter "Holland family history").

6 Holland journal.

7 Ibid.

8 Holland family history.

Holland returned to Gettysburg for the 50-year anniversary of the battle in 1913 and the National Park Service featured him on the now-removed "Lee's Shattered Army" marker near the Virginia monument. He reflected on a moving anecdote that happened at the anniversary: "While at the peace meeting in Gettysburg in 1913, standing where General Armistead fell, a man and his wife approached the spot where I fell just fifty years before, this being to the left of where Armistead fell and some ten steps in advance, where I stuck a stick in the ground to indicate the place.

"The man proved to be a member of Cushing's Battery of Philadelphia, if I am not mistaken. He said to his wife, 'Here is where I killed the only Rebel I know of during the war. I may have killed others, but this is the only one I know I killed.' She said: 'It is too bad that you killed him.'

"At this I knew I was the one referred to, and I thought I would relieve his mind. So I said to him: 'I am the man you killed, but I am a pretty lively corpse.' He stepped back, and I saw he was shocked, so I said: 'Here is where the ball entered my left cheek, and here is where it came out at the back of my head.'

"He then grasped my hand and inquired my name and gave me his. He introduced me to his wife, and they very insistently invited me to go over to the hotel where they were stopping and take dinner with them. But, owing to pressing business at the time, I could not go. I had been made adjutant general of Pickett's Division for the bogus charge and was pressed for time. However, this man and I began a correspondence and kept it up."[9]

Holland died at age 84 in Missouri in 1925, 62 years after crossing that wall and keeping a protective eye on the Confederate general as he lay in front of that door in the summer kitchen.

One Final Note

First Lieutenant Thomas C. Holland of the 28th Virginia was grateful for the care he received at Spangler from 34-year-old, German-born surgeon Charles W. Hagen of the 54th New York. Holland remembered, "I was treated kindly by him as long as I remained at Gettysburg." What Holland might not have known at the time, though, is Hagen became sick himself at Spangler.[10]

Lieutenant Colonel Hans Boebel of the 26th Wisconsin was shot twice in the right leg on July 1 and, in his words, spent "four days among the idiots in

9 Holland, "With Armistead at Gettysburg," *Confederate Veteran* 29, 62.

10 Holland journal.

the County Poor House near Gettysburg." His wounds went untreated, and an ambulance picked him up and took him to Spangler on July 4, where Dr. Hagen amputated his leg that same day. Hagen, however, sliced his right index finger while examining Boebel's wounds and soon after developed blood poisoning, a common and deadly illness in Civil War hospitals. Blood poisoning is caused by bacteria entering the bloodstream, resulting in shivering, fever, fast heartbeat, rapid breathing, heart palpitations, low energy, confusion, and extreme pain. It can develop into sepsis, a life-threatening infection in the major organs.[11]

It's not known how long Hagen stayed at Spangler, but he was declared unfit for duty in August. He remained in the army until October 1864, but the illness still troubled him. He didn't practice from 1864 to 1872 because of it and received a pension due to "blood poisoning and its effects." He said in 1880, "I was [and am still in some degree] suffering from blood poisoning resulting from the examination of a gunshot wound through the knee joint of Hans Boebel." In 1888, a fellow surgeon testified that Hagen "was forced in consequence of ill health to give up his practice sometime ago and has been unable to leave the house for over three months." An examination in 1890 found him to be emaciated with sallow and clammy skin. The five-foot-ten-inch Hagen saw his weight drop from 185 pounds in 1881 to 140 in 1892.[12]

Hagen lived to age 80 despite suffering from ill health for most of his adult life after that finger slice at Spangler in 1863. He died of a stroke in 1909 in Newark, New Jersey. Like Hagen, Boebel was born in Germany. After Hagen saved his life with the amputation and post-surgical treatment in the Spanglers' house, Boebel went on to become a civic leader in Milwaukee and lived to age 73.[13]

Spangler Farm Short Story

By Richard D. Schroeder, M.D., LBG #166
and Francis P. Feyock, CRNA, LBG #104

The sudden death at Spangler of Confederate Brig. Gen. Lewis Armistead two days after what seemed to be survivable wounds requires consideration that a pulmonary embolism caused his death. An embolism is a blood clot that forms

---

11 F. J. F. Schantz, "Recollections of Visitations at Gettysburg After the Great Battle in July, 1863," in Ralph S. Shay, ed., *Reflections on the Battle of Gettysburg*, Vol. 13, no. 6 (Lebanon County, PA, 1963). "Recollections" is an address written by Schantz in 1890. The manuscript was provided by Agnes S. Haak and Mildred C. Haak, granddaughters of the Rev. Schantz; Charles W. Hagen Invalid Pension Claim 182065, National Archives and Records Administration, Washington, D.C. (hereafter "NARA"); www.familydoctor.org/condition/blood-poisoning/, accessed Jan. 21, 2023.

12 Hagen invalid pension claim, NARA.

13 Ibid; Ancestry.com.

elsewhere in the body, often in the veins in the legs, and then travels to other locations. An embolism lodges in a blood vessel and leads to the blockage of the blood vessel. A pulmonary embolism (PE) occurs when a blood clot that originated somewhere else in the body travels into the lungs and blocks the circulation through the lungs.

Blood clots form due to three reasons:

1) Slow blood flow. An example of this is when someone sits or lies down for a long period of time and doesn't move their legs to help with blood flow, as undoubtedly happened with Armistead.

2) Abnormalities in how blood normally clots can also result in abnormal formation of clots. Some diseases change the number of clotting cells.

3) Finally, an injury to the blood vessel wall could result in blood clot formation. Normal clotting of blood is an essential bodily function that prevents persistent bleeding. However, blood clots can form in abnormal circumstances and cause health problems.

Deep vein thrombosis (DVT) is a blood clot that forms in the deep veins of the body, usually in the legs, and is a common source of pulmonary embolism. One of the most common causes of DVT is inactivity and a lack of mobility. This occurs often after injury or surgery. Inactivity can cause blood to stagnate and pool within the body, especially the legs. As a clot develops, it can increase in size, break free in the leg veins, and travel to the lungs. As the clot, now a pulmonary embolism, increases in size, blood flow is obstructed to the lungs.

Decreased delivery of oxygen can cause many symptoms, including restlessness, confusion, and sudden unexpected death. Surgeon Henry Van Aernam of the 154th New York described Armistead as "wild nervous flighty" at Spangler and Confederate 1st Lt. Thomas C. Holland of the 28th Virginia said Armistead was "distressed" and "so uneasy" in the summer kitchen. Those descriptions could indicate Armistead suffered a lack of oxygen delivery.[14]

Armistead's wounds should not have been fatal. He was largely immobile while in the summer kitchen at the Spangler farm, which increased his risk of developing a pulmonary embolism. His surgeons were surprised by Armistead's sudden death. This death, given the injuries to his arm and leg and his lack of mobility, could be explained by a pulmonary embolism.

The normal function of the human body relies on the delivery of oxygen to the cells and the removal of carbon dioxide. This delivery and removal system is accomplished by the heart and lungs. The rhythmic patterns of breathing accompanied by the constant flow of blood produced by the heart accomplish this task with amazing efficiency over long periods of time.

---

14 Edwin Dwight Northrup interview of Henry Van Aernam, Aug. 4, 1890, in Edwin Dwight Northrup Papers, #4190, Box 35, Division of Rare and Manuscript Collections, Carl A. Kroch Library, Cornell University; Holland journal.

Armistead was placed at the door of the summer kitchen. *Ron Kirkwood*

However, this system has limited reserve for oxygen delivery and carbon dioxide removal. Human brain cells are susceptible to a loss of oxygen and begin to die within 4 minutes of the disruption of the supply. A pulmonary embolism can produce a sudden and catastrophic disruption in oxygen delivery to the human body.

DVT and PE remain significant concerns in modern medicine after injury or surgery, so aspirin and other blood thinners as well as devices such as compression stockings are prescribed to try to prevent their development. However, a small percentage of patients still develop PE and a very small number of people die from this complication. Given the state of medical knowledge in 1863, there is good reason to consider that Armistead died of a pulmonary embolism on the George Spangler farm.[15]

15 www.hopkinsmedicine.org/health/conditions-and-diseases/pulmonary-embolism, accessed December 2022.

Dr. Richard Schroeder practiced as an orthopedic surgeon with a specialty in orthopedic trauma for 33 years at a Level 1 trauma center in Johnstown, PA. He has been a Licensed Battlefield Guide at Gettysburg National Military Park since 2016. Francis P. Feyock is a retired Certified Registered Nurse Anesthetist, owner of 763 Leadership Group, and an adjunct faculty member for The Lincoln Leadership Institute at Gettysburg. He also has been a Gettysburg LBG since 2016.

Chapter 2

First Order of Business:
The Shell Fragment in Fred Stowe's Head

"You may imagine the anxiety with which we waited for news from you after the battle."
— *Harriet Beecher Stowe in a letter sent to her son at Gettysburg*[1]

Doctor Daniel G. Brinton could see the Confederate shell fragment encased in blood in Fred Stowe's head when the 23-year-old son of world-famous author Harriet Beecher Stowe arrived at the George Spangler farm on July 3. This was no glancing blow in which the fragment struck and fell to the ground. The fragment penetrated Stowe's head. Stowe, the assistant adjutant general for Brig. Gen. Adolph von Steinwehr (Second Division, XI Corps), took the direct hit while standing only a few feet from Von Steinwehr on Cemetery Hill during the cannonade prior to Pickett's Charge. Stowe must have been unconscious or squirming in agony or a combination of both after such a blow upon his arrival at the XI Corps hospital following a quick ambulance ride.

The fragment stretched from in front of Stowe's right ear to above and behind the ear. Doctors measured it at two to two-and-a-half inches in length and a quarter-inch wide, plenty big and violent enough to cause great damage to a human head. Stowe was chloroformed, and Brinton took out the fragment by the route it went in, "with difficulty through the orifice of entrance," a Spangler surgeon reported in Stowe's 1866 pension claim.[2]

Brinton told his mother in a letter home that Stowe had been hit "in the parastoid process of the temporal bone, by a fragment of shell which I extracted on

---

1 Harriet Beecher Stowe to Fred Stowe at Gettysburg, July 11, 1863, Sterling Library, Yale, New Haven, CT.

2 Frederick W. Stowe Invalid Pension Claim 69920, NARA.

Harriet Beecher Stowe

Library of Congress

July 3. Though I left him doing well, I am not without anxiety as to the result." The temporal bone protected Stowe's brain and undoubtedly saved his life.[3]

Stowe was loaded with painkillers and placed in the Spanglers' summer kitchen. Both he and the mortally wounded Confederate Brig. Gen. Armistead were undoubtedly in no condition or mood to converse when Armistead joined Stowe in that space later on July 3. Back home in Massachusetts, Mrs. Stowe and her husband—the Rev. Calvin Ellis Stowe, a respected scholar and theologian—knew nothing of Fred's status for days, an agony amplified for these parents of seven by the fact that they had already suffered devastating deaths of two children: Samuel at age 18 months in a cholera epidemic and Henry at 19 in a swimming accident.[4]

Happily, they saw a list on Page 3 of the July 6 *Lewiston* (Maine) *Sun Journal* that reported, though not entirely accurately, "The son of Professor Stowe is wounded in the head, but not dangerously." Then the Stowes heard from family friends and a nephew and later a Christian Commission agent at Spangler that Fred was recovering. Further family tragedy ensued, though, as related in Mrs. Stowe's letter to Fred in Gettysburg:

July 11, 1863

My Dear Fred.

You may imagine the anxiety with which we waited for news from you after the battle. The first we heard was on Monday morning from the paper, that you were wounded in the head. On hearing this your Father set off immediately to go to you and took the twelve o'clock train to Boston and the five o clock New York cars to go right on to Baltimore.

---

3 Brinton to his mother, July 9, 1863, in Dr. Daniel Garrison Brinton Papers, 1863-1899, Ms. Coll. 177, Chester County Historical Society Library, West Chester, PA.

4 www.harrietbeecherstowecenter.org/harriet-beecher-stowe/harriet-beecher-stowe-life, accessed Nov. 21, 2021; www.findagrave.com/memorial/92647337/henry-ellis_beecher-stowe, accessed Nov. 21, 2021.

Capt. Frederick Stowe

Harriet Beecher Stowe Center

Before he left Andover we got a telegraph from Robert [nephew Robert Edes Beecher] saying that you were wounded, but not dangerously and would be sent home in a few days.

At Springfield that night a gang of pick pockets hustled your father among them as he was getting out of the cars and took from him his pocket book containing 130 dollars and all the letters which your sisters and I wrote to you.

He went on to Baltimore and when he arrived there was so sick as to have to send for a Doctor who told him that he was going to be very sick and must go back immediately where he could be taken care of. He how ever saw a Mr Clark (uncle of one student Clark) who was going on to Gettysburg to attend to the wounded, and Gen H. Wilson, who both promised to look for you.

Several other friends also volunteered and Papa returned to Brooklyn where Jack Howard nursed him and this morning Saturday the 11th he is home and in bed—quite unwell but not so but what good news from you would revive him. Do get some one to write for you and tell us how to direct, and what we shall do for you. Do let us know when we may expect you. We have been looking for you every night all your sisters waiting at the cars. We <u>must</u> see you and return thanks together that your life is saved God bless you. At last you have helped win a glorious victory the cause is triumphant! God be thanked!

Your loving mother,

H B S

Mrs. Stowe added: "We have heard of you thro Mr. Wood and Miss Gillis. Why did you not write to us and send <u>us</u> your address instead of to them? We got it thro them or we should not be able to write now."[5]

---

5 Harriet Beecher Stowe to Fred Stowe, July 11, 1863, Sterling Library, Yale.

The Christian Commission agent replied for Fred that "He is quiet and cheerful, longs to see some member of his family, and is, above all, anxious that they should hear from him as soon as possible."[6]

Fred was transferred from Gettysburg to a New York City hospital in mid-July, but a full recovery would never come. Dr. Brinton wrote in November 1863 that, "I do hereby certify that I have carefully examined this officer and find that he is suffering from the sequelae [after-effects] of a shell wound of the mastoid process of right temporal bone, consisting in partial deafness of that side, chronic Inflammation of the mastoid cells, and occasional attacks of severe cerebral pain, exacerbated by exposure and fatigues, the wound having been received in the performance of his duty at the Battle of Gettysburg, July 3, 1863."[7]

The lingering effects of the injury would remain apparent. His brother, Charles, recalled "After weary months of intense suffering it [is] only imperfectly healed; the cruel iron had too nearly touched the brain of the young officer."[8]

A surgeon testified in August 1864: "Hearing of that ear is destroyed entirely. Applicant looks well but shows satisfactory evidence that his general health is poor; he has a good deal of headache & is unable to do much of any kind of work."[9]

Mrs. Stowe wrote to a friend in November 1864 and talked of a plan to send her son to sea: "I left my poor Fred at home. I do hope he will get a good ship. The sea air works marvels in our family. That wound in his head will never heal unless by a general tonic to the whole system. . . . I feel a weight of solicitude for the poor fellow."[10]

Mrs. Stowe's worries continued through February 1865: "My other daughters are with me, and my son, Captain Stowe, who has come with weakened health through our struggle, suffering constantly from the effects of a wound in his head received at Gettysburg, which makes his returning to his studies a hard struggle."[11]

And then there was another surgeon's examination report in 1866: "Long attacks of lethargy. . . . He enlisted again after being first discharged, against the knowledge of his parents, but could not do the duty. . . . His ambition and patriotism were altogether beyond his strength. He is now engaged in the study of medicine, in which it is evident his wound causes great difficulty. . . . He has

---

6 Charles Edward Stowe and Harriet Beecher Stowe, *Life of Harriet Beecher Stowe: Compiled From Her Letters and Journals* (London, 1889), 372.

7 Stowe pension claim, NARA.

8 Annie Fields, *Life and Letters of Harriet Beecher Stowe* (Boston, 1897), 278.

9 Stowe pension claim, NARA.

10 Fields, *Life and Letters of Harriet Beecher Stowe*, 274.

11 Ibid, 277.

been at times compelled to suspend his studies, and finds it much more difficult to concentrate his thoughts than previous to the injury." The pain in his head grew constant, "permanently incapacitating him for business," and he began to receive a pension of $10 a month in August 1866.[12]

The Stowes kept trying to help Fred. He sailed to Spain with his father in 1868, "mainly for the health of the young man." Later, the Stowes purchased a plantation in Florida for Fred to manage, hoping the fresh air would revitalize him. After only a short stint in Florida he fled to California in 1870 and was never heard from again.

"That he reached [San Francisco] in safety is known," brother Charles said, "but that is all. No word from him or concerning him has ever reached the loving hearts that have waited so anxiously for it, and of his ultimate fate nothing is known."[13] "Where is my poor Fred?" Mrs. Stowe agonized. "I never forget my boy. Can a woman forget her child?"[14] A family that devoted itself to fighting society's evils always seemed to attract such devastating family misfortune.[15]

Fred would have been about 30 years old if he indeed died in San Francisco in 1870. The family that had done so much for their country and fought so hard against slavery had now seen three sons die young.

One Final Note

Widow Sarah Monfort of York Street in Gettysburg wrote an intriguing letter to a relative in Ohio in July 1863. She wrote that she went to the XI Corps hospital at Spangler and at some point Fred Stowe left the hospital and was taken to her home for treatment for "about 10 days." There are no medical or pension records that support this claim and on the surface it seems unlikely. The practice, after all, was for ambulances on July 4–5 to search town and take wounded men from homes to the field hospitals, not the other way around. But there is a documented case at the National Archives and Records Administration in Washington, D.C., of Capt. William J. Rannells of the 75th Ohio doing just that. Rannells was wounded in the left buttock on Barlow Knoll on July 1, taken to a Confederate hospital, and then picked up and removed to Spangler after the Confederate retreat. But he only spent one night at Spangler before he was taken to a residence in town where he was treated by a surgeon who was "a stranger to him." The reason for

12 Stowe pension claim, NARA.

13 Fields, *Life and Letters of Harriet Beecher Stowe*, 333.

14 Ibid., 333.

15 *Vermont Journal*, July 11, 1868.

the transfer remains unknown. Another fact that backs Widow Monfort's story is that Stowe's first cousin—1st Lt. Fred Beecher of the 16th Maine—was being treated next door at the home of Widow Monfort's mother after his wounding on Cemetery Hill. Harriet Beecher Stowe wrote to her brother, Henry Ward Beecher, on August 20, 1863: "Fred Beecher not yet fully recovered from a wound. . . . Rob escaped unhurt—he writes that Fred and he were side by side when he was struck down—the wound was not dangerous however, and he got into a private house at Gettysburg where a widow and her daughter nursed him carefully."

"Rob" was Fred Beecher's brother, 2nd Lt. Robert Beecher, who was on Cemetery Hill with the 73rd Ohio and another first cousin of Fred Stowe, who like his cousins was on Cemetery Hill at the time of his wounding. Mrs. Stowe's letter raises the possibility that Widow Monfort confused cousins Fred Stowe and Fred Beecher, and that Stowe remained all the while at Spangler. But even though such a scenario makes sense, the most likely case is that Widow Monfort got it exactly right and Fred Stowe spent a few days at Spangler, then she had him taken to her house after visiting the XI Corps hospital because his first cousin was next door, after which he transferred to an Army general hospital in New York City from York Street just a couple of blocks from his departure point at the Gettysburg train station. Perhaps Spangler surgeons considered Stowe to be out of danger after a few days in the summer kitchen and determined that joining up with his cousin would do him good. Widow Monfort mentioned in a later letter that doctors boarded with her, so they might have joined her in caring for Stowe.[16]

Spangler Farm Short Story

Blacksmith Shop Road was officially so named by Cumberland Township in 1963, exactly 100 years after it was used by thousands of Army of the Potomac troops to rush from the Baltimore Pike and the Spangler farm to the Union line. Prior to that, the Spanglers and anyone else living on what is now Blacksmith Shop Road simply had an address of RD 1. After 1963, the Andrew family and today's owner, the Gettysburg Foundation, were assigned the address of 488 Blacksmith Shop Road. Other well-known Cumberland Township roads to receive names in 1963 include Hospital Road, Black Horse Tavern Road, Herr's Ridge Road, and Sachs Road. Granite Schoolhouse Lane—the other road cutting through the Spanglers' farm to the line both then and today—is believed to have been named in the late 1800s.[17]

---

16 www.sparedshared22.wordpress.com/2021/05/18/1863-sarah-elenor-thompson-monfort-to-henry-jacob-brinkerhoff/, accessed Feb. 8, 2023; William J. Rannells Invalid Pension Claim 198116, NARA.

17 *The Gettysburg Times*, May 30, 1863.

This blacksmith shop once stood at the modern-day intersection of Blacksmith Shop Road and the Taneytown Road. *Ron Kirkwood*

The blacksmith shop featured in the road's name was owned by prominent Gettysburg-area resident John W. Epley. It sat on the west side of the intersection of Blacksmith Shop Road and the Taneytown Road, parallel to Wheatfield Road. The oldest part of the building was constructed about 1870, with enlargements after that. Epley owned the shop from 1904 until his death at age 81 in 1960, and his resume included being the master farrier for the world-famous horse breeder Hanover Shoe Farms.[18]

The shop was carefully taken down in 1969 and put back together piece by piece at Landis Valley Village & Farm Museum in Lancaster County, PA, where it can be visited today. Epley's tools hang from the ceiling and sit on work benches just like they did decades ago and are in use by modern-day Landis Valley blacksmiths, working over the same hearth Epley did in the historic building that gave Blacksmith Shop Road its name.[19]

18 Landis Valley Village & Farm Museum; *The Gettysburg Times*, Aug. 1, 1960.

19 Landis Valley Village & Farm Museum.

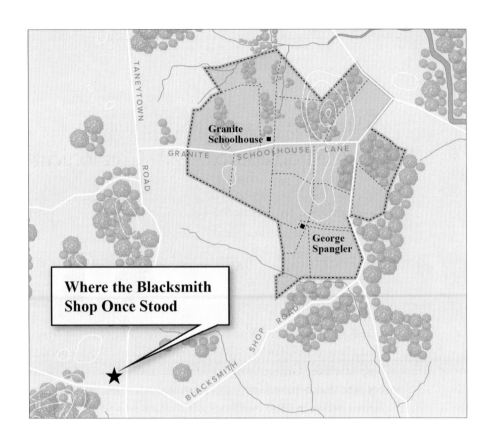

TANEYTOWN ROAD

Granite
Schoolhouse ■

GRANITE   SCHOOLHOUSE   LANE

■ George
Spangler

Where the Blacksmith
Shop Once Stood

★

BLACKSMITH   SHOP   ROAD

Chapter 3

A Stumble Leads to Spangler:
Pvt. James R. Middlebrook, 17th Connecticut

"It is enough to make ones heart bleed to witness the amputations."

— *Pvt. James R. Middlebrook, 17th Connecticut*

a slip and stumble on the Plank Road at Chancellorsville on May 2 ultimately sent Pvt. James R. Middlebrook of the 17th Connecticut to the XI Corps hospital on the George Spangler farm two months later. He suffered a hernia on his left side that required immediate medical attention, but medicine couldn't do much for a hernia in 1863 except for a belt that held the bulge in place, which is what 17th Connecticut surgeon Dr. Robert Hubbard prescribed.[1]

The pain and decreased mobility caused by the rupture were immediate, so Middlebrook, age 30, standing six feet and weighing 175 pounds, reported to the regimental hospital June 22–24 as the Army of the Potomac worked its way north. It's not known if he rode in an ambulance or marched to Gettysburg, but he made it, and he even fought in the first day's battle. That was the day the 17th Connecticut and the rest of Brig. Gen. Francis Barlow's XI Corps, First Division was outmanned and overrun on what today is known as Barlow Knoll. Middlebrook, of Company D, also made it to East Cemetery Hill, but without his knapsack and "all my things," which were lost in the hasty retreat. Without his ammunition, food, and other critical supplies, and suffering from the hernia, Middlebrook reported to the XI Corps hospital.[2]

---

1 James R, Middlebrook Invalid Pension Claim 151920, NARA.

2 Middlebrook Carded Medical Record, RG 94, Records of the Adjutant General's Office, Entry 534, 17 Connecticut, Kiser, G. to Philips, G.D., NARA; Middlebrook, Louis F Scrapbook, 1897-1906, Box MS 73139, Connecticut State Historical Society, Hartford, CT; Middlebrook pension claim, NARA.

"I came here July 2nd by permission of our Major," he wrote from the Spangler hospital on July 9 to wife Frances back home in Trumbull, "because I did not think prudent for me to stay with the Regt as I am."[3]

It is not known what time Middlebrook arrived at the XI Corps hospital on July 2 or if he hitched a ride in an ambulance or walked in pain the 1.6 miles from East Cemetery Hill down the Baltimore Pike to the Spangler farm, but it seems likely that he reached the edge of George Spangler land by 2 p.m. Walking south along the Baltimore Pike after passing the Nathaniel Lightner house, Middlebrook could look up at a hill to his right that someday would be called Powers Hill, three-fourths of which was owned by the Spanglers and the rest by the Lightners.

The border of Spangler-Lightner land is marked today as it was then by a stone wall, as well as a modern-day marker for Maj. Gen. Henry W. Slocum's XII Corps headquarters. When he passed that wall on July 2, Middlebrook arrived on the Spangler farm at its most crowded, signaling its crucial importance to the Army of the Potomac. As far as Middlebrook could see, the Spanglers' spacious 166 acres were packed with artillery, infantry, cavalry, and two hospitals. And all of those men and animals and all of that equipment assembled at Spangler were about to help Maj. Gen. George G. Meade win the biggest battle of the Civil War.

To Middlebrook's immediate right at the base of the hill along the Baltimore Pike were dozens of white canvas-topped XI Corps ambulances covering one of George Spangler's two wheatfields. The rest of the XI Corps ambulances were at East Cemetery Hill and the Spanglers' other wheatfield not far from their barn. Above the Powers Hill ambulances in plain sight were roughly 1,800 men of Brig. Gen. Thomas Neill's Third Brigade, Second Division, VI Corps. Meade had ordered Neill to the Spanglers' hill and told him to hold it "at all hazards."[4]

Artillery batteries were posted at the summit to guard the key Baltimore Pike and the back side of the army. Also at the top, Middlebrook could see an Army of the Potomac signal station with flags waving and messengers hustling about.

The intersection of the Baltimore Pike and the not-yet-named farm path that would become Granite Schoolhouse Lane sat 200 feet farther south in 1863 than it is today. Looking straight south as he reached that intersection, Middlebrook saw a mass of 11,000 men from the V Corps eating and resting after an overnight march and occupying Spangler, Musser, Diehl, and Bucher fields while awaiting their orders to get to the line. Those orders would famously come later that afternoon when they rushed from and through Spangler to defend Little Round Top and the area around it.

3 Middlebrook, Louis F Scrapbook.

4 www.ehistory.osu.edu/books/official-records/043/0680, accessed Dec. 22, 2021.

Pvt. James R. Middlebrook

Carolyn Ivanoff

Middlebrook passed several companies of the 4th New Jersey at the intersection of Granite Schoolhouse Lane and Blacksmith Shop Road that were guarding the artillery ammunition train, a mass of 100 wagons and hundreds of mules, horses, and men who provided ammunition to all Army of the Potomac artillery batteries at Gettysburg. Straight down Granite Schoolhouse Lane to the west he could see a cavalry artillery battery and the First Division, II Corps hospital setting up around Granite Schoolhouse in the middle of the Spanglers' vast farm. On his way he also would have seen 19 light batteries of the Army of the Potomac Artillery Reserve swallowing Spangler fields west of their barn.

It might have been comforting for Middlebrook to witness this much power arrayed around Spangler's fields awaiting deployment. Here was the massive reserve power of the Army of the Potomac on full display, and the bulk of it was on George Spangler's farm. But any comfort turned to horror when he traveled up the Spanglers' lane and witnessed the scenes in and around the Spanglers' big Pennsylvania barn, house, and other outbuildings. Because after just one full day of fighting, George and Elizabeth Spangler and their four children were already overrun by a fully developed corps field hospital.

At least three, and likely four, amputation tables were in full motion under the forebay just outside the front wall of the barn. Piles of limbs mounted, as did the hordes of flies that they attracted. The moaning, screaming, praying, and swearing of the wounded and dying filled the air. In that frantic scene, Middlebrook put his own health troubles aside to volunteer as a hospital worker. Not only was he put to work right away but he stayed at Spangler until August 5, one day before the hospital closed, comprising one of the longest and most dedicated tenures of any hospital staffer there.[5]

5 Middlebrook pension claim, NARA.

Middlebrook was an eloquent and frequent letter writer home throughout the war, and in his first of two letters from the Spangler farm he tried to describe the nightmare that he was experiencing. His first letter was written July 9 on U.S. Christian Commission stationery:

Dear Wife:

I almost blame myself for not writing to you sooner, but the fact is, I have not had . . . time to do it until now. . . . Thank God I am safe. When I came here I thought to do something for the soldiers & I am now doing all I can for them—Dressing wounds, giving them water & waiting on them to make them as comfortable as we can. Our hospital is a large barn & is full some 200 on the first floor where I am & under as many more & lots of them in Tents around outside then are some 80 men in the barn with legs & arms off & it is enough to make ones heart bleed to witness the amputations—I feel it my duty to do all I can for them. I cannot see them suffer shall stay as long as I can stand it.

The members of the Christian Commission are here from Philadelphia & Baltimore & citizens from other places doing all they can to comfort the wounded & may God Bless them. You know nothing of the Horrors of War & cannot until you go & see it for yourself. . . . There are a number of Ladies here every day & one who belongs to some Regt. who wears the soldiers uniform throughout, one Lady was here with the American Costume on yesterday. . . . I have not had a Blanket to sleep under, of my own since the Battle. I found one on the way here from the Battle Field but gave it to a wounded man to cover him—have not had a change of Clothes since—must go somewhere and get some soon.

The folks at home don't know how much they might do for the soldiers & never know it—will write you again soon. It's growing dark & I must close. Good Bye. God Bless you.[6]

Middlebrook left behind 7-year-old son Robert in addition to Frances when he enlisted in August 1862 with the 17th Connecticut. James and Frances had been married eight years. He closed his letters lovingly with such comments as "Ever your affectionate Husband," "A (Kiss) for you both," and "May God Bless & protect you all, & may it be his good pleasure to bring us together in the old Home, once more, kiss that dear Boy for me, & tell him to kiss his dear Ma Ma for me." He frequently called Frances "My Dear Wife" or "My Better Half."[7]

He wrote to Frances again from Spangler on July 18:

Dear Wife: I suppose you have heard that I am safe & sound am still in the Hospital of the 11th Corps, how soon we shall get away is uncertain and I have hardly found time

---

6 Middlebrook, Louis F Scrapbook.

7 Ibid.; Middlebrook pension claim, NARA.

to write—I beg your pardon for not writing sooner but have not been out of sight of the Barn since I came here. . . . I tell you it is Truly heartrending to see the wounded men & what do people say now to the times—the Copperheads I mean I suppose they rejoice— but . . . their days are numbered—providence has once more given success to our arms— may he continue so to do & speedily bring this war to a close.[8]

The 17th Connecticut was hit hard at Gettysburg. In three days of fighting at Barlow Knoll and East Cemetery Hill, the regiment suffered 197 casualties out of 386 men for a rate of 51 percent. 63 of those men are known to have been treated at Spangler, the seventh-highest total of the more than 50 regiments and batteries that sent casualties to the XI Corps hospital. Middlebrook was also considered one of the wounded, though decades after the war he couldn't recall the names of the doctors who treated him.[9]

Dr. Hubbard was at Spangler every day until he took a mass of wounded men to Baltimore in mid-July. He said Middlebrook "was more or less disabled" by the hernia "and had frequently to be relieved from duty." Second Lieutenant Albert Peck of the 17th Connecticut said Middlebrook "remained seriously and permanently disabled from said injury, so as to require his frequent, and at times protracted relief from duty, and the wearing of a truss continually."[10]

Middlebrook toughed it out through the end of the war and even with his disability was promoted to corporal in January 1864 and lieutenant in June 1865, suggesting the respect in which he was held. He was mustered out in July 1865 at Hilton Head, SC, having survived almost three years of Civil War service, two of those years with a hernia.[11]

---

8 Middlebrook, Louis F Scrapbook.

9 Travis W. Busey and John W. Busey, *Union Casualties at Gettysburg: A Comprehensive Record*, Vol. 3 (Jefferson, NC, 2011), 697, 1224; Middlebrook pension claim, NARA.

10 Middlebrook pension claim, NARA.

11 Hernias were a common and debilitating ailment in the Civil War. Another example with Spangler ties was 44-year-old 2nd Lt. Warren Onan of the 154th New York, who delivered numerous wounded men to the XI Corps hospital in his role as chief of ambulance of the Second Division. Four months after Gettysburg, in Georgia, Onan fell off his horse and was dragged with his foot in the stirrup while the horse jumped a ditch. Onan suffered a left inguinal hernia, the same injury as Middlebrook. Also like Middlebrook, Onan suffered an additional hernia on the right side after the war, and the pain from the double hernias limited his ability to move, causing weight gain: "Waying over 250 lbs I cannot find a truss that will hold either in & in consequence when on my feet suffer grate pain," Onan wrote in his application for a military pension. Former 154th New York Assistant Surgeon Corydon C. Rugg added: "The hernia was very severe and Mr. Onan a large and corpulent man that it would require a very strong pressure"; Warren Onan Invalid Pension Claim 254535, NARA. Despite his health concerns, Onan became a successful businessman and justice of the peace in Minnesota and lived to age 91.

Middlebrook returned to Trumbull and was commissioned into the Connecticut National Guard on January 3, 1866, as a lieutenant, to serve five years. He was discharged on December 11, 1871. He also spent many years as an officer on the Executive Committee of the 17th Connecticut Volunteer Association. He suffered an even worse rupture on his right side at some point after the war that was almost three times the size of the left hernia, giving him the agony of a double inguinal hernia. He gave up farming and maintained a law license, which, in combination with a variety of jobs such as hat salesman, allowed him to refrain from physical employment.[12]

Middlebrook's son Robert became a leader like his father. He graduated from Yale Law School and made a career as a respected lawyer, judge, police commissioner, and community leader in Kansas City, MO. He's honored in the book *Men Who Made Kansas City*.[13]

Middlebrook's only other child was Louis, born in 1866. Following family tradition, he made a name for himself, serving as an ensign and captain in the Navy, a naval aide to Connecticut Gov. George P. McLean, and as an author of dozens of books, most of which focused on maritime topics. He also was an early member of the Marine Historical Association, now the popular Mystic Seaport Museum in Mystic, CT.

James R. Middlebrook died in 1908 at age 75 after a productive, if painful, life. He is buried in Long Hill Burial Ground on Middlebrooks Avenue in Trumbull. He was receiving an invalid pension of $20 a month at the time of his death. Frances received a widow's pension of $12 per month after he died. The Middlebrook name can still be seen throughout Trumbull on buildings honoring a venerable family of accomplishment that settled in Connecticut colony in the mid-1600s and provided leaders in law, medicine, farming, and journalism.[14]

It was the fight and work in Gettysburg and at Spangler that Middlebrook remembered most in one of his last letters to Frances soon after the end of the war: "Make up your mind to travel some when we get Home," he urged on July 12, 1865, before being mustered out. "I think of going to that place long to be remembered—Gettysburg."[15]

12 Middlebrook Family Papers 1782-1929, MS 73139, Folder 17, Connecticut State Historical Society; 1860, 1870, 1880 and 1900 U.S. Census; Middlebrook pension claim, NARA.

13 www.vintagekansascity.com/menwhomadekc/middlebrook_robert_brinsmade.html, accessed Dec. 22, 2021.

14 Middlebrook pension claim, NARA.

15 Middlebrook, Louis F Scrapbook.

One Final Note

Private Middlebrook mentioned a female visitor at Spangler in a letter home who "was here with the American Costume on yesterday." The American costume was a style of dress championed by women's rights activists and dress reformers such as Harriet N. Austin and Elizabeth Smith Miller of New York in which a loose skirt of about knee length was worn with some form of trousers underneath (see accompanying photo). Austin, Miller, and other reformers promoted this outfit because it maintained full bodily coverage while being more healthful than the common ground-length dresses and body-squeezing corsets of the day.

Interestingly, both Austin and Smith Miller had connections to Spangler and either could have been spotted there by Middlebrook. Smith Miller was the daughter of one of the richest men in the country, the powerful anti-slavery activist Gerrit Smith of Peterboro, NY, who took in and helped raise 1st Lt. Joseph Heeney of the 157th New York as a child. Smith's son, Greene, traveled to Gettysburg to check on Heeney at Spangler but arrived after the 21-year-old died. It's possible that his American costume-wearing, women's right activist sister Elizabeth made that journey with him.

In addition, Harriet N. Austin was from Dansville, NY, also the home of Spangler surgeon Bleecker Lansing Hovey and nurse Marilla Hovey, so it's possible she could have visited the XI Corps hospital.

While the American costume never gained full acceptance, it was known well enough in 1863 that any number of women could have shown up at Spangler from around the region or country in their statement-making attire.

Nurse and living historian Jackie Greer models an American costume at the George Spangler farm. *Ron Kirkwood*

An Expert's Closer Look: James R. Middlebrook's Hernias

By Ryan Neff, M.D.
Fellow of American College of Surgeons

Hernias are basically a hole or defect in the abdominal musculature that leads to a bulge or mass. The muscle is the strength layer to the torso compartment known in common tongue as the stomach. This "stomach" or abdominal cavity is anatomically known as the peritoneal cavity and contains internal organs of the abdomen and pelvis. Numerous muscles and bony structures such as the spine, ribs, and pelvic bones, for example, form the boundary to the peritoneal cavity. If a hole develops in a muscle (or wall of the peritoneal cavity), the intra-abdominal pressure forces contents outside of the cavity creating a hernia. This protrusion of organs through the muscle results in a bulge that can be commonly felt in individuals and seen as an asymmetry when comparing right and left groins. In early hernias as with Pvt. Middlebrook's, the "bulge" can be pushed back in but unfortunately the constant intra-abdominal pressure leads to a recurrence of the bulge. When the bulge is pushed back inside the cavity, one commonly feels a hole in the muscle. As hernias progress over time the bulge becomes larger and more difficult to return its contents to the peritoneal cavity resulting in more discomfort to the patient. This phenomenon can lead to a severe episode of pain known as a strangulation of the hernia contents. A strangulated hernia is an emergent situation that can lead to a life-threatening infection if not treated immediately.

Current treatment of hernias, especially groin hernias such as with Pvt. Middlebrook, would be an outpatient surgery with four weeks' recovery that includes no strenuous exercising or lifting greater than 15 pounds. The main objective is to return organs to their peritoneal origin and repair the hernia to prevent future bulges. Commonly, surgical mesh or a patch is used to repair the hernia in a tension-free manner as opposed to previous suture closure, which had higher failure rates. Full recovery, including return to soldier's duties, is expected with an uneventful surgery that is not complicated by preceding strangulation. In pre-surgical times, treatment of hernias was aimed at preventing strangulation which meant keeping the bulge as small as possible. This reduced the amount of material (organs or fat) coming through the hernia or muscle defect thereby avoiding lack of blood flow and necrosis/infection of the hernia contents. Common recommendations were to prohibit activities or movements such as heavy lifting or smoking (as this produced coughing) which led to increase in intra-abdominal pressure. A hernia truss is an apparatus that aims to provide support to the muscle defect/hernia so that fewer intra-abdominal contents protrude through the hole. Trusses can be effective in thin patients but the more subcutaneous fat a patient has makes it difficult for the truss padding to effectively oppose the hernia. The more movement a hernia patient exhibits also leads to failure of the apparatus to stay in place and thereby prevent further bulging.

Leaving Pvt. Middlebrook's hernia untreated as they did (except for the truss) would significantly decrease his effectiveness as a soldier and greatly limit his ability to carry equipment into combat. Living with two inguinal hernias as he did after the war would be challenging and absolutely affect daily activities, causing him to limit physical efforts secondary to discomfort/pain.

Dr. Ryan Neff is Section Chief–General Surgery, Mercy Hospital St. Louis, where he has been practicing since 2008. He received his medical degree from Sidney Kimmel Medical College at Thomas Jefferson University in Philadelphia. He is a native of Red Lion, Pennsylvania, not far from Gettysburg.

Spangler Farm Short Story

Family members and friends who didn't know the status of a wounded, dead, or missing soldier could write to the United States Sanitary Commission for answers. The Sanitary Commission was formed as a private agency by Congress in 1861 to aid the sick and wounded and monitor the army's sanitation in camps and field hospitals. The Commission did not receive government funding. In 1862, the Sanitary Commission began to collect information on sick and wounded soldiers in army general hospitals in an effort to answer questions from concerned members of the public. It also searched via letters, telegrams, and in-person contact for soldiers about whom it did not have information. Three inquiries about soldiers treated at Spangler offer examples of this process:

Sergeant Samuel Comstock, age 21, 17th Connecticut, Company H, arrived at Spangler on July 4 after sustaining a compound fracture in his left thigh from a gunshot on July 1. He was transferred from Spangler to Camp Letterman outside of Gettysburg at some point before the XI Corps hospital closed on August 6, but his aunt didn't know any of that, writing to the Sanitary Commission branch office in Philadelphia on August 20: "Sir, I have your direction from Mr. Wilson of Washington, who thinks you may be able to answer my inquiries. I have a nephew, Samuel Comstock of the 17th Regt. Connt. Vols. Compy. H who was hurt at Gettesburg. I have not been able to ascertain where he is or the nature of his wounds & his condition. I suppose he is in some of the Hospitals at Philadelphia or at Gettesburg. Can you inform me where he is? What is the nature of his wounds, & what his prospects for recovery are? His mother is dead & his father is in London [New London] & his remaining friends here would be very glad to know about him. I have been recently in Philadelphia & Washington & could find little satisfactory respect to him." The Sanitary Commission always made a point of writing back, though its response in this case is not recorded, so it's not known when Sgt. Comstock's aunt and friends found out that he died September 27 at Camp Letterman.

Private James Farrell, age about 36, 119th New York, Company I, had his right leg amputated at the thigh at Spangler and—shockingly and sadly—his wife, Mary Ann, still did not know his status in February 1864, writing: "When last heard of he was in Field Hospl. at Gettysburgh & thence transferred to some Hosp'l unknown. Had . . . a leg amputated . . . not heard from him since. Is he on your books, or can you suggest another source of information?" The Sanitary Commission responded: "Doing well in Christian St. Hospital Philadelphia." The native of Ireland was discharged from that Philadelphia hospital in March 1864 and lived another 21 years.

Corporal James Brownlee, age 21, 134th New York, Company G, arrived at Spangler on July 4 with eight wounds from the Brickyard, one of which broke four ribs. The Sanitary Commission told an inquirer on August 27 that Brownlee was "At Camp Letterman severely wounded." The five-foot-eight-inch, blue-eyed native of Ireland lived to age 62 even though Union surgeons considered his disability permanent. (See Chapter 17 for more information on Cpl. Brownlee.)[16]

The Sanitary Commission saved the lives of thousands during the Civil War with its dedication and care. Tracking down and communicating the status of wounded soldiers for family members and friends grew into an important part of its mission.

---

16 United States Sanitary Commission Hospital Directory archives, Mss. Col. 19877, Vol. 26, The New York Public Library Manuscripts and Archives Division, New York, NY.

Chapter 4

Eight Men in a Tent:
Part 1

"I shall keep out of danger."

— *Drummer Thaddeus Reynolds of the 154th New York in a letter to his parents from Gettysburg on July 2, 1863*

Eight man canvas tents were popular in field hospitals after the battle of Gettysburg. Commonly, these were "wall tents" with a wall extending 4 to 5 feet straight up from the ground on all four sides with the canvas "roof" angling up from the two longest sides into a peak at the top. A row of four wounded men on cots, straw, or a gum/rubber blanket lay in a row on each side of the tent, leaving room for a walkway in the center. Pine branches were sometimes hung in the tent as a natural air freshener to cut down on the gagging smell of vomit, infection, feces, and other body fluids. Sometimes, pine branches were used for bedding.

Outside, a shallow trench might be dug around each tent to prevent water from pouring in. These eight-man tents were lined up in neat order with "city streets" between them, making for easy movement between tents for hospital staffers and visitors. Townspeople, chaplains, nurses, wounded soldiers, and others sang and preached in these streets for the comfort and enjoyment of all.

Tents began to arrive at most hospitals around Gettysburg on July 4, which also was the day that masses of wounded Army of the Potomac men arrived at the XI Corps hospital at the Spangler farm. Tents continued to stream in for the next few days, but in the meantime hundreds of men at Spangler were forced by the absence of tents and the overcrowding of the Spangler barn and outbuildings to lie in the mud during the drenching thunderstorms of that miserable Independence Day.

July 4th was the day ambulances began to pick up wounded men from the 154th New York and carry them to Spangler. Those men had been outmanned, overpowered, and almost surrounded at Kuhn's Brickyard three days prior on

Tents at Camp Letterman. *Tyson Brothers/Library of Congress*

July 1. Most of the healthy casualties of the 154th on that desperate day were made prisoners and sent south while the wounded were taken to downtown Gettysburg hospitals, where they, too, were considered prisoners of war. These men were picked up and taken to Spangler after the Confederates skedaddled.

At some point, eight men of the 154th New York were placed together in one tent in the tent city in a rutted Spangler field. Five of those eight men died in that tent. The other three lived, but they didn't go home whole. They and their families were impacted the rest of their lives by what happened at Gettysburg and the XI Corps hospital.

All eight soldiers enlisted in hilly, rural Cattaraugus and Chautauqua counties in western New York, south of Buffalo and just north of Pennsylvania. Each of those men had loved ones and families. They sent a good portion of their pay home monthly prior to Gettysburg, keeping only a little for themselves. In addition to money, they expressed their love to family members in their letters. They told their families not to worry, because they were fine. They were optimistic about their chances of going home.

Sadly, it didn't end up fine for any of them. The suffering in that eight-man tent at Spangler had to have been far worse than what we can comprehend today. This tent likely would have been an intense focus for chaplains, nurses, and hospital workers who were trying to ease the misery of its damaged occupants. This tent was a sacred space where many of these men came to die, where the chaplains and nurses comforted them as best they could, where Bible verses were read, and where they talked to the men about their lives in an attempt to keep their minds distracted from excruciating pain.

Practically speaking, the odor in this tent would have been strong enough to cause someone not prepared for it to pass out. Many of these men could not move, so they rolled over to vomit. The same with feces. One of them—Pvt. James F. Chase—suffered a wound that commonly caused feces to gush out at the site of the injury. On top of all that was the putrid smell of infection. Those factors, combined with the boiling heat of July in a small, enclosed space, probably made even the most experienced hospital worker and chaplain stop in his or her tracks upon entering that tent.

Even so, and even though every one of these men was critically wounded, we have evidence that they cared for one another and tried to help their suffering comrades as best they could. And we have evidence that even though they were dying in that tent they sometimes seemed less worried about their own death and more concerned about how it would burden their families back home.

Here are those eight men:

Corporal Albert Mericle, Company H. Age 19. From Randolph, NY. Flesh wound abdomen, fracture right leg. Corporal Mericle died July 10 at Spangler.[1]

Drummer Thaddeus Reynolds, Company I. Age 19. From Olean, NY. Flesh wound left hand and hip; two fingers amputated. Reynolds was wounded on Cemetery Hill and died July 12 at Spangler.

Private John Paugh, Company I. Age 42. From Hinsdale, NY. Flesh wound mid right thigh. Private Paugh died July 12 at Spangler.

Private James F. Chase, Company D. Age 24. From Ischua, NY. Right hip and "privates." Private Chase died July 31 at Spangler.

Sergeant Lewis Bishop, Company C. Age 23. From Allegany, NY. Shot in both legs. Left knee fracture, amputation at the thigh of left leg. Sergeant Bishop died July 31 at Spangler.

Sergeant John A. Bush, Company D. Age 31. From Machias, NY. Four inches of fractured bone extracted in upper right arm. Sergeant Bush lived.

Corporal Gilbert M. Rykert, Company C. Age 22. From Hinsdale, NY. Four inches of fractured bone extracted in upper right arm. Corporal Rykert lived.

1 Pennsylvania Register 554 (*Register of the Sick and Wounded*) from the U.S. Surgeon General's Office, NARA.

Sergeant Francis Strickland, Company I. Age 32. From Salamanca, NY. Right arm amputated. Sergeant Strickland lived.

Thaddeus Reynolds went by Thad, and like his father was a house painter. He was a reliable letter writer, corresponding frequently about the money he was sending home to parents David and Elizabeth (usually $20 every couple of months), telling them not to worry about his safety, and requesting that they "Kiss Clara for me," his 2- or 3-year-old sister. "I would like to see her or have her here for a little while," he wrote. "I would like to have you all here for a little while."[2]

Reynolds stood five feet four inches with dark hair and a dark complexion. He was thin when he went off to war at 138 pounds, but he boasted in one letter home in February 1863 that "I am perfectly well and hearty as a buck. As far as weight is concerned I am on the increase. I now weigh 157 pounds. I am very fleshy and have done a great deal of hard work for the past three months more than I ever did at home in double that time."[3]

He assured his parents about his safety in numerous letters, telling them:

> You need not worry about me because I shall take all the pains I can to keep well and clean. I shall not have to go on picket duty or any thing of that kind all I have to do when I am in battle is to carry of the dead. . . . I am armed with a sword and brace of six shooters with a dirk [a dagger] so that if there is any pluck In me at all I can defend my self without much danger."[4]

He seemed to worry more about his parents' health than his own: "I received your last letter of the 5th friday night and was very sorry to hear of the ill health of both Mother and Father," he wrote. "I pity Mothers misfortune and hope that nothing very serious will come of it. I was in hopes that father was going to get better after using so much medicine. But never mind keep up good courage and hope for a better future," he exhorted. He seemed to focus on happy times in the future, predicting that "there is good times a coming when we shall all gather together once more around the family circle and never be separated again by war. Although I am far away from home and in the enemys country I still expect to

2 Letter to parents from Fairfax Court House, VA, Oct. 19, 1862, 2013.22.8.0370.004.pdf (sbu. edu), accessed Jan. 8, 2022.

3 Ancestry.com; letter to parents from Stafford Court House, VA, Feb. 14, 1863, 2013.22.8.0370.006. pdf (sbu.edu), accessed Jan. 8, 2022.

4 Undated letter to parents from Jamestown, NY, 1862, 2013.22.8.0370.003.pdf (sbu.edu), accessed Jan. 8, 2022.

Drummer Thaddeus Reynolds

Dennis Frank/St. Bonaventure University

see home again and to enjoy the pleasures and privileges of a free man." He added, "I do not call my self free here in the army."[5]

Reynolds somehow found a moment on July 2 at Gettysburg to write to his parents and recount what he had witnessed after the 154th was routed at the Brickyard on July 1: "When the fire opened myself & another orderly were ordered to fall back to the rear with the ambulences. We did & went to the Hospital. What we saw there was the horror of war: I saw some very bad wounds and help dress them Some were shot as much as three times in different places. Some had an arm shot off some had legs shot all to pieces and hands and fingers all torn to pieces with shells."[6] Even then, he assured his parents he was OK, signing off from Gettysburg with "I shall keep out of danger." But danger found him the next day. That July 2 letter would be the last letter home of his life.[7]

Army of the Potomac assistant surgeons had the dangerous duty of running aid stations directly behind the line at Gettysburg. There they provided first aid and performed triage before sending the wounded to field hospitals farther behind the line. 154th New York Assistant Surgeon Dwight W. Day was working on Cemetery Hill on July 3 and Reynolds was holding the doctor's horse when Reynolds was hit by Confederate fire in the left hip and left hand. Reynolds got to the XI Corps hospital the day he was wounded because he was hit behind the Union line, unlike his comrades from the Day 1 Brickyard fight who still lay out of reach behind enemy lines. He could have been placed in the Spangler barn if there was room, but it's equally likely that Reynolds had to suffer on the bare ground outside without protection from that July 4 rainstorm until enough tents arrived.

5 Letter to parents from Falmouth, VA, Feb. 15, 1863, 2013.22.8.0370.007.pdf (sbu.edu), accessed Jan. 8, 2022.

6 Letter to parents from Gettysburg, July 2, 1863, 2013.22.8.0370.010.pdf (sbu.edu), accessed Jan. 8, 2022.

7 2013.22.8.0370.010.pdf (sbu.edu); Ibid.

154th New York tentmate Strickland said Reynolds was "badly wounded by a shell—three fingers were taken off his left hand & all the flesh from his left hip."[8]

Great Valley, NY, resident James W. Phelps visited the XI Corps hospital, and he takes the story from there in a harrowing letter to Reynolds' father on July 24:

> My dear sir: I reached Gettysburg on Wednesday the 8th inst. & found your son that day at the 11th corps Hospital 2½ miles from town in a tent with seven other Cattaraugus men, badly wounded. I was personally acquainted with but one of them I had a conversation with your son that afternoon. He knew himself to be dangerously wounded but did not suffer much, considering the extent of his wounds. He rec'd his wound . . . while in the cemetery lying on his left side with the left hand and arm under him holding the horse of the officer he was with. . . . The injury to the hip was very great, although he got back some distance without assistance, yet Dr. Day told me he was surprised he could have lived so long as 3 or 4 days. A part of the left hand was amputated when I saw him first. Thursday & Friday he was quiet & slept some, Saturday Lockjaw showed itself, but when I left him Saturday eve, he was quite comfortable Sunday morning at 6 o clock I was on the ground & found him much worse, his wounds pained him very much & the Dr. directed he should be kept under the influence of Chloroform, which was done until he died at about 5 P.M. . . . On Saturday he spoke particularly of you, your situation, your poor health & he said that he 'feared his death would kill his Father.'[9]

Phelps also wrote that 26-year-old Assistant Surgeon Henry K. Spooner of the 55th Ohio "was very attentive and kind to your son" at Spangler "although he was not immediately under his care."[10]

We'll never know with certainty, but Reynolds might have survived without the onset of lockjaw, more commonly known today as tetanus, and easily treated with antibiotics. Lockjaw was an infection caused by a bacterium that entered the body through wounds, getting its name from one of its symptoms, i.e., stiffness of the lower jaw and neck. A patient with lockjaw died an agonizing death with convulsions and windpipe spasms that cut off breathing, which is why surgeons sometimes put the patient under with chloroform in his final hours, as they did with Reynolds at Spangler, to prevent a torturous death.[11]

8 Chuck Strickland and Peggy Strickland, *The Road to Red House* (Breinigsville, PA, 2007), 124.

9 Letter to David Reynolds from Great Valley, NY, July 24, 1863, 2013.22.8.0370.011.pdf (sbu.edu), accessed Jan. 8, 2022.

10 Ibid.

11 www.vermontcivilwar.org/medic/medicine3.php, accessed Apr. 24, 2017.

Reynolds' father was 84 years old and still a house painter and his mother was 78 in the 1900 U.S. census, long after their son died at Spangler in 1863. They had gone on to long lives despite their son's loving worries about them in letters home.[12]

Reynolds was the second to leave a void in that Spangler tent. The first was 19-year-old Cpl. Albert Mericle, who died two days before Reynolds. Mericle and Sgt. Lewis Bishop were highly respected and had the honor to be chosen as the flag bearers for the 154th New York. That honor put them front and center when the regiment was overwhelmed in the bloody Brickyard fight. State flag bearer Mericle took crippling blows to the abdomen and right leg on July 1. Bishop was the national flag color bearer for the 154th and had somehow passed through the furious assault by Stonewall Jackson's men at Chancellorsville without injury two months earlier, though his flag and staff took 20 bullet hits. He wasn't as fortunate at Gettysburg, where he was hit in both legs when the regiment was overrun.

Albert Mericle stood five feet eight inches with blue eyes and dark hair, but judging from his pension file his most prominent characteristics were his unrelenting work ethic and commitment to the care of his parents. Mericle's father, Cornelius, was crippled in a threshing machine accident in 1855, so Albert went to work at age 12 and became the bread winner for his family, single-handedly supporting himself, his parents, and five younger siblings at home.[13]

"Albert was doing farm work and working for a railroad before the war," his mother, Betsy, said in her pension application after her son died at Spangler. "The boy did all the plowing & all the farm work & the crops raised belonging to us were all used in the family. In the winter of 1861 & 1862 he cut the fallen timber . . . into wood drove it into the village of Randolph & sold it for flour, sugar, shoes, etc., etc., for my family. I had it all for the family except what he had to use for his own clothes."

Albert received $125 in bounty money when he enlisted in August 1862, all of which went to his parents. He even bought a cow and gave it to his mother before going off to war. A female pension witness called the family "extremely poor." She testified: "Albert told me in Jamestown after he enlisted that the reason he enlisted was to get his mother a home; that he was going to help his folks and particularly his mother, that he had enlisted for that purpose and that he was going to send his money home to his mother."

Albert's mother testified that she received $25 from her son in the spring of 1863 and that she received a letter from him prior to Gettysburg in which he

12 1900 U.S. Federal Census, Ancestry.com.

13 New York Civil War Muster Roll Abstract, Fold3.

promised more soon, but she said Albert told a nurse at Spangler that he was robbed by Confederates of three months' pay after his wounding.[14]

Lieutenant James W. Bird of the 154th saw at the XI Corps hospital that Mericle was shot through the bowels, a wound that was usually a death sentence in the Civil War, as it was for Mericle. Bird said Mericle was attended by 154th New York surgeon Dr. Henry Van Aernam.[15]

Mericle's sacrifice, however, meant his mother would receive a pension and he would continue to be the prime supporter of his family even after his death at Spangler. But the family's sufferings were not over: The government dropped the pension in 1872 when a resident of their area reported that the Mericles were not dependent on Albert for support. Mother Betsy Meracle testified in 1880 that she is poor and "suffers on account of withholding of said pension." The pension was returned at $8 a month in 1880 and raised to $12 in 1886.[16]

Mericle's fellow flag bearer, Sgt. Lewis Bishop, 23, had gone home to Allegany on a leave of absence to marry Lucy Hall on April 12, 1863. The honeymoon lasted a few days, and then Bishop left New York and his young bride to return to the 154th and the war. The newlyweds would never see each other again.[17]

Bishop was thrown into the fight at Chancellorsville less than a month after his wedding and somehow survived without injury when his flag and staff took a bullet-ridden beating. He was not so fortunate when he was front and center in the mayhem at the Brickyard in Gettysburg two months later, taking enemy hits in both legs.

Second Lieutenant Warren Onan of the 154th commanded the ambulance corps of the 2nd Division, XI Corps at Gettysburg and is likely the one who picked up Bishop on July 4 and took him to Spangler. Onan wrote:

> Lewis Bishop while in the line of his duty and in the faithful performance of his duty as color bearer was wounded by a musket ball passing through both legs and that I took charge of said Bishop and provided for him as well as possible at the time but that it became necessary to amputate one of his legs.[18]

---

14 Albert Mericle Mother's Pension Claim 90581, Fold3.

15 James W. Bird to Matthew B. Cheney, Nov. 30, 1893, and to Northrup, May 20, 1891, in Edwin Dwight Northrup Papers, Box 35, Carl A. Kroch Library, Cornell University.

16 Pension claim of Mericle's mother, Fold3.

17 Lewis Bishop Widow Pension Claim 16290, Fold3.

18 Ibid.

Bishop's left knee was splintered, requiring the amputation of that leg on July 1 before he was taken to Spangler. His bravery became known, attracting attention at the XI Corps hospital.

"I was for some time with Louis Bishop," wrote The Rev. Franklin F. J. F. Schantz, a Lutheran minister from Lehigh County, Pennsylvania, who made two visits to Spangler. "He was the bold soldier who would not give up his flag when one of his legs was shot off. He stuck to his flag."[19]

Bishop fought for survival for almost a month before dying July 31 at Spangler. He was one of the last two of the five mortally wounded men of the 154th New York in that tent to die and one of only a few wounded men left at Spangler at that time because most of those who were able had by then been moved to the Camp Letterman general hospital outside of Gettysburg or elsewhere. The XI Corps hospital at Spangler closed on August 6.

Lucy Bishop was married to Lewis for 111 days and they spent no more than a week together after their marriage. They had no children. She received a widow's pension of $8 per month starting in 1863.

Corporal Albert Mericle, drummer Thaddeus Reynolds, and Sgt. Lewis Bishop were buried in the rough cemetery in George and Elizabeth Spangler's orchard with each of their names painted on a piece of wood that served as a grave marker. They were exhumed in the following months and reburied in the New York section of Soldiers' National Cemetery in Gettysburg on the same hill where Reynolds was mortally wounded on July 3. Mericle's name is misspelled on his gravestone.

Spangler Farm Short Story

As noted above, 26-year-old assistant surgeon Henry K. Spooner of the 55th Ohio was recognized in a letter to the father of dying 19-year-old drummer Thaddeus Reynolds. Reynolds' father was told that Spooner had been "very attentive and kind to your son" at Spangler "although he was not immediately under his care." That letter written by hospital visitor James W. Phelps—who was at Spangler for a few days starting July 8—indicates that Dr. Spooner was one of the few surgeons with a long-term assignment there. Additionally, visitors from Ohio saw him at Spangler on July 10: "Here we found Doctor Spooner, of the 55th, with his coat off and sleeves rolled up, attending to his patients in a most faithful manner."[20]

---

19 F. J. F. Schantz, "Recollections of Visitations at Gettysburg After the Great Battle in July, 1863," in Shay, *Reflections on the Battle of Gettysburg*.

20 Letter to David Reynolds, 2013.22.8.0370.011.pdf (sbu.edu), accessed Jan. 8, 2022; *Huron Reflector*, July 21, 1863.

Assistant Surgeon Henry K. Spooner, 55th Ohio *Ancestry.com*

Spooner might have had company during his extended time at Spangler because the book *History of Seneca County Ohio* and the newspaper *The Galion Inquirer* place Hattie Spooner—24-year-old wife of Henry—in Gettysburg with her husband during and after the battle. *The Inquirer* even says the Spooners' 17-month-old daughter, Sophie, was with them in Gettysburg. As difficult a situation as that would have been for all three, the entire family seems to have been together at the Spangler XI Corps hospital.[21]

The Inquirer reported in 1913 that a group unsuccessfully tried to get the then 51-year-old Sophie's expenses covered so she could attend the 50th anniversary of the battle in Gettysburg with veterans of the 55th Ohio as the daughter of an assistant surgeon in the regiment and one who had been in Gettysburg as an infant. The newspaper recounted, "On July 2, 1862 [1863] Mrs. Spooner, accompanied by their daughter . . . joined her husband on the field of battle remaining with him through the terrible engagement." The *History of Seneca County Ohio* reported that "Mrs. Spooner was with her husband at Gettysburg, Chancellorsville, Lookout Mountain and at the barracks at Washington, at which latter place she attended the reception given President Lincoln."[22]

No letters, diaries, or official records could be found that verify the presence of the Spooner females at Spangler, and the Seneca County Historical Society couldn't find evidence of it, but it remains an intriguing thought. If true, that adds the Spooners to the list of complete families at the XI Corps hospital with the Spanglers, Barlows, and Hoveys.

Spooner was transferred to the 61st Ohio in November 1863 and promoted to surgeon and in 1865 was in charge of the XX Corps First Division field hospital before being mustered out. He and Hattie divorced in 1874.[23]

21 A. J. Baughman, *History of Seneca County Ohio* (Chicago, 1911), 836; *The Galion Inquirer*, June 21, 1913.

22 Ibid.

23 Henry K. Spooner Invalid Pension Claim 105473, NARA; RG 94 (Adjutant General's Office), Personal Papers of Medical Officers and Physicians, Spilman, R.S.—Spring, C.E., Box 544, NARA.

Chapter 5

Eight Men in a Tent: Part 2

"We have not a very good place to lie. Our bed is on the ground."

— *First Sergeant Francis Strickland, 154th New York, in a letter home from the XI Corps hospital at Spangler*

July 3, 1863, in a school in downtown Gettysburg, 1st Sgt. Francis Strickland of the 154th New York woke up to his right arm being amputated midway between his elbow and shoulder. The chloroform had worn off. Surgeon John H. Wilson of the 73rd Pennsylvania momentarily stopped cutting when he saw that his patient had awakened, then decided to plow ahead anyway without anesthesia. "He's a grizzly dog," surgeon Wilson said. "I guess he will stand it."[1]

We know that Wilson did indeed call Strickland a "grizzly dog" because Frank Strickland—as he preferred to be called—heard it from the operating table and wrote about it later. In fact, Strickland was aware of everything that happened to him during the rest of that amputation. "Sawing the bone was the easiest part," Strickland recalled, surprisingly nonchalantly, about the bone saw cutting through his arm. "Did not hurt near as much as tying the arteries and sewing the skin."[2]

Grizzly dog indeed.

We don't know why it was decided to keep operating on a lucid Strickland instead of putting him back under as was normal in the Civil War when anesthesia wore off. The patient was under anesthesia 95 percent of the time during the war. It is highly likely, though, that anesthesia supplies were running low at this makeshift hospital behind enemy lines and had to be rationed. This probably also

---

1 *The Medical and Surgical History of the War of the Rebellion 1861-1865*, Vol. X (Washington, D.C., 1870), 732; Strickland and Strickland, *The Road to Red House*, 107.

2 Strickland and Strickland, *The Road to Red House*, 108.

happened at the XI Corps hospital at Spangler, because major generals George Gordon Meade and Winfield Scott Hancock banned most medical wagons from Gettysburg to allow for clear roads for quick troop and machinery movement, exacerbating medical shortages. That sometimes meant a return to Revolutionary War amputation practices of putting a stick in the soldier's mouth and hoping he could survive what he was about to bear.

154th New York Assistant Surgeon Corydon C. Rugg found Strickland at the Brickyard with a gun-shot wound through his right elbow at dusk, July 1, and stopped the bleeding. Rugg then left but returned later and transported Strickland to a church hospital, where he stayed for two days. Rugg later assisted Wilson with Strickland's amputation after Strickland was moved to the school.[3]

On July 4, 1863, one day after his amputation, 32-year-old Frank Strickland of Salamanca, NY—with wife Catharine and five children ages 9 and under at home with no idea of what was going on with their father and husband—rode in an ambulance to the hospital at the George Spangler farm, where he would join a tent of seven other soldiers from the 154th battling for their lives. He was provided with clean hospital clothes and his first decent meal since the two hardtack crackers he had eaten after his wounding on July 1. Unlike most of his comrades in that tent, Frank would survive his wounds and nightmarish amputation and eventually go home to his wife and kids.[4]

Strickland was born February 19, 1831, in Yorkshire, England, and was 17 when he and his family emigrated to New York in 1848. Four years later, he and his North Evans next-door neighbor Catharine Camp were married just south of Buffalo. They moved to nearby Salamanca just above the New York-Pennsylvania state line where they lived in a log house. There they operated a sawmill and farm and grew their family. Despite his responsibilities to that family and growing business, Strickland answered President Abraham Lincoln's call for volunteers and enlisted, bidding goodbye and going off to war in September 1862. He received a $100 town bounty and $17 a month as a sergeant.[5]

At five feet nine-and-a-half inches tall, Frank was taller than the average Civil War soldier. His muster roll listed him as a farmer with blue eyes, brown hair, and light complexion, and his letters home showed him to be a better writer and speller than most soldiers of the time. He gave Catharine loving nicknames in those letters, including "Caty," "Katy," and "Ever Dear Wife." He wrote home from Virginia in January 1863 that "I dream some nights of being at home with you but wake in the

---

3 Strickland Invalid Pension Claim 27224, NARA.

4 Strickland and Strickland, *The Road to Red House*, 108.

5 Ibid., 6; Strickland Compiled Military Service Record, NARA.

1st Sgt. Francis Strickland

Charles L. and Peggy Strickland and Mark Dunkelman

morning only to be disappointed. I hunted the Camp all over to find something that I could send to the children in a letter from Santa Claus but could not find anything."[6] He often closed with "Yours for Ever" or "Your ever affectionate husband."

Frank's letters home showed him to be mature and thoughtful, exemplified by his comments after much of the XI Corps was run over at Chancellorsville in May 1863. The corps had suffered substantial loss of reputation and manpower due to the poor generalship there of Maj. Gen. Oliver Otis Howard. Strickland contextualized those losses poignantly: "Although this is not the way I should converse with you at present could I have my choice," he wrote, "yet it is a privilege which thousands of my fellow soldiers are deprived of forever. And whilst I write I feel as though I was very much favored in having seen this privilege."[7]

Trauma followed trauma on July 1 at Gettysburg only two months after Chancellorsville, when the 154th left Cemetery Hill to cover the retreat under fire of two defeated and outmanned XI Corps divisions that were rushing back through town. There's nothing left of Kuhn's Brickyard today except the house on North Stratton Street where the Kuhn family lived, now marked by an artillery shell in the house's south wall. But that site played a critical role on Day 1 of the largest battle of the Civil War. The brave work and sacrifice there of the 154th New York, 134th New York, and 27th Pennsylvania of Col. Charles R. Coster's XI Corps, Second Division, First Brigade against an overpowering enemy of eight regiments provided the retreating Northern troops just enough time to reach the safety of Cemetery Hill, likely preventing the Confederates from taking that strategic hill and with it the rest of the line.

Strickland described the aftermath of his Gettysburg wounding in a letter to fellow 154th Sgt. Samuel D. Woodford, who was taken prisoner at the Brickyard: "When you were peremptorily ordered to the rear as you were just preparing to

6 Strickland and Strickland, *The Road to Red House*, 49; New York Civil War Muster Roll, Fold3.

7 Strickland and Strickland, *The Road to Red House*, 85.

The Brickyard today. *Ron Kirkwood*

take care of me there at the brick kiln my feelings were such as I cannot describe, perhaps you can imagine," he recalled. Describing what must have been an awkward scene, he wrote "Shortly after you left, some Rebs came in, spread some blankets, laid down 2 wounded rebs and put me between them, where I lay still bleeding till about dark when Dr. found me, dressed my arm and entirely stopped its bleeding." Relief came when "[a]bout midnight Dr. Rugg came with a one horse wagon and carried me to a church in town."[8]

Strickland recounted later about being removed from the church to a nearby school where his amputation took place. The church very likely was Trinity German Reformed Church at East High and North Stratton streets, just a few blocks straight up Stratton from the Brickyard. The site of that congregation is now the modern-day Trinity United Church of Christ. A sign in front of the church describes the scene during the battle, which reads in part: "For several days surgeons worked at operating tables in the 'lecture room.' Citizen volunteer nurses recalled newly painted walls 'splattered' and pews 'soaked' with blood, 'and they had to bore holes in the floor to let the blood run away.' Eventually, many wounded were transferred to the public school next door."

Strickland's move to Spangler began a years-long recovery and suffering from his wound and amputation. Ten days after his wounding and eight days after his amputation he wrote to Catharine that "My health is pretty good and my wound

8 Ibid., 124.

is gaining slowly." Care standards at the hospital had begun to improve, save for the sleeping accommodations: "We have plenty of things to eat or as good as the circumstances will permit. We have not a very good place to lie. Our bed is on the ground. We have straw ticks to sleep on and woolen blankets to sleep on. I am in good spirits and I can walk out once in a while. So keep up good cheer and I will soon be at home with you."[9]

Strickland's generally upbeat accounts were seconded by others. Great Valley, NY, resident James W. Phelps wrote to Catharine on July 23 after returning from Spangler that "Mr. Strickland . . . seems to be doing well now, much better on Monday the 13th when I left him than when I saw him first" and that "[a] spoonfull of choice G. Hyson Green tea is prized highly by the wounded & faint men. A little can be sent in any letter. Papers sent often will be thankfully recd," he added, in a bid to keep up morale.[10]

Strickland was transferred on July 24 to Mulberry Street Hospital in Harrisburg to continue his rehabilitation. This school-turned-hospital was near where the present-day Harrisburg Hospital stands on Front Street with a view of the beautiful, milewide Susquehanna River that casually flows past town. Pennsylvania's capital city was dotted with temporary soldiers' hospitals in schools, churches, warehouses, and businesses, and the large Mulberry Street Hospital was one of the biggest, receiving many former Spangler patients. The Cotton Factory Hospital a few blocks north on Front Street also overlooked the river and took in many Spangler patients.[11]

Frank taught himself to write with his left hand at Mulberry Street Hospital. As always, uppermost in his mind was his dear Catharine, whom he entreated to "keep up good courage for I hope soon to be with you again."[12] His wounds continued to vex his recovery, as when he became "rather severely allocated with Billious Fever." Thankfully, by late August "I am recovered of that. My arm remains rather painful at times."[13] By early September his spirits had recovered as well, even in the midst of ongoing suffering. "Good Evening Howdy do!" he wrote to Catharine. "I feel some better than when I last wrote you. . . . I have suffered a great deal since I

9 Strickland and Strickland, *The Road to Red House*, 111.

10 Ibid., 112.

11 As the name indicates, the Cotton Factory Hospital was a cotton factory before the war, but it was turned into a hospital when the cotton supply was cut off. The building was changed to a silk mill after the war and is currently the site of the YMCA.

12 Strickland and Strickland, *The Road to Red House*, 113.

13 Ibid., 115. Answers.com: Bilious fever is an old term no longer commonly used. It was used in the 18th and early 19th centuries by doctors to describe symptoms that included fever with nausea and vomiting.

wrote last," he noted. "I got so that I couldn't eat and you know how a Strickland is when he cant eat. But after I got the inflammation out of my arm the second time it began to heal and I feel better." Yet even then Strickland's case reminds that recovery was not a linear process, as in one unfortunate occurrence when "dame fortune once more looked upon me with disdain and caused a bench (on which I was sitting) to tip up throwing me flat upon the floor upon my stump. Oh dear! How it hurt. It broke it open about an inch." His doctors "were soon on hand and after they found that the arteries were not broke they gave me medicine to still the pain and put me to sleep which made me forget my troubles for awhile but it pained me severely for a few days." As with every soldier, his thoughts remained elsewhere: "I think if I was at home now and had Katy to tend to it, it would soon be well."[14]

He wrote his final letter home from Harrisburg on October 1: "I am gaining in flesh now, but it is not on what I get in the hospital, but the apples and peaches & grapes which I eat. I weigh 147 lbs. . . . I have got my Photograph taken so that you may see what kind of an animal you have got out here. The picture you sent me looks very pretty. . . . They are discharging all the one arm and one legged men now those who wish."[15]

Strickland was discharged from Mulberry Street Hospital five days after writing that letter. The government offered him a spot in the Invalid Corps, but he declined. Years later, his son Theron wrote cinematically and movingly about his younger siblings' reaction to their dad's return to Salamanca from Spangler and then Harrisburg:

> At length the father returns, but to the little ones he is a stranger now. Instead of a sturdy red-faced man, dressed in the plainest-pioneer study, as of yore, he is now pale and thin, and wears a suit of blue, trimmed with yellow braid and large brass buttons. The mother is the only one to give him a cordial greeting; the children, abashed and shy, cling to the mother's dress, continually keeping their eyes on the so-called, "new Papa." At length one of them ventures timidly to inquire: "Mama, why does he let that sleeve hang empty? Why don't he put his arm in it?" Here the father takes them on his lap and tells them all about it; how his strong right arm had been shattered by a ball and had to be cut off and buried. Instead of weeping as did the mother, they only sat with open mouths and wondering eyes, listening to "Papa's story," and then wanted to feel of the empty sleeve, which they hardly dared to touch.[16]

14 Ibid., 117.

15 Ibid., 120.

16 Ibid., 122; Strickland Compiled Military Service Record, NARA.

Frank was elected collector of taxes in the town of Evans in 1864 and that same summer traveled to New York City to be fitted for an artificial limb—a new technology at the time—but he wasn't strong enough to wear it so he went home without a new arm.

Frank and Catharine had three more children after the war, though one of those three died in infancy. With his one good arm, Frank ran his shingle mill in Red House, which was broken away from Salamanca, maintained his farm, and received a pension. A respected leader in the area, Frank took the census in 1870 and was elected superintendent of the poor for Cattaraugus County. He served in that role for many years and was elected the first town supervisor of Red House in 1869 and justice of the peace in 1875, a position he held until his death in 1880 at age 49. Catharine outlived Frank by 23 years and never remarried.[17]

Frank and Catharine's daughter Ida married at age 15 in 1872, their first child to marry. Tragically, in 1874 Ida gave birth to premature twin boys who did not survive. Ida died three days later.[18]

One Final Note

Pension records at the National Archives and Records Administration show that Strickland suffered from 1862 until his death in 1880 with lung damage, which dogged him relentlessly, sapped his strength, and eventually killed him. Because of this, he struggled to keep up with the 154th on the march to Gettysburg. Those same records also offer a glimpse into Strickland's character and his caring, sacrificial nature. Pvt. James D. Frink of the 154th tells the story of his tentmate until Frink was taken prisoner at Chancellorsville:

> About Oct. 12, 1862 while on a march from Arlington Heights Va. to Fairfax [Court House] Va. we camped one night in a severe rain storm. There were some sick in our tent and others crowded in on account of the rain. . . . Francis Strickland let the sick ones have his blanket, and the tent was so crowded that he lay with his feet and part of his body out of the tent exposed to the rain storm. He contracted a severe cold on account of the exposure and the lack of proper shelter, and the cold settled upon his lungs. From this time on until I left him at the battle of Chancellorsville he was continually suffering from a cough and lung trouble which was aggravated by various other severe exposures. . . . On the march from Fairfax to Falmouth Va. about Dec. 10–16, 1862 he was sick from cough and lung trouble and was aided by riding

17 Strickland and Strickland, *The Road to Red House*, 126, 130, 132-134.

18 Ibid., 133.

in ambulance one day, and I with another comrade got him out of the ambulance at night and got him quartered in a house where we cared for him. . . . During all this time since the exposure of Oct. 12, 1862 aforesaid, said Francis Strickland had complained at times of pains in chest, and had bad coughing spells and was excused considerable from doing full duty. . . . (After the war) I know he was continuously troubled with a cough."

Assistant Surgeon Rugg of the 154th adds: Strickland was "constantly suffering with a severe cough and pain in the chest until about May (1863). . . . Relapse came because of exposure at Chancellorsville. (lying in the trenches for 2 or 3 days) During this march (to Gettysburg) said soldier would become fatigued & taken with severe cough and shortness of breath. . . . (After the battle) I found him at all times suffering with his lungs accompanied by frequent hemorrhages from the lungs which I am satisfied were the result of exposures incident to camp life."

Dr. John Colegrove of Salamanca took up the diagnosis years later. "In 1875 I first became acquainted with said Francis Strickland," Colegrove began. "I knew him then as a one-armed soldier pale and thin and troubled with a bad cough. From this time I doctored in the family of said Strickland, and met and conversed with him often and kept up an acquaintance with him till the time of his death in 1880." Colegrove finally took the measure of a diagnosis, adding "I several times examined said Strickland's lungs, and found them affected with tubercular disease."[19]

Rugg's testimony indicates Strickland was suffering from the lung troubles and cough while recovering from his arm amputation in the eight-man tent at Spangler. Frank wrote many long, detailed letters home but rarely reported on his own health and suffering, though he did mention it in a December 9, 1862, letter that said, "I am a great deal better today but cough some yet" and reported "very bad discharging blood & yellow matter very freely."[20]

Spangler Farm Short Story

Surgeon Henry Van Aernam of the 154th New York had a keen military eye, even with his gruesome workload at Spangler. In this excerpt from a July 30 letter to his wife, Amy Melissa, after he left Spangler, Van Aernam described the battlefield in great detail and how Army of the Potomac leadership used Spangler and surrounding farms to help win the fight. Note how Van Aernam describes the Union line as a horseshoe or shoe—common for the time—rather than the fishhook as it's usually called today.

19 Strickland pension claim, NARA.

20 Strickland and Strickland, *The Road to Red House*, 41.

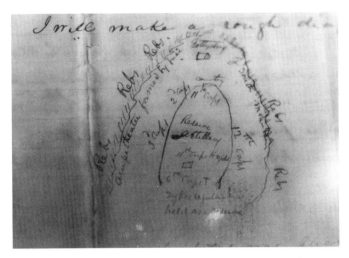

Surgeon Henry Van Aernam drew this map of the Gettysburg
battlefield and sent it to his wife. *Dennis Frank/St. Bonaventure University*

"Our line of Battle was in the shape of a horseshoe—with a rather sharper turn
than a circle at the toe of the shoe which was (the toe) directly south of Gettysburg,
and almost in the suburbs of the village," Van Aernam described. "The key of our
position—the toe of the shoe—was on a height about like the hill east of Ben
Howard's house, on which was an old burial ground in which the 'rude forefathers
of the hamlet sleep,'" he added poetically. Van Aernam understood the tactical array
that had produced the tremendous casualties he treated:

> [A] little east of the old burial ground, and right in the very toe of the shoe, modern
> taste had built a very beautiful cemetery—"Evergreen Cemetery"—among the trees
> and the monuments sacred to the memory of the dead, on those three eventful days
> were planted those huge Batteries that defended the position and decided the events
> of the issue after that long, terrible struggle. The cemetery occupied the highest point
> in the semi-circle, or crest of high ground—before and in front of which was a broad
> plain sown with wheat or meadlowland—this plain running up to the base of South
> Mountain which encloses the Village of Gettysburg in a great amphitheatre—along
> the base of the mountain is a dense forest in which the Rebel army were concealed
> from sight, except when the battle was raging.

It is clear from Van Aernam's narrative that the doctors who labored to save
the lives of the fallen were not immune from the dangers. "The situation of our
hospital was such that the shells that passed over our line of battle, either in front
or right or left, would fall in the hollow of the shoe, and, as on the 2nd and 3rd
day, the great struggle was to break through our left," Van Aernam wrote. "Shells,

consequently, fell very thickly about our hospital, especially on the 3rd day. For a while, from 1 to 3 or 4 o'clock it was a perfect shower."

Van Aernam must have followed developments closely. "In the hollow of the shoe, 300 pieces of Reserve artillery was placed, which could be sent to any spot needed in 20 minutes," he observed. "[B]etween the heels of the shoe were stationed as a reserve the 6th Corps—a part of the 5th Corps volunteers and Sykes regulars—during the contest if our line was weakened at any point, some of these reserve troops were sent to their aid. The line of battle was well chosen and a strong one," he added approvingly, "being the crest of a gentle elevation—say some 20ft above the valley in front. The troops were handled like chess men in the hands of skillful players. Aid was always thrown to the right spot in the right time."[21]

Like Van Aernam and so many non-combatants, Spangler chaplain the Rev. Henry Dyer Lowing of the 154th New York also showed a keen military eye in letters home and described in great and accurate detail the landscape, lines, and fight at Gettysburg. In a letter written to his father on July 22 in Virginia, the chaplain remembered: "We had a narrow escape at Gittisburg. The first day of the fight we were whipped and they drove us out of the town and we were compelled to fall back to our position on the hights East of the Town. This in the end proved to be our salvation." He also mentioned the slow pace of the Army of the Potomac's chase of Robert E. Lee after the battle: "At Hagerstown and Williamsport I believe we might have made a big haul if we had a little more dash. Our carefullness in military matters does not prove to be the safest course. . . . For some good reason yet to be seen an over ruling Providence permitted them to escape."[22]

---

21 Van Aernam to Amy Melissa Van Aernam, July 30, 1863, Box 1, Henry Van Aernam Correspondence (Transcribed), 1862-1864, U.S. Army Heritage and Education Center, Carlisle, PA. There actually were 106 pieces of reserve artillery by the author's count.

22 Henry D. Lowing Letters, provided by his 2X great-grandson Robert Lowing of Lancaster, PA, and Mark Dunkelman.

Chapter 6

Eight Men in a Tent:
Part 3

"My troubles seem without end."

— *Almira Paugh after the death at Spangler of her husband, John, 154th New York*

Sergeant John A. Bush was one of the fortunate 50 soldiers of the 154th New York who were not in Gettysburg on July 1. Those 50 had been detailed to a reconnaissance mission in northern Frederick County, Maryland, so they missed the slaughter of the 154th at Kuhn's Brickyard. Their lives were spared.

That scout team hustled overnight to Gettysburg upon hearing word of the fight, arriving the morning of July 2 and setting up with other XI Corps regiments on East Cemetery Hill. But the 31-year-old Bush's luck would run out that evening when his upper right arm was shattered by a 2½-inch shell. Even so, Bush was fortunate one more time because he was hit behind his own army's line, not the enemy's, as happened at the Brickyard when three XI Corps regiments were overrun. That meant he could be taken directly to the corps hospital down the Baltimore Pike at the Spangler farm immediately after his wounding instead of being trapped for days under Confederate control as had those comrades who were wounded on July 1. That kind of good fortune could save a life.[1]

Private Ben Bentley—of Company D, like Bush—rushed to his side and helped him get to Spangler. Bush must have been quite a load as a strong six-feet-tall farmer, but he was "carried back a mile over in valley . . . to hospital" where he was taken to 154th surgeon Henry Van Aernam. Van Aernam removed four inches of bone from Bush's upper arm soon after his arrival at the farm. Bush arrived at Spangler early enough in the battle that he likely was placed in the barn or another

---

1 Hiram H. Hardesty, *Presidents, Soldiers, Statesmen*, Vol. 2 (New York, 1899), 1494.

Sgt. John A. Bush

Dennis Frank/St. Bonaventure University

outbuilding when there was still indoor space available to await the arrival of tents in two or three days.[2]

The long-term success of this Spangler resection was not positive, Van Aernam admitted in 1866: "A shell . . . passed through his right shoulder, shattering the upper portion of the humerus of that arm so severely that it required an extensive exsection to save his life. I performed the operation upon him the same evening [of Bush's arrival] in the Field Hospital of the XI Army Corps by removing nearly five inches of the upper portion of the humerus. He has recovered from the operation but his arm is nearly useless. . . . It hangs dangling at his side, and he has no ability to raise it. I am of the opinion that it now disables him quite as much for performing manual labor, as it would if amputated." 154th New York Assistant Surgeon Dwight W. Day was at Spangler and he shared Van Aernam's view after an 1866 examination: "Muscles of the arm are atrophied & the area is very weak," he testified.[3]

After the resection, Bush couldn't move his arm away from his body, at right angles at the slightest, or move the arm backward at all when it was hanging by his side. He still had full motion of his wrist, he could touch all fingers with his thumb and pick up and use a knife to prepare food, but he couldn't carry the food to his mouth without assistance from his left hand. Also, the right arm was now 3 inches shorter than the left. It's not known why Bush and Van Aernam chose resection over amputation, but perhaps they did so in the hope that Bush could return to his work as a farmer.[4]

2 John A. Bush to Edwin Dwight Northrup, Aug. 30-31, 1888, Edwin Dwight Northrup Papers, #4190, Box 35, Division of Rare and Manuscript Collections, Cornell University; Hardesty, *Presidents, Soldiers, Statesmen*, 1494; Bush Invalid Pension Claim 59342, NARA.

3 Bush pension claim, NARA.

4 Ibid.

The site of Sgt. Bush's resection.

National Archives and Records Administration

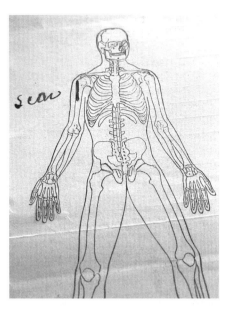

Bush's wife, Helen, and two children under age five were at home when he left for the war, so he likely was used to caring for others. His instinct for care superseded his own critical wounding when the tent arrived and the eight men from the 154th New York filled it. Drummer Thaddeus Reynolds, age 19, lay next to Bush, and Bush kept an eye on him. "John Bush . . . badly wounded in the arm lying next to him although helpless himself watched him & called attention to him when he required during the last two days especially," Great Valley, NY, resident James W. Phelps wrote to Reynolds' father.[5]

Bush was transferred to Camp Letterman and was treated there through November and then hospitalized in Elmira, NY, and Harrisburg (where he also was dealing with tonsilitis on top of everything else) and York, PA, before being discharged from the army in York in January 1865. Through all of those moves and rehabilitation, Bush kept the shell fragment that Dr. Van Aernam removed from his arm at Spangler as a souvenir.[6]

Bush lived a long life despite his serious wound, dying in 1912. He was receiving a total disability pension of $46 a month at the time of his death. Sadly, his loved ones did not enjoy such long lives: wife Helen died at age 44 and children Lura and Jesse died at 45 and 13, respectively. His second wife, Elizabeth, died in 1899 about a year and a half after they married.[7]

Doctor Van Aernam not only tended Pvt. James F. Chase at Spangler as he did Sgt. Bush, but he also was Chase's family doctor before enlistment and delivered James and wife Susan's daughter, Caroline, in March 1862. The 25-year-old Chase enlisted five months after Caroline's birth.

5 Letter to David Reynolds from Great Valley, NY, July 24, 1863, 2013.22.8.0370.011.pdf (sbu. edu), accessed March 4, 2022.

6 Hardesty, *Presidents, Soldiers, Statesmen*, 1494; Bush Carded Medical Record, 154 New York, Abbey, O. J. to Drayton, G. W., NARA.

7 Bush pension claim, NARA.

The five-foot-nine-and-a-half inch, blue-eyed farmer Chase was another victim of the July 1 Brickyard fight and went into the Spangler tent as one of the eight men of the 154th New York on July 4. Chase lasted in agony in that tent until July 31 with wounds to his hip and abdomen. One source at Spangler said, "Excrement oozed out of the entrance and exit holes." As with head and chest wounds, abdominal penetrations such as Chase's were almost always fatal in the Civil War. Infection inevitably followed, and when he wasn't drugged with pain-killing morphine Chase must have been in agony for all of July from the combination of his horrific wounds and infection.

Records show his treatment at Spangler as the basic "water dressing" with no mention of treatment for the internal injuries, though he undoubtedly received nursing to make him as comfortable as possible. It's a testament to Chase's strength and will that he lasted so long with such debilitating wounds, intense July south-central Pennsylvania heat and humidity, and the gagging smells that accompanied his and other wounds in that tent. Of those who died, only Sgt. Lewis Bishop, Company C, lasted as long in that tent as Chase, also dying July 31.[8]

Chase's father, James Sr., was notified of his son's condition and rushed to Spangler from Lyndon, NY, but he didn't get there in time. When he asked of his son's whereabouts upon his arrival, the father was told he had been buried a day earlier. XI Corps hospital staffers showed the heart-broken father his son's grave in the Spanglers' orchard, with his name, company, and regiment painted on a piece of wood. James Sr. took possession of his son's clothing and effects.[9]

Susan and James were married three years before his death at Spangler, with James off at war for the last year of that marriage. Susan received an $8-a-month pension plus $2 a month for Caroline, who was 1 year old when her father died. Chase is buried in Soldiers' National Cemetery in Gettysburg.

As the surgeon for the 154th New York, Dr. Van Aernam undoubtedly felt it was his responsibility to treat as many men of his regiment as he could. As with Bush and Chase, the surgeon was the first to treat Pvt. John Paugh. Paugh was older than most soldiers, arriving at Spangler at age 42. He was a farmer with blue eyes, brown hair, and a light complexion who stood five feet four-and-a-half inches tall. Paugh's wife, Almira, and four daughters ages six through twelve were at home while he was at Spangler.[10]

8 James F. Chase, New York Civil War Muster Roll Abstract, Fold3; www.findagrave.com/memorial/20918616/james-f-chace, accessed Mar. 4, 2022; Pennsylvania Register 554, *Register of the Sick and Wounded*, NARA.

9 Susan Chase Widow Pension Claim 120701, Fold3; CMSR 228, NARA.

10 Almira Paugh Widow Pension Claim 83676, Fold3; John Paugh, New York Civil War Muster Roll Abstract, Fold3.

Paugh suffered a "flesh wound" of his right thigh in the Brickyard on July 1 and was treated with water dressing at Spangler. Van Aernam called it a "gunshot wound severely" and dressed it, then handed off duties to 154th New York Assistant Surgeon Day when Van Aernam left Gettysburg with the Army of the Potomac on July 5. A flesh wound to the thigh that doesn't require amputation is a wound that requires less treatment. But in Paugh's case, the scourge of Civil War hospitals, gangrene, set in. Gangrene is the death of body tissue caused by the cutting off of blood supply or an infection. If it was an infection, it would have added to the thick smell in that tent as the worst infections could be smelled eight to ten feet away. Either way, Paugh died July 12 and Dr. Day blamed gangrene. Van Aernam received a letter from Day on July 18 informing him of Paugh's death. Paugh and drummer Thaddeus Reynolds both died on the 12th, so they were the second and third men to die in that tent after Cpl. Albert Mericle on July 10.[11]

Paugh was buried in the cemetery in the Spanglers' orchard, but that wasn't the end of his story as his death ignited financial woes back home in Hinsdale. Almira now had four girls to support with no income. "They have no home now," Almira wrote of her daughters in 1866. "I have had to separate them. My troubles seem without end." One person writing in support of her pension application in 1866 stated, "Please secure to her what belongs to her by law for the sustenance of her and her four orphan children." A pension was awarded in 1866 and Almira reassembled her family with the $8 a month she began to receive for herself and $2 a month for each of her three youngest children until they reached age 16.[12]

Almira died in 1928 at age 98 at the home of a granddaughter in Bradford, PA, where she lived the final eight years of her life. Almira was receiving a pension of $50 a month at the time of her death and was survived by two of her daughters, ten grandchildren, ten great grandchildren, and two great-great grandchildren. Of course, John knew none of those 22 grandkids. Almira never remarried. John was exhumed from his Spangler grave and is buried in the New York section of Soldiers' National Cemetery.[13]

At age 22, Cpl. Gilbert M. Rykert was the third youngest soldier in that miserable tent. Only drummer Thaddeus Reynolds and Cpl. Albert Mericle, both 19, were younger. Rykert was single, five feet nine inches, with brown hair and

---

11 Paugh widow pension claim; "water dressing" was the application of an ointment to a wound covered with a wet cloth. It was the most popular treatment at the Spangler hospital and an example of why Civil War-era hospitals needed to be near a supply of cold, fresh water to keep wounds clean.

12 Paugh widow pension claim.

13 Paugh widow pension claim; "Mrs. Paugh, Aged Nearly 100 Years, Dies In This City," *Bradford Evening Star and Daily Record*, Jan. 30, 1928.

Cpl. Gilbert M. Rykert

Buffalo *(NY)* Courier

blue eyes when he left for war in 1862, leaving his job as a wagon maker.[14]

Rykert was hit in the right arm at the Brickyard, and several inches of bone were removed on July 3. His pension claim stated that the ball passed "through the right arm severing the bone about four inches below the shoulder." It further noted that "in consequence of said wound he had to have from four to five inches of the bone removed rendering his arm useless."[15] Rykert was transferred from Spangler to Camp Letterman on July 25 and from there to the Cotton Factory Hospital in downtown Harrisburg on September 7. He was discharged from the army in January 1864 with "no control of arm." Rykert's father, the Rev. Gilbert Rykert Sr., died in June 1864 so chances are strong that father and son reunited after young Gilbert returned home before Gilbert Sr.'s death.[16]

Surgeons who examined Rykert's wound were unanimous in support of his invalid pension claim:

February 1864: "Arm shortened, muscles much destroyed, wounds nearly healed—hand and arm entirely useless."

July 1867: "[The arm] in present situation is entirely useless for all practical purposes and is the source of much suffering to him. Disability permanent. No probability of it being restored by surgical interference."

September 1877: "Evidences of ball having passed into back side of right arm. . . . Arm shriveled, dangling and useless, but there is partial use of hand."[17]

Rykert received a monthly pension that climbed to $24 by 1886 thanks in part to the support of those surgeons. He married Arietta Smith in 1868 and had

14 Gilbert M. Rykert, New York Civil War Muster Roll Abstract, Fold3.

15 Gilbert M. Rykert Invalid Pension Claim 29244, NARA.

16 Rykert Civil War Muster Roll Abstract; Rykert Carded Medical Record, 154 New York, Murke, J. to Wingsnwthwing, A., NARA.

17 Rykert pension claim, NARA.

three sons. Rykert remarried in 1898 after Arietta's death in 1895. He worked as a telegraph operator and for Lake Shore Railroad in Westfield, NY, and, because he was hard of hearing, it was as a railroad employee in 1900 that his carriage was struck by a train. He was thrown 80 feet and likely killed instantly at age 60.[18]

A history of Chautauqua County, NY, called Rykert "a gallant soldier, an honest, faithful, conscientious employe, and an upright, honorable and respected citizen, ever doing all in his power for the prosperity of the town in which he resides."[19]

Students of the battle of Gettysburg know well the sacrifice of the XI Corps' Second Division, First Brigade under Col. Charles R. Coster at the Brickyard. Casual visitors to Gettysburg might not be so aware. The fight took place away from the battlefield's easily identified topography, and its location is now obscured by development. But the isolated site is far from forgotten. It can be found at Coster Avenue on the Gettysburg National Military Park battlefield map in northeast Gettysburg and is worth a visit with its monuments, markers, and a beautiful mural of the fighting by author, historian, 154th New York expert, and artist Mark H. Dunkelman. On summer weekends, a visit can be concluded with a trip to the Gettysburg Foundation's George Spangler Farm & Field Hospital to further study the 154th New York and the site where eight men endured so much suffering in that one tent.

An Expert's Closer Look: Resections

By Jon Willen, M.D., Retired Infectious Disease Specialist

Sergeant Bush and Corporal Rykert each had bone removed from an arm at Spangler instead of the more common amputation. Incomplete XI Corps hospital records list only seven resections at Spangler including Bush and Rykert, but there were undoubtedly many more.

In some cases, surgeons on both sides performed resections or excisions (the terms are interchangeable), removing several inches of shattered bone or a damaged joint using a chain saw. Obviously, these saws weren't anything like what you envision in today's chain saws. Rather, they were small steel chains with sharp edges, a couple of feet long, with a handle on each end. Their flexibility allowed the surgeon to cut through the bone without damaging surrounding tissue, which wouldn't have been possible with a bone saw used for amputations.

---

18 Obed Edson, *Chautauqua County, New York* (Philadelphia, 1891), 108-109; *Buffalo* (New York) *Courier*, Apr. 15, 1900; *The Buffalo Commercial*, Apr. 9, 1900; Rykert pension claim, NARA.

19 Edson, *Chautauqua County, New York*, 109.

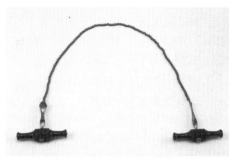

An example of a chain saw used for resections. *www.fleaglass.com*

Surgeons tried to avoid amputation when only the bone and muscles, not the nerves and arteries, were damaged. This shortened and deformed the limb, but often left some function.

Union surgeons performed at least 4,656 resections, but these operations suffered a higher fatality rate than amputation. Because the surgery weakened the limb it was more often performed on arms than legs. Sometimes, resections were done to preserve the limb at the insistence of the soldier, especially officers. A resection, with a less functional and shortened limb, would actually be more difficult for a soldier postoperatively than an amputation and subsequent prosthesis. There were instances of soldiers undergoing a resection and later undergoing an amputation.

Resections were usually not done in the height of battle, as they took at least 45 minutes compared with 15 minutes or less for an amputation. I suspect the reason that Bush and Rykert underwent resections by Dr. Van Aernam was that they arrived at the Spangler farm early, and hence there were fewer patients requiring attention.

Dr. Jon Willen is a retired infectious disease specialist. He has been a medical re-enactor and lecturer on Civil War medicine for 25 years, portraying Union and Confederate army surgeons, often at the George Spangler farm. Dr. Willen serves as a board member of the Civil War Roundtable of the District of Columbia, the Lincoln Group of the District of Columbia, and the Society of Civil War Surgeons, and he is a docent at both the Smithsonian National Museum of American History and the National Museum of Health and Medicine.

Spangler Farm Short Story

Major General George Meade had only been in command of the Army of the Potomac for a few days when he arrived in Gettysburg at 1 a.m. July 2. He explored the battlefield overnight, but still did not have a complete picture of the enemy's strength and placement. Even with those deficiencies and with no sleep, he was supposed to finish setting up his line for what would become the biggest battle of the Civil War. And he didn't just do that, he did it to great success. And he involved the George Spangler farm.

"So soon as it was light," Meade wrote of July 2, "I proceeded to inspect the position occupied, and to make arrangements for posting the several corps as they should reach the ground." That would have been soon after 4 a.m. The V Corps arrived on the Hanover Road about then and later that morning was moved by Meade. "My troops took position on the right of our line," V Corps commander Maj. Gen. George Sykes wrote, "but it being thought too extended, they were subsequently massed near the bridge over Rock Creek, on the Baltimore and Gettysburg pike, and within reach of the Twelfth Army Corps." There the corps stayed on Spangler, Musser, Bucher, and Diehl land until Meade ordered the corps "to our extreme left." The VI Corps then occupied that land after the V Corps rushed to the line through Spangler land. The Sixth raced to the line through Spangler soon after.[20]

The V Corps was partially on Spangler land because that is precisely where Meade placed the men. Meade had a detailed sketch made on a map showing where each corps was to be placed and then sent it with an aide to each corps commander. After that was done, he sent artillery chief Brig. Gen. Henry J. Hunt to the line for a second time to make sure the artillery was properly posted.[21]

Meade's overnight placement July 1-2 of the V Corps and VI Corps on and behind Spangler land on the Baltimore Pike paid crucial dividends when those corps rushed on the double-quick down Blacksmith Shop Road and Granite Schoolhouse Lane to save the line on and in front of Little Round Top in the late afternoon/early evening of July 2. And the line that he ordered precisely arranged by sketch was plenty strong enough to hold off Robert E. Lee's army for two consecutive days. Meade undoubtedly had no idea and didn't care who owned the farms he seized, but even with no sleep he was wide awake to the military value of Spangler and neighboring land.

XII Corps commander Maj. Gen. Henry Slocum gave full credit to Meade's quick thinking and placement of the V Corps in the Spangler neighborhood:

> The Fifth Corps was massed between the extreme right and left of the line occupied
> by the army, and held in readiness to move to the support of any part of the line.

20 Maj. Gen. George G. Meade, www.nytimes.com/1863/11/12/archives/general-meades-official-report-of-the-battle-of-gettysburgh.html, accessed Dec. 26, 2023; Maj. Gen. George Sykes, Official Records, Series I, Vol. XXVII/1, Warrenton, VA, July 31, 1863. We know that the V Corps was on the I. M. Diehl farm on July 2 in addition to Spangler, Bucher, and Musser because that's what Two Taverns-area native Cpl. Isaac N. Durboraw of the 30th Pennsylvania Infantry/1st Pennsylvania Reserves wrote later. His Company K was recruited in Gettysburg and came home to fight this battle. Durboraw knew the neighborhood and its residents so well that Peter Baker of the east side of the Baltimore Pike invited Durboraw across the road to his house to eat, which Durboraw did, then returned to his unit just in time to join the V Corps' rush to Little Round Top, Houck's Ridge, and the Wheatfield. The Diehl farm was directly across Blacksmith Shop Road from the Spanglers' lane and stretched to Rock Creek and is the site of a quarry today. Coco Collection, Gettysburg Field Hospital Research No. 9, Misc. Accounts, Box B-75-2, Folder 0-201 to 0-210, GNMP.

21 George Gordon Meade, *With Meade at Gettysburg* (Philadelphia, 1930), 96.

About half an hour before the attack on our left, this corps [the Fifth] was moved by order of the commanding general to the support of that part of the line. This attack was made by the enemy in strong force, and with great spirit and determination. Had it been successful, the result would have been terribly disastrous to our army and to the country. The arrival of the Fifth Corps at the point of attack at so critical a moment afforded it an opportunity of doing service for the country the value of which can never be overestimated.[22]

---

22 *OR*, Serial 43, Page 759, Chapter XXXIX.

Chapter 7

The XI Corps Hospital

"All the suffering and distress I saw there was awful."
— *Gettysburg resident Sarah Monfort after visiting the XI Corps Hospital*

men of the First Division, XI Corps ambulance corps waited along the Emmitsburg Road just south of Gettysburg in the early afternoon of July 1. The division's infantry and artillery had been ordered north of town, but the 30-some ambulances accompanying them were told to sit tight while the line was sorted out. These ambulance workers were used to going in, too, and they could hear the battle on the other side of town and even see some of it, but they waited as ordered. Common Army of the Potomac strategy was to send stretcher bearers to the line with the troops, then have them carry the wounded to the ambulance collection point out of range of Confederate artillery behind the line. The instructions were different on this day at Gettysburg.

When the order finally came to rush the ambulances through town to the aid of Brig. Gen. Francis Barlow's retreating First Division regiments and get them to the Spangler farm hospital, it was too late. At that point, the fighting men weren't the only ones trapped in town by the quickly moving Confederates. So, too, were the division ambulances and their teams. The race was on to save their own lives in addition to those they were assigned to rescue.

Stretcher bearer Pvt. Jacob Smith of the 107th Ohio—23 years old and a native of Germany—described the frenzy and panic:

Just as we reached the heart of the town on our way to the front, we encountered our forces falling back in confusion and disorder, filling the street so that it was an utter impossibility to make further progress forward, or to turn our teams about again. The enemy were close behind in hot pursuit. At this juncture the only way left for us to escape was to tear away

Ambulance worker Jacob Smith,
107th Ohio

U.S. Army Heritage and Education Center

a couple of panels of fence between two houses alongside of the street, and pass between the buildings, and then other way up the back street. The fence was quickly removed, the wagons turned in and we passed through. The enemy were so near that in turning the corner back of the building more than half of the Ambulance men in our squad were captured. This I think was about the only time in service that I considered it really necessary to disobey orders; the enemy halted us, but I thought it my duty to get along as rapidly as possible, and by considerable effort and fast running I succeeded in getting out of their reach and inside of our lines on Cemetery Hill.[1]

Spangler neighbor Nathaniel Lightner was in and outside of town with a friend during this hysteria and witnessed Union troops "rushing pell-mell forward, without any apparent order, with fixed bayonets, eager-eyed, stripped, perspiring, and panting in the hot sun. . . . A mad rush of more troops, wagons and ambulances followed, filling up streets, orchards, fields and every place."[2]

The Northern troops were ordered to Cemetery Hill to regroup, but most had no idea where the hill was. Some of Smith's captured ambulance corps comrades never made it back to the army, instead dying of disease and starvation in a Confederate prison. In all, Army of the Potomac Medical Director Jonathan A. Letterman estimated that one officer and four privates of the ambulance corps were killed at Gettysburg and 17 wounded, not including unknown numbers of men taken prisoner.[3]

But because Smith made it, because he somehow scrambled out of that deadly frenzy in downtown Gettysburg, he was able to spend five days delivering wounded and dying men to the XI Corps hospital and also to work in that hospital on the

---

1 Jacob Smith, *Camps and Campaigns of the 107th Regiment Ohio Volunteer Infantry, From August, 1862, to July, 1865* (Navarre, OH, 2000), 87–88.

2 "Horrors of Battle," an interview with National Lightner, National Museum of Civil War Medicine, Frederick MD.

3 Jonathan Letterman, *OR*, Series I, Vol. 27, Part I Reports, Oct. 3, 1863, 198.

night of July 1. His work delivering wounded to Spangler began immediately after he made it safely behind the line.

"In our retreat through the town and when near our lines we loaded our wagons with wounded who had managed to get back that far," Smith wrote after the war. "We hauled them about a mile to the rear of the battle line out of the reach of immediate danger, and after unloading them started back to the front for another load," he recalled. "We were not long in finding sufficient wounded soldiers to fill our wagons and these we took back to where we had unloaded the first load." He remembered the scene well: "The place where we had taken the wounded was alongside of the Baltimore pike, close to the point where Rock Creek crosses the road, and just about a mile in rear of our lines upon Cemetery Hill."[4]

Private Francis Stofflet, Company D, 153rd Pennsylvania, was hit three times in the Day 1 horror north of town, including once in the left elbow, which caused a compound fracture. The 22-year-old teacher who lived with his family near Allentown went to the almshouse and treated his own wounds with cold water from a pump. His diary offers a harrowing description of that July 1 fight:

> The bullets soon began to whiz. They have such a bewitching, embarrassing tone! The rebel artillery open upon us on our left. Our artillery branch reply. . . . Thrice struck by bullets myself, all harmless except one which pierced my left arm at the elbow. I walked, and bled, and fought. . . . The onslaught, the beginning of the conflict was terrible. One sees pictures of battles; they give no adequate idea of the carnage. The moan, the roar and the tumult are absent. You hide from one bloody scene only to be introduced to another and more horrible one.[5]

The five-foot-eight-inch Stofflet was transferred from the almshouse to Spangler on July 5, but he didn't stay there long. "The doctor examined my wound and advised me to continue bathing my arm in cold water," his diary records. "After lingering a day around the field hospital, picking up a scrap here and there to eat, orders came for the transfer of the sick and wounded that it was safe to handle to the Baltimore and Philadelphia hospitals." Along with other sick and wounded he was "transferred first to Baltimore, where as many as could be accommodated were left, the rest among them myself, were taken on to Philadelphia and there

4 Smith, *Camps and Campaigns*, 88–89.

5 Francis Stofflet, "Diary of Francis Stofflet Private Co. D 153rd PA. Vols. 1862-63," Easton (PA) Area Public Library, 17; www.findagrave.com/memorial/59502289/francis-stofflet, accessed Sep. 28, 2023.

distributed among the hospitals. Here the sick and wounded received excellent care," he was careful to observe.[6]

Nine hundred and eighty men known to have been taken to Spangler were wounded on July 1, by far the heaviest day of the battle for the XI Corps, though many wouldn't arrive at the XI Corps hospital until July 4 or 5 after the Confederate retreat. That total of 980 is more than three times the July 2 number of 307, most of which came from East Cemetery Hill and Cemetery Hill. Of those 980 on Day 1, only 18- or 19-year-old musician Pvt. Adam Snyder, Company H, 107th Ohio, is known to have died July 1 at the XI Corps hospital, though many more undoubtedly did but are unrecorded. Snyder was first buried in the Spangler orchard and now rests in Soldiers' National Cemetery in Gettysburg.[7]

The temperature in Gettysburg that day was 76 degrees under cloudy skies at 2 p.m. about the time George and Elizabeth Spangler's farm was claimed for a hospital. We'll probably never know who rode up the lane and informed the Spanglers that their farm was now a hospital under government control, but likely candidates are XI Corps Medical Director George Suckley, or because it was claimed first for a Second Division hospital, Second Division Surgeon-in-Chief Daniel G. Brinton, and First Brigade, Second Division Surgeon-in-Chief Henry Van Aernam of the 154th New York. Letterman could have joined Suckley in turning Spangler from a division hospital into a corps hospital with all three divisions represented as there are reports of his direct involvement with hospitals throughout the battle.[8] Whoever that officer was bearing that news, it changed the Spanglers' lives forever.

Corporal Horace Anguish of the 157th New York, First Brigade, First Division, XI Corps, was 22 or 23 years old at Gettysburg and described by a comrade as a "quiet and saving man" because he sent "all or nearly all of his pay home to his mother" in Madison County, NY, near Syracuse. Anguish was hit in the arm near the Mummasburg and Carlisle roads on July 1 and was one of the fortunate wounded who made it behind the line to Spangler that same day, perhaps because he was ambulatory or because stretcher bearers were present. But his arrival began a nearly month-long, painful stay at the XI Corps hospital.[9]

6 Ibid.

7 Pennsylvania Register 554, Record Group 94, NARA; Jacob Anguish Father's Pension Claim 233821, NARA.

8 Misc. Farms & House Hospital folder, Gregory A. Coco Collection, Gettysburg Field Hospital Research No. 6, GNMP.

9 Harriet Anguish Mother's Pension Claim 248647, NARA.

157th New York Assistant Surgeon J. Mortimer Crawe tended Anguish at Spangler for that entire July, and it was Crawe who wrote to Anguish's parents as their son's life faded:

Near Gettisburg Penn July 26th 1863

Jacob Anguish

Dear Sir

At the request of your Son, I write to inform you of his condition. He was wounded at the battle near this place by a Minie ball which entered the arm mid way between the Elbow & Shoulder, tearing the flesh & breaking the bone into fragments, and entering the cavaty of the Chest. We endeavered to save his arm by performing a Resection, (That is taking out the bone from the joint above . . .) but yesterday secondary hemorrhage set in & on examination it was found that the blood vessles were so much diseased as to require the Amputation of the arm, it being the only hopes of saving his life, even this being small. We will do all in our power to make him comfortable & to save his life, at the same time you must not flatter yourselves. The chances being very much against him. He has born his sufferings like a true soldier as he is & always has been & you may be proud of such a son who has nobly done his duty as a soldier in defence of his country. Hoping that God will sustain & strengthen you & yours watching over your son in this his hour of need.

Remain

Truly Yours

J. Mortimer Crawe, Assistant surgeon, 157th New York,

Surgeon in charge, 1st Division, 11th Corps hospital.

Anguish died five days after that letter was written. He was buried in the Spanglers' orchard and his body now lies in Soldiers' National Cemetery.[10]

With the ambulances' lanterns aglow, crews worked long after dark carrying men to Spangler from July 1 into July 2. "Going all night bringing off wounded," 27-year-old ambulance worker Sgt. Martin Luther Buchwalter of the 73rd Ohio wrote in his diary.[11]

The armies took a reprieve from heavy combat on the night of July 1, so the hospital staff at Spangler focused on the wounded and dying with no fear of Confederate artillery. The temporary hush on the battlefield revealed the horrible din of the hospital: ambulance wagons and their horses bouncing and clanging

10 Ibid.

11 Richard A. Baumgartner, *Buckeye Blood: Ohio at Gettysburg* (Huntington, WV, 2003), 120.

onto the farm to drop off their wounded and dying and then rushing back to the line; the frightening and relentless echo of the bone saw as it ground back and forth in front of the barn; surgeons shouting orders; patients crying and screaming and moaning; comrades praying; soldiers killing the Spanglers' livestock for food; and window shutters and doors being torn down and broken for operating tables and fires. The Spanglers could hear it all from the upstairs bedroom in which all six were confined, only yards from the barn. Some of it happened directly beneath that bedroom window. What kind of terror and horror had suddenly exploded on their once-quiet and peaceful farm?

"My heart is sick contemplating the mutilations," Van Aernam wrote to his wife about his work at Spangler. Like the Spanglers and the wounded, the surgeons at the XI Corps hospital were victims of this battle as well, exemplified by Van Aernam and Enoch Pearce of the 61st Ohio. Both were sick at Spangler with the deadly Civil War curse of chronic diarrhea, the No. 1 killer of the war. Both worked through it when possible.[12]

Van Aernam became ill in November 1862 and never recovered. He was hospitalized in 1862 and 1864, finally being discharged in November 1864. The repeated diarrhea caused a prolapsed anus among other long-term difficulties.[13] Van Aernam's description of the camp and hospital life that caused his health issues typified the miserable conditions at Spangler. "[T]he offal and skins of the cattle slaughtered for beef were left just where the animals were killed, all of those vile things were left unburied," he wrote, "and the sink holes of the men were uncovered with earth, and the stench from all these sources, pollutes and poisoned the air." It got worse: "[T]he surface water running into the little brooks and creeks, from the frequent showers, where the water to supply the troops was obtained, washes this putrefying mass carrying it into the brooks and creeks and contaminated all the water thoroughly that could be had for the use of the army." With characteristic understatement, Van Aernam summed up the state of camp and hospital hygiene as "bad, as bad could be."

A physician witness described Van Aernam's condition before, during, and after Gettysburg in his application for a pension. The account provides a detailed and painful picture of how he likely was suffering at Spangler, describing, from the onset of "[f]ever and diarrhea after Thoroughfare Gap" to the "hardships and exposure at Fredericksburg" that "brought on the diarrhea again." Van Aernam

---

12 Van Aernam to Amy Melissa Van Aernam, July 30, 1863, in Mark Dunkelman, *Brothers One and All* (Baton Rouge, 2004), 144.

13 Henry Van Aernam Invalid Pension Claim 464173, NARA. According to the Cleveland Clinic, failure of the muscles that hold the rectum in place leads to rectal prolapse. This can be caused by chronic diarrhea.

Surgeon Henry Van Aernam
New York State Military Museum

"never fully recovered. He has always since then, been compelled to have the strictest watch over his diet. The least indiscretion at table, either in the quality or quantity of his food, always followed by diarrhea of two or three days duration dyspeptic troubles of a longer period."

Van Aernam's sufferings were terrible indeed. "The prolapsed anus has been a constant source of annoyance to him," the pension application continued. "Standing upon his feet for any considerable time, getting fatigued from any cause, or when debilitated when unwell, when walking or doing anything that required a stooping position or riding in a carriage over a rough road, any of these always bring it on bad." His symptoms were "attended with agonizing spasmodic efforts to evacuate the contents of the bladder, and not unfrequent by the contents of the lower rectum are evacuated . . . as well as the contents of the bladder. At frequent, and if not responded to at once, the spasm and pain are excruciating." The miserable doctor required attention "whether in church or at the meal table. . . . After his sickness in 1862 he never regained his health or strength but remained at the front with the command, until he could go no further."

Spangler surgeon Bleecker Lansing Hovey of the 136th New York sometimes shared a tent with Van Aernam. "At Chancellorsville, Fredericksburg, Gettysburg and many other battles and campaigns . . . Van Aernam was present doing duty as a Surgeon when suffering from disease," Hovey recalled. "The objective symptoms of impaired health were well marked by emaciation, loss of physical endurance, sallow and jaundiced skin and general wasting, the result of long and continued diarrhea." Van Aernam wrote in 1890 that "my condition is such as to require the constant attendance and aid of another person."[14]

The battle claimed other victims from the medical staff. Surgeon Enoch Pearce of the 61st Ohio was at the bedside of Assistant Surgeon William S. Moore of the 61st when he died at Spangler. "Dr. Moore . . . was mortally wounded by a cannon shot which took effect on his left thigh," the 30-year-old Pearce wrote

14 Van Aernam Pension Claim, NARA.

Surgeon Enoch Pearce, 61st Ohio
www.sparedshared20.home.blog

in a letter on July 20. "It very extensively extending from the glutal region nearly to the knee. . . . There was very severe shock. . . . He died on the 6th of July the entire limb being either in a state of mortification or gangrene which extended to the gluteal serotal and iliac regions."[15]

Remarkably, Moore was the only surgeon to die at the battle of Gettysburg, and according to Pearce's wife, Beulah, Moore's death combined with the workload at the Spangler hospital and elsewhere played a role in the downward spiral of her husband's health. She said Pearce was in good health when she saw him in the winter of 1862-63, but then "I next saw him in Washington City after the Battle of Gettysburg probably August 1863 . . . at which time he showed the effects of hard service, looking very thin and much worn—the effects of overwork he being not only Brigade Surgeon but the only Medical Officer of the Regiment his first assistant having been killed at the Battle of Gettysburg and 2nd assistant previously mustered out on account of physical disability." And sure enough, like many others, as Beulah also recorded, Pearce suffered "chronic diarrhea in that campaign."[16]

Mrs. Pearce saw her husband again four months after Gettysburg. "His appearance evinced a man of greatly impaired health, he was very thin, of a yellow pallor, and his step was very slow & feeble, and would become fatigued by the least exertion, being very weak and debilitated he finally became confined to bed. Complained of general aching and great soreness, particularly of the groins, was restless & very sleepless, he was in bed I think some three weeks." His doctor called him "a played out man."[17] Pearce was discharged in spring 1864 and recovered and lived to age 83. His younger brother, John Pearce of the 61st Ohio, served as a hospital steward at Spangler.

15 RG 94, Adjutant General's Office, Personal Papers of Medical Officers and Physicians ("Medical Officer's Files") Peables, A.M.—Pease, C.M. Box No. 446, Letter to the Army Medical Board, July 20, 1863, Warrenton, VA, NARA.

16 Enoch Pearce Invalid Pension Claim 348146, Fold3.

17 Pearce Pension Claim, Fold3.

So prevalent was the curse of diarrhea that even visitors to Spangler were susceptible. 64-year-old George Schlabach got severe diarrhea while visiting his dying son at Spangler, which he attributed to the unsanitary conditions on the farm. His son—Pvt. Benjamin Schlabach, Company D, 153rd Pennsylvania— died at the XI Corps hospital of wounds to his hand and hip.[18]

Hospital steward William R. Kiefer of the 153rd Pennsylvania bounced between the aid station on East Cemetery Hill where his regiment was deployed and the Spangler hospital during the battle before going to work full time at Spangler. Kiefer kept a diary at the XI Corps hospital that now resides in the Easton Area Public Library. Here is a first excerpt:

> Thurs. 2nd. Am at the Eleventh Corps Hospital waiting on our wounded. Several of the 153rd Regt. here, wounded. Sharp skirmishing all day. Line extended from Gettysburg five miles south; heavy cannonading on left wing toward evening, a fine day.
>
> Fri. 3rd. The conflict is raging, a terrible slaughter must ensue; am out in front near cemetery; some 1500 wounded now at the Hospital; many brought in. . . . Brought in Philip Ensly.
>
> Sat. 4th. About the Hospital, no fighting to-day but skirmishing not forgotten. Rain this evening. Many wounded lying on the ground and not covered, horrible sight here. Many amputations.[19]

Kiefer helped the ambulance corps load wounded at the Evergreen Cemetery gate, and there war's horrors became personal for him. "Among those I have a distinct recollection of finding two of my acquaintances, Samuel Lantz and Philip Ensley. I found John Koken near a fence where I dressed his wounds and as soon as there was room for him had him carried to the improvised hospital in the [Spangler] barn." Kiefer said the arched, brick, cemetery gate house was "crowded with wounded men. Numbers of them died and were temporarily buried, while the wounded were conveyed by wagons to the barn hospital."[20]

Private John Koken, Company F, 153rd Pennsylvania, was shot in the right breast, and Kiefer met up with him and helped him again at Spangler. "Comrade John Koken . . . was a good soldier. We were school boys together, living in the same neighborhood from early childhood," Kiefer recalled. "While I was around

18 Jeffrey D. Stocker, "We Fought Desperate": A History of the 153rd Pennsylvania Volunteer Infantry Regiment (2004), 339.

19 William R. Kiefer, "Diary of William R. Kiefer, Drummer Co. F 153rd PA Vols. 1862-63," Easton Area Public Library, 37.

20 Kiefer, History of the One Hundred and Fifty-Third Regiment Pennsylvania Volunteers Infantry, 97.

Hospital steward William R. Kiefer, 153rd Pennsylvania

Jeffrey D. Stocker, We Fought Desperate

the hospital, assisting in the care of 1500 wounded, I strolled out back of the barn (our hospital) and wholly unexpected I found my friend John lying under shelter of a few boards which had one end laid on a fence. It was along side a barrack. He was very glad to see me, and his case was pitiable enough. He had been wounded in the chest, and the great profusion of blood had saturated his clothes, pocket book and all." Not all service at Spangler was medical, and Kiefer wrote about Koken's "$60 bills so covered with blood that they required soaking and washing. I laid them out on the boards, with some pieces of garments, also, to dry," Kiefer described. "He requested me send his money home. He was subsequently removed to a hospital, I think, in Newark. He lived many years and was employed in railroading."[21]

The five-foot-five-inch, 24-year-old Koken was shot through his body not quite one year after he married 21-year-old Sarah on July 15, 1862. The ball entered the upper part of the nipple, passed through a portion of his lung, traveled 10 inches, and exited through his back about 2 or 3 inches lower than the chest entry wound. Koken was treated with water dressing at Spangler and survived despite the hemorrhaging from his mouth that Kiefer witnessed. Koken was still bleeding and coughing in February 1864, but he survived because of what one doctor described as "a fine constitution." He was awarded a pension of $6 a month and went on to have at least five children and work as a brakeman for the Lehigh Valley Railroad. The wound finally caught up to him for good when he died of internal bleeding at age 53 in 1892 at his home in Easton. Sarah owned neither property nor money to bury her husband, so she applied for a widow pension, which she received until her death in 1919.[22]

Kiefer continued to witness scenes of torment. "At the time I was nursing in the 11th Corps hospital," he relayed in another anecdote, "I spent a night of the most awful heart strain I had ever experienced:

A young man lay under the eaves of the barn during a torrent of rain with but slight covering surrounded by hundreds of others. His cries for help were truly the most heart-

21 Ibid., 191.

22 John Koken Invalid Pension Claim 27008, NARA; Sarah Koken Widow Pension Claim 366479, NARA; *The Philadelphia Times*, July 7, 1892.

rending one could listen to. His shrieks became unendurable. I hunted about to learn from what direction the calling came and finally found him under some boards which had been hastily laid up for shelter. I asked him where he was wounded and he could not tell, except that he had great pain between his shoulders. I removed his shirt to ascertain the location and character of his wound and by the dim light of the lantern I succeeded in finding a wound between his shoulder-blades, the shape of the incision being exactly that of a bayonet. From the size of the hole the weapon must have pierced deeply into his body.[23]

Private William J. Dunbar, Company G, 153rd Pennsylvania, suffered a bayonet wound in the back so he's likely the man Kiefer found. The five-foot-three-inch, 22-year-old farmer was treated with water dressing by Spangler doctors, survived the wound, and was mustered out with the rest of the 153rd later that month. Dunbar died in 1924.[24]

July 1 had been a beautiful day in Gettysburg with a slight breeze accompanying the 76-degree temperature at 2 p.m. July 2 dawned with the same slight breeze but with a slightly warmer day at 81 degrees by 2 p.m. Residents of south-central Pennsylvania are familiar with high heat and humidity in July, so the weather on the first two days of the fight wasn't part of the abundant misery at the XI Corps hospital.[25]

XI Corps surgeons spent July 2 playing catch-up from the mass of wounded delivered the previous day. They fell further behind because of wounded brought from Cemetery Hill from Confederate artillery and sniper fire throughout the day, violent skirmishes in the modern-day Colt Park neighborhood west of the hill, and the dusk charge on East Cemetery Hill of five Louisiana regiments under Brig. Gen. Harry T. Hays and three North Carolina regiments from Brig. Gen. Robert Hoke's brigade. Also arriving on July 2 was Spangler neighbor and close friend Jacob Hummelbaugh, though he was seeking sanctuary rather than medical attention. In addition to being in perilous proximity to combat, Hummelbaugh's farm was claimed as a First Division, II Corps aid station on the afternoon of the 2nd. Hummelbaugh left a partially eaten meal on the table and a half-barrel of flour in the attic when he escaped to Spangler, so hospital attendants who took over his house used the flour to make "slapjacks" for the hungry troops and staff. Soon, the house and temporary hospital was filled mainly with III Corps wounded, so

23 Kiefer, *History of the One Hundred and Fifty-Third Regiment Pennsylvania Volunteers Infantry*, 183.

24 William J. Dunbar Invalid Pension Claim 212059, NARA.

25 Misc. Farms & House Hospital folder, Coco Collection, Gettysburg Field Hospital Research No. 6, GNMP.

Hummelbaugh likely spent the night with the Spanglers, putting all seven of them in that one bedroom surrounded by flies, blood, screams, and tears.[26]

First Lieutenant Horace Clark of the 73rd Ohio was leading his men in the July 2 skirmishing west of the Emmitsburg Road and shouting "Stand fast, boys, don't give a foot," when he was hit in the left thigh by a piece of shell that then fell into his boot. He was taken to Spangler and treated with water dressing before being transferred to a more sanitary Baltimore hospital, where he still possessed that shell fragment.[27]

The 55th Ohio was on the Taneytown Road next to the 73rd Ohio and near the intersection with the Emmitsburg Road when 30- or 31-year-old Pvt. William E. Pollock of the 55th was torn up by the premature explosion of an Army of the Potomac shell. It had come from the hill behind him in an often-overlooked deadly section of the battlefield. The five-foot-six-and-a-half inch machinist from Monroeville, just south of Sandusky, had left his wife of seven years, Sarah, and 6-year-old daughter, Ida, back home in Ohio when he was hit. He was taken to Spangler, where hospital worker Pvt. Sumner A. Wing of the 55th Ohio tried to help him. "I remember William E. Pollock, a stalwart man of Company C, who was mortally wounded," Wing recalled later. "He was torn by a piece of shell—a terrible wound. I remember just how he looked, with his pale, pleading face. Poor fellow, we could do but a little for him." Sources are conflicted about when Pollock died at Spangler, either July 3 or 5.[28]

Kiefer continued to bear witness to scenes of unendurable agony, and "some special cases which were very affecting." One of those cases involved a young New Englander whose groans and cries "were so distressing that it was enough to unnerve the stoutest heart." Kiefer remembered him as a handsome youth suffering a mortal wound "in the region of the chest. [A]t every effort of coughing," Kiefer remembered, "the suppuration was so offensive that to every one near him it was unendurable. I visited him as often as my urgent work upon others would allow, and words cannot express the distressing pleas he made for my assistance."

These were not isolated incidents. "The barn floor was constructed with a partition making it a double threshing floor, with bays on either side," Kiefer continued. "The maimed were placed with heads next to the bays and the middle partition leaving a passageway at the feet of the patients. I had the care of about

---

26 A. T. Hamilton, "The Surgeon's Story," in *The Story of Our Regiment: A History of the 148th Pennsylvania Vols.*, ed. Joseph Wendel Muffly (Des Moines, IA, 1904), 172.

27 Baumgartner, *Buckeye Blood*, 84.

28 Hartwell Osborn, et al., *Trials and Triumphs: The Record of the 55th Ohio Volunteer Infantry* (Chicago, IL, 1904), 252; Sarah Pollock Widow Pension Claim 10266, Fold3; Ancestry.com.

fifty men in the ward assigned me. Soldiers of both armies were treated with equal kindness." But compassion was not nearly enough. "While all was done that it was possible to do on the first day or two," Kiefer wrote, "no words can portray the pitiable condition, the more distressing because of the insufficient means immediately at hand, to relieve the large number of helpless men. The amputation work under an open shed presented the most ghastly sights that could be witnessed."[29]

Like Kiefer, 153rd Pennsylvania Chaplain Philip W. Melick bounced between multiple locations. Chaplains had the freedom to roam and minister widely, from praying with dying men, to leading services, to writing letters for soldiers, to holding their pay, to providing food and water, to cleaning and wrapping wounds during and after battle. Melick tended the men at the Spangler hospital, tried to do so at the 153rd's location on East Cemetery Hill (but was discouraged from reaching there by Confederate sniper fire), and rested and left his belongings at the Henry/Abraham Spangler house on the Baltimore Pike. At the George Spangler hospital he "attended to the wants of the wounded soldiers in the barn as well as I could" and "slept and prayed with the soldiers in the barn." He didn't mention the difficulty of ministering to irreligious soldiers, including the one in the stable who yelled "put the preacher out" as Melick attempted to lead a Sunday service. He wasn't at the XI Corps hospital long, leaving Gettysburg with the army on July 5. He was discharged soon thereafter.[30]

As is commonly known, July 3 was the hottest day of the battle with a high temperature of 87 degrees, bright sun, and high humidity. This only added to the misery at the XI Corps hospital. All the Spangler livestock had already been taken, their crops appropriated, the family's clothing, furniture, and tools seized by the army, the well fouled, and most of their 166 acres trampled. Surgeons and hospital workers were having a difficult time bearing it. "We worked with little intermission & with a minimum amount of sleep," Dr. Daniel G. Brinton, Surgeon-in-Chief, Second Division, XI Corps, age 26, wrote in his diary. "On one day I arose at 2 AM & worked incessantly till midnight. I doubt if ever I worked harder at a more disagreeable occupation. What I saw of the fight was consequently little, but our anxiety was correspondingly great."[31]

---

29 Kiefer, *History of the One Hundred and Fifty-Third Regiment Pennsylvania Volunteers Infantry*, 99-100.

30 Ibid, 224; Rev. Philip W. Melick, "Diary of Rev. Philip W. Melick, Chaplain, 153rd PA Vols. 1862-63," Easton Area Public Library, 131-134.

31 Brinton, "From Chancellorsville to Gettysburg, a Doctor's Diary," *The Pennsylvania Magazine of History and Biography* 89, no. 3 (1965): 313.

Chaplain Philip W. Melick,
153rd Pennsylvania

Jeffrey D. Stocker, We Fought Desperate

On top of all that, and making everything even more unbearable, records indicate that 14 men died on July 3 at Spangler, making it the most agonizing day in the five weeks and two days of XI Corps hospital agony at Gettysburg. And there undoubtedly were more whose name or date of death have been lost to history. Here are those 14 men:

Carr, Orson S., Sgt., Co. E, 13th VT.

Crubaugh, Jeremiah, Pvt., Co. C, 75th OH.

Dietrich, Franz Louis, 1st Lt. & Adj., 58th NY.

Ervin, James, Pvt., Co. G, 73rd PA.

Gasler, Joseph, Pvt., Co. K, 107th OH.

Hamman, Gottfried, Pvt., Co. K, 74th PA.

Hanson, Austin, Cpl., Co. F, 17th ME.

Heald, Nathan, Pvt., Co. F, 73rd OH.

March, William, Pvt., Co. D, 13th VT.

Mayberry, Andrew, Cpl., Co. D, 20th ME.

Moody, William, 3rd Lt., Co. A, 2nd MS.

Reynolds, James M., Capt., Co. B, 61st OH.

Weisensel, John C., Cpl., Co. E, 45th NY.

Wilbur, Philip C., Pvt., Co. E, 134th NY.[32]

Ambulances fanned out across Gettysburg in the driving thunderstorms of July 4 and picked up almost all the XI Corps men who were wounded on July 1 and took them to Spangler. A few more arrived July 5 in two days of incredibly efficient, difficult, and tender ambulance work. "I know of no battle-field," Army of the Potomac Medical Director Letterman wrote after the battle, "from which wounded men have been so speedily and so carefully removed, and I have every reason to feel satisfied that their duties could not have been performed better or more fearlessly."[33]

July 4–5 is when the U.S. Sanitary and U.S. Christian Commissions—separate entities—estimated there were 1,800 or 1,900 wounded soldiers at the XI Corps hospital. Thirty-two of those men died at Spangler between July 4 and July 9, then nine more died on July 10 and 10 more on July 12 as deadly and

32 Compiled by historian and archivist James P. Fielden.

33 *War of the Rebellion: Official Records of the Union and Confederate Armies*, Series I, Vol. 27, Part I Reports, Letterman, (Culpeper Court-House, VA, 1863), 198.

unforgiving infections cursed the hospital and the suffering men. Many more died after being transferred from Spangler for better care in bigger, cleaner hospitals. July 3 had the highest one-day death total, but July 4–5 featured overpopulation at the farm, driving rain, mud, manure, more death, exhaustion, and agony. The battle of Gettysburg was fought mainly on July 1–3, but the crescendo of suffering at the XI Corps hospital took place July 3–5.[34]

XI Corps Third Division commander Maj. Gen. Carl Schurz visited Spangler on July 4: "To look after the wounded of my command, I visited the places where the surgeons were at work," he recalled. "At Bull Run, I had seen only on a very small scale what I was now to behold. At Gettysburg the wounded—many thousands of them—were carried to the farmsteads behind our lines. The houses, the barns, the sheds, and the open barnyards were crowded with moaning and wailing human beings, and still an unceasing procession of stretchers and ambulances was coming in from all sides to augment the number of the sufferers."[35]

Widow Sarah Monfort of York Street in downtown Gettysburg visited the farm shortly after the battle. "All the suffering and distress I saw there was awful," she said. "The poor fellows came around us. . . . We handed out cakes and bandages, but it went such a little ways. It made me so sorry that I had so little."[36]

Private Chauncey G. Pinney, age 26, Company D, 154th New York, was one of the July 4 arrivals at Spangler. A Minie ball hit Pinney in his left side on July 1, fractured a rib, and penetrated the lower portion of his left lung before lodging in his right side. "A portion of the lower tube of the left lung protrudes through the wound—he will probably die," 154th New York Assistant Surgeon Dwight W. Day wrote to his parents after leaving the XI Corps hospital. But Pinney was still alive and at Spangler on the hospital's last day there on August 6, aided by his younger brother, 23-year-old Pvt. Curtis S. Pinney, who survived the battle unscathed and was allowed to stay with his brother. "Curtis . . . is taking care of his brother" at Spangler, Dr. Day wrote.[37]

Chauncey was transferred to Camp Letterman on August 6, where surgeons did a thorough examination: "The patient had suffered little from the effects of the injury," one wrote. "The ball was excised and the wound was dressed with simple

34 Fielden research; *Report on the Operations of the Sanitary Commission During and After the Battles at Gettysburg* (New York, 1863), 24; Rev. John B. Poerner, "Third Report of the Committee of Maryland," 265.

35 Carl Schurz, *The Reminiscences of Carl Schurz*, 3 vols. (New York 1908), 3:38-39.

36 www.sparedshared22.wordpress.com/2021/05/18/1863-sarah-elenor-thompson-monfort-to-henry-jacob-brinkerhoff/, accessed Oct. 4, 2023 (link provided by Carolyn Ivanoff).

37 Chauncey Pinney Invalid Pension Claim 59308, NARA; 2013_22_8_0130_011.pdf (sbu.edu) by Mark Dunkelman, accessed Oct. 4, 2023.

Pvt. Curtis S. Pinney, 154th New York

Dennis Frank/St. Bonaventure University

cerate and tightly supported by adhesive plaster. Tonics were administered, with an opiate occasionally, and at night. From the wound of entrance there was a protrusion of about an inch in size, which was at first believed to be a hernia of the lung, but subsequently proved to be tissue which [was burned away with] caustic."[38]

Both Pinney boys survived the war, though Chauncey required intermittent hospitalization. Curtis settled in the wilds of the Jordan River Valley of the northern Lower Peninsula of Michigan, where he was an original homesteader. Pinney Bridge State Forest Campground between Mancelona and Boyne Falls is named after him. Despite his wounds and being the older brother, Chauncey outlived Curtis, who died at age 74 in 1915 in Charlevoix County, Michigan. Chauncey was left partially paralyzed on his right side, blind in his right eye, and partially blind in his left eye, but he lived to age 84 and died in 1921 in Bradford, Pennsylvania.[39]

Corporal John H. Benedict, Company C, 17th Connecticut, age 23, lay on the battlefield July 1–3 before being taken to the almshouse on the 3rd and Spangler on the 5th. "I saw John Benedict lying flat on his stomach on the ground, with all his accoutrements on, and as I passed I said, 'Hullo, John, is that you? Are you wounded?'" Pvt. William H. Warren, Company C, 17th Connecticut, recalled after the first day of battle. "'Yes,' he said, 'help me, take off my knapsack and other things.' While I stopped but a moment to help him, a reb saw me and told me with an oath to go to the rear or he would shoot me, so I said, 'John, I am sorry I cannot help you but I have to go to the rear or I will be shot.' It made me feel bad to leave

---

38 *The Medical and Surgical History of the War of the Rebellion* (1861-65), Vol. II, Part 1 (Washington, D.C., 1875), 584.

39 Pinney Invalid Pension Claim, NARA; www.findagrave.com/memorial/47066203/curtis-sherwood-pinney, accessed Oct. 4, 2023; www.findagrave.com/memorial/83458898/chauncey-g-pinney, accessed Oct. 4, 2023.

Cpl. John H. Benedict, 17th Connecticut

Carolyn Ivanoff, We Fought at Gettysburg

one of my own company in that position without assistance."[40]

Benedict stayed on his feet for a few moments after being hit in the right arm before passing out and falling face first onto the ground because of loss of blood. He was then hit in the leg while lying on the ground. Private John McHugh and Benedict were both from Danbury and they were transferred to Spangler together and placed in the same tent. "The two Johns were in the hospital together for twenty days," Warren wrote, "being cared for all the time by the Sanitary Commission citizens, and citizens' doctors, as well as army doctors, they worked night and day and did all they could for the wounded."[41]

Benedict and McHugh were transferred to York, Pennsylvania, on July 20 and survived. Before the transfer, Benedict made a point of visiting the Spangler hospital graves of 17th Connecticut comrades Daniel Purdy, Frank Benson, and Joseph Whitlock "beside a fence." Benedict received an invalid pension starting in 1865 with increases in 1878 and 1884. He was denied an increase in 1897, and in response, with clear bitterness, said, "I tried to do my duty while in the service and have tried to be a respected citizen since as well as before the service. I must say to you I am very much surprised to receive your letter rejecting my application for increase. It makes me feel I was a fool to go down thare and get shot."[42] Benedict did indeed receive pension increases after that and died in 1921 at age 81.[43]

---

40 William Warren Manuscript, Bridgeport History Center, courtesy of Carolyn Ivanoff, *We Fought at Gettysburg; Firsthand Accounts by the Survivors of the 17th Connecticut Volunteer Infantry* (Gettysburg, PA, 2023), 57.

41 Warren manuscript and Ivanoff, *We Fought at Gettysburg*, 247.

42 Ibid, 247-248; John H. Benedict Invalid Pension Claim 81671, NARA.

43 Benedict Pension Claim, NARA.

Corporal Aaron W. Lee, Company G, 17th Connecticut, said he wasn't placed in a tent at Spangler like his comrades Benedict and McHugh. Instead, he lay in "open fields" from the 4th through the 8th before being taken to Satterlee Hospital in Philadelphia on the 9th. He said gangrene developed in his wounded left thigh and this injury was dressed for the first time at Satterlee.[44]

Private Stephen C. Romig, Company F, 153rd Pennsylvania, age 17, was struck in the left knee on East Cemetery Hill and treated on the threshing floor upstairs in the Spangler barn. But he had problems other than just his knee. "On our way to Gettysburg from Emmitsburg," he remembered after the war, "we traveled through muddy roads, as it had rained considerable and it seemed to be the most peculiar sort of clay, being of a very sticky nature. I did not give attention to it until I was wounded and lying in the hospital. For several days my feet annoyed me very much," he said, "and I asked a nurse to remove my shoes. He tried to take them off but finally said it was impossible. I told him to cut them off as the mud had become so hard and dry that there was no way of removing them. He got the shoes off but he forgot to wash my feet, and the soil remained on them until it wore off. On the long march to Gettysburg the shoes had become literally worn out; the bare skin being exposed."[45]

The 17th Connecticut sent out a squad in search of stragglers on the morning of July 5, and Pvt. William W. Paynton of Company A described the hospital scene and who he found at Spangler:

> There was a large orchard in the rear of the barn, and under nearly every tree was a shelter tent, or a rude shelter of boards constituting an improvised hospital and occupied by one or more wounded soldiers. While strolling around amongst these, I came upon an old friend that had been one of our "Big-Six" mess at Brooks Station, Va., the winter of '63; he was in attendance upon Corp. W. W. Westlake of Co. A. who had been wounded in both legs, and both had been amputated above the knees. I stopped to speak a few words of cheer and encouragement to Westlake, who was a good, brave boy, having just been promoted and was a popular comrade as well as a good soldier. He died in a few days later during a second amputation. As I turned to leave my old mess-mate wanted me to take him with me; he said he was sick—that he was sick of the situation. He had straggled away, and a surgeon had detailed him to attend Westlake, but he said he was unfitted for the task, and he wanted to return with me to the regiment. He said he had been there two days and nights and had not had a mouthful to eat, he was almost starved. I gave him all the "Tack" I had, which was three, and we started together from the orchard to meet the

---

44 Aaron W. Lee Invalid Pension Claim 171081, NARA; Warren manuscript and Ivanoff, *We Fought at Gettysburg*, 205.

45 Kiefer, *History of the One Hundred and Fifty-Third Regiment Pennsylvania Volunteers Infantry*, 184.

rest of the detail. Just then I saw another chap, a member of Co. C that I thought might as well go with me, so I approached him and said, "What are you doing here?" he replied that he was detailed by a surgeon as a nurse in the hospital. I looked him over and made up my mind that he was lying. "Is that so?" says I. "What are you doing with that waist belt and cartridge box on?" He still maintained that he was detailed nurse. Then I asked him where was the hospital badge which all field nurses wear, consisting of a strip of white cotton cloth tied around the arm above the elbow. This was a "stunner" to him, and when I told him of my mission, and unless he could take me to the surgeon that detailed him to verify his statement, he must go with me to the Regt. I brought my musket to a charge and ordered him forward, and he wilted, and I took him to the Regt.

On our way out we passed a corner of the barn, and I noticed two large hogsheads that stood close to the roadside. Curiosity prompted me to look into them; I was horrified to find them filled with human limbs, arms, legs, hands and feet that had been amputated from the bodies of the brave boys in blue, that their lives might possibly be saved. I turned away with a shudder; such is war![46]

The horrors of what had taken place began to be revealed to a larger public audience in the immediate aftermath of the battle. Friends and family members began to swarm Gettysburg to search for missing and dead loved ones once the railroad was returned to serviceable shape on July 7, and 13-year-old West Railroad Street resident Leander H. Warren and his team of horses and wagon were there to help, delivering them to Spangler and other hospitals. "Gettysburg only had a few public houses at that time," young Warren remembered, "so many of the people had to walk the streets all night because they could not find a place to stay. In every barn south and east was a hospital and the people who were looking for their friends wanted someone to take them, so I made good use of our team. Sometimes I could find their friends, but not very often. It was a terrible sight to go around to the barns that were converted into hospitals. The men were lying in rows on straw and a blanket for a bed."[47]

The Adams Sentinel wrote on July 21: "We learn from one of our undertakers in town, that the number of coffins manufactured here for the transportation of the dead soldiers home by their friends, amounts probably to six or seven hundred already, and we presume this mournful business will be kept up for some time yet. The town is full of inquiring relatives for those near or dear to them. Some have to go away cheerless and unsatisfied, the last resting place of their friends not

46 Ivanoff, *We Fought at Gettysburg*, 245-246.

47 Leander H. Warren, "Recollections of the Battle of Gettysburg," ACHS Research Civilian Accounts, A-Cr Biggs, Basil folder, Adams County Historical Society, Gettysburg.

being identified, from the vast amount that were hurried into their mother-earth, without a mark to tell who lies there."

On the surface at least, the horrors of the XI Corps hospital lessened just a bit by Thursday, July 9. Hundreds of patients had been transferred to better facilities and initial amputations had been performed. Deaths remained troubling, however, with five on this date and many more to come. This is when visitors from Ohio reported what they saw at Spangler: "At the 11th Corps hospital . . . we found several members of the 55th and 107th Regiments, and though strangers to most of them, all were glad to see us, and we were highly gratified to find most of the wounded in excellent spirits, and well cared for. Here we found Doctor Spooner of the 55th, with his coat off and sleeves rolled up, attending to his patients in a most faithful manner. On the whole our wounded are well cared for and are doing better than could have been expected under the circumstances."[48]

Hospital worker Kiefer of the 153rd Pennsylvania was apparently becoming inured to the daily atrocities he witnessed. He offered a day-by-day overview of his work July 5–16 at Spangler:

Sun. 5th—Busy all day nursing, was detailed for nursing; unpleasant weather. Put up a few Hospital tents, not half enough.

Mon. 6th—About hospital all day, except in p.m. Went out towards town, getting the wounded better cared for. A fine day.

Tues. 7th—Busy all day attending to the wounded, a large number sent off to-day. A number of citizens came with eatables. Term expired.

Wed. 8th—Nursing all day. John Seiple died of lockjaw about 4 o'clock a.m. Many wounded taken away. Seventy or more legs and arms amputated. Rain last night and this morning, clear tonight.

Thurs. 9th—In Hospital to-day. Many citizens came to see us today. Jno. Seiple buried in cemetery in Gettysburg by some of his friends. To Gettysburg this morning and back to the Hospital. Fine day.

Fri. 10th—To Hospital nearly all day, at work assisting. A fine day. (Kiefer note from 1903: A barn was used for the Wards, Bay's stalls, Out-Sheds, Barracks and Orchards.)

Sat. 11th—Busy all day nursing, except in p.m. Visited part of Battle ground. Fine day.

Sun. 12th—In Hospital all day; much to do. Cloudy, rain this afternoon.

Mon. 13th—Nursing all day, rain part of day.

---

48 *Norwalk Reflector*, July 21, 1863; Fielden research.

Tues. 14th—Nursing all day, rain a.m.

Wed. 15th—Relieved from Hospital and went to town. Fine day.

Thurs. 16th—Starting for Harrisburg this morning, arrived towards night.[49]

Someone died and a family lost a loved one on George Spangler's farm on every one of those days mentioned by Kiefer. In fact, someone died at the XI Corps hospital every day except July 23, July 26–27, July 29, August 3, and August 5–6. A total of 49 men are recorded as having died between July 12 and July 19. Finally, the grief began to subside, as 26 men died between July 20 and August 4 with a daily high of six during that period on July 21. The last two men known to have died on Spangler property were Pvt. Henry Muller, Company B, 41st New York (right hip and mid-3rd right arm) and Pvt. August Raber, Company F, 107th Ohio (flesh wound left forearm), on August 4. Muller and Raber were 20 or 21 years old. Many more died later elsewhere.[50]

Private Daniel H. Purdy, age 21, Company C, 17th Connecticut, died July 14 of shoulder and lung wounds sustained on July 1. The Rev. Jacob M. Hinson of Philadelphia was by his side in his tent at his death and informed Purdy's father in a letter:

Philadelphia, July 23rd, 1863

Mr. Alson Purdy, Dear Sir:

It becomes my painful duty to send you sad tidings. I was a delegate of the U.S. Christian Commission to the battlefield at Gettysburg; among the sufferers, I found your son; he was shot through the lung. His mind was fixed on home and heaven. When I first met with him, I inquired about his home and relatives, he said, "I have a father and mother and two little sisters; how I would love to see them." He asked me to pray with him; I complied. He said, "I feel comfortable in my mind, a good hope." A telegram was sent to you and I asked him in case you did not come, what word he had to leave for you. He said "Tell father his son done his duty as a soldier for his country and his Lord." (Just here I would mention that he prayed with one of his dying companions.) "Tell mother not to worry and take good care of the children; tell the girls to love and obey their parents, both in sight of God and man."

He received as good care as the time and circumstances could afford. While your son has fallen, his messages to you are words of comfort, and you should not mourn as those

49 Kiefer diary, 37.

50 Fielden research.

having no hope. He died July 14th, about four o'clock p.m. at the 11th Corps Field Hospital near Gettysburg.

Yours obediently, J. M. Hinson, Pastor of Port Richmond M. E. Church, Phil.[51]

Purdy is buried in Soldiers' National Cemetery.

Private Robert Corl, Company H, 134th New York, was 18 when he died at the XI Corps hospital on July 19. The six-foot mechanic from Schenectady had been wounded in the right ankle and left shoulder. Corl's mother, Melinda, had died one year earlier at age 36 or 37. Corl's body was removed to Schenectady, arriving July 23, the same day that Pvt. David Proper's body arrived home after temporary burial elsewhere in Gettysburg. They were buried in a joint funeral on July 24 with a procession of veterans, private carriages, drum corps, and fire departments. "The funeral was large and the exercises unusually interesting," wrote the *Schenectady Evening Star and Times*. "Brave soldiers! They have yielded up their lives on the altar of their country. They could not have a nobler epitaph than the mere statement of the fact."[52] Private Corl was one of seven men to die at the George Spangler farm on July 19, 1863.[53]

Doctor Jacob Y. Cantwell, 82nd Ohio, age 38, surgeon-in-chief, Second Brigade, Third Division, XI Corps, was either personally present at these deaths or nearby because he announced so many of them. And he worked at Spangler for all of July and likely the first week of August. This labor took a most definite toll. "Dr. Cantwell . . . has worked faithfully and energetically ever since the first day's fight, and is now almost worn out," reported *The Ashland* (Ohio) *Union* newspaper on July 22, 1863, adding perhaps with a bit of a stretch in an era of Civil War medicine that was still finding its way, "He performed . . . some of the most difficult operations in surgery, and all successfully. The following is a small list of his operations [at Spangler]: Removal of the entire upper jaw; ligation of the sub-clavian artery; four resections of shoulder joint; one resection of hip joint; one hundred and fifty amputations, besides innumerable smaller operations. The appointment of Dr. Cantwell as chief operator of the corps was a decided compliment," the newspaper proudly reported, "there being in the corps Surgeons from Philadelphia, Boston and New York. The wounded are all being very well taken care of."

---

51 Ivanoff, *We Fought at Gettysburg*, 241.

52 *Schenectady Evening Star and Times*, July 25, 1863; New York, U.S., Civil War Muster Roll Abstracts, 1861-1900, Fold3; www.findagrave.com/memorial/71767561/melinda-corl, accessed Oct. 5, 2023.

53 Fielden research.

U.S. Assistant Surgeon Austin D. Kibbee
Ancestors.familysearch.org

XI Corps Medical Director George Suckley was equally impressed with Cantwell, telling him as he left him at Spangler: "Your operations are performed with judgement, skill, dexterity and humanity. I now leave knowing well that our poor wounded cannot be left in better hands."[54] Like other surgeons who worked several weeks at Spangler, Cantwell required a leave of absence after the closing of the XI Corps hospital to restore his physical and mental well-being after what he had just been through. As further evidence of his skills, he was promoted to brevet lieutenant colonel by the end of the war.[55]

U.S. Assistant Surgeon Austin D. Kibbee, age 32, was at Dr. Cantwell's side during those surgeries, and he, too, needed medical care after such a lengthy and taxing time at Spangler. A medical certificate dated August 14, 1863—one week after the closing of the XI Corps hospital—shows he was examined and found to be suffering from remittent fever and unfit for duty, becoming yet another casualty of the Spangler hospital nightmare.[56]

Hospital worker Pvt. Emory Sweetland, age 27, 154th New York, told wife Mary Jane in a letter written July 17 that his work was slowing down at the XI Corps hospital: "My Own Dear Wife . . . I don't have quite so much to do as I did at first. I draw & divide among the nurses the bread, eggs, preserves & . . . for the wounded. Also I draw clothes for them & see to having their clothes washed (I have two men that don't do anything but wash) I have to see that the nurses tend to the wounded & keep them clean & I am much encouraged by recent events to think the end is nigh."[57]

54 "Letters Received by Commissioner Branch, 1863-1870," C715-C1109 C769-Cantwell, J. Y., Fold3.

55 Compiled Military Service Records No. 453, NARA.

56 Austin D. Kibbee Invalid Pension Claim 1056968, NARA.

57 "Civil War Letters From Emory Sweetland, Little Valley, Cattaraugus County, New York, to His Wife Mary Jane (Holdridge) 1862-1865." Originals remain in the family's possession. Transcribed by Mark Dunkelman and Sweetland descendant Margaret (Nyhart) Smith, and accessed at 2013_22_8_0428_012-115_10.pdf (sbu.edu) on Oct. 5, 2023.

Hospital stewards Emory Sweetland, 154th New York (left), and David W. Knowles, U.S. Army. Knowles likely served at Spangler with Sweetland. *Dennis Frank/St. Bonaventure University*

Sweetland also is one of our witnesses to the availability and importance of newspapers at the XI Corps hospital, writing in the same letter, "The pappers say Lee is across the river. I doubt it some yet we heard cannon yesterday in the direction of Antietam." XI Corps ambulance worker Jacob Smith of the 107th Ohio said newspapers were being used by soldiers on July 5 to find out exactly what happened in the battle in which they had just fought. "This morning shortly after sunrise," he wrote, "we were visited by a newspaper boy. Everyone was anxious to get the news. We were still ignorant with regard to the probable number of killed and wounded, and what the mortality of the enemy's forces were. It was but a short time until he had disposed of all his papers and the supply was far from satisfying the demand. However, by going together in groups and one of the number reading and the others listening, we soon learned the most important news. Aside from our own great victory over the enemy, we, today had the cheering intelligence given us that General Grant had captured Vicksburg."[58]

Sweetland wrote on July 22 from Spangler: "God has been good to us dear wife in preserving our lives in these perilous times. We ought to be verry thankful & love him more for his goodness to us. I have a verry pleasant place here considering that I am among wounded men." And on July 26: "About a week ago our steward went away & now I am acting steward & ward master at the same time. I dont know how long that I shall stay here Louis Bishop our color Serg' is dying to day. He is a noble brave man. he went home before the battle of Chancellorsville & was married to a girl at Olean. . . . the weather is quite warm & the flies verry thick." Bishop lasted until July 31.[59]

---

58 Smith, *Camps and Campaigns of the 107th Regiment Ohio Volunteer Infantry*, 124.

59 Smith and Dunkelman, "Civil War Letters From Emory Sweetland," 2013_22_8_0428_012-115_10.pdf (sbu.edu), accessed Oct. 5, 2023.

Sweetland was transferred from Spangler to Camp Letterman on August 5, where he was placed in charge of 60 patients and 20 nurses. He was present at Abraham Lincoln's Gettysburg Address. Camp Letterman was closed for good in late November, and Sweetland transferred to other hospitals. He later developed a close friendship with surgeon Van Aernam.[60]

Men such as Sweetland and Kiefer worked at Spangler and hospitals at other battles because it was their job. For others, Spangler was their first hospital assignment, including Sgt. William H. Howe, 134th New York; Cpl. George Dickens, 17th Connecticut; Cpl. John Irvin, 154th New York, and dozens more. Still others who arrived at the XI Corps hospital with minor injuries were put to work once they were able, such as Pvt. James R. Middlebrook, 17th Connecticut (hernia); Pvt. Albert A. Simons, 154th New York (rheumatism and cracked ribs); Sgt. Orrin P. Warner, 134th New York (hit in the head by a splinter of a rail); Pvt. Justus Silliman, 17th Connecticut (head); Musician Alfred J. Rider, 107th Ohio (feet); and Pvt. James D. Quilliam, 154th New York (face). Simons was a doctor and Warner a medical student before the war so they were obvious hospital choices, though Simons, according to 154th New York Assistant Surgeon Corydon Rugg, "used opium and morphine and drank to the excess . . . and he was morally as well as physically a wreck." Simons had been convicted of burglary in October 1857 and sentenced to two years in Auburn State Prison. He was pardoned in October 1858. Rugg also recalled incidents during the war in which Simons had stolen "drugs and whiskey during the night by hiding them under his shirt." Simons said he was taken to the XI Corps hospital by Dr. Van Aernam and worked there until it closed in August. Van Aernam said Simons was a "dresser of wounds or nurse" at Spangler. He worked as a physician after the war, but said, "I tried to practice medicine a little and did practice for a while what I could." His application for an invalid pension was denied by the Pension Bureau. Simons had two sons who became physicians.[61]

Dickens of the 17th Connecticut helped grieving family members find their dead loved ones at Spangler. One case recounted by the Rev. Hiram O. Nash of Ridgefield, Connecticut, ended tragically like so many others. Nash had traveled by train to Gettysburg to visit his nephew, Pvt. Rufus Warren, Company C, 17th

60 2013_22_8_0428_012-115_10.pdf (sbu.edu), accessed Oct. 5, 2023; 2013_22_8_0428_003_10.pdf (sbu.edu), accessed Oct. 5, 2023.

61 Alfred A. Simons Invalid Pension Claim 343165, NARA; Ancestry.com; www.findagrave.com/memorial/80120081/albert-a-simons, accessed Oct. 5, 2023; George H. Warner, *Military Records of Schoharie County Veterans of Four Wars* (Albany, NY, 1891), 287; www.museum.dmna.ny.gov/unit-history/infantry-2/134th-infantry-regiment/newspaper-clippings, accessed Oct. 5, 2023; Ivanoff, *We Fought at Gettysburg*, 85, 220.

Connecticut, age 21. "On the 17th [a Friday] I set out with the intention of seeing him alive if possible. . . . Reached Gettysburg about daylight Sunday a.m. Learning of the direction of the 11th Corps Hospital, we set out, some eight or ten of us, on the Emmitsburg Turnpike some two miles, until we reached the Taneytown Road, which turned to our right about half a mile and brought us to the camp. With indescribable emotion we approached the camp, and soon with intense solicitude we inquired the fate of our poor nephew, and was met with the answer by George Dickens, a member of his company, that he expired on the morning of the 17th about the time we left our home." Nash and his party were then "conducted to his grave which we found decently marked with a head-board, name, company, date of death, etc. This we secured and brought home with us. We returned to the village and made all necessary preparations." Nash returned to the hospital that afternoon to get a fuller report of the circumstances of his nephew's death. He learned that Warren had been "wounded by a cannon ball in the left leg, which had to be amputated just above the knee, which was done on the 4th with much fortitude." Nash was fortunate that Warren's last words had been preserved in the memory of his attending nurse: "'Tell them,' says he, 'to live as Christians and meet me in heaven.' And what should I say to the Regiment, should I see them again? 'Tell them to be praying men and stand by the flag of the Union to the last.'"[62] Nash had Warren's body prepared for transport and returned to Ridgefield on July 23. He was buried on July 26, nine days after his death at Spangler.[63]

Another Spangler hospital worker from the 17th Connecticut—Pvt. William Wurz of Company D—was in charge of about 18 wounded men, including three Confederates, and he said he had to mark their wounds with chloroform every half-hour to keep out the maggots.[64]

Exhumation of bodies of Union soldiers buried on the battlefield and all over Gettysburg as well as those at Spangler and other massive field hospitals south of town began October 1. First was the graveyard at the Presbyterian church, according to 13-year-old Leander Warren, who in July used his wagon to take visitors to hospitals in search of loved ones. Warren picked up empty coffins at the train station, carried them to the exhumations at the temporary graves, picked up filled coffins containing newly exhumed remains, and drove them to Soldiers' National Cemetery for reburial by another crew. Basil Biggs headed a crew of eight to 10 black men doing the exhumation work, and this crew also had a wagon and a man carrying filled coffins to Soldiers' National Cemetery. This work began less

---

62 Ivanoff, *We Fought at Gettysburg*, 304-305.

63 Ibid., 305.

64 Warren Manuscript, Ivanoff, *We Fought at Gettysburg*, 238.

than two months after the XI Corps hospital closed on August 6 and continued into March, but it's not known when Biggs, Warren, and the crews reached Spangler.[65]

Warren described the systematic, and racialized, approach to the grisly labor: "While the work of uncovering the dead on the field was done by negroes, the reburial at the national plot was in charge of white men. The semi-circular trenches were opened to a depth of about four feet and were just as wide as the length of the coffins. When one coffin was placed, it was covered by the earth from the excavation for the next grave. Thirty or forty men were working under the cemetery association."[66] Warren added, "Samuel Weaver oversaw the exhumations and he said he personally witnessed the exhumation and reburial of 3,512 Federal dead." Biggs used his earnings to buy a farm on the Taneytown Road.[67]

Former Spangler patient Pvt. Enoch M. Detty, Company G, 73rd Ohio, age 22, was the first identified soldier to be buried in the Ohio section of the new cemetery. Detty was taken to Spangler on July 2 with a gunshot wound of the neck, then died of chronic diarrhea October 26 at Camp Letterman. A funeral was held for him that day at Letterman and he was then immediately taken to Soldiers' National Cemetery, according to Daniel W. Brown, the state agent who superintended the removal of the Ohio dead from the battlefield. Detty is buried in Grave A-1 in the Ohio section. Detty's father, David, received a $12 monthly pension starting in 1881.[68]

Jacob Smith, the 23-year-old ambulance worker for the 107th Ohio who only escaped capture in the madness of downtown Gettysburg on July 1 because of his quick feet and then delivered so many wounded and dying men to the XI Corps hospital, returned to Gettysburg 36 years after the battle at age 59. This was common for these survivors to remember what they accomplished and honor the friends they lost on America's most historic battlefield. "In my walk over the battlefield," Smith recalled of his return trip, "I found that part over which I had labored during the fight, in nearly all of its parts to be about the same in appearance as when first gone over, with only some slight changes caused by time and growth of trees and shrubbery. Any person wishing a pleasant recreation, can do no better than come here and see the grandeur displayed in the care and

65 "Re-burial of Union Dead in the National Cemetery," Adams County Historical Society, Civilian Accounts, A-Cr, Biggs, Basil folder.

66 Ibid.

67 Ibid.

68 https://www.npshistory.com/series/symposia/gettysburg_seminars/15/essay3.pdf, accessed Oct. 7, 2023; David Detty Father's Pension Claim 242588, NARA.

attention given the ground by the government, and also the extent of the great and world-renowned battlefield."[69]

It's highly likely that Smith made Spangler one of his stops on that visit all those years later. He definitely knew the way to the XI Corps hospital.

Final Medical Notes

Corporal William Barthauer, Company D, 45th New York, age 35, was wounded July 1 by "a conoidal ball which produced a wound of the scalp about an inch in length" in the rear of his head. He remained at Spangler until July 11, when he was transferred to Philadelphia. "He improved steadily until the 23d, when the parts in the region of the wound became highly inflamed, creating considerable sympathetic fever. Flaxseed poultices were applied, and on the 27th the wound suppurated freely. Milk punch was given during the day, the diet otherwise being restricted. The patient became prostrated, and on the 2d of August was attacked with a slight delirium. Death followed on the 6th of August."[70]

Private August Beck, Company D, 54th New York, age 42, was wounded July 2 "by a musket ball, which passed laterally through the thyroid cartilage, destroying the upper half and two-thirds of the anterior part, thereby injuring the chordae vocales. . . . When he attempted to speak, the air passed through with a hissing . . . sound. . . . On September 1st, [after transfer from Spangler to Philadelphia] the wound had entirely healed, but the patient had lost his voice."[71]

Private Carl Behling, Company E, 26th Wisconsin, age 22, "received a gunshot wound through the upper lobe of the left lung" on July 1. He was taken to Spangler and remained there until July 10, when he was transferred to Jarvis Hospital in Baltimore. "When admitted, he was suffering from a profuse, exhausting hemorrhage. It ceased, but recurred on the 23rd, continuing for two hours. On August 6th, after eating a hearty dinner, he was about to walk from his bed to the door, when a sudden and profuse hemorrhage occurred. Death resulted in 10 minutes."[72]

69 Smith, *Camps and Campaigns*, 127, 130.

70 *The Medical and Surgical History of the War of the Rebellion* (1861-65) Vol. II, Part 1, 159.

71 Ibid., 407.

72 *The Medical and Surgical History of the Civil War*, Vol. VIII (Wilmington, NC, 1991), 493.

An Expert's Closer Look: Diarrhea

By Terry Sharrer, Ph.D., retired curator for the
Smithsonian's National Museum of American History

Civil War soldiers had a sense of humor, even if it was often dark humor about their conditions, commanders, or cause. There must have been lots of funny stories about brothers in arms who had "the runs," "the trots," or the euphemistic "Virginia Quick Step." Not every soldier wore the same uniform or performed the same duty or suffered alike from battle, wounds, or capture, but nearly all the Confederates and more than three quarters of Union soldiers endured serious and repeated bowel complaints throughout the war and it was a common problem at the Spangler XI Corps hospital. By the time the armies reached Appomattox Court House, the sick rate for diarrhea and dysentery was 995 per 1,000 men. The Union Medical Department recorded 57,265 deaths from such causes, and without an existing record of Confederate mortality, it's a safe assumption that close to 100,000 from both sides died from diarrhea/dysentery—the war's greatest killer. As historian Drew Galpin Faust remarked, "Disease offered all the evils of the battlefield with none of its honors."[73]

The difference between the symptom "diarrhea" and the disease "dysentery" dawned dimly on Civil War surgeons and soldiers, though blood and mucus in the stool indicated the latter. Diarrhea presented in three forms: acute (usually lasting less than two weeks), persistent (lasting two to four weeks), and chronic (more than four weeks, as happened to many at Spangler). Most cases were the acute form, usually arising from ingesting an infectious organism (e.g., bacterial *Escherichia coli*; or protozoan *Giardia*—among many others). What made this so common was polluted water sources in winter camps and opportunistic infections from water and spoiled food during campaigns. Persistent diarrhea typically came from continuing imbalances of fluids and electrolytes that altered the motor and sensory functions of the colon, risking dehydration. A wounded soldier who also became dehydrated (or vice versa) was more likely than not to go into shock and die. Chronic diarrhea, such as afflicted Spangler surgeon Henry Van Aernam and Confederate cavalry Gen. Nathan Bedford Forrest, resulted from permanent nerve damage in the highly innervated gastrointestinal tract. Van Aernam suffered with it for the rest of his life and Forrest died at age 56, just 12 years after the war, never having recovered from wartime diarrhea.[74]

---

73 Drew Gilpin Faust, *This Republic of Suffering: Death and the American Civil War* (New York, 2008), 4.

74 Anthony Fauci, et al., *Harrison's Principles of Internal Medicine*, Vol. I (New York, 2008), 247-257; Roy Morris Jr., *The Better Angel: Walt Whitman in the Civil War* (New York, 2000), 84.

Though the era's physicians possessed few specific treatments for many diseases, they tried many medications thought to rectify the imbalances that caused diseases. Among their armamentarium for diarrhea/dysentery were alum, balsam of copaiba (from the sap of a South American tree), essence of Mayapple (used in today's anticancer etoposide), calomel (mercury chloride), and several laxative substances (including antimony pills, fluid extracts of prunes or rhubarb, and castor oil) in the mistaken belief that purgatives restored natural balances. In truth, such treatments mostly caused more dehydration. Perhaps the most widely used medicines for diarrhea/dysentery were the panaceas quinine and opium (by injection, pills, or laudanum). Opium, at least, tightened the sphincter muscle.[75]

One example offers a perspective. The 8th Virginia Infantry should have had close to 1,000 men, but when the Gettysburg Campaign began it rostered only 225 in 10 companies. Company B, which included my 2X great-grandfather Pvt. Ezekiel Carter, had 26 men. Of these, three were absent for sickness and two survived unhurt from Pickett's Charge. The rest were casualties, many with diarrhea—part of the regiment's 92 percent losses. Had more men been healthy, the number of dead, mortally wounded, and permanently disabled likely would have been higher. In that sense, diarrhea probably saved more lives than it took.[76]

Dr. Terry Sharrar was a curator at the Smithsonian's National Museum of American History in Washington, D.C., for nearly 40 years. Most of his writing then and since focuses on modern molecular medicine. After leaving the museum in 2008, he was the executive director of the Medical Innovation and Transformation Institute of the Inova Hospital group in northern Virginia. Today, he edits a weekly newsletter on medical automation.

Spangler Farm Short Story

Visitors to the farm sometimes ask if blood dripped from the top floor of the Spanglers' barn onto the wounded and dying soldiers in the stable below, but the truth is we don't know. There are no known reports of it. It likely wouldn't have happened through the upstairs double threshing floor because those boards were tight so good grain wasn't lost, but it could have taken place early on in the hospital in the north hay mow, which also is above the stable. That top floor of the barn was filled shoulder-to-shoulder with wounded and bloody men, so the blood supply would have been sadly strong enough for that dripping to take place.

Most, though, that you hear about the George Spangler farm is known to be true, particularly its seclusion, beauty, rolling hills, and productivity before the

---

75 Michael A. Flannery, *Civil War Pharmacy: A History*, 2nd ed. (Carbondale, IL, 2017), 110-119.

76 John E. Divine, *8th Virginia Infantry*, 2nd ed. (Lynchburg, VA, 1984), 18-28, 58.

war. Also, thanks to the Gettysburg Foundation, we know that the barn, summer kitchen, and smokehouse today closely resemble or match how they appeared when the property was taken over by XI Corps medical staffers. Also true about this hospital: the torturous flies and maggots; the blood and other body fluids and smells everywhere, almost impossible to escape; how the six Spanglers must have suffered living together in that one bedroom for five weeks and two days and how they were surrounded by heart-rending and nightmarish cries, screams, and moans; the sickening sight of amputated limbs in piles and barrels; the screeching and rattling sound of the bone saws and the quiet and tender murmur as a chaplain or nurse said farewell and prayed and tenderly held a soldier in his final moments before death; how death was an almost every-day occurrence on that property; and how young soldiers bravely died for their country and sacrificed for their family without experiencing marriage, children, and grandchildren of their own, or how their dependent families back home never recovered from the devastating loss of that loved one at Spangler and struggled to survive without the financial support of their son or husband.

The human and moral atrocities witnessed at the XI Corps hospital are painful and shocking to consider. How could so many men do this to so many other men and their families? How could they cause so much suffering and devastation? The truth in this case most definitely hurts, but because the Gettysburg Foundation saved this farm and its stories and we can visit this farm today, we can learn from the people involved in this XI Corps hospital tragedy at the exact spot it happened. Over there is where the amputations took place; Armistead died on this very spot; that dirt floor there was covered with bloody hay, human feces, and manure; and upstairs is where the men were crammed so closely together that they were spreading disease. So many generations removed, we are able at least to try to imagine this suffering and what it looked like at the George Spangler farm. The Gettysburg Foundation provided us with this remarkable gift, and that most certainly is the truth.

Chapter 8

Captain Samuel M. Sprole Goes AWOL

By Wayne Motts and Ron Kirkwood

"His place is clearly the insane asylum."

— Dr. Daniel G. Brinton, describing Capt. Samuel M. Sprole after treating him at Spangler

Unauthorized absences and desertion frustrated the aims and strategies of both armies in the Civil War. One estimate says one in five Union soldiers and one in three Confederates walked away from the war without permission. This massive number of men deciding they'd had enough crippled the armies' fighting abilities, so bounties were paid to track them down and bring them back. Punishment could be harsh, including execution or imprisonment. The U.S. government increased the bounty on deserters from $5 to $10 plus expenses within two weeks after the battle of Gettysburg because of a sharp increase in desertions.[1]

The incentives to leave, though, were often too strong to resist, no matter the potential life-threatening consequences, because of poor food, poor leadership, endless foot-mangling marching, deadly disease, filth, homesickness, a family in need back home, exposure to bone-chilling cold and beat-down heat, and, of course, perhaps overarching all, the lethality of battle. Most of us today cannot fully comprehend the terror of what the Civil War soldier faced in battle, with bullets and shells and screaming and death everywhere. It drove many men insane, and it's a wonder so many soldiers stayed and stuck it out under the conditions they faced every day in camp and battle.

Captain Samuel M. Sprole, 4th U.S. Infantry, age 23, did not stay and stick it out. He left the George Spangler farm on July 5, and insanity—or temporary

---

1 Quartermaster Records July 1863–November 1864, Vol. 174, William G. LeDuc Papers, Minnesota Historical Society, St. Paul, MN; www.gilderlehrman.org/sites/default/files/inline-pdfs/David%20Carr_0.pdf, accessed Jan. 5, 2023.

Capt. Samuel M. Sprole, 4th U.S. Infantry
FindaGrave.com

insanity—are possible causes. Doctor Daniel G. Brinton had the most medical contact with Sprole at Spangler and tried to help him, writing in his diary, "Capt. Sprohl, U.S.I., had been with me for parts of two days. His mental condition was more deplorable than ever, & to crown his other acts, he had left his command in time of battle. I took him to corps h.q. & tried to induce him to join his regt."[2]

Sprole was born in Carlisle, Pennsylvania, where his father—the Rev. Dr. William Thomas Sprole—pastored the First Presbyterian Church. Young Sprole followed his father to Washington, D.C. and then to West Point from 1847 to 1856 where Dr. Sprole served as chaplain, until being removed by Secretary of War Jefferson Davis because of animosity between the two men.[3]

Because of his father's position at West Point, young Sprole was tutored by professors there and with their recommendation was commissioned as a 2nd lieutenant on May 4, 1861. Ten days later he was made a 1st lieutenant in the 4th U.S. Infantry, nicknamed "The Warriors" and famous still today for its 200-plus years of service. The Fourth fought in the battle of Tippecanoe in 1812, the Indian Wars, the War with Mexico, the Civil War, World War I, World War II, in Iraq and Afghanistan, and in many other conflicts. Ulysses S. Grant fought with the 4th. The 4th U.S. Infantry was and is a fighting unit, but for whatever reason—insanity, cowardice, medical reasons—Sprole was about to prove himself no fighter.[4]

Sprole was made a captain by August 1862, based in New York City working mainly as a recruiter. He still hadn't seen any fighting when he was ordered to join his regiment in February 1863, but he became sick on the way and spent two weeks

---

2 Brinton, *From Chancellorsville to Gettysburg, a Doctor's Diary*, 314.

3 *New York Tribune*, June 13, 1883.

4 https://bit.ly/3SY7KEj, accessed Feb. 14, 2024; Letters Received by the Adjutant General, 1861-1870, Fold3.

in a Philadelphia hospital before being sent home. "He was brought home, and for three weeks was little else than a maniac," Rev. Sprole said. "His sickness seriously affected his mind, so much so, that we dreaded at one time the entire loss of his reason." He was still sick at home in Newburgh, New York, in April, according to family doctor Nathaniel Deyo, but the doctor's description of the symptoms in a letter of April 10 were vague: "I have carefully examined this officer and find him unable to proceed to his Regiment in consequence of debility caused by his late severe indisposition, from which he is now recovering. And I do further certify that to the best of my belief he will be able to proceed to join his Regiment on the 1st of May ensuing, should his present rate of convalescence not be interrupted."[5]

But the same doctor wrote on April 29: "His convalescence has not been such as I anticipated. . . . I have carefully examined him, and find him suffering from so much debility, as would render it hazardous . . . to join his Regiment."

Dr. Deyo followed up on May 19, still vague about the symptoms: "His convalescence has been more tedious than I anticipated in my previous certificate. He experienced a relapse some four weeks since, which has kept him in a condition . . . unfit . . . for duty in the field. His present feeble [condition] has been increased by a recent effort to join his Regiment, being compelled to return home for treatment after proceeding two thirds of the distance. His symptoms now are such, that should there be no unfortunate change, I believe, he will, in a comparatively short time, be once more restored to health & duty."

Army Surgeon Basil Norris saw Sprole on May 20 and wrote in June: "I found him suffering from partial insanity of such degree as to require special attendance. I learned that this officer set out to join his Regiment in the field contrary to the advice of his attending physician and the remonstrance of his family and friends." The physician noted Sprole "was accompanied by his Father the Rev. Sprole . . . who succeeded in persuading his son to return from Washington to his home in Newburgh, New York."

Sprole finally made it to the army at Aldie, Virginia, just west of Washington, D.C., on June 20, 1863. He reported to Brig. Gen. Romeyn Ayres, commander of the First Brigade, Second Division, V Corps, where being the senior captain present he was to take command of the 4th U.S. Infantry. Sprole, however, told Ayres he was not capable of commanding his regiment so Ayres gave him 10 days to learn the duties of the position before taking over. Ayres reported at the end of those 10 days that Sprole "informed me today that he does not consider himself either mentally or physically capable to enter upon the duties of his office—that he feels broken down. The regimental Surgeon, he states, declines to give him a

5 Letters Received by the Adjutant General, 1861-1870, Publication Number M619, Fold3.

medical certificate." Ayres felt his hands tied: "As I cannot assign an Officer to the responsible office of commander of a Regiment, who states that he is incapable to perform the duties of that station, I submit his case for such action as the authorities may deem suitable to be had."

After more than two years' service in an army at war and still not having seen action, Sprole requested to be placed on the retirement list, stating he was broken down. His father seconded his retirement appeal, saying, "His condition is an act of God, and a thing beyond his control."

Now, as Robert E. Lee bore down on Pennsylvania and the Army of the Potomac moved to catch up with him amid worries about the next big fight, Union generals were having their attention diverted to the Sprole retirement request. Ayres kicked it up to then-Second Division commander Maj. Gen. George Sykes, who then kicked it up to V Corps commander Maj. Gen. George Meade, who said, "I can see no reason for Capt. Sprole claiming to be placed on the retired list, but strong reasons for his being discharged . . . [including] inefficiency and incompetency." And then it went up to Army of the Potomac commander Maj. Gen. Joseph Hooker, who said, "I fully concur in the view of Maj. Gen. Meade."

Rebuffed at the highest commands, Sprole was now on his way with the army north to Pennsylvania. His introduction to warfare after sitting it out for two years couldn't come at a worse place than Gettysburg.

U.S. Army Assistant Surgeon Edward Swift Dunster wrote from Washington, D.C. on June 29 as Meade moved north that he disagreed with the generals' decision to deny Sprole his retirement. Dunster wrote that Sprole "has been at times . . . laboring under a peculiar form of insanity & from the communications I have received concerning him since he has been in the field I am satisfied that he has been suffering under another attack & that he is not morally or legally responsible for his words & actions." On the same day, Dr. Thomas Cuyler of Philadelphia offered his concurrence that Sprole "must be partially deranged." Surgeon Dunster added in a letter on July 2 that Sprole is "unmistakeably insane and it is desirable that he should be gotten away as soon as possible and placed under appropriate treatment."[6]

That fall, Sprole explained what he was feeling leading up to Gettysburg: "During the two weeks preceding the battle & at this time, my mind was utterly paralyzed and a prey to the most tormenting and distressing hallucinations."[7]

---

6 Letters Received by the Adjutant General, 1861-1870, Publication Number M619, Fold3.

7 Letters Received by the Commission Branch of the Adjutant General's Office, 1863-1870, Publication Number M1064, Fold3.

Even so, Sprole made it to Gettysburg on the morning of July 2 with the V Corps, now commanded by Sykes after Hooker was replaced by Meade. Ayres was now in charge of the Second Division, and it was that division that bivouacked on the part of George Spangler's land that extended to the east side of Blacksmith Shop Road, giving Sprole his first look at the Spangler farm and the XI Corps hospital in the distance. The division left Spangler later that afternoon and fought at Houck's Ridge and the Wheatfield along modern-day Ayres Avenue. There the 4th U.S. Infantry suffered 40 casualties out of its already severely depleted fighting force of 173 men in surviving companies C, F, H, and K.[8]

Sprole's father said his son was "injured by a musket ball in the fleshy part of his right leg near the end of the battle." Captain Sprole said of the July 2 fight that he was "cut off from the Regiment, in the confusion attendant upon some change of position and at the same time having my leg badly bruised by a spent ball, did not again join them. At this time I was so weak as to make it very difficult to proceed at all." Captain Julius Walker Adams Jr., who commanded the regiment because Sprole wasn't up to it, listed Sprole in his official report as "unattached."[9]

Sprole left the line at this point and went to a III Corps hospital and then the XI Corps hospital. There, he walked into one of the most crowded and severe scenes of suffering one could imagine. Doctor Brinton's description offers clues as to what Sprole saw at Spangler: "From the 1st of July till the afternoon of the fifth, I was not absent from the hospital more than once and then but for an hour or two. Very hard work it was, too, & little sleep fell to our share. Four operating tables were going night and day."[10]

Brinton began his personal care of the mortally wounded Confederate Brig. Gen. Lewis A. Armistead and Army of the Potomac Capt. Fred Stowe in the Spanglers' summer kitchen on July 3. So on top of all the wounded and dying and screaming and anguish and the famous officers he was attending, surgeon Brinton took responsibility for Captain Sprole.

"Capt. Sprole . . . came to our hospital on July 3 in a sad frame of mind," Brinton wrote on July 6 to U.S. Assistant Surgeon Dunster in D.C. "I ascertained he had absented himself from his command in the battle of that day. He was

---

8 John Bachelder Map of the Battlefield of Gettysburg, Library of Congress; Travis W. Busey and John W. Busey, *Union Casualties at Gettysburg, A Comprehensive Record*, Vol. 3 (Jefferson, NC, 2011), 1206.

9 Letters Received by the Adjutant General, 1861-1870, Fold3; Letters Received by the Commission Branch of the Adjutant General's Office, 1863-1870, Fold3; Capt. Julius Walker Adams Jr.' official report, *OR*, Series I, Vol. 27, Part I Reports, July 17, 1863, 639.

10 Letters Received by the Commission Branch of the Adjutant General's Office, 1863-1870, Fold3; Brinton, *From Chancellorsville to Gettysburg, a Doctor's Diary*, 313.

Surgeon Daniel G. Brinton

Britt Isenberg

& is in my opinion—& I form it after a long & careful conversation with him—insane on certain points, & entirely unfit for his position. I took him to Maj. Gen. Howard, 11th Corps commander, who gave him a personal letter to his (Sprohl's) division commander. I then urged him with all my power to join his regiment, but I feel quite sure he will not do so." Brinton was under no delusions about the perilousness of Sprole's position. "You see the scandalous nature of the act he has committed in military eyes, & the severe punishment he will undoubtedly meet unless immediate & active measures are taken by his friends to let the military authorities know his mental condition." Brinton strongly advised that Sprole's "place is clearly the insane asylum & not active life," adding "it would take but little to make him commit suicide at any time."[11]

Sprole said he left Spangler on July 5 and tried to "overtake the column now in pursuit of Lee. I found it impossible to proceed & returned to Gettysburgh; from there with a train of wounded men I got to Baltimore & eventually reached home." He was home in Newburgh by July 9, officially absent without leave.[12]

Major General Oliver O. Howard was an 1854 West Point graduate and a friend of Chaplain Sprole. Brinton must have convinced Howard to step in during their July 5 conversation on East Cemetery Hill because Howard wrote a letter on July 9 to Ayres in support of helping Capt. Sprole: "For the sake of an old friend, Professor Sprole, I appeal to you on behalf of his son Capt. Sprole. . . . He may have been guilty of some military offence, but he seems to me partially deranged—he came in to see me and said much in his own disparagement. He used to be a manly boy & I think should now be carefully examined." But Sprole was already far away from Ayres at home in New York when Howard wrote that letter in support of him.[13]

11 Letters Received by the Adjutant General, 1861-1870, Fold3.

12 Letters Received by the Commission Branch of the Adjutant General's Office, 1863-1870, Fold3.

13 Ibid.

With his son home, Chaplain Sprole added to the letter writing on July 11 with another official request for approval of his son's retirement, calling him "demented, doing and saying things so unlike himself. . . . My . . . boy is no coward, nor inefficient, nor lacking in zeal and devotion to the country," the anguished father wrote. "[B]ut God has seen fit to afflict him—his mind is under a cloud and he should not be held responsible for his acts nor his words. . . . He talks in the most disparaging manner of himself." In what must have been a phrase painful to write, his father called him "unsound in mind" and begged for his discharge so he could be "restored to his right mind."[14]

And then, suddenly, all the letter writing and medical evaluations paid off. Meade changed his mind and approved Capt. Sprole's resignation, coincidentally, on the same day Chaplain Sprole wrote that letter. He was officially discharged on July 14. Sprole considered himself recovered in November 1863 when he applied to have his resignation withdrawn to allow his return to the army, stating he "was deranged" when he offered it. "I solemnly protest that during this time I was not a responsible agent & ought not to be held accountable for any words or actions that may have transpired," citing "circumstances not within my control." Surgeon Dunster supported Sprole's reinstatement. He said Sprole "is free from all disability either mental or bodily that would in any way disqualify him from the performance of the most active or arduous duty."[15]

Sprole's reinstatement application went to the Judge Adjutant General's Office and Secretary of War Edwin Stanton and was turned down. Sprole kept trying and wrote a personal letter in March 1864 to President Lincoln. He told Lincoln that his case was "not fully examined" and his is a "righteous cause" and asked that "justice is done." Lincoln denied Sprole's application in April because of the vacancy he sought "being filled."[16]

Despite his less than illustrious time in the military, Sprole went on to a long and successful career in education after the war. In 1865 he took charge of the mathematical department and the discipline of the Mount Pleasant Military Academy at Sing-Sing, New York. In 1868 he took over as principal of the New York House of Refuge at Randall's Island and after four years of service there he accepted the principalship of Grammar School No. 32, Brooklyn, where he served for more than 30 years until his death at age 65 in 1905. That school is named after him still today. His obituary in the *New York Tribune* cited his "devotion

---

14 Ibid.

15 Letters Received by the Adjutant General, 1861-1870, Fold3; Letters Received by the Commission Branch of the Adjutant General's Office, 1863-1870, Fold3.

16 Letters Received by the Commission Branch of the Adjutant General's Office, 1863-1870, Fold3.

House of Refuge, Randall's Island,
New York, a wood engraving
Ballou's Pictorial Drawing-Room Companion

to duty" and he was credited in 1904 with saving many lives in a school fire thanks to the disciplined training that he used for teachers and students in case of such an event. One local historian judged Sprole as possessing "matchless skill in adopting new ideas through his school work and making them of practical value both to teachers and pupils."[17]

Despite these later positive judgments, controversy followed him after the war. In 1872 the *New York Herald* labeled him a "fiend" amid charges of holding down boys and beating them repeatedly with a strap at the New York House of Refuge, the first juvenile reformatory in the nation. A female teacher whom he suspended in Brooklyn for not following his instructions called him "ungentlemanly" and of "contemptible character" and the *New York Times Union* reported that she said Sprole frequently punished her students for simply turning their heads, a charge also made against Sprole at Randall's Island. Among other charges against Sprole she said he frequently spoke to her in a most disrespectful manner and that on one occasion Sprole said, "The pupils needed clubbing to get them to apply their minds, and if only he had the power of whacking them as he had on Randall's Island." *The Brooklyn Daily Eagle* called him "a well built man of middle age, with a stiff military manner and a voice which is superior to the acoustic shortcomings of any and every character" and said he flew into an "ungovernable rage" and had "theatrical attitudes and defiant words" at a hearing.[18]

Sprole and his first wife, Emma, had three children before her death in 1876. In 1889 he married Joanna Mitchell, 10 years his junior and who had been heading the primary grades department at Grammar School No. 32; they had two daughters. Sprole's brother, Lt. Col. Henry W. Sprole of the 1st Cavalry, killed himself with a shot to the head in the Philippines at age 55 in 1903. Military officials blamed it on temporary insanity. Another brother, William T. Sprole, died

17 Peter Ross, *A History of Long Island, From Its Earliest Settlement to the Present Time*, Vol. 2 (New York, 1902), 374; *New York Tribune*, Nov. 15, 1905; *The New York Sun*, Mar. 5, 1904.

18 *New York Herald*, June 13, 1872; "A Guide to the Records of the New York House of Refuge," New York State Archives, Albany, NY; *Brooklyn Daily Eagle*, July 7, 1881; *New York Times Union*, July 7, 1881; *Brooklyn Daily Eagle*, June 28, 1881.

in 1861 at age 26 after guarding Washington, D.C., with the 7th New York State Militia. His father blamed his son's death on exposure while in service.[19]

The Rev. Dr. William T. Sprole said the first six months of 1863 leading up to his son's time at Spangler and then departure from there and subsequent resignation left him "completely overwhelmed, heartbroken." His military background of service to country and putting comrades first as a leader at West Point probably only added to his grief.[20]

We can never know with certainty what caused Capt. Sprole to flee the battlefield and end up at Spangler. The fact that after more than a year in service he only became ill when ordered to join his regiment, and that he always managed to stay out of the fight, and that he got on a train and left Gettysburg, all suggest cowardice. But we also know of multiple doctors describing his behavior as a form of insanity, and they would know far better than we possibly could today. Sprole was a high achiever based on his academic career after the war and the fact that a school in Brooklyn remains named for him today. At the same time, bona fide accounts attested to his vigorous and sometimes violent temper, which could have been part of his mental health struggles. The federal National Institute of Mental Health in Bethesda, Maryland, says certain mental disorders tend to run in families, and having a close relative with a mental disorder could mean a family member is at higher risk. The fact that the suicide of Capt. Sprole's brother was attributed to temporary insanity could be a coincidence or it could be a genetic sign. It's impossible to know today. What we do know is Sprole was one of thousands of soldiers from both armies to walk away during the Civil War and many of us today might do the same thing in that life-threatening mayhem.[21]

One Final Note

As mentioned earlier, Dr. Daniel G. Brinton wrote to U.S. Army Assistant Surgeon Edward Swift Dunster on July 6, 1863, a day after he left Spangler, to request help for Sprole after treating him at the XI Corps hospital. Brinton knew

19 www.findagrave.com/memorial/152190798/samuel-mills-sprole, accessed Jan. 4, 2023; *New York Tribune*, Apr. 23, 1903; Letters Received by the Adjutant General, 1861-1870, Fold3.

20 Letters Received by the Adjutant General, 1861-1870, Fold3.

21 www.nimh.nih.gov/health/publications/looking-at-my-genes, accessed Jan. 5, 2023. A Carded Medical Record for Sprole could not be found at the National Archives. Carded Medical Records track a soldier's health history and hospital stays. It's unusual for a soldier who has been treated to not have a CMR. It is, of course, possible that he suffered a wound as he and his father stated but did not have it treated or recorded.

Dunster would be sympathetic because Dunster was engaged to Sprole's sister, Rebecca, and they were married that November by Sprole's father.[22]

An Expert's Closer Look: A Possible Diagnosis

By Michele Montenegro, MSW, LCSW

Although little documentation is available, and assuming his episodes were not due to substance abuse or an infectious disease that caused cognitive impairment, informed hypothesis can lead us to believe that rather than cowardice Capt. Samuel M. Sprole suffered from mental illness. He was commissioned to the U.S. 4th Infantry at the age of 21. When he was 23, it was documented that he was "little else than a maniac." In fact, his father stated he "dreaded at one time the entire loss of his reason." Most mental health professionals now concur that the majority of mental illnesses begin by age 24.

It is possible that Sprole was affected by bipolar disorder with psychotic features. Our understanding of bipolar disorder has greatly evolved since it was first described by the Greek physician Hippocrates, who lived around 400 BC during the Classical period. "Bipolar" is a description for two extremes in mood. While healthy emotions range across a spectrum, bipolar disorder represents clinically significant criteria for a major depressive episode and a manic episode. For several years, the *Diagnostic and Statistical Manual of Mental Disorders* classified these symptoms as manic depressive illness. This is how the disorder continues to be termed by many lay individuals today.[23]

A manic episode is characterized by "a distinct period of abnormally and persistently elevated, expansive, or irritable mood." It can include inflated self-esteem or grandiosity, erratic ideas that might have little or no connection, increased goal-driven activity, and excessive involvement in activities that have negative consequences. For some, a manic episode can produce remarkable works of art, beautifully composed music, or genius inventions. But it can also result in hospitalization to prevent harm to self or others, involvement with law enforcement, and time in prison.[24]

On the other hand, a depressive episode includes an almost daily depressed mood, apathy, fatigue, feelings of worthlessness, problems concentrating, and thoughts of death or suicide. Just as in mania, the symptoms in a depressive episode

---

22 *The New York Times*, Nov. 6, 1863.

23 www.webmd.com/bipolar-disorder/history-bipolar, accessed Oct. 12, 2023; American Psychiatric Association, *Diagnostic and Statistical Manual of Mental Disorders-II* (Washington, D.C., 1968).

24 *Diagnostic and Statistical Manual of Mental Disorders DSM-5-TR* (2022), 139–143.

cause "clinically significant distress or impairment in social, occupational, or other important areas of functioning."[25]

Each of these episodes might also include psychosis where a person has difficulty understanding what is real and what is not. In severe cases, the illness disrupts connection with reality. The minimum length of episode differs from each pole, typically with a significant length of time between each. During the time between, many individuals can return to a fully functioning level of behavior. Treatment for bipolar disorder is life-long and includes psychotropic medication to stabilize the mood.

In the several assessments we have of Sprole, the words used to describe him included "maniac," "hazardous," "frail," "insanity," "inefficient and incompetent," and "partially deranged." These descriptions lead me to believe that he was in fact detached from reality for some time. There was a time documented where Sprole was aware, stating that he felt "broken down" and mentally incapable. A surgeon noted that it would "take little to make him commit suicide" and at one time he was "suffering under another attack."

Interestingly, Sprole applied to be reinstated in late 1863. After everything he went through and put others through, this does not seem like a healthy or logical request. Perhaps the reinstatement request can be attributed to delusions of grandeur. Nonetheless, Sprole went on to a successful career in charge of others. Despite being successful, though, he continued to be described as ungentlemanly, morally indignant, abusive, angry, dramatic, and defiant.

Sprole was certainly an individual afflicted with a pathological condition during a time when little was known about mental disorders. We can only hypothesize what his true psychiatric diagnosis or diagnoses might have been.

Michele Montenegro, MSW, LCSW, is the founder and owner of arKardia Counseling & Consulting, LLC, in Gettysburg. She has been working as an independently licensed psychotherapist for more than 20 years and is highly regarded for clinically sound assessments and therapeutic work. In addition to psychotherapy, Michele provides consultation and facilitates workshops. To learn more, visit arKardia.com.

Spangler Farm Short Story

Gettysburg Foundation President Emeritus and Historian Wayne Motts has conducted extensive research on Sprole and did a Zoom presentation on him in 2020 for the Civil War Roundtable of Gettysburg. Motts' insightful 45-minute presentation is available on YouTube for anyone desiring more information on

25 Ibid.

Sprole. Motts is former CEO of The National Civil War Museum in Harrisburg and former executive director of the Adams County Historical Society and is well known in the Civil War community as an author, speaker, battlefield guide, and historian.

Chapter 9

Hidden History:
The Granite Schoolhouse Hospital

"Through much of that night I assisted at the hospital. I held the arm of Lieut. [Isaac N.] Vance of
Co. C while his hand was amputated. That to me was a most dreadful night."

— *Sgt. Benjamin Franklin Powelson, age 22, 140th Pennsylvania. First Lieutenant Vance survived his amputation.*[1]

First Division of the Army of the Potomac's II Corps arrived in Gettysburg with a reputation as fighting men. They were battled-hardened after fights in the Seven Days campaign, Antietam, Fredericksburg, Chancellorsville, and more. This included the famous Irish Brigade. These men were disciplined, highly trained, and daring.

But that fighting spirit, that bravery, and that willingness to sacrifice for the good of the nation's cause came at a high price. The division was a shell of its former self when it arrived along the Taneytown Road just outside of Gettysburg on the morning of July 2, 1863, within a few hundred yards of the George Spangler farm. Only 3,300 men were available for battle divided among 18 regiments. Their war losses were so severe that at Gettysburg the Irish Brigade's 63rd, 69th, and 88th New York regiments were each down to two companies and 90 men or fewer, so they combined into one smaller unit.[2]

The casualty numbers for the First Division remained high at Gettysburg. Those numbers told a grim story of the intensity of what this already depleted division faced in the late afternoon and early evening back-and-forth fighting at the Wheatfield, Rose Woods, and Stony Hill. Those few men still standing in early July 1863 were survivors, but many wouldn't survive the trip into Pennsylvania.

1 Benjamin Franklin Powelson, *History of Company K of the 140th Pennsylvania Volunteers* (Steubenville, OH, 1906), 29; *The Grand Junction* (CO) *Daily Sentinel*, Apr. 8, 1914.

2 Busey and Busey, *Union Casualties at Gettysburg, A Comprehensive Record*, Vol. 3, 1167, 1168, and 1172.

Of all the losses, here are the division's top five hardest-hit regiments in terms of percentage at Gettysburg:

61st New York (1st Brigade): 59.6% casualties.

53rd Pennsylvania (4th Brigade): 58.5%.

116th Pennsylvania (Irish Brigade): 56.1%.

27th Connecticut (4th Brigade): 52.0%.

64th New York (4th Brigade): 50.0%.[3]

As a whole, Maj. Gen. Winfield Scott Hancock's former division suffered 39.4 percent casualties at Gettysburg, including 955 wounded and 183 killed, and it was so bad on July 2 that some of the First Division broke and ran, shocking Hancock. The vast majority of those casualties took place on their lone day of fighting on July 2. By the end of that day, most of those wounded and dying men were either at the First Division, II Corps hospital next to Granite Schoolhouse on the George Spangler farm or they were waiting to be picked up and taken to the location a quarter-mile northwest of the XI Corps hospital in and around the Spanglers' barn. The Spanglers now had two major Union hospitals on their property, one a division hospital at Granite Schoolhouse and the other a corps hospital of three divisions.[4]

Captain Thomas Livermore had no experience in the ambulance corps. He was 19 years old and managing a few dozen men in an infantry company, but his character, intelligence, and bravery must have made an impression on 41-year-old II Corps Medical Director Alexander N. Dougherty. On June 30, Dougherty handed Livermore the reins of a headquarters horse and with them command over approximately 100 ambulances and 400 men of the II Corps ambulance corps. Livermore had a lot to learn—and quickly—for in two days he would be responsible for overseeing the movement of thousands of wounded men from three divisions to the correct division hospital, or in some desperate cases any close hospital that could be found.[5]

Upon arrival at Gettysburg on July 2, Livermore likely set up his mass of wagons, men, and animals on the vast Sarah Patterson and Jacob Swisher farms neighboring George Spangler's land to the west along the Taneytown Road. The Patterson farm became the Second Division hospital and the Swisher farm the Third Division hospital. The First Division medical staff set up next to and east of

---

3 Ibid., 1166, 1168, 1170, 1171.

4 Ladds, *The Bachelder Papers*, 1356; Busey and Busey, *Union Casualties at Gettysburg*, 1172.

5 Thomas L. Livermore, *Days and Events 1860-1866* (Boston, 1920), 233.

Granite Schoolhouse, just a right turn away from the ambulance park and down Granite Schoolhouse Lane in the middle of George Spangler's farm.[6]

Each infantry division maintained its own ambulance train under the charge of a lieutenant. The train followed its division on the march and then into battle, staying close behind the line, hopefully just out of artillery range. So when the fighters of the First Division took off toward the Wheatfield, the division's ambulances and stretcher carriers took off, too, under the direction of Lt. George C. Anderson of the 53rd Pennsylvania. It was Anderson's men who were responsible for getting the First Division wounded from the mayhem of the Wheatfield area to the care and relative safety at Granite Schoolhouse. Captain Livermore—a Galena, Illinois, native who had settled in New Hampshire with his parents before the war—oversaw this operation as well as those of the two other II Corps divisions. "I found some of the stretcher-carriers lagging behind," Livermore said of the First Division, "evidently afraid to go after the division. I accordingly made them go along with me until I had got them up to the division or close to it and well under the artillery fire, which was uncomfortably savage."[7]

Private Robert L. Stewart, Company G, 140th Pennsylvania, age 22, arrived at the Granite Schoolhouse hospital on the night of July 2, undoubtedly carried by one of Livermore and Anderson's ambulances. He suffered a leg wound caused by a fragment of a shell, and he described the hospital's location as "somewhere behind the position held by the Second Division [II Corps], and not very far from General Meade's headquarters." In fact, if Granite Schoolhouse Lane continued through its terminal intersection with the Taneytown Road it would land today between the modern-day Father Corby statue and the State of Pennsylvania Monument in the heart of II Corps country, just as Stewart described.[8]

The location was one of the advantages of placing this major division hospital in the center of the George Spangler farm and halfway down a rutted farm path connecting the Taneytown Road and Baltimore Pike that eventually would become Granite Schoolhouse Lane. From the northeast corner of farmer George Rose's Wheatfield, ambulances had only to travel down Millerstown (now Wheatfield) Road, turn left on the Taneytown Road and then right on Granite Schoolhouse Lane for a quick trip of 1.7 miles. A more direct route down the Trostle farm lane was quicker, though too close to the fighting.

6 Ibid., 243.

7 Ibid., 241, 247.

8 Robert Laird Stewart, *A History of the One Hundred and Fortieth Regiment Pennsylvania Volunteers* (1912), 121.

Capt. Thomas Livermore
Library of Congress

In many ways, this little piece of Spangler land directly under and to the west of Powers Hill was an ideal spot for a big hospital. The hill was directly above the hospital, gradually climbing to its summit and protecting it from Confederate fire on Culp's Hill to the east. There is a little brook coursing through the heart of the field—more of a "run" really—that often is dry today but would have been filled in July 1863 after recent rains. Also, there is another stream behind the hill and there are small springs that send their water like veins on a short journey into the run and can make the area mushy and damp, so there was plenty of water available.

This Spangler site also had space, wood for fires, a few trees for shade, and wheat for bedding. But it lacked something critical for the care and comfort of the wounded and dying men: It had no buildings to provide cover. Granite Schoolhouse was only a few yards west of the hospital site, but it was occupied by II Corps medical bosses so it wasn't available for hospital purposes. Plus, the school was small. That meant wounded and dying First Division, II Corps men who had already sacrificed so much were laid in the field or among the trees and their limbs were amputated there and that is where they were placed afterward to recover or die. At least make-shift hospitals in schools, homes, warehouses, stores, and farms offered buildings in which to place the men. It's possible that surgeons put up a canopy tent or two to protect their patients on the operating table, but if they didn't then the First Division, II Corps hospital had nothing, leaving the men and hospital staff entirely exposed to the elements. Even the manure-filled stable in the Spanglers' barn used by the XI Corps hospital was better than that.

As the final deadly insult, Confederate artillery from the West pelted the area, forcing the bulk of the hospital to be moved farther behind the line on July 3–4 to the Jacob Schwartz farm. If there was a hint of a bright spot, at least these men were receiving care in a hospital—horrific and basic as it might be—unlike their

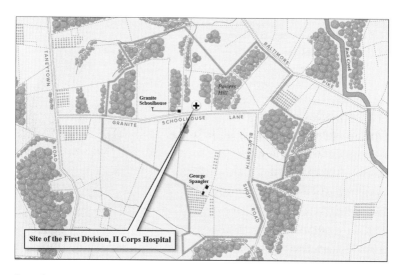

comrades who were trapped overnight July 2 into July 3 without care or water on the dangerous ground between the armies' lines in the Wheatfield.

Robert Stewart wrote a history of the 140th Pennsylvania—made up of recruits from four counties south, west, and north of Pittsburgh—that was published in 1912, almost 50 years after the battle of Gettysburg. In it he describes First Division hospital scenes and sometimes in the same sentence confuses the Granite Schoolhouse and Jacob Schwartz locations, which is understandable when writing so long after that confusing moment of his wounding. But he offers hints based on known facts today about which hospital he is thinking about as he writes, and it's likely that most of his following reminiscences are of the Granite Schoolhouse hospital.

"At times the stretcher carriers separated the dead from the living, but meanwhile others passed away in their place," Stewart wrote. "Those who could care for themselves sat or lounged on the ground at the foot of a tree or beside a great rock, but the larger number were lying on their backs in long rows without pillow or shelter, for as yet the hospital supplies, somewhere in the rear, had not arrived.

"Between the rows of prostrate men there were narrow lanes to permit the attendants to pass. At intervals in the open spaces were long rows of tables around which faithful surgeons with sleeves rolled up to the shoulder had been at work since daybreak in two or three reliefs, each one working so long as his strength would hold out," he wrote. "In all serious cases chloroform was administered and thus much suffering was prevented," recalled Stewart, and then the essential revulsion of many Civil War hospital recollections: "but, oh, the horror of the carving and the heaps of human legs and arms on the ground at the ends of the tables, and the pallid faces and the smothered moans of anguish, which could not be repressed."

Pvt. Robert L. Stewart, 140th Pennsylvania
A History of the One Hundred and Fortieth Regiment Pennsylvania Volunteers

These and other sights and sounds that may not even be mentioned will remain while life lasts as the saddest reminders of those days of turmoil, suffering and fraternal strife."[9] The five-foot-eight-inch, brown-haired Stewart became a respected minister, professor, and historian after the war. The native of Murrysville lived to age 75, dying in Los Angeles County in 1916.[10]

John B. Holloway of the 148th Pennsylvania was 25 or 26 years old at Gettysburg and a teacher in civilian life. A drummer, it was his job to get to the hospital once the fighting started and help wherever he could, including assisting at operating tables, burying amputated limbs, cleaning surgical tools, and providing water. He said what he saw at the First Division, II Corps hospital next to Powers Hill was his worst experience of the war.

"At the battle of Gettysburg I saw many distressing incidents," he wrote later. "Perhaps the most distressing case of suffering I saw was at this battle, in the case of a man who was shot through the throat from side to side, and his throat was swelling shut. He was at the field hospital in the woods by the hillside. He would roll and crawl and tumble about on the ground," as Holloway described the dramatic scene, "then get up and walk back and forth, beckoning with both of his hands to all who were about him. This continued until a surgeon . . . went to him, laid him on the ground, run an instrument into his throat and wind pipe, and inserted a silver tube. Then the man was relieved of his great sufferings, but he died in a short time." Holloway was also present at the treatment administered to General Hancock, witnessing the awful sight of "blood from his wound as it dripped from the wagon to the ground."[11]

Early July was prime time in 1863 for Adams County farmers to bring in their wheat crop, but multiple soldier accounts indicate that hadn't happened yet in the famous Wheatfield. "We were the first troops to cross the field, and the yellow

9 Ibid., 121.

10 Ancestry.com.

11 Joseph Wendel Muffly, ed., *The Story of Our Regiment, A History of the 148th Pennsylvania Vols.* (Des Moines, IA, 1904), 331–332.

Drummer John B. Holloway,
148th Pennsylvania
*The Story of Our Regiment, A History of
the 148th Pennsylvania Vols.*

grain was still standing," wrote Henry Meyer, 148th Pennsylvania, after the war. He was a private in Company A at Gettysburg. "I noticed how the ears of wheat flew in the air all over the field as they were cut off by the enemy's bullets."[12]

Most of that field of waving wheat probably more resembled a dirt patch by the time Col. John Rutter Brooke's Fourth Brigade lined up on Wheatfield Road north of the Wheatfield at about 6:30 p.m. as the last of the First Division's four brigades to go in. It took less than an hour for Erie County's 145th Pennsylvania of that brigade, under the command of Col. Hiram L. Brown, to lose 42.1 percent of its 202-man fighting force on July 2.

Within a half-hour the Fourth Brigade fought its way southwest through both the Wheatfield and through and to the far edge of Rose Woods, driving back the Confederates and taking prisoners along the way. But the Fourth Brigade ran into a wall of eight Georgia regiments plus the 15th South Carolina at the southwest edge of Rose Woods. The brigade found itself flanked by the larger Confederate numbers and forced to return to where it came from, crossing back through the Wheatfield and over Wheatfield Road, Plum Run, and to its starting point along Cemetery Ridge. In and out in under an hour, and losing the 145th's Col. Brown, and later his replacement, Capt. John W. Reynolds, to their wounds, the unit lost a total of 85 men along the way. Brown was hit in the arm and Reynolds in the head; both survived.

Brown was taken from the fight directly to the Granite Schoolhouse hospital, but Reynolds and some others of the 145th first went to George Spangler's barn and the XI Corps hospital by mistake. 145th Chaplain John H. W. Stuckenberg found them there after leaving Granite Schoolhouse in search of his regiment's men. "He was much excited—elated because our regt. had done so well & had driven the rebels before them," Stuckenberg said of Capt. Reynolds among the

Spangler farm buildings. "I found many more here of the wounded of our regt. As many as could easily be moved I directed to be taken to our corps hospital, others were made as comfortable as possible."[13]

Stuckenberg, age 28, also found 145th Pennsylvania Assistant Surgeon Daniel W. Richards, age 25, tending his men at the XI Corps hospital. Richards was an Easton native who enrolled less than a month before Gettysburg on June 12, making that fight his terrible initiation into the Civil War. His residence in Easton should have put him in the 153rd Pennsylvania, but the 153rd was a 9-month unit that was soon to be mustered out. Doctor Richards was assigned to the Erie regiment instead. Richards and Chaplain Stuckenberg became friends in those days before Gettysburg, with Richards getting the benefit of turns on the chaplain's horse during the march to Pennsylvania.[14]

It was dark or close to dark by the time Stuckenberg met up with Richards at the Spangler barn because of the late July 2 Wheatfield and Rose Woods fights. They both knew the 145th had suffered greatly and many of their men had to be missing so they left the XI Corps hospital and searched the battlefield together to see who could be found and helped. "We met a number of regts leaving the field and saw two guns drawn off by hand. It was dark and the road was not very good," Stuckenberg wrote. "We soon came to a house full of wounded men, with only one or two well ones to wait on them. We went on farther, over fields and rocks and stone walls and through woods not knowing whither our course would lead us. We met few soldiers, heard but little noise," he noted. "The very stillness was fearful and oppressive. A dread came upon as I neared the ground where the desperate fighting had taken place in the afternoon. At any moment I might stumble on some corpse or fall over some wounded man. We frequently stopped to listen for groans, but heard none till we came to another house."

They did find signs of hope. "I asked for the wounded of our regt and found one man answering to my call. I passed through between the wounded men outside the house, entered the house, with difficulty passed in the dark through a room in which were some wounded men, and entered another room. On a bed suffering terribly lay Forbes of Company G, wounded through the breast. [Pvt. Frank M. Forbes. Company I. Age about 22. Wounded through the right lung.] He begged us to dress his wounds," Stuckenberg reported, "but as there was no candle to be had, this was out of the question. I gave him some whiskey to stimulate him and

---

13 Chaplain John H. W. Stuckenberg, diary, Box B-70, Folder 72b, Gregory A. Coco Collection, GNMP.

14 David T. Hedrick and Gordon Barry Davis, Jr., eds., *I'm Surrounded by Methodists: Diary of John H. W. Stuckenberg Chaplain of the 145th Pennsylvania Volunteer Infantry* (Gettysburg, PA, 1995), 76.

J. H. W. STUCKENBERG

Left: Chaplain John H. W. Stuckenberg, 145th Pennsylvania, *Special Collections and College Archives, Musselman Library, Gettysburg College*; Right: Assistant Surgeon Daniel Richards, 145th Pennsylvania *Susannah Richards*

then left him [while] promising if possible to have him removed to our Hospital, where I had the pleasure of seeing him the next morning."[15]

Their task seemed overwhelming. "I left the many wounded at their house (no physicians to attend to them, no candle even, though they were taken away as fast as the ambulances could carry them) and went further to the front," Stuckenberg wrote. "Back of the house we saw the first corpse. Scarcely had we passed it when a bullet from the rebels whistled past us and warned us to proceed no further. Nor could we have gone much further, for our picket line was but a short distance in front of us. In again passing the house we had just left we heard subdued, but constant groaning near the barn. I found a rebel there, seriously wounded, who gave no answer to the question, whether I could do anything for him? He being perhaps unconscious and near his end."

---

15 Forbes was taken to the Granite Schoolhouse hospital on July 3 and then the Jacob Schwartz hospital. He was transferred to a Baltimore hospital on July 9 and then to a Philadelphia hospital on July 13, according to his Carded Medical Record at the National Archives, RG 94 Records of the Adjutant General's Office, Entry 534, 145 Pennsylvania Cohill, I.L., to Green, Joel, R. Forbes joined the Veteran Reserve Corps in 1864 and survived the war.

Stuckenberg and Richards had endured all they could. "In passing from the field we learned that a wounded man was lying all alone in the woods. We carried him to a place where he could easily be found, and sent a stretcher for him. We went back to the [Granite Schoolhouse] hospital, where I found quite a number of our wounded. I then went to bed. Seldom had I been so tired. Nature had endured all it could and now coveted the balmy restorer—sleep."[16]

Back at the Wheatfield, a slight breeze overnight carried the moans and cries of the helpless and trapped wounded to the Union men hunkered down for safety on the eastern side of the battlefield. With Confederates on the other side of that small field, it wasn't safe for either army to go in for their wounded. Second Lieutenant Gilbert Frederick, 57th New York, described those nighttime moans as "a sound indescribably desolate, which could not be shut out even by covering the head."[17]

Private Meyer of the 148th Pennsylvania added, "All night long were heard the monotonous tramp of moving troops, the low rumble of the wheels of the ambulances, the ammunition and supply trains, and the artillery over the stony roads."[18]

After leaving George Spangler's barn and going on his night-time search-and-rescue mission with Chaplain Stuckenberg, Dr. Richards worked at the Granite Schoolhouse hospital and then moved with it to the Jacob Schwartz farm on July 3–4 when all three II Corps division hospitals were consolidated there. Richards went on to have an unhealthy tenure in the Civil War. Gettysburg, in fact, might have represented the high tide of his own health. After that, medical records show he was treated August 29 to September 12, 1863, for remittent fever; September 14 to October 2, 1863, for diarrhea; October 3, 1863, for chronic diarrhea and granted leave of absence; June 1–2, 1864, scabies (intensely itchy condition caused by a tiny mite that burrows into the skin); June 21–27, 1864, debilitas (weakness, lameness, general disability); and September 4, 1864, intermittent fever. In May 1864, Richards was taken prisoner at Spotsylvania and, despite his health challenges, placed in charge of a ward in a Richmond prison hospital. The Confederates released him unconditionally on May 31 and he was discharged on a surgeon's certificate that November with liver trouble.[19]

16 Hedrick and Davis, *I'm Surrounded by Methodists*, 78-79.

17 Gilbert Frederick, *The Story of a Regiment: A Record of the Military Services of the Fifty-Seventh New York State Volunteer Infantry in the War of the Rebellion* (1895), 173.

18 Muffly, *The Story of Our Regiment, A History of the 148th Pennsylvania Vols.*, 538-539.

19 Carded Medical Records, RG 94 Records of the Adjutant General's Office, Entry 534, 145 Pennsylvania, Hu. McArthur to William H. Ross, NARA; "Personal Papers of Medical Officers & Physicians," Daniel W. Richards, 145th Pennsylvania, RG 94, Adjutant General's Office, Entry 561, Box 486, NARA.

Richards returned home to Easton where—like so many other former Spangler surgeons—he became a highly respected doctor and community leader until his death at age 61 in 1902. A history of Northampton County called him "one of the eminent men of his profession, and through his skill and ability added greatly to the sum of human happiness."[20]

Private Erastus A. Allen, Company I, 145th Pennsylvania, age about 22, was one of the many familiar faces seen by Richards and Stuckenberg upon their return to the Granite Schoolhouse hospital. "Allen . . . shot through [the] abdomen suffered terribly," Stuckenberg said. "Some of the intestines protruded through the wound and some of their contents would occasionally flow out, producing a horrible stench."[21]

Allen was listed in the 1860 U.S. census as an 18-year-old "boatman" living at home with his parents and siblings in Erie County. He enlisted in September 1862 and arrived in Gettysburg on July 2. He had earned accolades for his bravery at Chancellorsville two months earlier in Col. Brown's official report: "I cannot close this report," Brown wrote, "without referring to the gallant conduct of Private Erastus A. Allen, of Company I, who, while engaged in the fight on Sunday, volunteered to carry cartridges to the men of the Sixty-fourth New York Volunteers, who were destitute of ammunition and could not procure any. A box had been brought by someone and left at a distance from their lines. Private Allen, hearing the men call for ammunition, offered to take the contents of the box to them, and succeeded in doing so, although exposed to a heavy fire in the undertaking."[22]

Chaplain Stuckenberg tore apart a wool blanket during the downpours after the fight at Gettysburg and gave half to Allen and half to another patient in an attempt to ease their suffering. But Pvt. Allen lasted only until 8 p.m. July 4, when he died of his stomach wound at the II Corps division hospital. Stuckenberg said he participated in Pvt. Allen's burial on the morning of July 5 before leaving Gettysburg with the 145th. Allen was later exhumed and is now buried in the Pennsylvania section of Soldiers' National Cemetery.[23]

Captain John C. Hilton, age 22, was commanding the 145th's Company K when he was hit in the thigh in the woods near Rose Run. Captain Charles Lynch of Company D went to Hilton's aid and ordered two captured Confederates to carry Hilton out. Stuckenberg later found Hilton near the stream in the middle

20 Pennsylvania, U.S., Veterans Burial Cards, 1777–2012, Ancestry.com; William J. Heller, *History of Northampton County Pennsylvania and The Grand Valley of the Lehigh*, Vol. 2 (Boston, 1920), 254.

21 Hedrick and Davis, *I'm Surrounded by Methodists*, 79.

22 www.ehistory.osu.edu/books/official-records/039/0349, accessed Nov. 10, 2022.

23 Stuckenberg diary, GNMP.

of the Granite Schoolhouse hospital.[24] "I saw Capt. J. C. Hilton near the spot where the hospital was in the morning," the chaplain wrote. "He was wounded in [the] thigh, the bone being shattered up to the hip joint, and the surgeons said there was no hope for his recovery. I was informed of these facts and requested to announce them to him." Stuckenberg recalled a tender scene, with Hilton "lying on the ground, under the shade of a tree, by the side of a brook, attended to by one of his men. My task was a delicate, unpleasant and sad one. When I told him that probably his wound would be fatal, he told me he had feared it, but it seemed he never so fully realized it as then."

Stuckenberg's ministry was important at that point. Hilton's "eyes filled with tears, deep emotions were traced on his youthful countenance, he cast a glance upward and lay silent 'Chaplain, what does it take to constitute a Christian?'" Hilton was "very anxious about his soul. He had been piously trained, had been a good boy, it seems, but for some years had been rather careless. After conversing awhile on the subject of religion, he spoke about his mother and sisters," Stuckenberg recorded. "Were it not for them death would be easy. He loved them tenderly and wanted to live for their sakes. His deep feeling moved me deeply—he was overwhelmed with emotion—he, his servant and I all wept. He said he did not want to be taken to the hospital—he must die anyhow and would as soon die where he was as anywhere else. 'Bury me,' he said as if utterly hopeless of recovery, 'under this tree.'"[25]

But he didn't die, saved by an officer who refused to follow Hilton's instructions. Hilton takes his own story from there: "The enemies shell came screeching and crashing through the trees—it became necessary to hastily remove back to a safer position. When they came to me I refused to allow them [to] remove me, as I was told I could not live and by this time I was in excruciating pain; and for an hour or two I remained alone, when the Capt. came back with four stalwart men and pointed me out, and without paying any attention to my remonstrations, raised my stretcher, and 'taking step' hurried me to the rear amid the bursting shells."[26]

Hilton's right leg was amputated at the Schwartz farm a full 11 days after the initial wounding. Such a delay was ordinarily a death sentence because of the rapid spread of infection. Most primary amputations such as Hilton's were performed within the first two days of the wounding even under the strenuous and overcrowded conditions during and after Gettysburg, so it is highly possible that

---

24 Verel R. Salmon, *Common Men in the War for the Common Man: History of the 145th Pennsylvania Volunteers* (Bloomington, IN, 2013), 710 on Kindle.

25 Hedrick and Davis, *I'm Surrounded by Methodists*, 80–81.

26 Ibid., 130–131.

Hilton was given morphine for his pain and set aside somewhere out of the way to die. Those who it was thought could not be saved were not a priority.[27]

But Hilton defied the odds. He was transferred to Camp Letterman on August 5, where he was listed as "doing very well; the treatment consists of stimulants and nourishing diet, with water dressings to the stump." His stump had entirely healed to the point that he left the hospital on September 1, departing Gettysburg hale and hearty less than two months after being told it would be his final resting place. He transferred to the Veteran Reserve Corps that December and in 1865 received a brevet promotion to major.[28]

Not only did Hilton defy the doctors' prognosis by surviving, the battle would only be the beginning of his involvement with Gettysburg. He was a speaker at the dedication of the 145th's monument in Rose Woods in 1889 and chairman of the unit's Monumental Association. He served as president of the 145th's annual reunions, and also served on the National Committee planning the 50th anniversary commemoration of the battle in 1913.

Chaplain Stuckenberg died in 1903 in Europe and is buried in Soldiers' National Cemetery. Eighty-two veterans of the 145th gathered in Erie for their annual reunion shortly after his death and honored Stuckenberg by placing his photo on the 145th badge worn at the gathering. Remembering how the chaplain came to his aid, as well as so many others', at Granite Schoolhouse and elsewhere, Hilton spoke at the reunion and "dwelt at considerable length upon the past life and services of the late Rev. J. H. W. Stuckenberg. . . . He paid a high tribute to the deceased chaplain."[29]

Hilton died at age 84 in 1925 after serving many years as postmaster and is buried in Erie. He died of heart disease 62 years after being told at Granite Schoolhouse that his thigh wound was going to kill him.[30]

On the afternoon of July 3, the artillery bombardment unleashed by Confederate forces ahead of Pickett's Charge relentlessly pelted the Granite Schoolhouse Lane area, causing panic and death on that part of the Spangler farm and the hasty pickup and retreat of the hospital. "The hospital which seemed to have been almost in the rear of the point selected by General Lee for the concentration of his attack, was, for a time one of the most exposed sites behind the Union lines," Pvt. Stewart of the 140th Pennsylvania recalled. "In swift succession scores of shrieking shells

27 U.S. Surgeon General's Office, *The Medical and Surgical History of the War of the Rebellion*, Vol. 2, pt. 3, "Surgical History" (Washington, D.C., 1883), 273.

28 Ibid.

29 *The Evening Republican*, Meadville, PA, Aug. 21, 1903.

30 Capt. John C. Hilton Certificate of Death, Oct. 9, 1925, Ancestry.com.

burst in the air and on the ground scattering their deadly missiles in the midst of this mass of helpless sufferers, killing some outright and wounding others." We can glimpse the chaos through Stewart's recollections:

> In this emergency those who had the use of their limbs at once laid hold of the poor fellows who were helpless pulling and dragging them as best they could, to places of comparative safety. For a few moments the confusion and distress which prevailed was terrible beyond expression. Those who could not move were crying out for help and many who were partially disabled were attempting to drag their maimed or helpless limbs as far as possible from the immediate danger/one of the plunging shot and shells. In a marvelously short space of time the most exposed places were cleared—for all who could work at this task were desperately in earnest—and the new location to which all were transferred in one way or other, afforded a safe refuge for the rest of the day.[31]

The panicked retreat under bombardment forced the II Corps medical bosses to evacuate the school, thus making it newly available as hospital quarters for those men too seriously wounded to be moved. So that is where Lt. George A. Woodruff, the commander of Battery I, 1st U.S. Artillery, II Corps Artillery Brigade, was placed. Woodruff was shot through the intestines while placing a section of his battery to set up enfilade fire on the Confederates near the end of the infantry charge. He died July 4 in the school and was buried behind it. Woodruff maintained an intense interest in the battle and its outcome while at Granite Schoolhouse and received updates while there. Woodruff's brigade commander—Capt. John G. Hazard of the 1st Rhode Island Light Artillery—said of him: "To the manner in which the guns of his battery were served and his unflinching courage and determination may be due the pertinacity with which this part of the line was so gallantly held under a most severe attack."[32]

Surgeon Horatio Bardwell (H. B.) Buck, age 31, treated Woodruff at Granite Schoolhouse. Buck was the surgeon in charge of U.S. artillery batteries in the II Corps and was at Spangler only three months after his wedding. He went on to great acclaim as the superintendent and surgeon in charge of the Camp Butler U.S. soldier training ground and Confederate POW camp near Springfield,

---

31 Stewart, *A History of the One Hundred and Fortieth Regiment Pennsylvania Volunteers*, 121.

32 *The Bachelder Papers*, Vol. III, "Notes on the Services of Troops at the Battle of Gettysburg," in the John P. Nicholson Collection, Huntington Library, San Marino, CA, 1363 and 1975; Robert N. Scott, *The War of the Rebellion: A Compilation of the Official Records of the Union and Confederate Armies*, Series I, Vol. 27, Part 1—"Reports" (Washington, D.C., 1889), 481.

Illinois, where he saved the lives of countless men by improving the sanitary and medical conditions.[33]

After fits and starts trying to find a new location for the wounded and dying, all three divisions of the II Corps eventually landed together at one hospital near Rock Creek on the Jacob Schwartz farm. It sits about a 2-mile drive today from the site of the Granite Schoolhouse hospital traveling east down Granite Schoolhouse Lane, right on Blacksmith Shop Road, left on Hospital Road and left on Sachs Road to the location. Of the seven Union infantry corps at Gettysburg, the I Corps had the most casualties: 6,243 (a shocking 51.1 percent); the II Corps was next at 4,509 (40.1 percent). At the First Division, II Corps hospital, Medical Director Richard C. Stiles stated in his after-action report that "Surg. [Charles Squire] Wood, who was left in charge of the division hospital, informs me that about 800 of our wounded & 200 of the enemy's were cared for in our division hospital— that he performed 120 capital operations, 150 operations in all—Surg. [William Warren] Potter performed 54 amputations & resections; and Surg. [J.W.] Wishart almost 30, making almost 230 operations in all."[34]

One cannot see, or get, to the important Schwartz farm hospital today because it's hidden from the road on private land. It sits on the left side of the road immediately after Sachs Road crosses Rock Creek when driving out from Gettysburg in the area known as Red Hill, behind the III Corps hospital marker. It's just south of modern-day The Outlet Shoppes at Gettysburg. The II Corps also used space at the VI Corps hospital across Sachs Road at the John Trostle farm because the VI was not heavily involved at Gettysburg and suffered few casualties.[35]

It takes effort, but one is able to explore the site of the First Division, II Corps hospital when it was on the former Spangler farm because it's now on National Park Service land. Park in the little gravel lot off the east end of Granite Schoolhouse Lane near its junction with the Baltimore Pike. Walk west down the lane past Powers Hill, about a third of a mile, until you reach the bottom of a little valley where the often-dry stream wends under the lane. You've gone too far if you reach the monument to Batteries B and L, 2nd U.S. Artillery, 1st Brigade, Cavalry Corps on your left.

Look into the woods from the lane to your right (to the north) at the bottom of the valley and that's the site of the Spangler hospital to which this chapter is

33 George Irving Reed and Hyland MacGrath, eds., *Encyclopedia of Biography of Illinois*, Vol. 3, (Chicago, 1902), 234.

34 Busey and Busey, *Union Casualties at Gettysburg*, 1165 and 1183; Roland R. Maust, *Grappling With Death: The Union Second Corps Hospital at Gettysburg* (Dayton, OH, 2001), 453.

35 The location is at 39°46'57" N 77°12'22" W.

The former site of the First Division, II Corps hospital is overgrown today.

Ron Kirkwood

dedicated. This was a mainly open field in 1863, not thick and overgrown as it is now. This is where the men lay and many died. This is where Col. Edward E. Cross died (see Chapter 10). This is where Confederate shells from the west exploded and dying bullets whizzed overhead from Culp's Hill to the east.[36]

You may enter this field, but the site is uneven and not maintained so care is required. Thorns puncture and cling to clothing and stop you in your tracks. Many roots and rocks are there to trip you, and low branches hang at head height. Rain turns the area soft and muddy. If you do go in, note how Powers Hill gradually slopes down to you from the east, ending at the stream, making that part of the hospital a part of the hill. It was on top of Powers Hill directly above the hospital where Maj. Gen. Henry W. Slocum directed the dawn July 3 artillery assault that lasted most of the morning and helped drive the Confederates out of Union breastworks on Culp's Hill. When looking up at this site, try to imagine the frightening sound of all that artillery on that hill so close to the hospital as surgeons and nurses tried to work and wounded men tried to rest and heal. It seems almost impossible. Likewise, try to imagine this as an open field and a hospital with hundreds of men lying everywhere around you.

36 The location is at 39°48'18" N 77°13'19" W.

One Final Note

I was thrilled to discover after the publication of my first Spangler book that Dr. Daniel W. Richards of the 145th Pennsylvania is the 4X great-grandfather of three of my grandchildren—Elizabeth Ansell, Austin Ansell, and Katherine Ansell. My son-in-law is the Rev. Christopher B. Ansell of Swissvale, Pennsylvania, who is Dr. Richards' 3X great-grandson and who is following in his ancestor's path of community leadership. Christopher's mother, retired Dallastown, Pennsylvania, music teacher Dr. Susannah Richards, is the doctor's 2X great-granddaughter. In a strong family tradition, Dr. Daniel W. Richards' grandmother was named Susanna, his mother was Susannah, his wife was Susanna, he had a sister Susanna, and his 2X great-granddaughter is Susannah.

I'm also pleased that ownership of the wooden storage chest used by Dr. Richards after the war was transferred in 2022 from 2X great-granddaughter Susannah to noted historian, educator, and author Carolyn Ivanoff of Gettysburg and Connecticut. Then, once it was confirmed that Dr. Richards worked at both hospitals on Spangler property, Carolyn graciously donated the chest and it is now owned by Paul Semanek, the longtime and highly respected site coordinator of the modern-day George Spangler farm. The Gettysburg Foundation displays the chest on loan from Semanek at the farm where Dr. Richards worked at both the XI Corps and First Division, II Corps hospitals. Ivanoff often portrays Civil War women at Spangler, and it is fortunate that the Richards family chest came into her hands.

Spangler Farm Short Story

In the first paragraph that follows, 145th Pennsylvania Chaplain Stuckenberg describes the scene at the II Corps hospital on the Schwartz farm outside of Gettysburg on July 4. The paragraph after that discusses both that location and Civil War hospitals in general:

> Some of the wounded were in shelter tents which sheltered them poorly, others lay in the rain & mud, covered with a woolen or rubber blanket—or nothing at all. I labored to shelter them till I was wet through & returned to my tent very weary & sick. It was a sad sight to look at the hospital at any time, but especially when those severely & mortally wounded were thus exposed. And nothing could be done for them. After the rain I . . . got some hay & placed under the wounded.[37]

> What a hospital on or near the field of battle is can only be known by those that have seen one. There were between 2000 and 3000 wounded in our 2nd corps hospital.

In 1st Division there were two operating stands, where the Surgeons were constantly consulting about operations and were performing amputations. Heaps of amputated feet and hands, arms and legs were seen lying under the tables and by their sides. Go around among the wounded and you witness the most saddening and sickening sights. Some are writhing with pain, and deeply moaning and groaning and calling for relief which cannot be afforded them. The finest forms are horribly disfigured and mutilated. Wounds are found in all parts of the body. Here lies one with his leg shattered, the flesh torn by a shell, nothing but shreds being left. There lies one shot through the abdomen, the intestines protruding—his life cannot be saved, perhaps even opium gives him little temporary relief. He is but waiting to die. Here lies one with his arm almost severed from his body—waiting for amputation. There lies one young and once handsome shot through the face and head—his eyes swollen shut and covered with a yellow, putrid matter, his hair clotted with blood, his jaws torn, and a bullet hole through each cheek. Some of the wounds are dressed, some not. From some the blood still oozes, in others maggots are perhaps found. Perhaps they are poorly waited on, there not being nurses enough. No physician may have examined their wounds and dressed them. Their physical wants may not have been attended to. They long for home and their friends, but they cannot get to the one, the other cannot come to them. Through neglect, perhaps they die. They are buried in their clothes, without shroud, without coffin, perhaps without religious services and a board to mark their resting place. The hospital soon becomes foul, especially in summer—the stench sometimes being almost intolerable. Medicines may be scarce, the fool unpalatable—perhaps scarce. Near the battle field of Gettysburg many barns for miles were filled with wounded, many of whom had neither surgeons, nor nurses, nor food.[38]

Stuckenberg received a pension of $6 a month for the last six years of his life because of heart disease and rheumatism. He died in 1903. His widow, Mary, lived on Springs Avenue next to Meade School in Gettysburg for several years after her husband's death and founded the Woman's League of Pennsylvania College to support religious programs and activities at what is now Gettysburg College. Mary died in 1934 and is buried with her husband in Soldiers' National Cemetery.[39]

38 Hedrick and Davis, *I'm Surrounded by Methodists*, 84.

39 John H. W. Stuckenberg Invalid Pension Claim 941650 and Mary Stuckenberg Widow Pension Claim 672656, NARA; *Gettysburg Times*, Feb. 5, 1934.

Chapter 10

Colonel Cross' Death at the Granite Schoolhouse Hospital

"Colonel Cross, who was a fine looking man . . . begged for someone to shoot
him so he might be relieved from his great suffering."

— *Drummer John B. Holloway, 148th Pennsylvania*[1]

It's no wonder Col. Edward E. Cross of the 5th New Hampshire foresaw his death at Gettysburg. He suffered multiple wounds and illnesses and been moved in and out of hospitals in the 13 months leading up to the battle. Surely, all those close calls had to damage the psyche of even a hardened soldier such as Cross. Here's a rundown of Cross' pre-Gettysburg wounds and medical care:

June 1, 1862, Fair Oaks, Virginia: Disabled by a rifle ball in the upper left thigh. He developed a persistent fever and was admitted to a general hospital in New York City on June 23 for a 10-day recovery. Then he went on a 30-day furlough.

September 17, 1862, Sharpsburg, Maryland: Wounded slightly in the forehead.

December 13, 1862, Fredericksburg, Virginia: Wounded by two shells in five places. Transferred from the regimental hospital on December 20 to a Washington, D.C., hospital. 30-day furlough started on December 23.

February 5, 1863: Treated in Boston for a contusion of the chest, then went on a 20-day furlough.

February 23, 1863: Admitted to a Washington, D.C., hospital. Returned to duty on March 14.[2]

---

1 Muffly, *The Story of Our Regiment, A History of the 148th Pennsylvania Vols.*, 331.

2 Cross Carded Medical Record, RG 94 Records of the Adjutant General's Office, Entry 534, 5 New Hampshire Crown, A.J. to Frozzeller, C.H., NARA.

Being shot up at Fredericksburg and lying helpless for hours not far from the wall in the terror of Marye's Heights seemed to frighten Cross especially. "It came near being my last battle," he later wrote. "A twelve-pounder shell . . . burst in front of me. One fragment struck me just below the heart, making a bad wound. Another blew off my hat; another (small bit) entered my mouth, and broke out three of my best jaw-teeth, while the gravel, bits of . . . earth, and minute fragments of shell covered my face with bruises. I fell insensible," as he told it, "and lay for some time, when another fragment of shell, striking me on the left leg, below the knee, brought me to my senses. My mouth was full of blood, fragments of teeth and gravel, my breast-bone almost broken in, and I lay in mud two inches deep." His wounds constituted only part of the harrowing experience: "I lay on the field for hours, the most awful moments of my life. As the balls from our line hissed over me within a foot of my head. I covered my face with both hands, and counted rapidly from one to one hundred, expecting every moment my brains would spatter the ground. But they didn't."[3]

Many wouldn't have made it back from that, and perhaps most would have refused to come back. In Cross' case, a terrible fatalism took over. He told Maj. Gen. Winfield Scott Hancock on July 2 that "I will die today." Days earlier, he had told his aide, Lt. Charles Hale, that Gettysburg would be his final battle.[4] "The Colonel evidently had a strong premonition of his death," Hale said. "It did not seem to effect him much, in fact it effected me more than it did himself for I was then only a smooth-faced boy of nineteen, while he was a long bearded man of thirty-one, but having been more or less in contact with him from the time the regiment was organized, I had come to know him intimately and understood something of his moods." Cross even instructed Hale to take care of his books and papers after his death.[5]

But his many wounds, the horror of Fredericksburg, and even the premonitions of his own death appeared to do little to dim Cross' fighting spirit. The newspaperman and native of Lancaster kept coming back to lead his men, though at a deadly price. As with the entire First Division of the II Corps, the 5th New Hampshire was a shell of its former robust self when it arrived outside of Gettysburg on the morning of July 2. Once 1,010 strong at its organization in Concord in 1861, the

---

3 5-Participant Accounts—Edward Cross folder, GNMP.

4 St. Clair A. Mulholland, *The 116th Pennsylvania Volunteers in the War of the Rebellion 1861-1865* (Philadelphia, 1903), 149.

5 Charles A. Hale, "With Colonel Cross in the Gettysburg Campaign," 5-Participant Accounts–Edward Cross, GNMP.

Col. Edward E. Cross

Library of Congress

regiment counted a mere 179 men at battle strength as it rested on the Taneytown Road.[6]

Among its many battles, the 5th suffered particularly heavy losses at Fair Oaks, Antietam, and Fredericksburg. At Fredericksburg, it repeatedly charged through Confederate lead in frontal assaults and wasn't stopped until advancing close to the terrible stone wall, losing six color bearers and 13 officers.[7]

Cross was promoted to command the First Brigade of the First Division of the II Corps before Gettysburg, so in addition to the 5th New Hampshire he now had charge of the 148th Pennsylvania, 81st Pennsylvania, and 61st New York. The brigade rested with the division most of the day on July 2 as the armies took their positions, then got its orders and dashed toward the Wheatfield. At about 6 p.m., Cross led the brigade across Wheatfield Road on a charge into the eastern edge of the Wheatfield and the woods to the east of the field.

"The wheat had been trampled into the dirt by line after line before we came," Hale said. He saw Cross scanning the ground in front. "Our line was well warmed up, and the enemy along the edge of the woods by the wall below were getting all the hot lead they wanted. But we were catching it hot also, for wounded men were staggering back to the rear, and the dead were getting thick along the ground."[8]

Moments later, Cross was hit in the abdomen by a Confederate Minie ball that entered through the front of his body and exited the back. Cross "was lying among some small bushes on the edge of the wheat field," Pvt. George G. Walters of the 148th Pennsylvania said, describing the scene after the colonel was shot.[9]

---

6 William Child, M.D., *A History of the Fifth Regiment New Hampshire Volunteers, in the American Civil War, 1861-1865* (Bristol, NH, 1893), 9; Busey and Busey, *Union Casualties at Gettysburg*, 1166.

7 www.civilwardata.com/active/hdsquery.dll?RegimentHistory?1207&U, accessed Dec. 15, 2022.

8 Hale, "With Colonel Cross in the Gettysburg Campaign," GNMP.

9 Muffly, *The Story of Our Regiment, A History of the 148th Pennsylvania Vols.*, 439.

Lieutenant Colonel Charles Hapgood took command of the 5th New Hampshire upon Cross' earlier promotion to brigade command. He saw the Confederate soldier fire and hit Cross from behind a boulder and then duck out of view behind the boulder. Hapgood ordered Sgt. Charles H. Phelps to take out the Confederate, which he did moments later with an expert shot when the Confederate re-emerged. The 21-year-old Phelps was mortally wounded himself when the brigade was forced to retreat. He died two days later. Like Cross and so many others in the 5th New Hampshire, Phelps had been seriously wounded December 13, 1862, at Fredericksburg. He finally was able to return to duty less than three months before he was killed at Gettysburg.[10]

The II Corps' First Division ambulances were waiting not far behind the Wheatfield line, so Cross was loaded into an ambulance five minutes after he was hit.[11]

Cross was taken to the First Division, II Corps hospital between Granite Schoolhouse and Powers Hill in the middle of George Spangler's farm. 5th New Hampshire Assistant Surgeon William Child said wheat sheaves from a nearby Spangler field at the base of the hill were gathered by Cross' attendants and a comfortable bed was made. "Some camp-fires crackled and glimmered, flashed and cast weird shadows around the group of friends and attendants," Child recalled. "Now and then a shell went screeching across the sky, bursting with a sudden flash and stunning report. Many of his regiment, men who had followed him in a score of battles, were around; his surgeon, Major J. W. Bucknam, rendered skillful medical aid and friendly comfort." The poignant scene continued: "Standing nearby were the officers and men who had so often followed him into battle. All faces were sad, all hearts were sorrowful. The dying warrior had a kind word for all. To his officers and men he sent messages of love, of respect, of encouragement. . . . He gave messages of love to his sisters and brothers. . . . Shells were bursting near; spiteful picket firing was in every direction. Life was drawing to an end in that noble form. He constantly murmured, 'My brave men.'"[12]

"Colonel Cross, who was a fine looking man, had command of our Brigade," said drummer John B. Holloway of the 148th Pennsylvania, who was working at the hospital. "He was fatally wounded . . . and taken to the rear, and his sufferings were so great, during the night, that he begged for someone to shoot him so he might be relieved from his great suffering."[13]

---

10 Phelps Carded Medical Record, 5 New Hampshire A. S. Marston to J. Price, NARA.

11 Hale, "With Colonel Cross in the Gettysburg Campaign," GNMP.

12 Child, *A History of the Fifth Regiment, New Hampshire Volunteers*, 211-212.

13 Muffly, *The Story of Our Regiment, A History of the 148th Pennsylvania Vols.*, 331.

Lt. Charles Hale, 5th New Hampshire
U.S. Army Heritage and Education Center

Assistant Surgeon Child added: "In pain he lived on another hour and still another, until at 12:30 midnight that brave spirit went out on the great battle-field. He died on the field of honor, amid the turmoil of a great fight, surrounded by his comrades in arms."[14] "I sat right down on the ground, feeling that hope was dead," Cross' aide Hale said of hearing the news later that night about his commander.[15]

As he lay dying, Cross had asked to see new II Corps ambulance chief Thomas Livermore, a former member of Cross' regiment, at the Granite Schoolhouse hospital. "Nothing but the most imperative duty could have detained me from him," Livermore recalled later, "but the removal of the many wounded who might perish, if not cared for, was of that character, and I found myself unable to go to him until midnight. . . . I was oppressed with great regret that I had failed to see Colonel Cross before he died."[16]

Surgeon John W. Bucknam, age 29 at Spangler, had joined up four months after his wedding in 1861. He treated Cross for each wound he received since the start of the war, so it was only appropriate that Bucknam attended Cross at his death. Bucknam crossed the colonel's arms and closed his eyes upon his death. Cross' body was embalmed and buried the following week in Lancaster to great ceremony and mourning with "an immense concourse of people," flags at half-staff, a band playing solemn melodies, and multiple eulogies.[17]

Like other physicians on the scene, Bucknam had labored so tirelessly in the frightful conditions at the Granite Schoolhouse hospital on July 2–3 and the Jacob Schwartz farm on July 3–4 that he became permanently ill and was admitted to a Washington, D.C., hospital later that month with bronchitis. "Bucknam became disabled on or about the 4th day of July," fellow assistant surgeon Child remembered. "He was upon the operating staff and labored three days and two nights

14 Child, *A History of the Fifth Regiment, New Hampshire Volunteers*, 212.

15 Hale, "With Colonel Cross in the Gettysburg Campaign," GNMP.

16 Livermore, *Days and Events 1860-1866*, 254–255.

17 Ibid., 325; *Coos* (New Hampshire) *Republican*, July 14, 1863.

Surgeon J. W. Bucknam

U.S. Army Heritage and Education Center

without rest; thus injuring his health and contracting chronic diarrhea. . . . [which caused] a general debility."[18]

5th New Hampshire commander Hapgood said Bucknam "contracted chronic diarrhea at the battle of Gettysburg Pa. from own exertion and exposure . . . to such an extent as to prevent him from doing duty as surgeon."[19] His body ravaged by his time at Spangler, Gettysburg, and in the Civil War, Bucknam died at age 37 in 1870 in New Hampshire from "general prostration resulting from congestion of the lungs, chronic diarrhea." His wife, Celia, died eight days later.[20]

Cross is deservedly honored in New Hampshire and throughout the Civil War community for his courage, leadership, discipline, and military skill. A road is named for him next to the Wheatfield in Gettysburg National Military Park and he is memorialized with a monument and small stone marker where he fell. But he also receives his share of criticism for his temper and mood swings. Those attributes were common among most normal human beings in the life-threatening fury of the Civil War, but Cross so bothered the men of the 148th Pennsylvania that they still complained about him in writing and speeches decades after the war. The 148th's Pioneer Corps called him "the tyrant commander of our Brigade" in the 1904 history of the regiment and in the same book complaints were made against Cross for angrily striking one of their men in the back of the neck with a sword for comments made by another man.[21]

Major Robert Henry Forster explained his regiment's animosity in a speech during the dedication of the 148th's monument at the eastern edge of the Wheatfield in 1889, only yards from the monument honoring Cross and the 5th

18 Bucknam Carded Medical Record, 5 New Hampshire D. Bradbury to C. Crawford, NARA; Bucknam Invalid Pension Claim 73474, NARA.

19 Bucknam pension file.

20 Ibid.

21 Muffly, *The Story of Our Regiment, A History of the 148th Pennsylvania Vols.*, 461, 716.

New Hampshire. "Colonel Cross was undoubtedly a dashing, brave and impetuous soldier," Forster said in his remarks,

> but in other personal characteristics he was not noted for giving much consideration to the rights and feelings of the soldiers. For some cause, never, so far as I am aware, known or explained, he from his first association with us, seemed to have conceived a dislike to the regiment. Now, because of this dislike, or prejudice, or whatever it may have been, officers and men of our regiment were almost daily, from the day we broke camp on the Rappahannock until we reached Gettysburg, made to suffer wrong and injustice from him. One officer in particular, from the very outset of the campaign, seemed to have incurred his displeasure. That officer was Lieutenant-Colonel Robert McFarlane, commanding officer of the regiment in the absence of Colonel [James A.] Beaver, who had not recovered from the severe wound he had received at Chancellorsville. Colonel McFarlane soon became a victim to this displeasure; yet it is a truth, known to myself and others, that if he ever gave offense to Colonel Cross it was only in such efforts as he made to protect himself and those who served under him from imposition and injustice. However that may be, on the evening of the 30th of June, 1863, while in bivouac at Uniontown, Maryland, the company commanders were called together to meet Colonel [Henry B.] McKeen [of the 81st Pennsylvania], and were by him informed that he had come to the regiment by order of Colonel Cross to assume command of it. To say that all were astounded and shocked at this sudden and unceremonious announcement is to give mild terms to their feelings. It must be said, however, that if such an arbitrary and cruel act of injustice was to be perpetrated, a less objectionable officer than Colonel McKeen could not have been selected to place in command. He was an officer and soldier of excellent repute, highly esteemed by all who knew him, and in all respects one under whom a subordinate might cheerfully serve. Under the circumstances we could only repress our indignation and submit. Without a murmur of open complaint at the time, though the provocation was grievous, Colonel McFarlane quietly bore this humiliation. Courageous man and soldier as he was, he followed his regiment to Gettysburg and gallantly shared its dangers. On this wheatfield, after the fall of Colonel Cross, and Colonel McKeen, by virtue of his rank had become brigade commander, so acceptable to him had been Colonel McFarlane's conduct in the fight, that his first act was to direct Colonel McFarlane to resume command of the regiment, thus in a measure atoning for the wrong of his predecessor in command. From that moment until the battle ended, the regiment was in charge of Colonel McFarlane.[22]

Ambulance chief Livermore offered something of a rejoinder to Forster's criticism:

22 John P. Nicholson, *Pennsylvania at Gettysburg: Ceremonies at the Dedication of the Monuments Erected by the Commonwealth of Pennsylvania*, Vol. 2 (Harrisburg, PA, 1914), 739–740.

With Colonel Cross' death the glory of our regiment came to a halt. . . . It is true that the regiment maintained a good reputation to the end of the war and did some splendid fighting, but it was not the old regiment. Colonel Cross had been a severe teacher, but he had impressed those under him with his martial spirit, and I believe that the regiment as little contemplated retreating as he himself did. He was a very brave man, and clear-headed in a fight; he took the most excellent care of his men in a sanitary way, and was a good disciplinarian. He had his faults which injured him more than anyone else; such as jumping at conclusions, and criticizing and condemning men and measures without stint. If all the colonels in the army had been like him we should never have lost a battle. Other volunteer regiments, many of them, were composed of as good men as ours, but I do not think there were a half dozen in the army which were as good in every respect as ours, and we owed that to the colonel. . . . He clothed and fed us well, taught us to build good quarters, and camped us on good ground, and in short did everything well to keep us healthy, well drilled, and always ready to meet the enemy.[23]

Cross' aide Lt. Hale had taken his share of reprimands from the colonel. "I had come to know him intimately and understood something of his moods," Hale said. But the lieutenant also said it was his "privilege to be intimately associated with Colonel Cross during the last twenty-seven days of his life." As instructed, Hale secured and took care of the colonel's belongings after his death at Gettysburg.[24]

Pension records reveal Cross as a loving and caring son who went to great lengths to support his 58-year-old mother, Abigail. She filed a pension application in 1863 in which a merchant neighbor testified that Cross' father, Ephraim, "has been in limited circumstances" and that "Col. Edward E. Cross deceased, has in his belief supported and maintained his mother . . . and other members of the family for the space of two years—providing them a home, and procuring articles necessary for their support," adding "Col. E. E. Cross has for a long period supported his mother.[25]

Pension applications revealed, in fact, that Cross had long filled the financial breach his father created. Cross' father had invested in a new bank around 1850 that failed and then left for Canada for five years, leaving his wife behind without support. When mortgage foreclosure was threatened, young Edward "in order to secure a home for his mother and to prevent her from being driven from the house in which she had lived so many years furnished his father with the money to redeem the homestead, taking a mortgage of the same himself. And Cross made

23 Livermore, *Days and Events 1860-1866*, 255–256.

24 Hale, "With Colonel Cross in the Gettysburg Campaign," GNMP.

25 Cross' Mother's Pension Claim 21965, Fold3.

arrangements when leaving for the Army in 1859 and 1861 to pay for provisions at his expense."

The same witness said "several parties told me that they thought [the father] could do more than he now does were it not for his too free use of liquor. . . . It appears that the son was very much attached to his mother, perhaps more than he otherwise would have been if the father had been a sober man, but on account of his vicious habits, he took every means to get the property in his own hands and by so doing to secure a home for his mother and prevent his Father from squandering it for liquor."[26]

The *Coos* (New Hampshire) *Republican* said, "As a son and brother, he was kind, attentive and observing. His parents and relatives were always the source of remembrance and solicitude and his practical kindness was frequent and abundant."[27] Abigail received a $30-a-month mother's military pension until her death in 1883.[28]

The area where the monument to the 5th New Hampshire and Colonel Cross sits near the southeastern edge of the Wheatfield is in an area of hardwoods in a landscape today slightly more wooded than when Cross was mortally wounded there, according to National Park Service maps.[29]

One Final Note

The 5th New Hampshire suffered 83 casualties out of 179 men at Gettysburg for a rate of 46.4 percent, thus continuing its history of severe Civil War losses.[30]

Spangler Farm Short Story

Most of the Irish Brigade's wounded and dying men were taken from the battlefield to the First Division, II Corps hospital at Granite Schoolhouse on July 2–3. So it makes sense that their beloved chaplain, Father William Corby, was likely there on Spangler land with them. Father Corby was one of the most revered men

26 Ibid.

27 *Coos* (New Hampshire) *Republican*, July 14, 1863.

28 Cross' Mother's Pension Claim.

29 Cultural Landscape Report for Gettysburg National Military Park Record of Treatment: Volume I, (2018), Drawings 16A and 16B, Olmsted Center for Landscape Preservation, National Park Service, Boston, MA.

30 Busey and Busey, *Union Casualties at Gettysburg*, 1166.

of God on either side in the Civil War. The love by which he was held by his men translated after the war into a broad popular esteem, a respect that sent Corby to the presidency of Notre Dame University not once but twice. Father Corby was the only chaplain for the vaunted Irish Brigade at Gettysburg and granted the men general absolution moments before the battle on July 2, thus securing his fame for generations to come.

Civil War chaplains tended the soldiers where they were most needed, and Father Corby was known and appreciated by his soldiers for his dedicated and courageous work on battlefields and in hospitals. He sought medical help for them, offered confession, provided water, cleaned wounds, and prayed with the wounded and dying. And he stayed. He stayed until he felt he had done everything he could in the saddest possible conditions. "An inspection of a battle-field immediately after the battle has a very depressing effect on the mind, more so even than the battle itself," Corby wrote after the war. "You might see outside the *quasi*-hospital, in one great pile, legs, arms, hands, and feet, covered with the fresh blood of the owners—a scene that would sicken most persons to such an extent as to make them hope never to see the like again. The picture can be compared with nothing but a butcher shop, or slaughter-house, where meat is cut and piled up. . . . These scenes I witnessed, not once, but many times. Great distress wills one's mind when obliged to behold such misery, with no possible means to apply an immediate remedy; but such are the fates of war."[31]

It's our fate to have only circumstantial evidence, albeit strong circumstantial evidence, of Father Corby's attendance at Granite Schoolhouse. No matter that we are tantalizingly close and we know that Father Corby ministered at hospitals at many other battlefields, this writer could not find the one sentence from anybody at Gettysburg placing the chaplain at Granite Schoolhouse. Perhaps, in time, someone will come forward with that missing link.

Father Corby did write a few lines about his July 2, 1863, granting of general absolution at Gettysburg in which he forgave Irish Brigade soldiers of their sins a few moments before they went into battle, thus clearing their path to heaven. This event brought him fame and two statues, one at Gettysburg on the boulder on which he granted the absolution and one at the University of Notre Dame. His Notre Dame statue stands in front of Corby Hall. But he seemed not as impressed by the absolution as others: "Often in camp and sometimes on the march we held very impressive religious services, but the one at Gettysburg was more public, and was witnessed by many who had not, perhaps, seen the others. The surroundings there, too, made a vast difference, for really the situation reminded one of the day of judgment, when shall be seen 'men withering away for fear and expectation of what shall come upon the whole world,' so great were the whirlwinds of war then in

---

31 William Corby, C.S.C. (Congregation of Holy Cross), *Memoirs of Chaplain Life: Three Years With the Irish Brigade in the Army of the Potomac*, ed. Lawrence Frederick Kohl (New York, 1992), 63, 77–78.

Notre Dame's Father Corby statue is in front of Corby Hall on campus.
Ron Kirkwood

motion." An obviously non-Catholic Pvt. Henry Meyer of the 148th Pennsylvania called the absolution "some religious ceremony of a few minutes' duration."[32]

Photos show the Very Rev. Corby to be of slender frame in the Civil War. He was 29 years old at Gettysburg and a veteran already of just under two years of difficult war service. His beard reached straight out from the sides of his face and was full and long in front. The hair on top of his head was thin. But like his beard, his character and concern for his fellow man were full and strong. And that made him beloved in the Irish Brigade.

He returned to Gettysburg in 1888 for the dedication of the Irish Brigade statue on Stony Hill and was asked to be a speaker there. "At first I got on reasonably well," he said of his speech, recalling the event, "until, looking over those assembled, the surviving members of our illustrious and numerous band as it appeared at Alexandria, Va., in the fall of '61, I happened to make this statement, 'Here is what is left of us; where are the others?' when I filled up very unexpectedly and could not speak for several minutes. I had struck a very tender chord. The celebrant, although eleven years younger than I, wept like a child, and the brave old warriors before me who had stood the shock of the battles also wept. We were on the spot where many of the 'others' had fallen," Corby continued, "heroes whom we had helped to carry out of our ranks. The place, the circumstances, the remembrances, the old friendships renewed, contributed to emotions that perhaps may not be well understood except by the participants."[33]

Perhaps someday, if we are fortunate and someone uncovers a letter or diary or record placing Father Corby at the Granite Schoolhouse hospital, then we can finally honor him for his help, his healing, and his tender care and mercy on the George Spangler farm.

---

32 Ibid., 185; Muffly, *The Story of Our Regiment, A History of the 148th Pennsylvania Vols.*, 536.

33 Corby, *Memoirs of Chaplain Life*, 192–193.

Chapter 11

Soldier Stories:
The Loved Ones Left Behind

"Mary Vaughn . . . has been unable to support herself through old age and infirmity and
had no property or income with the exception of her said son's earnings."

— *The widow pension claim for the mother of Cpl. Robert Vaughn, 134th New York*

By the hundreds of thousands, the mothers, fathers, wives, and children left behind became the forgotten casualties of the Civil War. When a soldier died, devastated family members back home not only lost a precious loved one, but often their only means of support, thus causing even more pain. Sometimes, the deceased soldier's father had already died, and in other cases he was too broken down or ill to support a family, a burden often assumed by young men called to war. In these many cases, a mother and any other children were dependent on the soldier. The loss of this soldier, therefore, often produced generational misery.

Pension claims reveal the devotion and dedication to family by these men—and in many cases, boys—before they became soldiers. Through their hard work they supported themselves, their parents, stepparents, siblings, and half siblings. Sometimes they were as young as 10 or 12 years old when they began this effort. Often, they worked multiple physically demanding jobs, and they usually handed over all of their money to their parents. Then when this young man went off to war he sent most or all of his pay home and expressed concern about his family's well-being in letters. As pension records show, this kind of family love and devotion and self-sacrifice was common—perhaps even the norm—in the Civil War.

But who would step in and support the family if a soldier died? Their loss was twofold—not only a beloved family member, but the vital income that the family member produced. As it turns out, it was mostly the federal government that was obliged to step into the role of provider. One adult family member and all children of the soldier under age 16 could receive pensions. A wife normally was the lone adult pension recipient, with mothers of single soldiers and sometimes siblings and widower fathers awarded money in some cases. A family member of a deceased private could get $8 a month from the government with raises in ensuing years. Officers qualified for higher pensions. Each young child of a deceased soldier could receive $2 a month.

Qualifying for this money wasn't easy. A disabled husband, for example, would have to prove his disability in order for his wife to receive a mother's pension. Such proof required his own testimony and that of others. A mother needed to prove her financial distress, also requiring her own testimony and that of others. In the case of a soldier's death, his mother had to show how her son supported her before his death. The parents had to prove they were married, requiring a record or minister's testimony. They had to vow their loyalty to the United States. An officer in the deceased soldier's regiment testified to his death and that he had been a loyal, good soldier. Establishing a claim was so involved that applicants often hired an attorney to represent them. Rarely, someone in the family's community would testify against the potential recipient and say they didn't qualify for the money because the applicant family didn't need it. Sometimes an investigator was sent to the scene to make the determination.

Once approved, as happened in the vast majority of cases, the family member then received the pension for life with occasional monthly increases along the way. Remarriage ended a widow's pension. Recipients also could petition for an increase. Without a doubt, pension money saved lives and eased the pain as much as possible back home.

What follows are 10 pension examples from soldiers at Spangler.

"OLD, INFIRM . . . AND NO PROPERTY GOODS"
Private Joseph Balmes Jr., 26th Wisconsin, Company C
Pension No: 90579; Pension Applicant: Mother Anna Maria

Private Joseph Balmes suffered a gunshot wound "through his body" in his right hip on July 1 when the 26th Wisconsin and the rest of the Third Division of the XI Corps was overrun north of Gettysburg. Balmes was taken to an unknown hospital behind Confederate lines and arrived at the XI Corps hospital on George Spangler's farm on July 4 or 5.

Though Balmes suffered a compound fracture, surgeon general records indicate his treatment only as "water dressing." Doctors undoubtedly tried much more for him that wasn't included in scant hospital files. There is no mention of an amputation in the records, so either the location of his wound made an amputation untenable or one was performed at Spangler and not recorded, which was common. If he didn't have an amputation, the Madison-area native was doomed from the moment he was hit due to the inevitable blood poisoning or infection. He died at Spangler half a country away from his Wisconsin home on July 10 or 14, depending on the source.[1]

A mother could apply for a pension if her deceased son had no wife or children, so Balmes' mother, Anna Maria, age 52, applied in 1866. His father, James Sr., was 61. Though those seem like modest ages today, one witness in support of their pension application called them "old, infirm and have no property goods." Friends of five years vouched that Joseph Jr. was the Balmes' son, and their doctor and a neighbor were among those who testified for them and their need for a pension. Comments included "The rheumatism settled in both [James Sr.'s] legs so that often for weeks is unable to leave his bed . . . extreme pain in both legs . . . preventing him from supporting himself. . . . Joseph Balmes Sr. is wholly incapable of supporting her, being suffering from disease that totally disqualifies him from manual labor. That this applicant [Mrs. Balmes] is also unfit for manual labor, suffering from dropsy [an excess of watery fluid in the body]."

One witness testified that Joseph Jr. supported his parents before his enlistment in 1862 and gave them a wagon worth $75 that they sold "for the purpose of applying the proceeds to their own support." He also gave them $8 of his monthly $13 soldier pay. Anna Maria was approved for a pension of $8 a month starting in 1867, and despite her health challenges at that time she lived until 1902, receiving a $12-a-month pension until her death. Her son, Joseph, is buried next to three other Spangler patients from the 26th Wisconsin in Soldiers' National Cemetery in Gettysburg.[2]

DID HE MEET HIS SON?
Private Benjamin Bice, 134th New York, Company A
Pension No: 26368; Pension Applicant: Wife Mary Ann

Like so many others, Pvt. Benjamin Bice was wounded at the Brickyard on July 1. His thoughts undoubtedly focused on his wife, Mary Ann, and his two young sons back in Schenectady once he was moved to Spangler with a wound of the left shoulder. The blue-eyed, six-foot-one-inch shoemaker married Mary Ann in 1859. William was age two years, nine months, and Benjamin Jr. nine months old in July 1863. It is unlikely that Benjamin Sr. ever met his youngest son. Here's why:

1 Anna Balmes Mother Pension File, Fold3.

2 Ibid.

Ben Sr. went off to war in September 1862. Ben Jr. was born in November of that year and there's no record of the elder Bice being home for his son's birth. Ben Sr.'s absences from the army were listed as being in a hospital in Washington, D.C., December 9-15 for rheumatism and then in a hospital at Fort Schuyler in the Bronx from late December through April with an unknown illness. If there ever was a chance for Ben Sr. to meet Ben Jr. it was at Fort Schuyler, about 165 miles from home. But for that meeting to happen, Mary Ann would have had to board a train in Schenectady with a two-year-old and a nine-month-old and take that train 20 miles to Albany. Then she had to catch another train to go 20 miles from Albany to Mechanicville, then another for the 13-mile trip from Mechanicville to Troy and yet another for the 150-mile journey from Troy to Harlem. And then she still had to get 10 miles from Harlem to the fort out on Long Island Sound. It would be nice to think that this happy reunion happened, but that's a lot of hurdles, effort, and exhaustion for a wife and two boys under age three.[3]

Bice was transferred from Spangler to Camp Letterman in late July and he died there on July 31. How his wife and children must have dominated his thoughts.

Mary Ann received an $8 pension per month after her husband's death and each boy got $2. She remarried in 1867, at which time her pension was stopped, but each boy's pension was raised then to $8. Husband Henry Brand and his new family relocated to Chicago, where he died in 1905, leaving "no property or life insurance." Mary Ann also had nothing, so the government granted her a pension again, this time of $12 a month, which increased to $20 in 1916. She was getting $25 a month at the time of her death in 1919.[4]

Bice is buried in the New York section of Soldiers' National Cemetery, where he is surrounded by 13 other Spangler patients.

HE NEVER MET HIS SON, PART II
Corporal Peter Carl Sr., 107th Ohio, Company I
Pension No: 26368; Pension Applicant: Wife Lovina

Corporal Peter Carl Sr. of the 107th Ohio is another example of a mortally wounded soldier lying at the XI Corps hospital who because of the Civil War would not only sacrifice his life but also the chance to meet, raise, and love his child and grandchildren. Carl and wife Lovina were married in the Akron, Ohio, area on August 17, 1862, six days after he enlisted. He was mustered in about three weeks later and the newlywed went off to war, leaving his bride at home.

---

3 "Map of the Railroads of the State of New York," 1863, Library of Congress.

4 Benjamin Bice Widow Pension Claim 26368, Fold3; Bice, New York Civil War Muster Roll Abstract, Fold3.

Cpl. Peter Carl Sr.

FindaGrave.com

Carl Jr. was born March 20, 1863, while his father was away.[5]

The 107th Ohio suffered the fifth most wounded at the Spangler hospital, with at least 98 patients out of more than 50 batteries and regiments represented there, behind only the 26th Wisconsin, 157th New York, 134th New York, and 153rd Pennsylvania. Of those regiments, all but the 134th New York took the vast majority of those casualties in the Day 1 fight north of Gettysburg. Carl, who was about 23, was hit in the upper third of his right leg and eventually made it to Spangler, where records indicate he was treated with water dressing. He also could have had an amputation that was not recorded. An amputation at the thigh during the Civil War left the soldier with a not-quite-50 percent chance of survival.[6]

Carl was transferred from Spangler in mid-July and ended up at Davids Island in the Long Island Sound, where he died September 28 of gangrene. His death caused a spiral of events that would negatively impact Peter Jr., who was 6 months old when his father died. Lovina received an $8-a-month widow's pension until she remarried and moved away. She didn't take her three-year-old son with her, so Lovina's parents became Peter Jr.'s guardians in January 1867 and took over the pension income. Peter Jr.'s grandfather and Lovina's father, Andrew Kepler, was killed by one of Kepler's sons-in-law in 1871, with the son-in-law convicted of manslaughter but then pardoned when the shooting was later ruled accidental. So nine-year-old Peter Jr. was moved again, this time to the home of an aunt and her husband, which is where he stayed until adulthood. Despite the sad family hurdles he faced as a child, Peter Jr. grew up to have a family and live into his 70s. Peter Carl Sr. is buried in Brooklyn with a military headstone.[7]

5 Lovina Carl Widow Pension Claim 26368, Fold3.

6 Joseph K. Barnes, *The Medical and Surgical History of the Civil War*, Vol. 12 (Wilmington, NC, 1990), 877–878.

7 Ancestry.com; Lovina Carl pension claim; *The Summit County Beacon*, Dec. 13, 1871; "Annual Reports for 1874 Made to the Sixty-First General Assembly of the State of Ohio" (Columbus, 1875), 21.

FIRST SHE LOST HER HUSBAND, THEN HER SON
Captain John Costin Jr., 82nd Ohio, Company F
Pension No.: 10343; Pension Applicant: Mother Mary

Captain John Costin Jr. was wounded at Bull Run in August 1862 but survived and returned to his regiment. He would not be so fortunate at Gettysburg 11 months later. Costin was hit in the left hip north of Gettysburg on July 1, just two days after his 22nd birthday. He was taken to Spangler, but surgeons couldn't find the ball because it had penetrated so far. So Costin was treated with water dressing until he died July 11. He was taken care of by 82nd Ohio comrade and surgeon Jacob Cantwell, who was one of the few doctors assigned to work through July at the XI Corps hospital. Cantwell announced Costin's death.[8]

Costin's mother, Mary, already was a widow after her husband John Sr.'s death in 1856. Now she had lost a child, too. A witness in her pension application said she was dependent on John Jr. and his brother Timothy for support since her husband died. Timothy was one of the witnesses, saying, "They have known . . . John Costin Jr. to give her regularly sums of money, clothing, flour and provisions that she had no other means of support."[9]

Mary received a pension of $20 because John Jr. was a captain. She would have received nothing if her son had been married. Costin died before the military banned removal of bodies from Gettysburg later in July, so Timothy traveled 350 miles from his home in Mansfield to the Spanglers' farm to have his brother's body exhumed and returned to Mansfield for burial. There he lies today in Mansfield Catholic Cemetery.[10]

"I AM VERY MUCH OBLIGED TO YOU"
Private Benjamin Franklin Darr, 107th Ohio, Company A
Pension No.: 147435; Pension Applicant: Mother Mary

He was only 20 years old at Spangler. He was off fighting a war, but his letters home prior to Gettysburg show more concern for his family than his own well-being. They also show gratitude. Private Benjamin Franklin Darr of Navarre, Ohio, near Canton, was a grateful human being, as exemplified by these excerpts from a letter home that he wrote on June 6, 1863, from Brooks Station, Virginia.

---

8 Volunteer Carded Medical Records, Mexican and Civil Wars, 1846–1865, 82 Ohio AS—CU, John Costin card, NARA; Mary Costin Mother Pension Claim, Fold3; Ancestry.com.

9 Costin pension claim.

10 Ibid.

Your letter I received through the hands of A.J. Rider the 3rd of this month. I was as I always am glad to hear from you all that you enjoy yourselves well. The paper and envelopes and stamps and newspaper I received too and I am very much obliged to you for your trouble. . . .

I am well and enjoy myself pretty well at the present. . . .

Let me know how Grandfather and Grandmother gets along and all the rest of the folks, and how Samuel likes Sheep shearing. . . .

We did go for Richmond I did not happen to get a scratch of a wound. But I dare not brag about it.[11]

He sent $50 home in one letter and $15 in another. He also sent Confederate money home one time just so his family could see it.[12]

But on July 1, 1863, less than a month after that letter home, he was mortally wounded on Barlow Knoll north of Gettysburg. Darr was hit by a Minie ball in the left hip and eventually taken to Spangler for treatment. Scanty XI Corps hospital records indicate he was treated with water dressing. He held on, but died July 29. Records don't indicate the site of his death, but it could have been Spangler.

Darr's father, Godfrey, had a leg amputated in 1850, so oldest son Ben became the breadwinner in the late 1850s. He worked the farm that his family rented and took other jobs and gave the proceeds to his parents. One of Darr's employers said he "labored earnestly and faithfully for his parents and helped them pay rent, furnish provisions . . . [a]ll the products of his labor went towards the support of his father and mother and his younger sisters and brothers."

Mary Darr tried for years after Ben's death to support the family on her own with the aid of her minor children but couldn't. Her husband died in December 1869, so she filed for a mother's pension in May 1870 and began receiving $8 a month that December. She continued to receive a monthly pension until her death in 1891.[13]

Darr is buried in Ohio. The young, caring, thoughtful soldier was taken home.

11 Mary Darr Mother's Pension Claim 147435, Fold3.

12 Ibid.

13 Ibid.

NO MARRIAGE, NO PENSION
Private Charles Getter, 153rd Pennsylvania, Company D
Pension No.: 74321; Pension Applicants: Children William, Mary, and Catharine and guardian Samuel Seem

Charles Getter was a 38-year-old blacksmith from Bath, Pennsylvania, near Allentown and Easton, when he joined the 153rd Pennsylvania for 9 months in October 1862. He was also a widower after wife Catharine died on October 3, 1857, six years after they were married. They had two children at home.[14]

Getter was about to be mustered out with the rest of the 153rd Pennsylvania when he was wounded in the knee on July 1. XI Corps hospital records indicate his only treatment was water dressing, but he could have had part of his leg amputated, depending on the bone and tissue damage. Private Getter died from that knee wound in a Spangler field on July 18. A person visiting another wounded soldier in the 153rd saw Getter after his death when his "body was yet warm." Getter's brother, Levi, traveled to George Spangler's farm and took Charles' body home to northeast Pennsylvania for burial.[15]

Getter's death at Spangler sparked an intense and wide-ranging investigation into his life and family that was still going on in the early 1900s in an effort to determine who qualified for a pension. The U.S. Pension Office took the routine and normal in-person testimony, but Getter's case was so complicated that an investigator was sent to Bath to interview locals who knew him, including an elderly neighbor who spoke only German. Here's what the Pension Office uncovered about Getter after his death, his family, and who deserved to receive monthly support money from the government:

Charles and Catharine's son, William, was born June 3, 1851. His parents married two months later, on August 25, 1851, thus making William a "legitimate" heir in the government's view. Daughter Mary was born August 6, 1852. Catharine, however, died in 1857, leaving Charles and the children on their own, so her sister, Justina, a widow herself, moved in with the family as their housekeeper. Though unmarried, Justina and Getter had a daughter, whom they named Catharine in honor of Justina's sister and Charles' wife, on October 14, 1862. This was one month after Charles went to war, never to return and never to meet daughter Catharine. Justina died in 1865, leaving William and Mary and half sister Catharine on their own.

---

14 www.civilwardata.com/active/hdsquery.dll?SoldierHistory?U&784521, accessed Dec. 26, 2022; Ancestry.com.

15 Getter family pension claim 74321, Fold3.

A guardian of unknown relation was appointed for William and Mary in November of 1863. Each child received $8 a month, and the guardian $8 a month, until the children's 16th birthday. But it was less straightforward for young Catharine. She was born out of wedlock, which would hamper her the rest of her life. She said she was never told her birth date, her only memory of her mother was when her body was being taken out of the house, and her "grandmother did not treat me very well and she was rough to me. She told me that I was an illegitimate child." Catharine and her mother lived with her grandmother until her mother died, at which point someone else took her in.

Catharine attempted to prove she deserved a pension until 1907, but she could never find proof that her parents married. The Pension Office denied her application, stating "mother of claimant was not married to soldier." Catharine was 45 years old when she made that final failed attempt in 1907 to receive a pension.[16]

SINGLE-HANDEDLY SUPPORTING A FAMILY OF 8
Private Adam Goelz, 26th Wisconsin, Company H
Pension No: 115389; Pension Applicant: Father Lorenz

Adam Goelz was an 18-year-old kid from Milwaukee when he arrived at the XI Corps hospital with a wound from a bullet that entered beneath his left eye and exited through the lower back side of his neck. Goelz was wounded on July 1, but the date of his arrival at Spangler is not known.[17]

As debilitating as that wound sounds, Spangler hospital records list it as a flesh wound with a treatment of water dressing, or "simple dressings" as described on Goelz's Volunteer Carded Medical Record at the National Archives. Goelz was transferred from Spangler to USA General Hospital, Broad and Cherry streets, Philadelphia, on July 15 and from there he went to Mower USA General Hospital, Chestnut Hill, Philadelphia, on January 22, 1864. He returned to duty on June 5, 1864, but he was back in a hospital in Savannah, Georgia, in February 1865, still struggling with "old gunshot wound left side of face." He was placed on the hospital steamer *Cosmopolitan* in March and at some point after that went home to Wisconsin, and, ultimately, to die.[18]

Goelz's destiny was sealed with that musket ball wound on July 1, 1863. He died on August 22, 1865, at his father's home in Milwaukee, a little more than

---

16 Getter family pension claim 74321, Fold3.

17 Lorenz Goelz Father Pension Claim 115389, Fold3.

18 Carded Medical Records Volunteers, Mexican, and Civil Wars, 1846–1865, RG 94, Records of the Adjutant General's Office, Entry 534, 26th Wisconsin, Baltaser Davis to Philip Kuhn, NARA.

two years after what turned out to be his mortal wounding. The family doctor examined Goelz 10 days before his death and found him "suffering from a wound said to have been received on July 1, 1863, caused by a musket ball. . . . At the time I saw him he was suffering from pyaemia [blood poisoning] caused by the . . . gunshot fracture of bones composing the base of the skull, which finally resulted in death."[19]

Adam's death was another tragedy for the Goelz family. His mother, Elizabeth, died when he was five or six years old near Heidelberg in what would become Germany, and his father, Lorenz, was crippled and had no use of his right arm from wounds suffered in military service in Europe. The same family doctor called Lorenz "infirm and crippled" and "broken down by his wounds and general disability." Lorenz remarried in Germany and he and his new wife and family arrived in New York City in 1852 and settled in heavily German Milwaukee. By 1860, with his father owning no property except furniture and unable to perform manual labor, Adam had come to support five younger siblings and half siblings, as well as his father and stepmother, first as a farm laborer and then as a barrel maker. A witness in Lorenz's pension application called Adam "a strong, healthy young man, of industrious character . . . who labored steadily at his employment."[20]

Adam earned $1.25 a day, which he gave to his father. He sent various amounts of money home after his enlistment at age 17 in August 1862, starting with $5, then $10, then $15, and then $25. To help replace that after Adam's death, the government awarded Lorenz a father's pension of $8 a month.[21]

Private Adam Goelz is buried in Milwaukee. He is one of 139 wounded men of the 26th Wisconsin known to have been treated at Spangler, the most of more than 50 regiments and batteries represented there.

"WHO WILL CARE FOR MOTHER NOW?"
Private William L. Purbeck, 5th Massachusetts Battery
Pension No.: 25192; Pension Applicant: Mother Lydia

As he took his dying breaths on July 3, Pvt. William L. Purbeck of the 5th Massachusetts Battery could have been speaking for thousands of other Civil War soldiers when his thoughts turned toward home and he said in a soft voice, maybe to himself, perhaps to others: "Who will care for Mother now?"[22]

---

19 Goelz pension claim.

20 Ibid.; Goelz family descendant Gary R. Rebholz.

21 Ibid.

22 Cpl. Benjamin Graham in *History of the Fifth Massachusetts Battery* (Boston, 1902), 641.

Purbeck's mother, Lydia, had become a widow after her husband Aaron's death in 1854. Now, without her son, Mrs. Purbeck had no means of support.

Purbeck spent the morning and afternoon of July 2, 1863, with the Artillery Reserve on the George Spangler farm and fought later in the day next to the 9th Massachusetts on Wheatfield Road in an attempt to stem the collapse of Maj. Gen. Daniel Sickles' III Corps line. It was undoubtedly on the Trostle farm where Purbeck was mortally wounded in the side by a shell as the battery was falling back. He died July 3 at a non-Spangler hospital, and that's where he tearfully muttered "Who will care for Mother now?" His final heartbreaking words inspired a popular song of the era of the same name, the lyrics of which follow:[23]

> Why am I so weak and weary?
> See how faint my heated breath.
> All around to me seems darkness.
> Tell me, comrades, is this death?
> Ah! how well I know your answer.
> To my fate I meekly bow.
> If you'll only tell me truly:
> Who will care for mother now?
>
> Chorus:
> Soon with angels I'll be marching,
> With bright laurels on my brow.
> I have for my Country fallen,
> Who will care for mother now?
>
> Who will comfort her in sorrow?
> Who will dry the falling tear,
> Gently smooth her wrinkled forehead?
> Who will whisper words of cheer?
> Even now I think I see her
> Kneeling, praying for me! how
> Can I leave her in her anguish?
> Who will care for mother now?
>
> Chorus:
> Soon with angels I'll be marching,
> With bright laurels on my brow.
> I have for my Country fallen,

23 Ibid., 640.

Who will care for mother now?
Let this knapsack be my pillow,
And my mantle be the sky;
Hasten, comrades, to the battle!
I will like a soldier die.
Soon with angels I'll be marching,
With bright laurels on my brow;
I have for my Country fallen,
Who will care for mother now?

Chorus:
Soon with angels I'll be marching,
With bright laurels on my brow.
I have for my Country fallen,
Who will care for mother now?[24]

Purbeck's enlistment papers showed him to be 18 years old when he joined the army in 1862. But the 1850 and 1860 federal census and 1855 Massachusetts census list ages for him that would put him at only 14 or 15 in 1862 and 15 or 16 when he died at Gettysburg. Despite his youth, he supported his widowed mother before the war by working as a printer and after his death by a pension. Corporal Benjamin Graham of the 5th Massachusetts called the five-foot-five-and-a-half-inch soldier "little Purbeck" and "a good, smart boy" and remembered, "There was not a braver boy in the army."[25]

A witness testified in favor of Mother Lydia's pension claim that she had no property or means of support and suffered poor health and poor eyesight. She was awarded a pension, which she received due to her son's sacrifice, until her death in Boston in the late 1880s. William, as it turns out, was the one who would continue to care for his mother now.[26]

A LIFE OF POVERTY
Corporal Robert Vaughn, 134th New York, Company G
Pension No: 93881; Pension Applicant: Mother Mary

Robert Vaughn and his mother, Mary, were among the 4.5 million Irish who escaped the poverty and famine of Ireland between 1820 and 1930 and emigrated

---

24 Charles C. Sawyer, music by Charles F. Thompson, (New York, 1863). Lyrics provided by the Library of Congress.

25 Graham, *History of the Fifth Massachusetts Battery*, 641.

26 Purbeck pension claim.

to the United States. Mary was left a widow and Robert fatherless when he was about 12 in 1839 when John Vaughn died in Ireland, and it was in the mid-1850s that Robert and his mother decided to go to America and build a more prosperous life, settling in Schoharie County, New York. Records indicate they would remain doomed to poverty and tragedy in the U.S. just as they had been in Ireland.[27]

Robert was 35 years old, unmarried, blue eyed, and five feet ten inches when he enlisted in August 1862. He was a farm laborer who lived at home and fully supported his mother. He must have shown good character and soldierly ability because he was promoted to corporal a month after he enlisted. But as happened with so many other members of the 134th New York, Vaughn was hit July 1 at the Brickyard not long after the regiment rushed into town. And also like most others in the 134th, he was picked up and taken to Spangler after the battle.[28]

Vaughn was treated with water dressing at Spangler for a flesh wound on the back of his left knee. There are no records of an amputation, though one could have been done if Vaughn's wound was destructive enough. Vaughn lay at Spangler for a week or two before he gained the strength to make the trip to the much more sanitary conditions of the U.S. military's Portsmouth Grove Hospital in Rhode Island. But despite the better hospital and increased staff, Vaughn's condition worsened when he developed the Civil War hospital curses of blood poisoning and gangrene. It was those diseases that killed him on August 1, a month to the day after his wounding.[29]

It appears Mary learned of her son's death from a friend of his, who received a letter from a hospital chaplain in Rhode Island dated one day after Vaughn died:

Dear Sir: It becomes my sorrowful duty to announce the death at this Hospital . . . of Corporal Vaughn 134th N.Y. Vols. He received a gunshot wound in the left knee joint of the left leg at the battle of Gettysburg. Some days ago mortification set in & he departed this life on Saturday night at 9 o'clock. He mentioned you as a friend of his & I therefore write to inform you of the fact in order that you may carry the intelligence to any of his relatives of whom you may know. During the last few days of his life his pain & weakness were so great that he could with difficulty fix his mind on any subject, but in answer to my questions he told me that he felt himself to be a sinner in need of pardon . . . & that he prayed God to forgive & save him.[30]

27 www.loc.gov/classroom-materials/immigration/irish/irish-catholic-immigration-to-america/, accessed Mar. 28, 2022; Mary Vaughn pension claim, Fold3.

28 Vaughn, New York Civil War Muster Roll Abstract, Fold3.

29 Vaughn pension claim.

30 Ibid.

Mary had now lost her husband, son, and only means of support. She applied for a pension in 1865 when she was 70. A witness for her application testified that "Robert Vaughn lived at home with his mother prior to his enlistment and worked out as a farm laborer and gave the greater part of his earnings for the support of his said mother the remainder being used to provide the said Robert Vaughn in clothing." The witness confirmed that "Mary Vaughn had no other means of support as she has been unable to support herself through old age and infirmity and had no property or income with the exception of her said son's earnings and has since the death of her said son depending upon the charitable for her maintenance." The report concluded that "Mary Vaughn is now almost helpless." Mary was approved for a pension of $8 a month, retroactive to August 1, 1863.[31]

Robert Vaughn is buried in Cypress Hills National Cemetery in Brooklyn, New York.

ONE WEEK TOGETHER
Corporal Alva E. Wilcox, 17th Connecticut, Company D
Pension No: 13620; Pension Applicant: Wife Sarah

U.S. Assistant Surgeon Benjamin Douglas Howard studied the high rate of death from penetrating—or sucking—lung wounds in the Civil War and received permission to introduce the hermetical seal of these injuries at Gettysburg. The 27-year-old orphan and immigrant from England treated numerous soldiers on the battlefield by cleaning and closing the wound with metallic sutures, a liquid sealer, and several layers of linen that created an airtight dressing. This prevented a collapsed lung and allowed the patient to breathe without sucking or hissing sounds.[32]

Howard worked on Cpl. Alva E. Wilcox just inside the Evergreen Cemetery gatehouse on East Cemetery Hill on July 2, then sent the 27-year-old carriage maker from Bridgeport to the XI Corps hospital. "Corporal Wilcox, a fine man was shot in the arm & breast," Spangler hospital worker Pvt. James R. Middlebrook of the 17th Connecticut said. 17th Connecticut Lt. Albert Peck said Wilcox "had been wounded by a Rebel sharpshooter and the bullet had gone through his left arm near the shoulder, and had passed through his arm and had lodged in his abdomen, causing a mortal wound. . . . When I found Comrade Wilcox he was lying on his right side and sitting up a little and had a Testament in his hand which

---

31 Ibid.

32 www.civilwarmed.org/benjamin-howard/#:~:text=Following%20the%20Battle%20of%20 Antietam,abdomen%20by%20hermetically%20sealing%20it., accessed Dec. 21, 2021; Middlebrook, Louis F. Scrapbook; *Medical and Surgical History of the Civil War*, Vol. VIII, 497-498.

Cpl. Alva E. Wilcox

Carolyn Ivanoff

he was reading. He looked very pale. He was a large man and probably weighed 175 lbs. We had about all we could carry to get him over to the Cemetery as it was quite a long walk. . . . I wrote a letter to his wife and got a reply." Private Alonzo Scranton, Company D, 17th Connecticut, was at Spangler with a jaw wound from July 1 and he tended Wilcox in his comrade's dying hours. Wilcox died July 6 in Scranton's arms despite Howard and Scranton's best efforts. Scranton wrapped him in a blanket after he died and he was buried at Spangler and later removed to Evergreen Cemetery in Gettysburg on the same hill where he was mortally wounded. Later, his body was exhumed and returned to Connecticut.[33]

Wilcox left behind widow Sarah, whom he married on August 21, 1862, one week before he mustered in to the 17th Connecticut. They had no children. The 22-year-old widow began to receive a pension of $8 a month in the summer of 1863 and received $12 a month at the time of her death in 1914. Sarah never remarried and remained childless. Adding to her life of trials, doctors judged her in 1911 to be "insane," though we'll never know today her symptoms or their intensity.[34]

Spangler Farm Short Story

One ancient swamp white oak bears witness to what happened in the fields behind George Spangler's house and barn in 1863 because it was there. This tree straddles the Spangler boundary line with the Artillery Ridge Campground & Horse Park on the southwest edge of the modern-day farm and a couple hundred yards directly behind the Spanglers' house. That location put it at risk when Confederate shells landed near it in those fields and made it a direct observer of the invasion of the Spanglers' farm by the mass of men, animals, and equipment of the Army of the Potomac's Artillery Reserve directly in front. The tree undoubtedly provided shade

33 *Medical and Surgical History of the Civil War*, Vol. VIII, 504; Middlebrook, Louis F. Scrapbook; Ivanoff, *We Fought at Gettysburg*, 154-155, 238.

34 Sarah Wilcox Widow Pension Claim 13620, Fold3.

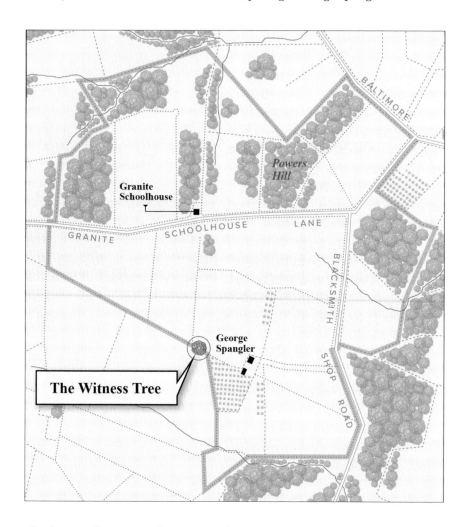

The Witness Tree

for those artillerymen as they awaited their assignment on July 2 just as XI Corps hospital staff and patients used it to escape the heat of the day. And this generous tree continues to give today, with its acorns attracting an abundance of wildlife.

Battlefield witness tree expert Greg Gober walked the 80 acres of the farm that the Gettysburg Foundation owns today and this is the one tree that stood out to him. "This guy right here," he said with glee when he knew he had found what he was looking for. He took out a tape measure and literally hugged the tree to get its measurements. He did some quick calculations and figured it to be at least 180 years old, but added with admiration, "I'm telling you that it's probably 200 years old. I guarantee you that's a witness tree. I guarantee it."

Retired Pennsylvania forester Bruce Kile doesn't know Gober and didn't know that he had visited the tree, but when Kile saw it he estimated its age at 180 to 200 years, exactly as Gober had done. If indeed that's its age, it could have another 100

Retired Pennsylvania forester Bruce Kile studies the Spangler witness tree.

Ron Kirkwood

years of life. Swamp white oaks prefer low elevations and wet ground, and this site offers both with a stream nearby.

What's left of an 1863 rock boundary wall that the Spanglers shared with neighbor Jacob Swisher runs directly into the tree, which Kile says could be a reason the tree was never taken down. "A property line is more likely to have a witness tree," he said. "Throughout the whole state of Pennsylvania it's always been rocks and trees that marked property lines, so people didn't cut down a property line tree because it was equally beneficial to adjoining property owners to tell you where the line was."

Swamp white oaks were prevalent in the Gettysburg area in 1863. Another prominent one that still stands is the Sickles witness tree on the Trostle farm.

Handily for farm visitors today, a dirt path travels from behind the Spanglers' house past their tree, which has stood tall and served so many for so long.

Chapter 12

Letters Tell the Story
of Pvt. James D. Quilliam

"Their wounds stink so that it spoils my apotite."

— *Private James D. Quilliam, 154th New York, describing the scene at the Spangler hospital*[1]

Private James D. Quilliam, Company E, 154th New York, had been a carpenter from Westfield, 66 miles southwest of Buffalo. He stood five feet six-and-a-half inches tall with brown hair and light eyes. When he went off to war he left behind a wife of seven years, Rhoda Dibble, and three children: William (age 6), Ida (4), and Frederick (2).[2] Like many Civil War soldiers, though he was poorly educated, he wrote thoughtful, earnest, and tender letters back home.

Quilliam had been lightly wounded in the mayhem at the Brickyard on July 1, and after a brief time in a Confederate hospital arrived at the Spangler farm on July 4, where he was enlisted right away as a hospital worker. He did not leave Spangler property until after the XI Corps hospital closed on August 6, making him one of the longest-tenured staffers there. He wrote of the wounded on July 27 from Spangler: "Their wounds stink so that it spoils my apotite." He transferred to Camp Letterman upon the closing of the XI Corps hospital.

Quilliam was religious, thoughtful, sacrificial, optimistic, and had little patience for self-pity. He especially disliked northern Democrats who supported a peace deal with the South, even if one of them was his sister Elizabeth. We know these things about Quilliam because of his many letters to family members, especially

---

1 James D. Quilliam Letters, Box 181, Folder 4, CCHS Documents, Chautauqua County Historical Society, Westfield, NY. All letters reprinted herein are from Folders 3, 4, 5, and 6. Quilliam's full complement of Civil War letters can be viewed at www.154th p-z (sbu.edu).

2 New York Civil War Muster Roll Abstract, Fold3; Quilliam Widow Pension Claim 143871, Fold3.

Pvt. James D. Quilliam, 154th New York

Dennis Frank/St. Bonaventure University

to Rhoda. Quilliam's letters reveal his love for his family. They also reveal his love for his country and his willingness to go to war, even to die, to defend it. And even though he was enduring life-threatening circumstances, he took pains to comfort Rhoda, who was struggling. Thankfully, Quilliam's descendants saved his letters and painstakingly transcribed them and they now reside in the protective hands of the Chautauqua County Historical Society in Westfield, available for the public to see.

Quilliam's grammar skills were poor, which he readily admitted and for which he took responsibility. He told Rhoda in a January 1864 letter from Lookout Valley, Tennessee: "Rhoda I am sory if I make as bad work spelling . . . for i can ask men that knowes how to spell any hard word and it is neglect if i spell bad." Because he was conscientious, he worked on his spelling and grammar and it improved between September 1862 and July 1864. He was not an unintelligent person, and he pursued his correspondence faithfully. He informed Rhoda where to send his mail each time the 154th relocated and asked her to write more often.[3]

All five of Quilliam's letters from Spangler will be printed here in near entirety as he wrote them and his descendants transcribed them. Excerpts from letters written before and after his time at the XI Corps hospital at Gettysburg also are included because—poor speller or not—Quilliam was a descriptive writer who can teach us much.

Comforter and Adviser

October 25, 1862, from Fairfax Court House, Virginia: To Rhoda, "[Y]ou say air very loansome you ought to make your self as comfortable as posable do not fret about me. . . . be cheerful and this time will not seem long i think that i will not begone more than a year and prehaps not so long"

November 30, 1862, from Fairfax Court House: To Rhoda, "i think that the war will soon be over and I can come home remember me to all my friends"

3 Quilliam Letters, Folder 5, Chautauqua County Historical Society.

March 27, 1863, from Camp John Manley, Virginia: "Dear Rhoda . . . sory to hear that you was not well i am afraid that you air worring about me to much it can do you no good and may do a great deal of harm i do not blame you for woshing that i was at home i want to come home as bad as you want me but i think how much better it is for us to come here and defind our homes then it would be to stay at home and let them come and distroy every thing that we have i know it is very bad for man to stay a lone especaly when you air not well but i am thankful that our house hath not been birned by an envading enemy as i have known and you laft to loock out for your self"

January 18, 1864: To Rhoda, "it is no worst for you to live alone then it is for thousands of others now i think that i have the most reason to complain and i never felt more chearful in my life now I think that you do very wrong is alowing your self to fret while you might just as well be cheerful and hapy"

Letters Written at the George Spangler Farm

July 5, 1863: "dear rhoda i arrived here on w nsday and was taken prisoner with the most of our regement but i got back kester day and am now at the hospatoll helpeing put up tents for the wounded i got hit with a ball . . . Just anought to start the blood"

July 13, 1863: "Dear rhoda i wrote you a few linds last week . . . to let let you know that i was well . . . nerly all one regement was taken exept about 50 men tha was out scouting and ware not in the battle on the first day I got dit with a spint ball under my eye hard anought to make it blead so I was taken with a bloody face and the rebs sent me to their hospatal with as many of the wounded as could walk the the payed but little attention to our wounded but were very kind we stayed there till the forth when the rebs went of and leaft us to our self we then came to this place where i have been very buisley wating on they wounded i do not know how long i shall stay here i have not hed a letter since i have ben here our regement is scattred . . . remember me to all my friends"

July 27, 1863: "Dear rhoda i again write you a few lind i to let you know that i am well i have but little time to write as i have got to be with they wounded from 5 to 6 i do not expect to stay here much longer they air taken the wounded as fast as they air able to go I do not get my letters here but when i get to the regement again i expect that i will get all that you have sent me give my love to all my friend and expect the same your self god nite"

July 28, 1863: "Dear Rhoda I am still at work in the hospatall and expect to be here about two weeks longer I want you to write as son as this comes to hand and . . . it is a greate whild since I have heard from you or ded any kind neuse from home but I think that they war will soon be over and I can be to home again but the lord knows best and will do all things well I do not like this work some wounded men cannot be be and air all the time finding fauld and their wounds stink so that it spoils my apotite but it is not so bad now as it was but I mus conclude hopeing to here from you soon"

August 7, 1863: "Dear Rhoda i receive a letter from you today it was the first i receved since i have been here you derected your letter just rite there is no 11 Corps hospatal here now all the Corps have been moved to one hospital you need not be very sory that i got hurt for it was not was not much and if there had not been blud on my face i would have hed to walk to richman and be shut up in some jayle tell the would peroal me i do not know when i woll get my pay i hope it wont be long but i hope that you know better then to pay 4 shillings a peace for hens 10 dollars 20 hens I wonder if some body could ask a dollar apiece for hens please send me some stamps I have no money if I had I could get them here give my love to all my friends"

Letters Written at Camp Letterman

Probably August 11, 1863: "Dear rhoda i receved a letter from you to day with stamps i was glad to here that you air well i am still at the hospital I am watting on 12 wounded rebbels it is not so hard work here as it was at the other hospital we have things a good deal handyer here i think that i will be hear some time yet for there is a great whild to get well i hope that the war will be over be fore i will leave here"

August 20, 1863: "Dear father and mother i received yours of the 9 yesterday and a nother to day contaning apice of paper and 12 stamps it truly is a great mercy that i have been spared but should i be call to dy in defince of liberty truth and Justes my life would not be spint in vain if i under stand your letter you object is to perswaid me that a soldier cannot be saved but you must first show me that it is rong to have any goverment for if it is write to have any goverment it must be rite to sustain it and in this case that cannot be dun without war I should like to know if daba and johnaton did not go to heven the same as all sinners they believed in a saviour to come and we believe in a saviour that hath come which is only a diferance in time not in fath pleace write soon"

August 23, 1863: "I fiered twise," James wrote to his uncle, William Quilliam, after the battle, "and hed my gun loaded redy to fire a gain when a spint ball hit me on the bone under the leaft eye then droped on the grown it made me quite disey for a spell . . . I thaught I would go back in the doctors care but thaught best to crawl along on the groynd but had not gon fir before they redgement started back double quick I got ut and went as fast any of them but when we got to they road it was full of rebbels and they were comeing up behind us so there we had to stay and but few got away they made us lay down our guns and marched us of they took us to a house . . . there we stayed tell the 4th when we found ourselves at libberty to go where pleace our doctor came to us and told us to go the 11 Corps hospatal as many as could walk and he would send tems to cary the rest and I went ther and they sat me to work I know nothin about how long I shall have to say here but I hope the war will stop soon so that I will not have to go back to verginia."

Quilliam was shipped from Gettysburg to Baltimore in September and to Columbus, Ohio, in October. He rejoined his regiment that month.

His Love for His Family

September 27, 1863: To Rhoda, "I must conclude with my love to uou all"

October 1, 1863: "Dear Rhoda I want you to have your likeness taken on a small plate and send it to me as soon as convenant"

On Religion

October 25, 1863, from Bridgeport, Alabama: To Rhoda, "I trust that the lord will give sucksses to our armey and that peace will again bless our land and we may enjoy our homes again I often think that if I will get home that I will know how to enjoy it after living so long more like a animal then like a man

March 13, 1864, from Lookout Valley, Tennessee: To Rhoda, "The Christian Commission started a Sunday school in its chapel tent. General Howard spoke to about 20 children and a few young ladies. The children ware very much interested . . . he spoke very kind to them and then asked them to kneel down and pray with him and he made a very plain and ernest prayer I think he is one of the best sunday school teachers I ever heard"

April 3, 1863, from Lookout Valley: To Rhoda, "General Howard is building a church here and some say that he is going to have school I sopose that he hates to see children grow up in igronance it would be quite a Ceurasaty [curiosity] for you to see the General in sunday school and old gray hed man with but one arm teaching girls from 15 to 20 to read in the pictorial primer"

April 8, 1864, from Lookout Valley: To Rhoda, "Last week I was down in Georgia . . . I asked one of the little [slave] girls if she could read she said that she could a little I gave hur a little hymn book which I had in my pocket then they wholl famely gathered around while one red the book that the yankeey soldier gave them"

On Slavery

January 27, 1864, from Lookout Valley: To his father, "We have grate reason to be thankfull that we air maid the honored instraments in gods hand of removing the curse of slavery from our land"

On Peace Democrats (Copperheads)

February 22, 1864, from Lookout Valley: To Rhoda, "no doubt Lincon will be reelected and every man that will not voat for him I think is an enemy to the best entrest of their Countery and air regardless of the lives of their country men and and the name of trater is almost too good for them when a man will enlist in the reble army he showes some honesty and courage at lest but those rebles at home have not honesty or courage aought to expose them selves to dainger but they stay at home and try to fill their pocket by emposeing on those who air gone to defind their conatrey but their time shall soon end I think"

April 3, 1864, about his sister Elizabeth, from Lookout Valley: To Rhoda, "I recieved a letter from Elizabeth full of copperdedinnn if a man had wrote me such a letter I think that I would have gaven a sausy answer espesualy if it had been a man that could enlist"

His Final Letters

Quilliam was wounded on June 15, 1864, at the battle of Pine Mountain during Sherman's Atlanta Campaign. His leg was amputated. He was able to continue to write home to Rhoda:

Undated, from General Hospital 1, Ward 7, Nashville: "My Dear Rhoda, it was with grate supprise a few days ago I learnt that I had to take the cars for nashvill I was carried on a bead but it was a long hard ride but I feel better now . . . I am doing as well as can be expected and think that I shall soon get wel"

July 6 from Nashville, as he continued to grow weak from his wound. The family's transcribers said this letter was difficult to read as the writing was unusually laborious: "Rhoda I am still here and think my wound I wrote to you same time ago and received no answer yet . . . be blessd shall have to get some body else to write I mus clos my love to you"

Somebody at the Nashville hospital wrote the following straightforward note to Rhoda on July 9th:

"Mrs. Quilliam, it becomes my painfull duty to inform you of the death of your husband Mr. James D. Quilliam a Private of Co. E 154th N.Y. He died in this Hospital on the [8th] day of July. He had no effects of any kind, he is deasently buried and was well cared for. the cause of his death was a gun shot wond this is all I can tell you of the your Deceased husband."[4]

And that is how Rhoda Quilliam found out she was a widow. And that her three young children's father was gone at such an early stage in their lives and that

4 Quilliam widow pension claim.

the chances were slim that they would remember him. He had, after all, left home for war when his oldest child was 6 and never saw them again. Rhoda applied for a widow's pension and received $8 a month plus $2 for each child until their 16th birthday. Her pension was stopped when she remarried in 1869. Rhoda died in Iowa in 1886 at age 48.[5]

Private James D. Quilliam, Company E, 154th New York, died July 8, 1864. He is buried in Nashville National Cemetery. He was 28 years old when he died.

Spangler Farm Short Story

There are two options today when driving down the lane to leave the George Spangler farm: turn left on Blacksmith Shop Road or turn right on Blacksmith Shop Road. The Spanglers, however, had a third option in 1863. They could go straight. Because directly on the other side of the intersection of their lane with what would someday be named Blacksmith Shop Road was a farm lane that ran from that intersection through the middle of Isaac Diehl's farm.[6]

You would never know it today with the dense woods and "No Trespassing" signs and a massive quarry just a few hundred feet in, but that Diehl lane in 1863 ran from its intersection with the Spangler lane through his fields to the banks of Rock Creek about a half-mile from the intersection. The lane made a sharp left turn at the creek and continued another quarter-mile to the Baltimore Pike, meeting it at the bridge that crosses the stream near the former Hoke toll house.

If the Spanglers had the option of going straight at the end of their lane, then obviously so did XI Corps hospital workers. That meant a short, direct, and quick wagon ride to the crucial and bountiful water required at a Civil War field hospital. Also, as Gettysburg locals well knew, Rock Creek was, like it or not, a bountiful source of leeches that commonly attached themselves en masse to swimmers. Those same nuisance leeches, though, were highly sought in Civil War hospitals for their ability to drain blood and fight infections, making that Diehl lane a path to healing and comfort. The Diehl lane is long gone today and almost 100 percent of it has been swallowed by the quarry.

5 Ibid.

6 Cultural Landscape Report, Record of Treatment: Volume I, Drawing 17A, GNMP; John Bachelder's 1863 Isometric Map.

Chapter 13

Powers Hill's Important Place
in U.S. History

"Upon my arrival upon the battle-field of Gettysburg . . . my brigade was detached by order of
Major-General Meade to support a height crowned by a battery, which the major-general
commanding the Army of the Potomac ordered to be held at all hazards."

— *Brigadier General Thomas Neill, Third Brigade, Second Division, VI Corps*

George Spangler's farm was not only a site of medical treatment for wounded soldiers. It was also militarily important. Traversing both Spangler and Lightner land was a 560-foot hill that came to be known as Powers Hill. It would become one of the four most important strategic hills in the Army of the Potomac's victory at Gettysburg. The hill was located directly behind the center of the Union line and close to both flanks, its clear lines of sight to all parts of the front, and its proximity to the Union's supply line and supply wagons and potential escape route along the Baltimore Pike giving it its strategic importance. Powers Hill belongs in the same conversation as Cemetery Hill, Little Round Top, and the two hills known today as Culp's Hill. Big Round Top has the great height at 785 feet and great fame, but it is a molehill in military significance compared with Powers Hill and the three others. Powers Hill was a key part of Meade's strategy at Gettysburg, and it was one of the many reasons, along with the use of Spangler land for infantry and artillery reserves and the roads through his farm, that George Spangler owned the most important farm in the battle of Gettysburg.[1]

Gettysburg historian, artist, and author John B. Bachelder probably named Powers Hill in 1863. There are no newspaper accounts, maps, or documents with the name before Bachelder used it on his 1863 isometric map of the battlefield, and he used it in letters to Union officers after the battle.

---

1 Powers Hill elevation measured on iPhone 11 Pro; www.nps.gov/gett/learn/nature/scenicvistas.
htm, accessed Oct. 23, 2023.

An almost bare Powers Hill is shown in the very top left of this circa 1880 photo taken from the area of Spangler's Spring. *Gettysburg National Military Park*

In one letter to Bachelder on April 21, 1864, XII Corps First Division commander Brig. Gen Alpheus S. Williams, who led the XII Corps for much of the battle while Maj. Gen. Henry Slocum commanded the right wing, wrote, "I marched Lockwood's and 1st Div. at once to the right flank, across the Baltimore Pike along the dirt road [Granite Schoolhouse Lane] that runs near the southern base of what you name as Powers Hill." Union officers often referred to it as Slocum's Hill during and after the battle in official reports because Slocum used the peak of the hill as his headquarters.[2]

Bachelder arrived in Gettysburg in July 1863 and spent months studying the battle and the area, so it's not surprising that he knew enough in 1863–1864 to name the hill for Solomon Powers, even though Powers didn't own his quarry land most of the years he worked the hill. Powers and his family lived at 63 W. High Street in downtown Gettysburg and operated his stone-cutting business there. Only in 1856 and 1857 did he own 28 acres on the hill where his prosperous

2 Ladd and Ladd, *The Bachelder Papers*, 146.

granite quarry was located when the land was transferred to him by Gettysburg resident Mary McAllister. She would later take care of wounded during the battle at her home on West Chambersburg Street. Powers must have leased the quarry land in the preceding and following years, including from 1858 onward from either Nathaniel Lightner or George Spangler. Most of the hill was owned by Spangler. In fact, Spangler Hill might have been a more appropriate name than Powers Hill. It makes sense that Bachelder likely named the hill, because he came up with the name "Hospital Hill" for the site of Camp Letterman; he named the "Copse of Trees"; and he invented the phrase "High Water Mark of the Rebellion" in his role as a board member of the Gettysburg Battlefield Memorial Association and superintendent of tablets and legends.[3]

By the 1870s, and increasingly through the 1880s and 1890s, newspapers, including those in Gettysburg, usually used the name Powers Hill, though the *Adams County News* called it "the Spangler hill" in 1910. Eventually, it was Bachelder's name for it that stuck.[4]

Born in New Hampshire in 1804, Solomon Powers moved to Baltimore where he met and married wife Catherine. Their first child, Cynthia, was born there in 1834. The Powers family moved to Gettysburg in 1838 and Solomon began his stone-cutting business. He and Catherine added five more daughters. Newspaper notices indicate Powers struggled with debt in the early 1840s, but in time he thrived and by the 1850s so much granite was coming out of the future Powers Hill and the Gettysburg area and being shipped to such places as York, Carlisle, Baltimore, and Frederick, Maryland, that local newspapers complained that a railroad was needed because wagons were too slow and couldn't keep up. Powers regularly advertised for wagon and shipping help. He provided granite work for the new Evergreen Cemetery and the steps for the 1859 Adams County Courthouse (still in operation today) besides the granite for many more local buildings. He became a leader in the borough and county and served on the board of the local temperance society, the 1862 committee to raise a militia, and the 1864 Relief Committee to "supply the wants of the destitute." He served on grand juries, coroner's juries, and was elected borough assessor in 1864. He was a bit of an entrepreneur with side businesses including selling soap, buying and selling hay, and moving bodies from all over Adams County to Evergreen Cemetery after it opened in 1854. He also held the contract to move the bodies of exhumed Massachusetts soldiers to the new Soldiers' National Cemetery in 1863 and 1864. During and after the battle, the

---

3 Tax Records Cumberland Township Box 1843-1859, Adams County Historical Society; https://bit.ly/48bQDn7, accessed Feb. 14, 2024; *The Gettysburg Times*, Oct. 24, 1989.

4 *Adams County News*, Apr. 9, 1910.

Solomon Powers

Adams County Historical Society

Powers family cared for wounded at their home and granite yard on the northeast corner of High and Washington streets in Gettysburg.[5]

"Solomon Powers and his wife, Catherine, were as widely known as any family in the surrounding country," *The Gettysburg Times* reported in 1926. "He had the only stone cutting shop in Pennsylvania and at one time had as high as sixteen apprentices."[6]

Indeed, like George Spangler, Solomon Powers was a man of prominence in Gettysburg and worthy of a hill named in his honor.

Spangler purchased most of the hill and connecting land on the northern side of today's Granite Schoolhouse Lane from Peter Weikert's heirs in 1861. The purchase of those 65 acres stretched the size of his farm to 166 acres and gave the Spanglers ownership of three-fourths of the hill. His land now met Lightner's land on the east side of the hill at the third wall north of Granite Schoolhouse Lane (39°48'28" N 77°13'5" W) as well as on part of the north side.

1863 maps show Granite Schoolhouse Lane's intersection with the Baltimore Pike at the southern base of the future Powers Hill about 50 yards south of the modern-day intersection, so Spangler used the land that includes where the lane now cuts through as one of his wheatfields. Reports indicate the Spanglers had cut this wheat and bound it into sheaves by July 2, and workers at the First Division, II Corps hospital between Powers Hill and Granite Schoolhouse on Spangler land recorded using the wheat as bedding for the wounded. Spangler had a Virginia worm fence from Granite Schoolhouse Lane's intersection with what would become Blacksmith Shop Road to the Baltimore Pike and a stone-and-rider fence plus a stone wall running from the Blacksmith Shop Road intersection westward to Granite Schoolhouse in the middle of the Spangler farm. Most importantly, at least in military terms, there were fewer trees at the top of the hill on Spangler land

---

5 *The Gettysburg Times*, Aug. 23, 1988; *Gettysburg Compiler*, July 26, 1841; *The Adams Sentinel*, Aug. 15, 1853; *Gettysburg Compiler*, Apr. 12, 1858; *Gettysburg Compiler*, Sep. 5, 1859; *The Adams Sentinel*, Dec. 27, 1864; *Gettysburg Compiler*, Mar. 21, 1864; *Gettysburg Compiler*, Jan. 16, 1894.

6 *The Gettysburg Times*, Aug. 2, 1926.

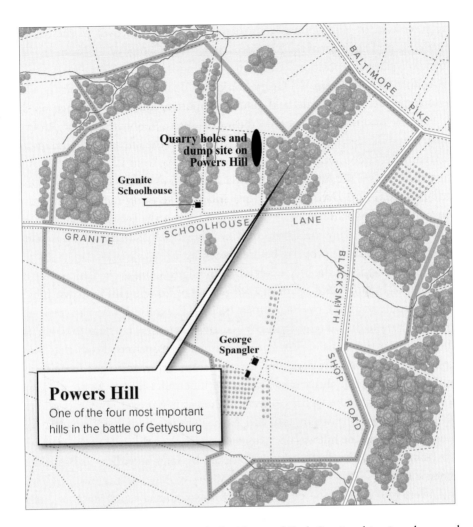

then than there are today, even with the National Park Service thinning the woods in recent years, as well as open fields on the Lightner side of the hill.[7]

Slocum arrived in Gettysburg during the late afternoon of July 1, but he didn't claim Powers Hill for his headquarters just yet, spending that overnight on Cemetery Hill. "After securing the cemetery," XI Corps commander Maj. Gen. Oliver O. Howard remembered, "he and I slept side by side that first weary night at the cemetery gate." Powers Hill was not involved in the fight on July 1, but it wasn't all quiet on that part of the George Spangler farm. Part of the XI Corps ambulance corps set up in the wheatfield at the base of the hill on July 1, and the 72 men of Battery K 5th U.S. Artillery of the XII Corps Artillery Brigade

7 Child, *History of the 5th New Hampshire Volunteers*, 211.

were placed on the hill, joined soon thereafter by the 800 men of the Second Brigade, Second Division of the XII Corps under Col. George A. Cobham Jr. "The brigade was placed in position," Cobham wrote in his official report, "by direction of Brigadier-General [John W.] Geary, commanding division, on the crest of a hill overlooking part of the battle-field, and in support of a battery stationed on the hill. Here the troops lay on their arms during the night." Cobham and the 5th U.S. Artillery used that Spangler land to protect the back of the line and offer aid in case of a disastrous Union retreat down the Baltimore Pike from Cemetery Hill. Also assigned to rest on the hill that night after a long day's march was the 8th Ohio (First Brigade, Third Division, II Corps) and its 209 weary men, putting more than 1,000 men plus horses, wagons, and artillery on the crowded Spangler and Lightner hill overlooking the Baltimore Pike. The 8th Ohio and 5th U.S. Artillery Battery K evacuated the property before dawn July 2.[8]

As those troops left the hill, a portion of the signal corps arrived and set up on the corner of Lightner and Spangler land on top of Powers Hill by dawn July 2, possibly manned by XII Corps signalman 1st Lt. J. E. Holland, who had spent July 1 at Little Round Top. Lightner discovered this station on his land at daybreak: "There I found the Signal Corps had established headquarters. From that point I could look down on my place and saw what was going on. I saw I could save nothing, so went back and moved my family nine miles further away, and came back and stayed with the Signal Corps until the battle was over." Lightner said the signal corps set up on his property and Bachelder's isometric map concurs, even though the peak of the hill was on Spangler land on the other side of the wall. The view from Spangler land, though, was blocked by trees according to Bachelder's isometric map.[9]

Powers Hill hosted one of six Army of the Potomac signal stations during the battle, the others at Meade's headquarters, Cemetery Hill, Little Round Top, Culp's Hill, and just north of Little Round Top at the VI Corps headquarters near modern-day Sedgwick Avenue. The Spangler/Lightner signal station was crucial to Union success at Gettysburg because the height of the hill and its open fields at the top made it visible from all other signal stations along the line. This signal station

---

8 *The Brooklyn Standard Union*, Apr. 30, 1894; Cobham official record, www.ehistory.osu.edu/books/official-records/043/0848, accessed Oct. 17, 2023; Busey and Busey, *Union Casualties at Gettysburg*, 1179, 1242, and 1245; Franklin Sawyer, *A Military History of the 8th Regiment Ohio Vol. Inf'y* (Cleveland, 1881), 123.

9 *War of the Rebellion: Official Records of the Union and Confederate Armies*, Series I, Vol. 27, Part I Reports, report of Capt. Lemuel B. Norton, chief signal officer, Sep. 18, 1863, 206; "Horrors of Battle," an interview with Nathaniel Lightner, *Washington* (D.C.) *Evening Star*, Nov. 4, 1893.

served as a central communications center and transmitted messages from stations not visible to other signal stations or army headquarters.[10]

Meade arrived early in the morning July 2 to set up his line, and that's when he decided to place his V Corps and VI Corps reserves near the base of Powers Hill. Meade has been rightly criticized for wanting to send the entire XII Corps from Culp's Hill to the aid of the III Corps during the late afternoon of July 2, with the hill saved only by Slocum leaving a brigade there under Brig. Gen. George S. Greene. Greene's Third Brigade, Second Division, lost ground on the night of July 2 but almost single-handedly held the hill with late help from the 61st Ohio and 157th New York of the XI Corps and the 71st Pennsylvania of the II Corps against three brigades in Maj. Gen. Edward Johnson's division. Meade, however, knew much more about the area than critics such as Brig. Gen. Williams gave him credit for. Williams incorrectly said, "It has always seemed to me that Gen. Meade had no proper understanding or appreciation of the operations of the right wing. He never came nearer our line than Slocum's Hd. Qrs. on Powers Hill, when driven out of his own camp on the afternoon of 3d July."[11]

Cobham's brigade also left Powers Hill on the morning of July 2, but the signal corps wouldn't have the hill to itself for long. The 19 batteries and 2,300 men and 2,300 horses of the Army of the Potomac Artillery Reserve began to arrive on the Spangler farm at 8 a.m. that day and continued to arrive into the early afternoon before being plugged into holes in the line from the Peach Orchard to the Codori farm to Cemetery Hill and East Cemetery Hill to Powers Hill. The 100 ammunition wagons and its hundreds of men and mules arrived at Spangler with the Artillery Reserve, and now Powers Hill was needed not only to protect the Baltimore Pike and the far right flank of the Union line but also the massive and all-important ammunition train in the valley under the hill, which supplied all the reserve ammunition for all the artillery of the Army of the Potomac. A Confederate breakthrough in the line on or south of Culp's Hill would expose the Baltimore Pike and the ammunition train and put the army in danger. The Spangler farm and the back of the line needed to be protected, and massive artillery help was on the way.

Two pieces of Lt. Charles Winegar's 1st New York Battery M (XII Corps) were placed below Powers Hill with the other two pieces across the pike on McAllister's Hill. The guns of Pennsylvania Light Independent Battery E (Lt. Charles Atwell, XII Corps) arrived on the slope of the hill by dawn July 2. Then artillery commander

---

10 "Cultural Report for Gettysburg National Military Park, Record of Treatment: Volume 1," National Park Service, U.S. Department of the Interior (Boston, 2018), 303; J. Willard Brown, *The Signal Corps, USA, in the War of the Rebellion* (Boston, 1896), 363. Flag signals and orderlies on horseback were the most-used signals at Gettysburg.

11 Ladd and Ladd, *The Bachelder Papers*, 223.

First Maryland Light Battery A's view of the
Culp's Hill neighborhood. *Ron Kirkwood*

Brig. Gen. Henry J. Hunt and Artillery Reserve commander Brig. Gen. Robert O. Tyler went to work at Spangler. They sent the 1st New York Light Battery K (Capt. Robert Fitzhugh) and the attached 11th New York as well as the 1st New Jersey Light Battery A (Lt. Augustin Parsons), and the First Maryland Light Battery A (Capt. James Rigby) from a Spangler field across Granite Schoolhouse Lane to Powers Hill, where they were personally placed in position by Meade and Hunt, further debunking Williams' charge that Meade didn't know the neighborhood. That means 26 guns were hauled to the top of Powers Hill or placed at its base by 9 a.m. In fact, 49 guns ruled Powers Hill and Cemetery Hill by noon July 2 in a massive show of force, defense, and concentrated fire. The height of Powers Hill was the key to Hunt's strategy.[12]

Slocum claimed Powers Hill for his right-wing headquarters early on July 2. The arrival on that Thursday morning of Maj. Gen. George Sykes' 10,900-man V Corps filled the Spangler, Musser, Bucher, and Diehl fields between Powers Hill and Rock Creek with reserves for a few hours of rest and made the hill Sykes' corps

---

12 *OR* 27, pt. 1, 872; General Alpheus Williams also was critical of Adams County residents in a letter after the battle, writing, "Entering Pennsylvania the next day, the troops arrived hot and dusty at Littlestown about 2 p.m. The inhabitants are Dutch descendants and quite Dutch in language. . . . The people are rich, but ignorant of everybody and [every] thing beyond their small spheres. They have immense barns, looking like great arsenals or public institutions, full of small windows and painted showily. Altogether, they are a people of barns, not brains"; Gary W. Gallagher, ed., *The Second Day at Gettysburg: Essays on Confederate and Union Leadership* (Kent, OH, 1993), 93; *Oversight Hearing on Gettysburg National Military Park General Management Plan and Proposed Visitors Center, Feb. 11, 1999* (Washington, D.C.), 61-62.

headquarters during the time he spent there with Slocum. As with the soon-to-follow VI Corps, they were placed there by Meade, who inspected the area after daybreak that morning, providing still more evidence against Williams' charge of Meade's ignorance of the area. Sykes left his staff on the hill when he departed for a 3:00 p.m. meeting at Meade's headquarters and shortly before the V Corps was ordered out to reinforce Sickles, though the staffers joined Sykes on the battlefield on their own initiative.[13]

At about 4:00 p.m. on July 2, Confederate gunners on Benner's Hill east of Gettysburg and elsewhere opened fire on Cemetery Hill. Batteries throughout the Army of the Potomac returned fire with such great effect that the Confederate guns were silenced and the fight exhausted itself by 6:00 p.m. Rigby's Battery A, Maryland Light Artillery tried to help by aiming at Benner's Hill from Powers Hill, but "finding the distance too great, I ceased firing for that day," Rigby wrote in his report.[14]

Brigadier General Thomas Neill's Third Brigade, Second Division, VI Corps, arrived as the artillery exchange concluded and was ordered to Powers Hill. Neill wrote later: "Upon my arrival upon the battle-field of Gettysburg, 6 p.m. July 2, after a march of 30 miles, my brigade was detached by order of Major-General Meade to support a height crowned by a battery, which the major-general commanding the Army of the Potomac ordered to be held at all hazards. I took position accordingly, and found General Slocum in command, who subsequently ordered me to take position supporting the front line, then held by Generals Geary and Wadsworth. At midnight was ordered to return to my original position, as directed by Major-General Meade, which was done." All but the 77th New York in Neill's brigade would be later sent across Rock Creek to defend the army's far-right flank on the Baker farm, known today as Neill Avenue or Lost Avenue. The 77th New York remained to defend Powers Hill and the Spangler fields.[15]

Neill's presence in the evening of July 2 put five regiments and about 1,800 men in the middle of the hill stretching from near Granite Schoolhouse Lane's intersection with Blacksmith Shop Road to the Baltimore Pike side, most on George Spangler land. From left to right were the 61st Pennsylvania, 77th New York, 49th New York, 7th Maine, and 43rd New York. That meant that at midnight July 2 going into July 3 the Spangler property from Granite Schoolhouse Lane's intersection with the Baltimore Pike to a couple hundred yards past the intersection with Blacksmith Shop Road, up to the top of Powers Hill, and then across Granite

13 OR 27, pt. 1, 592–593; Harry W. Pfanz, Gettysburg: The Second Day (Chapel Hill, 1987), 207.

14 OR 27, series I, report of Capt. James H. Rigby, Berlin, MD, July 17, 1863.

15 Ibid.; report of Brig. Gen. Thomas Neill, Aug. 3, 1863.

Maj. Gen. Henry Slocum

Library of Congress

Schoolhouse Lane to Spangler's fields on the south side was probably the busiest part of the battlefield that night. Because while Neill's men and horses attempted to rest on the hill at midnight, XI Corps ambulances streamed past carrying wounded from the night fight on East Cemetery Hill to the XI Corps hospital at George Spangler's barn, Army of the Potomac batteries from all over the line rumbled to and from the ammunition train in the Spangler field across the lane from Powers Hill, some Artillery Reserve batteries returned to their parking spot also across from the hill to rest, recover, and reload after their July 2 fight, and Slocum, XII Corps, and artillery commanders moved batteries around in preparation to go after the breastworks that were lost to the Confederates on Culp's Hill that day. In addition, the First Division, II Corps hospital sat at the base of the hill on the western side along Granite Schoolhouse Lane, crammed with hundreds of wounded from the Wheatfield and surrounding areas. That hill was enveloped.[16]

Both sides beefed up their strength on Culp's Hill during the night. The Confederates knew they had a better chance to take the strategic Cemetery Hill if they could finish taking Culp's Hill. Control of Culp's Hill would also open access to the Baltimore Pike, the rear of the Union line, and artillery wagons at Spangler. Slocum set the tone for the Union when after Williams reported at midnight the ground gained by the Confederates that night he replied, "Well! Drive them out at daylight." The Union held massive advantages of close-range artillery, including the 14 pieces now on Powers Hill: six each for Pennsylvania Light Battery E (XII Corps) and Battery A Maryland Light (Artillery Reserve) plus two from 1st New York Light Battery M (XII Corps). The strong and concentrated line of artillery extended from Powers Hill and McAllister's Hill northward on the Baltimore Pike to Kinzie's Knoll at the site of modern-day Hunt Avenue. The Maryland battery sat on George Spangler's land on Powers Hill, the New York battery on Nathaniel

---

16 Bachelder isometric map.

Pennsylvania Light Battery E. *Ron Kirkwood*

Lightner's, and the Pennsylvania battery probably on both properties. Maryland Light A used 3-inch ordnance rifles while the Pennsylvania and New York batteries fielded 10-pound Parrotts. Those guns could fire shell and shrapnel shell with strong accuracy up to 2,000 yards, and that was going to prove to be a problem for the Confederates on Culp's Hill, who had no artillery in the area to answer.[17]

Those 14 guns added about 250 artillerymen to the top of Powers Hill plus an equal number of horses and multiple caissons and limbers. Also crowded onto the hill that morning were Slocum and his staff, the signal station, the 77th New York, XI Corps ambulances, journalists, and untold miscellaneous personnel. Williams said the hurried overnight preparations "nearly exhausted the night. I slept half an hour on a flat rock near the Pike."[18] The longest and one of the most pivotal clashes in the three days at Gettysburg was about to erupt from Spangler and Lightner land.

At 4:00 or 4:30 a.m., depending on the official report, artillery along this line, including guns on Powers Hill, opened the cannonade on the Confederates on

17 Ladd and Ladd, *The Bachelder Papers*, 219.

18 Ibid., 220.

Culp's Hill when Brig. Gen. Geary fired his revolver into the air. "This tremendous assault," Geary reported, "at first staggered the enemy, by whom it was seemingly unexpected. Line after line of the enemy broke under this steady fire, but the pressing masses from behind rushed forward to take their places."[19]

Brigadier General Williams concurred: "We had the advantage of excellent positions for artillery at good range. The woods in front and rear and above the breastworks held by the rebels were filled with projectiles from our guns. . . . The whole line of woods were ablaze with continuous volleys." The fire seemed to be effective, as Williams continued: "The enemy suffered severely, much more than we did, as we were for the most part well covered, while they were greatly exposed and subjected to a tremendous artillery fire in addition to our sweeping infantry volleys." He added, as a grotesque afterthought, "I have seldom seen the dead lie thicker on any battlefield."[20]

Cincinnati Gazette war reporter Whitelaw Reid was on Powers Hill in the early-morning of July 3, and the cannonade began as he was leaving the hill. He described the scene with poetry and tactical precision. "At day break crashing volleys woke the few sleepers there were," he wrote.

> A fusillade ran along the line—each had felt the other, then came cautious skirmishing again. . . . As I rode down the slope and up through the wheat fields to Cemetery Hill, the batteries began to open again on points along our outer line. They were evidently playing on what had been Slocum's line of yesterday. The rebels, then were there still, in our rifle pits. Presently the battery on Slocum's hill gained the long-sought permission, and opened, too, aiming apparently in the same direction. Other batteries along the inner line, just to the left of the Baltimore pike, followed the signal, and as one after another opened up, till every little crest between Slocum's headquarters and Cemetery Hill began belching its thunder, I had to change my course through the wheat fields to avoid our own shells. Still no artillery response from the rebels. Could they be short of ammunition? Could they have failed to bring up all their guns? Were they, perhaps, massing artillery elsewhere, and only keeping up this furious crash of musketry on the right as a blind?[21]

Chaplain J. H. W. Stuckenberg of the 145th Pennsylvania was asleep at the First Division, II Corps hospital at the western base of Powers Hill when the cannonade opened, so he climbed to the peak to watch the artillery at work.

19 United States War Department, *The War of the Rebellion: Official Records of the Union and Confederate Armies* (Gettysburg, 1972), 828.

20 Ladd and Ladd, *The Bachelder Papers*, 220.

21 James G. Smart, ed., *A Radical View: The "Agate" Dispatches of Whitelaw Reid 1861-1865*, Vol. II (Memphis, 1976); Folder B-57-16 Miscellaneous—Union, GNMP.

"On our extreme right were three batteries, each one occupying a commanding position, which were almost incessantly throwing shells at the rebels," Stuckenberg recalled. "The rebels had fired no cannon at our right. I ascended a rocky hill—it was composed of large masses of rocks—to the middle one of the three batteries [Pennsylvania Light Battery E]. Gen. Slocum was here, in person directing the firing. A short distance before us was a rounded hill, covered with trees. On the side of the hill nearest us, the smoke was seen rising in columns from the forest—there the fighting took place." He remembered that "[t]he rattling of musketry was constant, rapid and terrific. The columns of smoke indicated the progress of the fight. It also served to indicate the position of the rebels to the artillerists. The shelling was rapid and must have produced terrible havoc in the rebel ranks." Triumphantly, he concluded, "Our men were victorious here. The rebels were repulsed, our rifle pits regained, the field covered with heaps of slain and wounded rebels whilst our loss was comparatively small."[22]

Sergeant David Nichol was an artilleryman on Spangler land on Powers Hill for the First Pennsylvania Light Battery E during that July 3 cannonade. He described what he witnessed in a letter to his father on July 9: "All this time we were busy throwing shell into their ranks and at one time, saved our men from being outflanked. The enemy came around the woods (about one brigade) exposing themselves to our View." A Confederate near Spangler's Spring called the region "artillery hell" because of the firing from Powers Hill and the Baltimore Pike.[23]

The artillery barrage first stalled the Confederates and then drove them back. But the fighting was often close and confused and combined with the smoke caused artillery friendly-fire casualties. Private George W. Warner, with the 20th Connecticut, lost both arms from the bursting of a shell yet somehow survived and fathered a large family. "At times," Lt. Col. William B. Wooster, 20th Connecticut, reported, "it became necessary to advance my left wing to successfully repulse the advancing column of the enemy, and again to retire my whole command to save it from being destroyed by our own artillery."[24]

Like the 20th Connecticut, other First Brigade, First Division, XII Corps regiments reported friendly-fire casualties. "A battery on a knoll just in rear of the Brigade on the Baltimore turnpike commenced firing, depressing their guns so as to rake the woods and breastworks lately occupied by the Brigade. One gun fell

---

22 Stuckenberg, *I'm Surrounded by Methodists*, 79–80.

23 Folder 6-PA1-ART-E, 1st Pennsylvania Artillery, Knap's Battery E, GNMP; www.npshistory.com/publications/gett/newsletter/v16n2.pdf, accessed Oct. 22, 2023.

24 *OR* 27, series I, report of Wooster, Warrenton Junction, VA, July 26, 1863.

short several times killing one man in the Regiment and several in the Brigade," Sgt. Henry C. Morhous of the 123rd New York observed.[25]

It was a persistent problem. "At daybreak," reported Lt. Col. James L. Selfridge, 46th Pennsylvania, "our artillery opened fire on the enemy, and several batteries in our rear, from an eminence, were obliged to throw their shot and shell immediately over my command, and from the premature explosions of our shells, and others from our batteries unexploded, falling in the midst of my command." Selfridge became so angry that he swore an oath, drew his pistol, and told brigade commander Col. Archibald L. McDougall that he was going to see the officer in command of that battery and if another shell fell short he would shoot the gunner. Word of the fire finally reached Slocum, and the situation abated.[26]

Still the salvo continued. "At eight o'clock there was a cessation for a short time; after which it was renewed with increased earnestness," Pennsylvania College professor Michael Jacobs recalled. "From 4 to 10 A. M., with terrible slaughter, our men pushed the enemy backward, until they drove them over our breastworks entirely broken to pieces. In this work of death, a battery of artillery placed on a hill to the right of the Baltimore turnpike, and some distance south of the Cemetery, was found to have performed a prominent part. . . . At 10 a.m., the fighting had nearly ceased on our right, after which it was not renewed on that part of the line."[27]

Slocum said the fight lasted until 10:30 a.m. "and resulted in our regaining possession of our entire line of intrenchments and driving the enemy back of the position originally held by him; in the capture of over 500 prisoners in addition to the large number of wounded left on the field, besides several thousand stand of arms and three stand of colors. Our own loss in killed and wounded was comparatively light, as most of our troops were protected by breastworks."[28]

Major St. Clair A. Mulholland of the 116th Pennsylvania said his men were rooting for the XII Corps on Culp's Hill from their location on Cemetery Ridge: "All morning," he wrote, "the men sat around calmly chewing hard tack and waiting for the result of the fight at Culp's Hill, looking over towards that high land, seeing great volumes of smoke arise from the timber, listening to the crash of the musketry, watching the streams of wounded that poured out of the dark woods, seeing the re-enforcements hurrying to the assaulted point, and joining in

---

25 Henry C. Morhous, *Reminiscences of the 123d Regiment, N.Y.S.V* (Greenwich, NY, 1879), 50.

26 *OR* 27, series I, report of Selfridge, July 18, Sandy Hook, MD.

27 Michael Jacobs, *Notes on the Rebel Invasion of Maryland and Pennsylvania and the Battle of Gettysburg* (Philadelphia, 1864), 40.

28 *OR* 27, series I, Slocum's report, Aug. 23, 1863.

the glad cheer that at eleven o'clock announced the victory of the Twelfth Corps and told the army that Culp's Hill was once more in possession of the Union Troops and the line was again intact."[29]

The 1st New York Light Battery M and Battery A Maryland Light reported no casualties at Gettysburg while Pennsylvania Light Battery E had one man mortally wounded and two wounded, though those casualties likely took place July 2, when the battery was on Culp's Hill.

The culmination of the Culp's Hill fight on the morning of July 3 ended Powers Hill's primary role at Gettysburg. Slocum's generalship on and around Powers Hill in preserving the Army of the Potomac's right flank and back side drew praise from XI Corps commander Howard, who proclaimed, "The most impressive incident of that great battle to me was General Slocum's own battle!" Howard relayed in great detail: "I was awakened from my cemetery bed the morning of the 3d of July, 1863, at 5 o'clock by the startling roar of Slocum's guns. For five anxious hours, with A. S. Williams maneuvering his Twelfth corps, Slocum also having some of the Sixth corps and many batteries, commanded the field." With a tactician's eye for the significance of what transpired, Howard continued:

> That dreadful struggle to our right went on till Ewell, with Early and Edward Johnson's large divisions, was forced to give up and abandon his prize of the night before. That prize was our intrenched line within a stone's throw of the Baltimore pike, and included the trains for our immediate supply; Slocum's resolute incidence on the 2d day of July upon leaving General Greene and his brigade, as just a little precaution, when General Meade asked that the whole Twelfth corps be sent to his left, then fast going to pieces, to be sent to its rescue, two miles away. This insistence, followed by Greene's marvelous night battle and, more still, Slocum's organized work and engagement of the ensuing early morning, in my judgment, prevented Meade losing the battle of Gettysburg. It was a grand judgment and action of Slocum—a step all important to victory.[30]

Slocum was 35 years old when he helped win the battle of Gettysburg from his base on Powers Hill. *The New York Times* said: "At Gettysburg Gen. Slocum exhibited great skill and gallantry. He had command of the right wing of the Army of the Potomac in that memorable engagement, and contributed much to the success of the Union arms. On the second and third days the brunt of the fight fell heavily on his troops, and he repulsed the enemy with great vigor."[31]

29 St. Clair A. Mulholland, *The Story of the 116th Regiment, Pennsylvania Infantry* (Philadelphia, 1899), 139–140.

30 *The Brooklyn Standard Union*, Apr. 30, 1894.

31 *The New York Times*, Apr. 15, 1894; https://bit.ly/3wjuZA4, accessed Feb. 14, 2024.

Slocum was placed in command of the XX Corps later in the war, and his corps was the first to enter Atlanta after its fall. Slocum returned to New York City after the war and served three terms in Congress. He died at age 66 in 1894. His pallbearers included Gettysburg generals Howard, Sickles, Daniel Butterfield, and George S. Greene of Culp's Hill fame, who was 92 years old at the funeral. Slocum is memorialized in two statues today, one on Stevens Knoll between East Cemetery Hill and Culp's Hill and the other in Brooklyn.[32]

The Army of the Potomac wasn't done with Powers Hill after Culp's Hill was won, however. The pre-Pickett's Charge cannonade on the afternoon of July 3 sent Meade's staff scrambling from the Leister house, and he eventually landed on top of Powers Hill to observe the battle from there. He likely occupied Lightner land for the best view, and also to take advantage of the signal station there for communication purposes.

Powers Hill received Confederate shells from in front of Seminary Ridge on July 2–3. "Such cannonading," Cpl. Charles H. Rems of 1st New York Light Battery M wrote home, "as there was on the afternoon of the last day of the fight this world never saw." Sergeant Nichol of Battery M's Powers Hill neighbor Pennsylvania Light Battery E added, "The enemy shells came very close to us," and he reported six horses killed on the hill.[33]

Meanwhile, Provost Marshal General Marsena Patrick and the 4th New Jersey patrolled the base of the hill to gather skedaddlers on Granite Schoolhouse Lane during the cannonade while Meade was at the top. Patrick maintained a checkpoint on the Baltimore Pike side of the base of the hill on July 4 where he collected Confederate prisoners who needed hospital care, and the Powers Hill signal station was discontinued on July 5.

After spending the night of July 3 along the Taneytown Road, Meade returned to Spangler land at 5:30 a.m. July 4 and set up his headquarters at the base of Powers Hill along the Baltimore Pike. *Cincinnati Gazette* reporter Reid was there, too. "Headquarters were established anew under the trees in a little wood near Slocum's Hill," Reid recounted. "Detachments of rebel prisoners every few moments passed back under guard. . . . Everyone was in the most exuberant spirits. For once this army had won a real victory."[34] But Meade still had work to do on the hill: "The

32 *The Brooklyn Daily Eagle*, Apr. 16, 1894.

33 Donald W. Croop, *The Valiant Men of Battery M*, Wilson Historical Society, Wilson, NY, Folder 6-NY1 AR(M), Battery M, 1st NY Light Artillery, GNMP; Folder 6-PA1-ART-E, 1st Pennsylvania Artillery, Knap's Battery E, GNMP.

34 Whitelaw Reid, *Two Witnesses at Gettysburg: The Personal Accounts of Whitelaw Reid and A. J. L. Fremantle* (Malden, MA, 2009), 68–69.

cavalry generals were again in request," Reid continued, "and heavy reconnaisances were ordered. The bulk of the rebel army was believed to be in full retreat."[35]

Meade stayed at Spangler only the morning of July 4 before he was driven inside and off the property by thunderstorms. This farm and this hill, however, had served his army well and in a variety of ways.

The Spanglers received $150 in 1895 for the placement of monuments to the 77th New York Infantry and Pennsylvania Light Artillery E on Powers Hill and the 4th New Jersey Infantry monument below the hill at Blacksmith Shop Road and Granite Schoolhouse Lane. The monument for Battery A Maryland Light went up on Powers Hill in 1888 and for 1st New York Light Battery M in 1889. Slocum's headquarters marker was placed along the Baltimore Pike in 1920. Captain James Rigby returned to Powers Hill for Battery A Maryland Light's marker dedication ceremony and delivered an address.[36]

Solomon and Catherine Powers celebrated their 50th anniversary on July 3, 1883. He died a prominent man in Gettysburg two months later at age 79. Beniah Spangler purchased 5 acres on the hill in 1887 and opened a quarry and Nathaniel Lightner and son Edward both quarried on the hill before business eventually died out. Edward cut most of the stone for the 77th New York and 4th New Jersey monuments on and at the base of Powers Hill on Spangler land. More than a dozen quarry holes remain on the north, northeast, northwest, and west sides of the hill, a couple as large as 30 or 40 feet long and at least 10 feet deep, serving as modern-day reminders of the stone once pulled out of there. Chisel marks remain on several of the stones.[37]

Powers Hill has not received the recognition accorded to Cemetery Hill, Little Round Top, and Culp's Hill, and visitation to it is rare. Cemetery Hill, Little Round Top, and Culp's Hill enjoy ample parking, paved pathways to walk, and signs and markers galore. All three hills are well-pointed out and described on the official battlefield map handed out to visitors. Powers Hill, meanwhile, isn't even mentioned on the map, so those who don't know where the hill is have to ask or find it on their own or miss it altogether because they are unaware of its significance.

Powers Hill parking is in a semi-hidden stone lot across Granite Schoolhouse Lane from the hill. The lot holds three or four cars, and while walking away from it there are no directions provided to the one little dirt path that leads to a summit often hidden by tall Indian grass (*Sorghastrum nutans*). Unlike the other hills,

---

35 Ibid., 71.

36 Cumberland Township tax records, Adams County Historical Society; *Gettysburg Compiler*, Apr. 10, 1920, and July 31, 1888; *Gettysburg Times*, June 27, 1939; *The Baltimore Sun*, Oct. 26, 1888.

37 *Gettysburg Times*, Dec. 20, 1937.

Members of New York Battery M returned to Powers Hill in 1889 to dedicate their monument. Note how the Lightner land at the site of the monument on top of the hill was being farmed at the time. *Wilson (NY) Historical Society*

including the less-important Benner's Hill, there is no sign at the base announcing that you have found Powers Hill. The dirt path to the top finally reveals impressive and important monuments, flank markers, and artillery—if one is physically able to climb over a pair of 3-to-4-foot-high rock walls to get there. No opening has been provided in these walls, making for a dangerous climb over rocks and preventing access for many to the peak of this historic hill. Big Round Top is steep and mainly suited for physically fit climbers, but even it does not have rock walls blocking the path to the top as does Powers Hill.[38]

If one safely clears the obstacle course and makes it to the top of Powers Hill, modern-day trees block what would have been Meade's view of the battlefield to the west. Some of Culp's Hill can be seen in the opposite direction but not much. The best view, sadly, is of the water towers behind the grocery store on the former site of Camp Letterman. Unlike just about everywhere else on this beautiful, detailed, and much-admired battlefield, it is impossible to interpret the battle from the top of Powers Hill because of all the trees, even though it was a critical hill. Modern trees have been removed from the eastern slope, but most of the sight blockers that weren't there in 1863 remain everywhere else on the hill.

---

38 The trail is 0.16 miles down Granite Schoolhouse Lane to the west from the parking lot.

The hill today. *Ron Kirkwood*

Finally, as kind of a last insult to this historic hill, what's left of a lane that had once served for the removal of granite and which had climbed from the Baltimore Pike to the rear of the north and northwest sides of the hill can still be seen up there on National Park Service land leading to a sad end at a former dump site. There, broken-down and rusted barrels and cans, clumps of barbed-wire and other fencing, and varieties of other garbage litter the landscape. Whoever did this didn't bother to make sure all the garbage they were trucking in and putting up there on protected land was buried. Solomon Powers' hill has not received the prominence that he did, and this dump site adds salt and sadness to this hill's historic wound.

There is, though, much to be celebrated and grateful for in the preservation of Powers Hill, some of which has occurred in recent years. The junk cars that used to sit on former Spangler land along the Baltimore Pike are gone, as is the junkyard across the street. The houses and buildings at the base of the hill along the pike have been removed and the eastern slope has been mainly cleared of trees as has some of the land at the top. And thanks to American Battlefield Trust and its aggressive and appreciated preservation efforts, the Lightner portion of Powers Hill is now under the control of Gettysburg National Military Park and the hill is surrounded by protected land. Plus, a new informational marker is planned, offering another indication that the hill is being cared for and education about it matters.

A small portion of the trash field on the back side of the hill. *Ron Kirkwood*

There are only a few issues left to resolve for Powers Hill to get the treatment it warrants, starting with accessibility, the garbage dump, signs at the base of the hill, and mapping. With so much already accomplished and preserved, then you begin to have a hill that would make John Bachelder, Solomon Powers, Henry Slocum, George Spangler, and Nathaniel Lightner proud. Then you have a site worthy of its critical role in the battle of Gettysburg and United States history.

This National Park Service marker is to be placed on Powers Hill. *Gettysburg National Military Park*

One Final Note

No report about Powers Hill would be complete without mention of Capt. Clermont L. Best, previously XII Corps artillery chief who was inspector general on Slocum's staff at Gettysburg. In this position, Best spent most of his time on Powers Hill with Slocum, and it was Best whom Slocum put in charge of placing the Union artillery on the night of July 2 on and around Powers Hill and along the Baltimore Pike, an emplacement that would drive the Confederates off Culp's Hill on the morning of July 3. In doing so he was all over the hill in carrying out Hunt's vision of concentrated firepower and was awarded brevet lieutenant colonel for gallant and meritorious service at Gettysburg. Lieutenant Edward D. Muhlenberg commanded the XII Corps artillery at Gettysburg and also received praise for his work along the Baltimore Pike. Indeed, Slocum's artillery was in splendid hands with Best and Muhlenberg and they used Spangler, Lightner, and other area farms to great military effect.[39]

Best graduated from West Point in 1847 and was 39 years old at Gettysburg. He remained in the military until his retirement as a colonel in 1888. He died at his home in New York City in 1897.

Spangler Farm Short Story

The Park Service began removal of post-1863 buildings from Powers Hill after it purchased 5-plus acres of former Nathaniel Lightner land from Leonard and Noreen Shealer and their family in the fall of 2010. The Shealers owned this property since 1951 and were living in a house that was built around 1900. This land sits on the Baltimore Pike next to and just to the north of the Slocum headquarters monument and across the wall from it. The Park Service cleared 5.63 acres on that side of the hill in 2012.[40]

This practice of living on or having businesses on the battlefield was common earlier in the century, particularly along the Emmitsburg Road, when little attention was paid to historic preservation. But if someone was going to live on Powers Hill, it's good it was the Shealers. Leonard Shealer's great-grandfather, Martin Shealer, owned a farm at the intersection of Hunterstown Road and what is now Shealer Road that was used for a hospital for Confederate Maj. Gen. Jubal Early's division. There were at least 42 graves found on that property. Leonard served with Gen. George S. Patton in World War II and met Noreen in England. They raised children Peggy, Ron, Susan, and Mike on that hill, and Mike went on to become

39 Bachelder Day 3 map of Gettysburg, Library of Congress; https://bit.ly/3wo7SUK, accessed Feb. 24, 2024.

40 "Cultural Report for Gettysburg National Military Park, Record of Treatment: Volume 1," 305.

From left, siblings Ron Shealer, Sue Hartman, and Mike Shealer grew up on the Baltimore Pike at the base of Powers Hill. They are standing next to the 1st New York Battery M monument, which was on their property. *Ron Kirkwood*

a licensed battlefield guide. He retired as a teacher and moved back to Gettysburg and became the Gettysburg Foundation's much-respected site coordinator at the George Spangler farm just across Granite Schoolhouse Lane from where he grew up.

"My father was the one who was responsible for getting through to all four of us kids the importance of Powers Hill during the battle of Gettysburg," Mike recalled. "My dad wasn't really a historian, but he knew a lot of facts about the town since he grew up there. I was always very proud of knowing what all happened on the hill where I grew up. I thought every kid was lucky enough to have cannons and monuments in their backyard."

Mike's sister, Susan, added, "We were taught to be respectful of the hill. We knew it was special."

Mike and Susan's brother, Ron, started metal detecting in the 1970s on the family property and on the Andrew farm that once served as the Spanglers' home. "There were bullets all over the Andrew farm" that had been dropped or dumped, he said, including explosive bullets used by the XI Corps. He also found pack hooks, buttons, belt buckles, and shell fragments on the Spangler/Andrew farm. Mike found part of a Hotchkiss shell in the Shealer driveway that had been fired from the peak of Powers Hill and didn't make it far.

The Shealers' property ran from the Baltimore Pike to the top of the hill and included the monument and artillery up there today for the 1st New York Light Battery M. "I had a lot of fun up there," Ron said. "I built a tree house. Explored in the woods. There were always deer. Everywhere. My dad used to let people hunt up there. I think I always knew when I was a kid that I was growing up on the battlefield, but I wasn't aware how important that site was until a little later." Ron also pointed out the remnants of a lane or trail that once climbed the hill next to the Slocum marker, wondering if that's how the artillery was taken up. Farmers regularly made their own lanes, so the artillery could have gone up there or on another lane on the hill from the 1800s.

Ron's oldest son, Corry, gets his dad's Spangler-Andrew-Shealer metal-detecting collection someday.

Chapter 14

Artillery Reserve Notes:
Henry Hunt Chooses Spangler

"[Meade] directed me . . . to see that the artillery of the corps was properly placed,
and to make the best dispositions as to the Reserve Artillery, on its arrival."

— *Brig. Gen. Henry J. Hunt*

Even today, it's easy to see why eight batteries of the Army of the Potomac Artillery Reserve stopped at the intersection of the Taneytown and Two Taverns roads for a short night's rest on their way northward to Gettysburg and the George Spangler farm on July 1. Looking west from this intersection on the Taneytown Road as you head north today is a large, flat, green field. Look northeast from the same location and you see the same thing: space. Perfect for the purpose. Subtract the woodlands on the edges of today's fields and you have even more flat, open space in 1863, enough to comfortably hold the First Regular and Fourth Volunteer brigades and their artillery, equipment, and hundreds of men and horses.

The Taneytown Road crosses the southward-bound Rock Creek as it takes its time rolling past the edge of these fields, providing a bounty of water for men and animals within only a few steps no matter the side of the road on which you're parked. It's only appropriate that the first two Artillery Reserve batteries to leave Taneytown for Gettysburg would stop at Rock Creek, the most important waterway in the battle, one that meandered by, and was involved in the fighting on Barlow Knoll and Culp's Hill. The creek continued onward a short distance from George Spangler's farm past this portion of the Artillery Reserve at the modern-day village of Barlow. These artillerymen and their comrades would see a lot of this stream's watershed in the coming days. This camp was a mere 3½ miles from a right turn onto Granite Schoolhouse Lane, and then only steps from Spangler. That put those eight batteries in their Spangler parking lot ready to fight the next morning.

Brig. Gen. Henry J. Hunt

Library of Congress

The other 11 Artillery Reserve batteries left Taneytown at dawn July 2 for the rough trip down the Taneytown Road. "We moved rapidly over a road so rough and stony that a Battery ahead of us had a badly packed limber chest blown up and a man killed," Capt. John Bigelow of the 9th Massachusetts Battery remembered. "The Command arrived [at Spangler] about eleven in the forenoon and was parked in the rear of Cemetery Hill, on the outskirts of Gettysburg."[1]

Chief of Artillery Brig. Gen. Henry J. Hunt knew the Artillery Reserve's location by sunrise July 2, even though he had arrived in Gettysburg only a few hours earlier with Maj. Gen. George Gordon Meade's command. He assured a concerned Meade that eight batteries were close and that he sent riders to guide them in. He also knew where he wanted them: the George Spangler farm. Hunt and Meade were all over the line together in the overnight hours and early light of July 2, and Meade gave Hunt full authority to move and place his army's artillery as he thought best. Hunt couldn't miss the vast open fields of the 166-acre Spangler farm directly behind and within a half-mile of the developing Union line, so that's where he placed his 106 cannons, 2,300 men, an equal number of horses, and the army's 100-wagon ammunition train. The six Spanglers must have felt like they had been invaded and overrun.[2] XI Corps commander Maj. Gen. Oliver O. Howard said Hunt had the Artillery Reserve "carefully placed in the angle between the Baltimore pike and the Taneytown road."[3]

---

1 John Bigelow, *The Peach Orchard—Gettysburg* (Minneapolis, 1910), 51.

2 Hunt to Maj. Gen. Oliver O. Howard, Dec. 29, 1876, Hunt Papers, Box 4, Library of Congress.

3 Oliver O. Howard, *Autobiography of Oliver Otis Howard*, Vol. 1 (New York, 1907), 425.

Hunt wrote after the war: "[Meade] directed me . . . to see that the artillery of the corps was properly placed, and to make the best dispositions as to the Reserve Artillery, on its arrival. These orders recognized, in fact necessarily vested in me all the powers of a commander-in-chief of the artillery."[4] Hunt also said Meade told him: "'This is your affair take the proper measures to provide against the attack, and make the line safe with artillery until it is properly occupied.' This, with his previous instructions, left me no room to doubt his intent as to my duties and powers, and it was under a full sense of the responsibility thus imposed that I immediately assumed the active command of the Artillery and exercised it during the remainder of the battle."[5]

The artillerymen awaited their orders once the Artillery Reserve gathered in the Spangler fields. Many experienced pre-fight jitters. Bigelow described a tense scene: "Frequent puffs of smoke high in the air, from exploding shells, and an irregular, sputtering infantry fire, extending from the right at Culp's Hill, around Cemetery Hill and to the left, near the Round Tops, indicating that the opposing lines were in close proximity, nervous and preparing for conflict. The day was very warm," he observed, "and canvas covers were stretched, as shelter from the sun's rays. The gunners examined their chests; horses were fed and watered by detachments, officers, from Batteries parked around us, called, bringing news of latest happenings, and many of the men visited a barn, near by, already well filled with wounded."[6]

Hunt or one of his staffers returned to Spangler often on July 2–3, and they teamed with Artillery Reserve commander Brig. Gen. Robert O. Tyler to move batteries and ammunition all over the line as needed. After being placed and fully gathered there, the 19 light batteries of the Artillery Reserve dashed from Spangler July 2–3 and fought from the Peach Orchard to Trostle to the Plum Run Line to Codori to Cemetery Hill to East Cemetery Hill to the Spanglers' own Powers Hill. These batteries were heavily involved and heavily important almost everywhere. The Artillery Reserve at Gettysburg, Hunt said, was "an invaluable resource in the time of greatest need."[7]

---

4 Ladd and Ladd, *The Bachelder Papers*, Vol. 1, 426.

5 David L. Ladd and Audrey L. Ladd, *The Bachelder Papers: Gettysburg in Their Own Words, Vol. II, September 6, 1880 to April 12, 1886* (Dayton, OH, 1994), 426-427.

6 Coco Collection, Gettysburg Field Hospital Research #1, Box B-69, Folder: B-69-1B, GNMP.

7 Henry J. Hunt, *Battles and Leaders of the Civil War*, Vol. III (New York, 1884), 304; Brig. Gen. Tyler had his Artillery Reserve headquarters at the Frey farm at the western edge of the Spangler farm on the southeast side of the intersection of Granite Schoolhouse Lane and Taneytown Road, according to John Bachelder's 1863 isometric map of the battlefield.

Lieutenant Tully McCrea of Battery I, 1st U.S. Artillery, II Corps Artillery Brigade, was involved in the fight on July 2 and July 3 at Ziegler's Grove, and he said Hunt's guidance and freedom to carry out his own vision was a difference maker. "If the same thing had occurred in some of the other battles," he wrote, "it is more than probable that history would have had a different story to record. One of the main features of this battle was the grouping of the batteries, thus giving to their fire the effect of concentration and mass."[8]

Confederate Col. Edward Porter Alexander commanded Lt. Gen. James Longstreet's First Corps artillery at Gettysburg and later as a railroad executive echoed McCrea in telling Hunt that "if your orders had not been so judicious & as well adhered to & carried out history might have been a little different."[9]

Army of the Potomac Maj. Gen. George McClellan concurred in the assessment of Hunt's capacities: "I appointed Hunt to the position of chief of artillery. If Hunt had been permitted to take command of a Brigade of Infantry he would long before the close of the war have been in command of a Corps at least."[10]

Under the heaviest of fire, Hunt moved each battery July 2–3 with thought and precision. He was already considered a military genius, and Gettysburg added to his reputation. "He was the finest Artillery Officer of the war, and commanded the love and respect of every member of his branch of the service," the 9th Massachusetts' Bigelow, now a brevet major, wrote after the war.[11] Hunt was the most respected artillery commander of his day. He saw the military value of George Spangler's farm and seized it and because of that it played a critical role in his success, vision, and legend at Gettysburg.

The Army of the Potomac Artillery Reserve used George Spangler's farm as its base July 2–3. The following are notes on some of those artillerymen and their time at the farm.

*   *   *

First Lieutenant Henry D. Scott of the 5th Massachusetts said "all was quiet" when the battery arrived on July 2 behind the Spanglers' barn and parked next to

---

8 Catherine S. Crary, *Dear Belle: Letters from a Cadet & Officer to his Sweetheart, 1858-1865* (Middletown, CT, 1965), 211, Folder: 1st US Artillery, Battery I, 6-Us1-Art-I, GNMP.

9 Henry Hunt Papers, 1863-1889, Correspondence Regarding Gettysburg, Alexander to Hunt, Jan. 27, 1879, Box B-11, GNMP.

10 Henry Hunt Papers, 1863-1889, Correspondence Regarding Gettysburg, McClellan to Lt. Col. Theodore Lyman III, May, 27, 1884, Box B-11, GNMP.

11 Bigelow, *The Peach Orchard—Gettysburg*, 40.

the 9th Massachusetts. "All the Artillery Reserve hitched up and bunched in the rear of the line of battle near the Baltimore turnpike, he remembered.

> Nothing could be seen from where we were of the line of battle. . . . Hitched up at 4 p.m. Fighting commenced at 5 p. m., when the ball opened in earnest. Ordered to the front. I was talking with First Lieut. Christopher Erickson of the Ninth Mass, about the probable result of the coming contest, when the batteries, one by one, began to start out in a hurry. A staff officer rode up to Captain [John] Phillips to direct the Battery to the front. The order to strip for action came quickly. All incumbrances were thrown aside, and we started out on a trot across the field, passing by the foot of Little Round Top, over stone walls and other obstructions. We could see, as we advanced, the terrible fight that was going on. The air was already full of sulphurous smoke.[12]

Scott was hit in the face in this fight, a single ball piercing both cheeks. He was sent to a hospital, recovered, and returned to the 5th Massachusetts in September.[13]

Captain Phillips added: "I suffered pretty severely in this day's fight: 3 men were left dead on the field, and one died the next morning in the hospital. Some 30 horses were killed." Spare Artillery Reserve horses were retrieved from Spangler as needed during the fight.[14]

Out of ammunition, Phillips' battery returned to Spangler. "I retired across the Taneytown road, and unhitched for the night," he said. "By midnight I got the whole battery together and went to sleep." The 9th Massachusetts, 15th New York Independent, and Pennsylvania Independent Batteries C and F also returned to their morning parking spot, meaning the Spanglers hosted the entire First Volunteer Brigade of Lt. Col. Freeman McGilvery on the night of July 2 into July 3.[15]

"The Artillery Reserve lost heavily in this fight," Scott recalled. "I have often talked with General Henry J. Hunt chief of artillery on the part the artillery took. He thought they did not get half the credit belonging to them."[16]

Corporal Thomas Chase wrote in his diary that the 5th Massachusetts returned to Spangler on the afternoon of July 5 to the same field west of the barn where it parked on the morning of July 2. While there, a furious thunderstorm hit at about 3:30 and lasted an hour. Through this, the artillerymen could see that the population of the XI Corps and other hospitals had dramatically increased

---

12 Luther E. Cowles, ed., *History of the Fifth Massachusetts Battery* (Boston, 1902), 629.

13 Henry D. Scott Compiled Military Service Record, Fold 3.

14 Cowles, *History of the Fifth Massachusetts Battery*, 625.

15 Ibid., 628.

16 Ibid., 632.

1st Lt. Henry D. Scott, 5th Massachusetts

Library of Congress

since their time there three days ago. "The hospitals were crowded with the wounded. Every available house, barn, or church was crowded," 1st Lt. Scott said. The men searched the battlefield after the storm for missing and dead comrades.[17]

*   *   *

The four batteries of the Artillery Reserve's Third Volunteer Brigade— 1st New Hampshire Light, 1st Ohio Light Battery H, 1st West Virginia Light Battery C, and 1st Pennsylvania Light Batteries F and G—rested from 2 to 4 hours on July 2 at Spangler before seeing heavy action that afternoon and evening on Cemetery Hill and East Cemetery Hill.[18] "No better place will occur," 1st Lt. Charles B. Brockway of F and G wrote to the *Toledo Blade* newspaper, "to disabuse the minds of your reader of the idea, generally prevalent—that the term 'Reserve Artillery' applies only to such as is held in reserve and only used when an emergency occurs & it becomes necessary to make use of the 'Reserve.' The very contrary is the case—to so great an extent—in fact, that it has become quite usual to say 'the Reserve is always first in and last out of a fight.'"[19]

However long these batteries were at Spangler, *Cincinnati Gazette* reporter Whitelaw Reid witnessed them there: "In the fields," he said, "stood the reserve artillery, with horses harnessed to the pieces and ready to move on the instant. Cavalry, too, was drawn up in detachments here and there."[20]

---

17 Ibid., 632, 657.

18 1st Lt. Charles B. Brockway of F and G told the *Toledo Blade* in an undated letter that the battery got a 2-hour rest (Harry Pfanz Research Collection Box 3, B-57, Folder B-57-13 Artillery, Union Army of the Potomac, GNMP) while Capt. R. Bruce Ricketts of F and G said it was a 4-hour break at Spangler (*OR, The War of the Rebellion: Official Records of the Civil War*, Serial 43, 894).

19 Pfanz Collection, Box 3, B-57, Folder B-57-13 Artillery, Union Army of the Potomac, GNMP.

20 Pfanz Collection, Box 3, Folder B-57-16 Miscellaneous—Union, GNMP.

1st Lt. Charles B. Brockway,
1st Pennsylvania Light Batteries F and G
FindaGrave.com

*   *   *

The left eardrum of Capt. James H. Rigby of 1st Maryland Light Battery A was perforated by the explosive sound of the firing of his cannons at Antietam in September 1862. That eardrum was still perforated July 2–3, 1863, on Powers Hill. Such ear injuries often heal themselves, and today they can be fixed with surgery. But not in the Civil War. Not when Civil War artillerymen wore little to no ear protection against explosions so loud that their chest and head pounded and sometimes their ears bled. That meant Rigby spent September 1862 to July 1863 with loss of hearing and pain and other likely symptoms such as ringing in his ear, vertigo, and nausea. His ear issues were the norm for artillerymen in the Civil War.[21]

It didn't help Rigby's ears when in defense of his country he fired his six guns intensely from Powers Hill on the morning of July 3. Gettysburg resident Jane Smith lived on the other side of town, recalling of the battle for Culp's Hill: "May I never again be roused to the consciousness of a new-born day by such fearful sounds! It seemed almost like the crashing of worlds."[22]

Infantrymen weren't immune from ear damage. Private Henry Meyer of the 148th Pennsylvania said the July 3 artillery barrage presaging Pickett's Charge "caused blood to flow from the ears and noses of men" and that when citizens visited the battlefield on July 4 "a number inquired of me to know why the soldiers talked so very loud to each other; so fierce, when they seemed not angry with each other. I said we are all very hard of hearing, nearly deaf, [from] the awful noise of battle."[23]

Like many soldiers and artillerymen, the Civil War never left Rigby after he left Spangler. He lived with the pain of it and problems caused by it every day for the rest of his life. He said at age 57 in 1888 that he "is now totally deaf in left

21 James H. Rigby Invalid Pension Claim 437824, NARA.

22 Jane Smith, diary, published July 2, 1913, in the Gettysburg *Star and Sentinel*, File V-8, Civilian Accounts Crawford, GNMP Library.

23 Muffly, *The Story of Our Regiment, A History of the 148th Pennsylvania Vols.*, 467.

ear and right ear considerably affected." Also impacted was his overall health. He stood five feet eleven-and-a-half inches tall in April 1889 but weighed only 140 pounds. A doctor said Rigby's "[g]eneral physical appearance very bad. Extreme emaciation." He died of a heart attack in downtown Baltimore four months after that doctor's report.[24]

*   *   *

Stable Sgt. Nelson Lowell, age 36, was left behind near the Spanglers' barn when the 9th Massachusetts sprinted to the Trostle farm. He was in charge of the spare horses that were left behind. But he could hear the intensity of the fight peaking and was getting reports of his comrades' tenuous situation so, unwilling to miss the fight, he mounted his horse, abandoned his duties and the relative safety at Spangler and took off for the higher calling of helping his batterymates. He arrived on the field at about the time the 9th was beginning its 400-yard retreat from today's Wheatfield Road to the Trostle yard. He reported to Bigelow, who was relieved to see him and put him right to work. "The chief of the sixth piece is wounded, go and take charge of that gun," Bigelow ordered.[25]

Lowell wasn't quite sure of what, exactly, he had been put in charge. As he recalled later, "I found the No. 1 wounded and helpless; No. 2, bruised by piece of shell . . . all the horses gone but the off pole horse, whose driver, E. [Pvt. Eleazer] Cole, was holding the pole yoke and guiding the horse, so that the limber kept out of the way of the gun. Near the gateway [in front of the Trostle house] the other horse was shot, and limber overturned; ammunition gone. I immediately joined the next serviceable gun, which was Gunner Wm. [Cpl. William] Tucker's, who was almost alone."[26]

*   *   *

The Artillery Reserve's 1st New York Light, Battery G left Spangler and fought in the Peach Orchard in late afternoon on July 2, then returned to Spangler that night to reload after being pushed back. Captain Nelson Ames described some of what was going on that night at Spangler: "During the night the ammunition chests were replenished. New horses were secured and put in place of those that

24 Rigby pension claim, NARA; *Baltimore Sun*, Aug. 6, 1889.

25 Levi W. Baker, *History of the Ninth Massachusetts Battery* (South Framingham, MA, 1888), 79.

26 Ibid.

were killed and wounded. The battery was put in as good condition as was possible under the circumstances, and was again ready for action."[27]

*   *   *

In an example of smart battle management, messengers remained at Spangler and on neighboring fields after the ammunition train and few remaining Artillery Reserve batteries escaped the farm during the pre-Pickett's Charge cannonade that pelted the west and north Spangler fields. The train moved farther to the rear and the batteries to the line. "I rode to the Artillery Reserve to order fresh batteries and ammunition to be sent up to the ridge as soon as the cannonade ceased; but both the reserve and the train had gone to a safer place," Hunt remembered. "Messengers, however, had been left to receive and convey orders, which I sent by them; then I returned to the ridge. Turning into the Taneytown pike [from Granite Schoolhouse Lane], I saw evidence of the necessity under which the reserve had 'decamped,' in the remains of a dozen exploded caissons, which had been placed under cover of a hill, but which the shells had managed to search out. In fact, the fire was more dangerous behind the ridge than on its crest."[28]

*   *   *

Ordnance officer Lt. Cornelius Gillett, 1st Connecticut Heavy Artillery, arrived at Spangler on July 2 in command of the Army of the Potomac's ammunition train. He parked his 100 wagons and hundreds of men and mules in the north Spangler fields across the lane from Powers Hill. Gillett immediately began to provide ammunition to any Union battery in need and continued to do so while staying up all through the night of July 2 into July 3 after an intense day of artillery fighting. He was so busy in his two days on the Spangler farm that his men distributed 19,189 of the train's 23,883 rounds while there.[29] Spangler took hits from Confederate artillery especially during the July 3 cannonade, prompting Gillett to report, "A mule in one of the teams was struck by a solid shot and killed. [M]any of the animals became so unmanageable that there was danger of a stampede."[30]

Gillett got what was left of his train off Spangler land and to safety farther behind the line on the afternoon of the 3rd. He survived Gettysburg and the Civil

27 Nelson Ames, *Captain Nelson Ames' Battery G* (Marshalltown, IA, 1900), 76.

28 www.ehistory.osu.edu/books/battles/vol3/373, accessed Jan. 8, 2023.

29 Gillett official report, Aug. 23, 1863, 878.

30 Ibid., 879.

The Army of the Potomac artillery ammunition train was centered on this George Spangler field. The photo is taken looking north with Powers Hill in the background. With 100 wagons and hundreds of men and animals, the train undoubtedly spilled into neighboring fields until wagons were moved farther behind the line as they were emptied. This train provided ammunition for all Army of the Potomac artillery batteries. Capt. Nelson Ames, Battery G, 1st New York Light of the Artillery Reserve, said of the night of July 2 here at Spangler: "[We] fell back to the ammunition train near the Baltimore turnpike. During the night the ammunition chests were replenished. The battery was put in as good condition as was possible under the circumstances, and was again ready for action."[31] *Ron Kirkwood*

War. He would not, however, live long in peacetime following the war. He drowned December 24, 1866, in Cow Creek near Fort Reading in northern California at age 28 or 29.

*   *   *

Captain John Bigelow of the 9th Massachusetts Battery raised the money, designed the monument, and led the drive for a permanent marker on the Gettysburg battlefield where Maj. Gen. Winfield S. Hancock was wounded on

---

31 Gregory A. Coco Collection, Gettysburg Field Hospital Research #1, Personal Accounts, Union, Box B-69, Folder: B-69-1B, Capt. Nelson Ames, Battery G, 1st NY Light Artillery, Gettysburg National Military Park Archives.

July 3. The fact that he did all of that is not a surprise, because Bigelow was a proven leader both during and after the war and one who sacrificed much for his country in battle. His stature in life far eclipsed his five-foot-seven-and-a-half-inch frame, and his maturity and leadership at Gettysburg belied his mere 22 years of existence.

Bigelow arrived at Spangler on the morning of July 2 with the Artillery Reserve and the 9th Massachusetts that he commanded. The former Harvard student parked his unit directly behind and close to the barn for a few hours of food and rest for the men and their horses. Bigelow's arrival at Spangler came almost a year to the day after his left forearm was shattered by a musket ball at Malvern Hill on July 1, 1862, while he was with the 1st Maryland Light Artillery. He also was crippled by a horse's kick in the knee earlier in the war. Bigelow led the 9th Massachusetts from Spangler to the Trostle farm in mid-afternoon July 2. His battery ended up being the last one standing in a furious fight in which the 9th held its position just long enough to allow the hole in the Army of the Potomac line left by the retreating III Corps to be plugged behind it. The dead horses shown lying in the Trostle yard in the famous Timothy O'Sullivan photo from after the battle are from the 9th Massachusetts. Bigelow was wounded in the left hand and right side just above the hip in the fight and was treated at the III Corps hospital. He was in and out of duty and sick call for the rest of the war. He went home as a brevet major in January 1865 to continue his healing and his leadership.[32]

Bigelow moved to Philadelphia and became a machinery designer. He returned to Spangler with other members of the 9th Massachusetts in 1884 and after parking there walked as a group from Spangler to the battlefield and placed their three monuments on Wheatfield Road, in the Trostle yard, and at Ziegler's Grove. He returned in 1885 to offer a dedication speech. He worked passionately in 1887 to establish a monument at Hancock's wounding site, as indicated by excerpts from his letters to John B. Bachelder, Superintendent of Tablets and Legends for the Gettysburg Battlefield Memorial Association:[33] "Every time that I have passed the spot where Genl. Hancock was wounded at Gettysburg," he wrote, "I have felt that some more durable and appropriate marker should be placed there than a simple wooden stake. . . . I have now collected a sufficient money to build a mon't like enclosed design, on which I have estimates. . . . If satisfactory, I will place the order at once."[34]

---

32 Baker, *History of the Ninth Massachusetts Battery*, 55; John Bigelow Invalid Pension Claim 172757, NARA.

33 Ibid.

34 Ladd and Ladd, *The Bachelder Papers*, 1519.

Bigelow got the OK after three more letters to Bachelder and his monument to Hancock's wounding was dedicated on Hancock Avenue in 1888. The design and wording of the monument remain today as they were when Bigelow submitted them to Bachelder in 1887. Bigelow was "fully disabled" by the time he created the Hancock monument according to his pension claim and must have been in a great deal of pain from his war wounds, but he lived until 1917, dying in Minnesota at age 76. If he was physically able, he could have attended the 50-year anniversary of the battle in 1913 to get one last look at the Spangler farm where his Gettysburg work began and the four battlefield monuments that he played such a significant role in placing.

Spangler Farm Short Story

By Greg Kaufmann, Historic Gettysburg Adams County

The pole rafters and cedar shingles stand out in the Spangler barn's vast upper reaches, but a visitor paying close attention to the high roof peak can spot the presence of a track. Scanning along this track to the north gable end, the visitor sees the hay trolley. In addition, the visitor can see pulleys and ropes that are part of the entire hay carrier system. This isolated hay trolley holds an honored place in the history of agricultural technology, but we can probably be sure George Spangler and son Beniah did not think about that in the 1870s or '80s as they learned of these systems and made the decision to install one.

Advances in agricultural technology in the mid-1800s contributed to a growth in the production of crops, especially hay, the main feed for the horses and oxen that powered the plows and wagons. Harvesting with scythes, loading it into wagons, and unloading it into hay ricks or mows was manpower-intensive. Normally, six or seven men were needed to lay up hay in the barn's mows, but that changed after the Civil War as the Second Industrial Revolution (1870-1914) capitalized on the technology developments driven by the war. Many agricultural historians consider the hay carrier of the kind George Spangler employed one of the primary outcomes of that revolution. While earlier primitive systems of ropes, pulleys, and slings were used in building the haystack often seen outside a barn, the first patent for a hay trolley was issued to William Louden in September 1867. The basic parts of a hay trolley system are the trolley itself with wheels to run on the track, the carrier drop pulley to which a harpoon or fork would be attached with which to "pitch" (or grab) the hay in the wagon, and the track on which the trolley ran. Early barn tracks were comprised of wood beams; around 1890, metal tracks started being introduced, and this is what the visitor sees in the Spangler barn.

This hay trolley is similar to the one owned by the Spanglers.

Greg Kaufmann

Another important development, the introduction of malleable iron (as opposed to its predecessor, cast iron), allowed for stronger, longer-lasting hay carriers to be built. By the time the hay trolley reached its zenith in the first half of the twentieth century, roughly 40 companies were producing these systems. The Spangler hay trolley appears to be from F. E. Myers & Bro. of Ashland, Ohio; their "OK Unloader" line was perhaps the most popular line of hay trolleys produced over the years.

Prior to hay trolleys, the job of putting up the hay in a mow usually took one man handling the horse team, two in the wagon pitching over into the mow, and three-four men in the mow taking the hay and moving it to fill the mow. This is where one would pitch the hay up to a level where another man was at a higher level and so forth until there would be three or four levels reaching up into the roof peak.

When the hay trolley came along, one man handled the horse team, one man was in the wagon helping direct the fork, and only one man was in the mow "cleaning up" the hay after the pitch was dropped from the hay trolley into the mow. The unloading and storage of the harvested hay proceeded much more rapidly, which is why this technology is considered one of the first automated, labor-saving devices in American industrial history.

One notable modification in the Spangler barn speaks to the increase in the size of the hay pitch that a fork or grapple could grab. As you enter the threshing floor, the bent (series of tall beams) to your right that divides the threshing floor from the south hay mow has had its tie beam partially removed. This modification opens the space for a larger pitch (i.e., an individual load of hay on the trolley's forks) to be maneuvered into the mow, but unfortunately it also weakens that bent.

Over time, these trolleys became bigger and more versatile and steam engines and tractors came to replace horses powering the trolley system. The use of these trolleys grew through the early 1900s, reaching their peak in the 1940s. Indeed, you can find these systems included in the Sears & Roebuck catalog as late as 1952. Their use continued into the 1980s, when the weight of the new round hay bales proved to be too much for the trolleys. Today, many old barns such as the Spanglers' retain evidence of these trolleys. In some cases, the owners might have used a trolley when they were young. Most barn owners today, though, do not have that experience but nonetheless treasure these trolleys as they learn their history.[35]

Greg Kaufmann is a retired colonel, U.S. Army Aviation, and holds a Ph.D. in Liberal Studies from Georgetown University. Living in the historic environment of Gettysburg, he was smitten by the majestic barns in the area and fell in with the Barn Preservation Project of Historic Gettysburg Adams County, where he serves on the Board of Directors, guiding other preservation-related programs.

---

35 Hay Trolley Heaven website: https://haytrolleyheaven.com; Hay Trolley Heaven Facebook page; Barry N. Merenoff, *The Mechanical Advantage: Reference Books for the Pulley & Hay Carrier Collector-Hay Carrier Systems* (New Haven, MI, 2003-04).

Chapter 15

A Fatal Shot in the Dark:
Pvt. Joseph Beal, 33rd Massachusetts

"I . . . walked about 2½ miles from the village to the 11th Corps hospital, found Joseph
in a cloth tent it is a tent hospital on the farm of a Mr. Sprangle."

— *Family friend Joseph C. Lewis on Pvt. Joseph Beal, 33rd Massachusetts*

Beal and Maria Greeley were married on Christmas Day, 1854, in East Bridgewater, Massachusetts, about halfway between Boston and Plymouth. Maria was 21 and Joseph was still a teenager at 19.

Their first child, Martin Herbert, was born soon after in 1855, but he lived only 6 months. Their second child, Augusta Jane, arrived in 1857. She would be the Beals' only surviving child. Joseph was a shoe cutter, a skilled trade in a booming industry in Massachusetts. But on July 30, 1862, Joseph accepted a bounty of $25 and enlisted in the 33rd Massachusetts for three years. Beal stood five feet seven inches with a light complexion, gray eyes, and dark hair. Maria was 29 years old, and Augusta Jane was 5, when Beal left his home and family for the Civil War. He would eventually find the George Spangler farm.[1]

The 33rd and Beal were on guard duty elsewhere and missed Antietam in September 1862. They arrived late at Fredericksburg in December and missed that, too. Still having not seen combat, the 33rd went into winter quarters outside of Fredericksburg. Ten-day furloughs flowed freely in that camp, and Beal got one and returned home to his wife and daughter in March 1863. Those were peaceful days for the 33rd so it must have been a happy and meaningful reunion with Maria and Augusta Jane in Massachusetts, perhaps even a time of hope.[2]

---

1 Ancestry.com; Massachusetts, U.S., Marriage Records, 1840-1915, Ancestry.com; Company Muster Roll, Fold3; Compiled Service Records of Volunteer Union Soldiers Who Served in Organizations From the State of Massachusetts, Fold3.

2 Ibid.

Beal was obliged to return to the army. He and the 33rd, now under Brig. Gen. Francis Barlow in the Second Brigade Second Division, were detached to the III Corps at Chancellorsville and thus did not participate in the frantic and disastrous XI Corps retreat from Stonewall Jackson's surprise attack. That's 3-for-3 in missing major combat: Antietam, Fredericksburg, and most of Chancellorsville. That streak of good fortune continued through Day 1 at Gettysburg when the 33rd watched in reserve from atop Cemetery Hill as most of the rest of the outmanned XI Corps frantically retreated from north of town to the safety of the hill. The 33rd then stayed relatively safe behind a stone wall on the Taneytown Road at the base of Cemetery Hill for the rest of July 1.

Good fortune, though, would not last. The 33rd received its first heavy combat of the war on July 2, and it would be deadly. The men were moved to the top of East Cemetery Hill along the Baltimore Pike, where they hunkered behind stone walls during the heavy artillery fight in the late afternoon. This not only would be the 33rd Massachusetts' indoctrination into major combat but also the day that Maria's husband and Augusta Jane's father received the head wound that eventually killed him at Spangler.

The artillery opened first. "[G]uns opened from the heights around Cemetery Hill, till the sharp flashes ran all around the encircling ridges which seemed to throb with fire and smoke, and the hills roared with heavy echoes," Col. Adin Ballou Underwood of the 33rd wrote after the war about the barrage. "Whizz came a round shot over the heads of the Thirty-Third men on Cemetery Hill, and plunged into the earth with a dull sound. A shell came shrieking and hissing in its track and exploded itself into destructive atoms; in almost a moment of time a hundred shot and shell were tearing about, bursting into fragments that hurried away many a brave life. Splinters of gun carriages, pieces of tombstones, even human legs and arms and palpitating flesh were flying around in every direction." Underwood said the artillery fire came from so many directions that he changed his men's position "from one side of a wall on Cemetery Hill to another, twice, and left them on the front side, as on the whole the safest."[3]

After the artillery fight, the 33rd Massachusetts and 41st New York were sent 400 to 500 yards from Brickyard Lane near the base of East Cemetery Hill and modern-day Wainwright Avenue to Culp's Meadow straight out from the hill. They were forced back when the five regiments of Brig. Gen. Harry Hays' Louisiana Tigers Brigade and the 6th North Carolina, 21st North Carolina, and 57th North Carolina under Col. Isaac Avery began their movement toward the

---

3 Adin Ballou *Underwood, The Three Years' Service of the Thirty-Third Mass. Infantry Regiment, 1862-1865* (Boston, 1881), 123.

hill in a sunset charge, sending the 33rd Massachusetts and 41st New York to the south end of a line of nine XI Corps regiments serving as the first line of defense at the bottom of the hill.

The North Carolina line marched closer, producing a "sheet of fire flashes along the dusky lines as they stop and fire a round and then start on," Underwood wrote. "Instantly a gun belches at them from the right and then from the left, and in a twinkling of time the thirty odd guns about the Cemetery are trained from the left, where they have just been firing over the tombstones onto [the] men, down now with depressed muzzles to the front, onto these troops of Early's division that are rapidly coming on." With a descriptive vigor that seems characteristic of the age, Underwood continued:

> The darkness is lighted up with flames from the cannons' mouths, that seem to pour down in streams upon them. The roar and shriek of the shot and shell that plough through and through their ranks, is appalling. The gaps bravely close up and still they advance. Canister cannot check them. They near fifty yards, when a rapid and awful fire is poured into them from the Thirty-Third and other infantry, until there are almost as many upon the ground as in their lines. It wavers some, but steadies up again, this brave brigade of Hoke's North Carolinians in front of the Thirty-Third, and then doggedly pushes forward again. It looks as if in a half minute it will be on the Thirty-Third men; they set their teeth, coolly get their bayonets ready and grimly wait for it, one solid Mass. regiment that kept its position lighted up during that night attack, with an unbroken line of fire, when it was all dark in gaps beyond. Hoke's men get up so near that the regiment starts up to use its bayonets; a rebel flag is waving almost directly over its head, when in an instant there are flashes like lightning from the muzzles of a Maine battery on the right, the roar of guns, and down drop the color and color bearer, and heaps of these brave traitors. Groans and shrieks fill the air. A fearful destruction of life! . . . The line in front is gone, all but the rows of dead and dying.[4]

That is how the 33rd Massachusetts came to know major combat.

The Louisiana Tigers had broken through and climbed that steep hill and in some places the combat grew desperate, hand to hand, or ramrod to hand. The men of the 33rd took fire from above and behind them. Underwood sent his adjutant "to the Cemetery gate to tell them there they are firing into their own men. When he returned," Underwood wrote, "he whispers, 'It is the rebels.'"[5]

It was at this spot, the site of today's 33rd Massachusetts monument, that many were hit from behind, including Pvt. Joseph Beal, Company I. A ball ripped

4 Ibid., 129–130.

5 Ibid., 130.

into his head behind his right ear and exited through his right eye. Others were also hit in the back of the head. In all, we know of almost 30 men of the 33rd Massachusetts, including Beal, who were carried down the Baltimore Pike that night from East Cemetery Hill to Spangler. "At the time of his being wounded I was quite near [Beal] and sent him to hospital . . . and by the surgeon pronounced mortally wounded," 33rd Massachusetts 1st Lt. Charles B. Walker wrote later.[6]

As July passed, hundreds left the XI Corps hospital for Camp Letterman or a sanitary brick-and-mortar hospital in a big city. But Beal remained behind. He was still alive but could not be moved. With Maria and Augusta Jane worried and waiting at home with no word, longtime Massachusetts family friend Joseph C. Lewis made the 430-mile journey from Boston to Gettysburg to check on Beal. He arrived in Gettysburg on Saturday, July 25, and kept a journal of his time at Spangler.

"I . . . walked about 2½ miles from the village to the 11th Corps hospital," Lewis wrote, "found Joseph in a cloth tent it is a tent hospital on the farm of a Mr. Sprangle. The hospital that Mr. Beal's was in was only a temporary one . . . wounded were moved from this hospital to a general hospital as fast as they were in condition to be moved and this hospital was simply a corps hospital. I found him about sunset he is wounded in the head just over the right ear about an inch back of his ear it was maid by a ball passed through his head and out his right eye. . . . I found him quite strong and very rational by spells. Don't seem to be in much pain takes no medicine.[7]

"Sunday 26th some weaker. 12 o'clock failing but very rational just wrote to Maria 8 o'clock . . . slowly. Monday 27th sinking fast. Won't take anything to eat . . . don't talk much don't understand anything. 10 o'clock . . . feet coald but hands still warm his left side num no feeling in it has no controle . . . 11 o'clock . . . he is sinking very fast has no sense of any thing Tuesday morning not much change Wensday a new Dr. took charge of our tent this morning Dr. Colwell [Dr. Jacob Y. Cantwell, 82nd Ohio] has had charg of him till this morning was ordered medicine for first time 10 drops arromatic spirrits . . . a day by the new Dr.

"One o'clock fails very fast is in great distress can't speak can't live long talked some this morning but some wild. Thursday morning was in great distress all night but is very easy now 8 o'clock a.m. just came from breakfast found Joseph's breaths very short for the first time 10 o'clock Joseph is gone died 10 minutes of 10 . . . 11 o'clock carried him down to the barn am going to the village to get a coffin 1 o'clock have got back with a coffin 2 o'clock just got back from the grave he is well

6 Maria A. Beal Widow Pension Claim 22694, Fold3.

7 Ibid.

The grave of Pvt. Joseph Beal, 33rd Massachusetts, in Soldiers' National Cemetery.
Ron Kirkwood

buried in a deacent coffin had everything done for him that could be done both by the Drs. and attendants started for home at 5 o'clock p.m."[8]

Beal died on July 30 at Spangler, one year to the day after he enrolled. He was 28 years old. He is now buried in the Massachusetts section of Soldiers' National Cemetery. "Beal was a good soldier, and faithfully performed all his duties," Lt. Walker wrote. Beal's death was reported in the August 29, 1863, *Boston Evening Transcript*, but for some reason his regiment didn't seem to know where he was, reporting him as absent until the January–February 1864 muster roll finally listed him as dead.[9]

Maria received a pension of $8 a month plus $2 for Augusta Jane until her 16th birthday in 1873. Maria died in 1883 at age 49. After missing Antietam, Fredericksburg, most of Chancellorsville, and much of the first day at Gettysburg, the 33rd Massachusetts went on to fight in numerous battles and suffer heavy losses, including as part of Sherman's campaign through the South. The regiment was mustered out on June 10, 1865. The next day the 33rd embarked on the train ride home through Washington, Baltimore, Philadelphia, and New York, "being received all day with cheers and waving of handkerchiefs," Underwood said. "Slept on the 'Plymouth Rock' . . . marched next morning through the streets of dear old Boston . . . had a public reception . . . with speeches . . . were furloughed home, and then the Thirty-Third Mass. Infantry Regiment passed into history."[10]

8 Maria A. Beal widow pension claim.

9 Maria A. Beal widow pension claim; Company Muster Roll, Fold3.

10 Maria A. Beal widow pension claim; Underwood, *The Three Years' Service of the Thirty-Third Mass.*, 299.

The north hay mow. *Ron Kirkwood*

One Final Note

The fact that Beal was carried "down to the barn" after his death adds to the likelihood that a portion of the Spanglers' barn was set aside as the hospital's "dead house" after enough wounded were shipped away to create room. Usually in a tent, a dead house is where bodies were prepared for burial and gathered to wait until workers had time to perform the burial. Effects to be sent home also were secured in a dead house.

The stable downstairs was occupied by the wounded for most of the hospital's time at Spangler, leaving one of the two semi-walled hay mows upstairs as likely spots for private and secure temporary placement of the dead. The barn's south hay mow is elevated and not private, so the north hay mow is the most likely spot for the XI Corps hospital dead house.

Spangler Farm Short Story

If George Spangler expected compensation for the heavy damage to his farm during and after the battle of Gettysburg then the United States government expected assurances of his loyalty, even requiring the Oath of Allegiance. This oath included solemnly swearing "that I will support, protect, and defend the

Constitution and Government of the United States . . . against all enemies, whether domestic or foreign; that I will bear true faith allegiance, and loyalty to said Constitution and Government."[11]

"I was loyal and my sympathies were full with the U.S.," Spangler wrote in the 1870s. Peter D. Swisher lived on his father Jacob Swisher's farm on the Taneytown Road in 1863 on land that is now mainly occupied by Artillery Ridge Campground & Horse Park, and he confirmed his next-door neighbor's loyalty: "Mr. Spangler was a truly loyal man," Peter Swisher said. Quartermaster Agent John T. Dahlgren was convinced: "Claimant was loyal," he said.[12]

Peter Swisher said he was on the Spanglers' farm "the first day of the battle, and, after the battle, nearly every day while the hospital was on the place" and he continued to support the Spanglers' claims for compensations: "Saw cattle and horses in the corn," he said, "don't know whether the cattle belonged to the army or not, but the horses did. . . . The timber was also considerably damaged by shells thrown by the rebels. . . . The farm was very badly cut up by troops marching over it, and by its being driven over a great deal."[13]

Big-ticket items in George Spangler's request for compensation from the federal government included $796.20 for 7,962 rails, $380 for loss of corn, $375 for damage to the house and barn, $300 for damage to land, and $200 for loss of 20 tons of meadow grass. Spangler also said he was owed $5 for one sheep. "My farm . . . was all [well] fenced before the occupation by the troops," Spangler said. "The rails charged for were burned, some by the soldiers and some for purposes of the Hospital." Quartermaster Agent Z. F. Nye said, "This farm was so close as to be almost considered a part of the battlefield" before turning down all but $90 of the Spanglers' $2,800 claim.[14]

George Spangler was loyal to the United States government just as Peter Swisher proved he was loyal to his neighbor, but Spangler's only receipt was for $90 worth of hay. In the end, the federal government was more interested in receipts than loyalty.

11 General Order No. 48, Quartermaster General's Office, Washington, D.C., M. C. Meigs, Brevet Major General, Quartermaster General, Nov 1, 1864.

12 Record Group 92, Quartermaster Claims From the Civil War, George Spangler Farm, Entry 812, Claim R-241, Box 275, NARA.

13 Ibid.

14 Ibid.

Chapter 16

Soldier Stories:
Southerners

"Employ white men in every place that you can and do a good service for your country and your race."

— The Caucasian *newspaper, Alexandria, Louisiana, August 15, 1874*

Forty-six Confederates are confirmed as having been treated at the XI Corps hospital on the George Spangler farm, though it's possible a few more were there who were missed by record keepers. The stories of many of those Confederates were told in *Too Much for Human Endurance.* Here are other soldier stories of note.

A FAMILY OF PROMINENCE AND TRAGEDY
Corporal Jonas S. Cloninger, 28th North Carolina, Company B, Age 22

Jonas Stanhope Cloninger was a boy of 12 when his brother, Laban, only 23 years old, died of typhoid in 1853. Jonas was 19 when he married Sarah Adderholt. At 20, he became the father of baby son Julius. At 21 years old, Jonas fought alongside older brothers Sidney and Wiley in Company B of the 28th North Carolina. He was 22 when both of his brothers were killed at Fredericksburg. And finally, still only 22, Jonas Cloninger lay at the George Spangler farm with an elbow wound sustained during Pickett's Charge. He had already experienced more major events and family tragedy than most people of far greater years.[1]

Jonas and his brothers, 1st Lt. Wiley Cloninger and Pvt. Sidney Cloninger, were members of the Gaston Invincibles company from the hill and mountain country of Gaston County, NC, near Charlotte. Wiley died at Fredericksburg when he was run through by a bayonet. His death was described poignantly by

---

1 Cloninger family history provided by Jonas' 2X great-grandson, Robert Russell "Rusty" Cloninger Jr.

Cpl. Jonas S. Cloninger

Robert Russell "Rusty" Cloninger Jr.

Brig. Gen. James Henry Lane in 1901: "It was here that 1st Lt. W. W. Cloninger, of Company B, as he lay at the field hospital . . . asked . . . why he had been neglected so long. When told that he was mortally wounded, and the Surgeons considered it their first duty to attend to those whose lives might be saved, he replied: 'If I must die, I will let you all see that I can die like a man.' Folding his arms across his breast, that hero, far away from his loved ones, lay under that tree . . . and, without a murmur, quietly awaited death." His brother Sidney lasted until January 9.[2]

Jonas Cloninger was taken prisoner at Hanover Court House in May 1862 and again at Fredericksburg that December, eventually released each time. He was back with the 28th in plenty of time for Gettysburg and survived the regiment's heavy fighting on Seminary Ridge on Day 1. On July 3, Cloninger and the rest of the 28th formed on the left of the Pickett's Charge line in Brig. Gen. James H. Lane's brigade, Maj. Gen. Isaac Trimble's division, and he was hit in the right elbow while reloading his rifle and taken prisoner for the third time in 14 months. He was taken to Spangler, where his wound was treated with water dressing. The five-foot-five-inch, light-haired, hazel-eyed Cloninger was transferred from the XI Corps hospital to Davids Island in New York Harbor on July 17 and was exchanged in September. He joined the Confederate Invalid Corps and retired from service in May 1864.[3]

Jonas is admired and honored by his descendants still today, who generation-by-generation have passed down photos, records, stories, and his family Bible that records the birth of his children. These materials now rest in the safe and attentive hands of Robert Russell "Rusty" Cloninger Jr. of Gastonia, North Carolina, Jonas' 2X great-grandson. Rusty provided the photo of his ancestor that is shown in this

2 Ibid.; Walter Clark, ed., *Histories of the Several Regiments and Battalions From North Carolina in the Great War 1861-'65* (Goldsboro, NC, no date), 475–476.

3 Fold3.

chapter and relates this story: "During the U.S. Civil War, Jonas was a barber. His grandson Fred Meynardie Cloninger [1893-1985], told his son Nard Brown Cloninger that he heard Jonas say there were so many lice that he would have to stop cutting hair periodically and wash the blood from his scissors in a mud hole." Jonas became a farmer after the war, and another family story relates how Jonas' sons Burt, Lee, and Meynardie held federal licenses in the 1890s to distill alcohol (moonshine), which was trucked to Charlotte and shipped to England.[4]

Jonas' family Bible reveals that he and Sarah had nine children, starting with Julius in 1861 and finishing with Loy in 1886. In a continuation of Jonas' history of family heartbreak, Julius died in 1883 at age 21 of typhoid. Jonas died of heart failure at age 84 in 1924.[5]

Today the Cloninger name is prominent throughout Gaston County, North Carolina.

A MONTH AT SPANGLER
Sergeant William W. Coe, 21st North Carolina, Company M, Age 23

William Coe was wounded in the lower third of both thighs during the 21st North Carolina's failed attempt to take East Cemetery Hill during the evening of July 2. He was taken down the Baltimore Pike to Spangler that night, where his right leg was amputated because of a compound fracture. And there he remained. Coe was there when Confederate Brig. Gen. Lewis Armistead arrived at Spangler on July 3, he was there when Armistead died two days later, and he was still there after most of his comrades had been shipped to East Coast prisons and prison hospitals by the middle of July.

After a month of suffering, the resident of the Greensboro area was taken to Camp Letterman on August 2 as the XI Corps hospital prepared to close. He was one of the last patients to be removed from Spangler. Coe developed chronic diarrhea at Letterman and died September 17. He was initially buried there and now rests in Oakwood Cemetery in Raleigh, North Carolina.[6]

Coe enlisted as a private in June 1861 and was promoted to sergeant in January 1863. He was likely treated in the Spanglers' wagon shed with other Confederates or in a tent or both.[7]

---

4 Cloninger family history.

5 Ibid.; *The Greensboro Daily News*, Oct. 2, 1924.

6 Fold3; John W. Busey and Travis W. Busey, *Confederate Casualties at Gettysburg, a Comprehensive Record*, Vol. 2 (Jefferson, NC, 2017), 969.

7 Fold3.

NORTHERN AT HEART
Corporal Theophilus Judd, 2nd Georgia Battalion, Company C, Age 28

Theophilus Judd's parents had been born in Connecticut, and he was born and raised there, too. But he relocated to Macon, Georgia, in the mid-1850s, purchased property, and worked as a carpenter. He enlisted in the 2nd Georgia Battalion as a private but was promoted to corporal by the time of Gettysburg.[8]

So here was this Northern man on July 2, 1863, charging across the Emmitsburg Road, storming the Codori farm, and breaking through the Union line on Cemetery Ridge near the Copse of Trees one day before many thousands more of his comrades repeated that effort in the much more famous charge of July 3. As was common in the battle of Gettysburg, the Confederates couldn't hold the ground they took on July 2. So when Judd was hit in the right shoulder in this advanced position and the Confederates fell back, he found himself wounded behind the Army of the Potomac line. The Northerners picked him up and got him to the nearby XI Corps hospital on July 2.

Though wounded, the five-foot-eight-inch, sandy-haired Judd probably felt relieved to be in Union hands and back on Northern ground, because he didn't wait long to make his intentions clear. He healed and rested at Spangler for almost three weeks before being transferred to Baltimore on July 21. There, he took the Oath of Allegiance in August. On September 1, he was a free man.[9]

His Confederate Compiled Military Service Record says he "Was born in Connecticut and has always been a Union man, was living in Georgia about five years before the war broke out, and did belong to a company of militia formed in time of peace. When the war broke out he was compelled to enlist with said Co. for 9 months and before that time was expired he was conscripted and compelled to remain in the rebel service. He will rather lose his property in Macon City, Ga than fight any longer against his country. Wishes to remain in Connecticut where his mother and other relatives are living."[10]

And that's what he did. He headed home to Connecticut. This was much easier for him than most Confederates because his family was north of the Mason-Dixon Line and not in danger of retribution in the South. He married wife Addie in August 1864 less than a year after his release, though Addie died in 1871 at age

8 Fold3.

9 Ibid.

10 Ibid.

26. Judd worked as a carpenter and stair builder and lived the rest of his life in the North, dying at age 75 in 1910. He was survived by four daughters.[11]

"SHOT THROUGH THE LEG"
Corporal James R. Kent, 11th Virginia, Company G, Age 24 or 25

James Kent began Pickett's Charge on the farm of George Spangler's half brother Henry Spangler west of the Emmitsburg Road. He reached and crossed the road with Kemper's brigade, only to be greeted by some of the deadliest fire of the Civil War. Many in that brigade of Pickett's division struggled through the storm of artillery and infantry fire to the wall, though it's not known how far Kent got. At some point he gave up and turned around, re-crossed the road heading west, and was hit in the upper third of his left leg during his retreat.

Captain John Holmes Smith of the 11th was with Kent when he was hit. "Sergeant James R. Kent, of my company, suddenly plunged forward in a ditch, and I asked of him: 'How are you hurt, Kent?' for I knew he was hit. He answered: 'Shot through the leg.' . . . Kent's leg had been fractured—the small bone—and he was captured."[12]

As were so many after Pickett's Charge, Kent was picked up by Union troops and transported to George Spangler's farm, the closest remaining major Army of the Potomac hospital to the line in the late afternoon of July 3. XI Corps surgeons classified the injury a flesh wound and treated Kent with water dressing. Kent, a farmer before the war, was deemed well enough to travel and didn't stay long at Spangler, arriving at Fort Delaware on July 7 on the day the railroad was repaired enough to make runs from Gettysburg. He was transferred to a Chester, Pennsylvania, hospital on July 19, where he was exchanged in August. He was promoted to sergeant in September and survived the war.[13]

THE LADIES' MAN/WHITE SUPREMACIST LEADER
First Lieutenant William C. McGimsey, 8th Louisiana, Company A, Age 23 or 24

At least one member of the Creole Guards company had the reputation as a bit of a ladies' man prior to Gettysburg. William McGimsey's pursuit of young Baton

11 Ancestry.com; *The Bridgeport Times and Evening Farmer*, May 12, 1910.

12 Gregory A. Coco Collection, Gettysburg Field Hospital Research #2, Personal Accounts, Box B-70, Folder: Rawley Martin-Col. 53rd Virginia Inf. Letter Aug. 11, 1897, GNMP.

13 Fold3.

Rouge socialite Sarah Morgan gets frequent mention in her diary,[14] and he got in trouble with his superiors in York a couple days before Gettysburg for similar efforts, as described by fellow 1st Lt. Joseph Warren Jackson of the 8th in a letter to his brother:

> June 29th—McGimsey and self took a french leave and went into town, had lots of fun, saw some pretty girls—and amused ourselves extensively until 10 P.M.—got back to camp that night & found that we would have to mch [march] before day—York is a place of about 15,000 inhabitants and has some magnificent buildings in it, the streets are very regular & well paved—The people are mostly Dutch [German] and were very friendly—Confederate money was taken *at par* and I shall ever remember York with pleasure.[15]

8th Louisiana Col. Trevanion D. Lewis placed McGimsey and Jackson under arrest for their unauthorized rendezvous with the ladies, so they rode from York to Heidlersburg northeast of Gettysburg on the 30th in an ambulance. But they were returned to the regiment in time for the battle, including their assault on East Cemetery Hill on the night of July 2 when McGimsey was shot through the lung. The fighting was so intense and the Army of the Potomac's defensive position on top of the hill so strong that Jackson said, "I felt as if my doom was sealed." Jackson, though, came out unscathed while McGimsey, like so many other Confederates that night, was put in an XI Corps ambulance and taken to the convenient and ever-more crowded Spangler hospital.[16]

McGimsey's presence at Spangler was not recorded by XI Corps surgeons but rather by a chaplain in the July 14 *Philadelphia Inquirer* who was visiting the hospital. The chaplain also reported Sgt. J. P. Murrell of the 8th Louisiana at Spangler with a lung wound. As was the norm at Spangler, the two Louisiana men were either treated in the Spanglers' wagon shed or a tent.

McGimsey was transferred from Spangler to Fort McHenry on July 12 and then to Fort Delaware on July 14 and to Johnson's Island in Lake Erie near Sandusky, Ohio, on July 29. He was exchanged in March 1865 and went on to become prominent in Louisiana politics after the war. He was appointed major of militia for East Baton Rouge in November 1865, elected a state fair officer in 1867, became an attorney in Alexandria, appointed to the Parish Executive Committee

14 Charles East, ed., *Sarah Morgan: The Civil War Diary of a Southern Woman* (New York, 1991).

15 Merl E. Reed, ed., "The Gettysburg Campaign—A Louisiana Lieutenant's Eye-Witness Account," in *Pennsylvania History: A Journal of Mid-Atlantic Studies 30*, no. 2 (1963): 187-188.

16 Ibid, 189.

The Confederate scabbard hanging in the middle of this photo was found on the George Spangler farm. Its top end is flattened, which could indicate it was pounded into the ground, possibly as a grave marker. *David Malgee, from his collection*

of the White Man's Party, and served as mayor of Alexandria in 1883 and 1884.[17]

The White Man's Party of which McGimsey was a leader was formed in August 1874 as a Southern response to the Republican Party's support of civil and political rights for blacks. The White Man's Party was willing to use lethal violence if necessary in its pursuit of white supremacy. The party called on white people to "stand by your race," according to *The Caucasian* newspaper of Alexandria. The newspaper further stated "Never before were we so thoroughly convinced that it is the duty of the white people of Rapides [parish], and the whole state, to give support and employment to all laboring white people over negroes, as we are now." The party's racism linked economic, cultural, and political benefits, claiming "A white mechanic is by far the most intelligent, and is in the 'long run' the cheapest, besides if they should cost a few dollars more, you get it back in keeping this class in the country, who will help you reduce taxes and protect your homes and property against negro domination and confiscation. Employ white men in every place that you can and do a good service for your country and your race."[18]

The Caucasian was a leading anti-Black voice that was founded in 1874 by George Waters Stafford, who like McGimsey was a first lieutenant in the 8th Louisiana and served with him throughout the war, including Gettysburg. McGimsey received favorable coverage in the newspaper and advertised in it, though *The Caucasian* went out of business after only a year. Stafford continued to champion White supremacy: He was a Democrat who served in the Louisiana state legislature and also commanded a mob of Ku Klux Klansmen who killed

---

17 Fold3; *Baton Rouge Tri-Weekly Gazette and Comet*, Nov. 14, 1865, and Feb. 2, 1867; *The Caucasian*, Aug. 15, 1874; *The Louisiana Democrat*, Jan. 8, 1885.

18 *The Caucasian*, Aug. 15, 1874.

up to 150 blacks in the Colfax massacre in Grant Parish north of New Orleans in 1873. Stafford and a few others were charged but a mistrial was declared and all went free.[19]

The 1880 U.S. census shows the 41-year-old McGimsey living with 30-year-old wife Mary, two stepdaughters, a son, and daughter in Alexandria. The 1900 census has the 60-year-old McGimsey living with 40-year-old second wife Lizzie and four daughters and a son in New Orleans. He died in 1912 at age 72.[20]

Confederate Final Notes

Captain John Scott Cochran, Company D, 5th Florida, was shot either in the lungs and shoulder or left thigh or perhaps all three depending on the source. He was one of the last men to be moved from Spangler to Camp Letterman in early August, then on November 10 was moved to West's Building in Baltimore, where he died of his wounds later that month.[21]

Third Lieutenant Charles Ellmer, Company G, 57th North Carolina, had his left eye destroyed by a gunshot. He was transferred from Spangler to Fort McHenry in Baltimore on July 12 and then to Fort Delaware two days later. He was exchanged in February 1865.[22]

Private George Hearn, Company G, 9th Georgia, was admitted to the Spangler hospital on July 2 with a compound fracture of the left side of his face after being hit by a Minie ball that entered his jaw and passed into his shoulder, fracturing the clavicle. He was transferred from Spangler to a Baltimore hospital on July 25. He was paroled in September and deserted in November.[23]

Second Lieutenant James Ingram, Company H, 20th North Carolina, was promoted from private to 1st sergeant to 2nd lieutenant and was a regular casualty throughout the Civil War but he kept coming back for more. He was wounded at Malvern Hill July 1, 1862, captured at Sharpsburg in September 1862, wounded at Gettysburg in July 1863 and taken to Spangler, wounded in May 1864, and captured at Third Winchester in September 1864. The six-foot, brown-eyed Ingram suffered a flesh wound of the back at Gettysburg and was treated with water

19 www.chroniclingamerica.loc.gov/lccn/sn86053765/, accessed Aug. 27, 2023; Edward Ball, *Life of a Klansman: A Family History in White Supremacy* (New York, 2020).

20 Ancestry.com.

21 *Philadelphia Inquirer*, July 14, 1863; Fold3.

22 Fold3.

23 Ibid.

dressing at the XI Corps hospital. He took the Oath of Allegiance to the United States in June 1865.[24]

First Sergeant John F. Puckett, Company E, 7th Tennessee, was wounded in the arm during Pickett's Charge. He was taken to Spangler, where he remained a couple weeks for treatment of a gunshot fracture of his upper left arm and injured nerves, a severe wound that normally required an amputation, but instead one medical record unsympathetically called it a "flesh wound." The five-foot-eleven-inch, blue-eyed farmer left Spangler and was received at De Camp General Hospital on Davids Island in New York City between July 17 and July 24. He was in a Petersburg hospital that November, by which time the bullet's entry point had healed but his arm remained paralyzed and the exit wound still discharged. Another medical record said his limb was "entirely useless." From Petersburg the litany of hospital stops included Richmond, Williamsburg, Petersburg again, and Kittrell's Springs, North Carolina, until his retirement from the military in February 1865. He died in 1873 at age 39.[25]

Spangler Farm Short Story

By Barbara J. Finfrock, Immediate Past Chair, Gettysburg Foundation

In 2009, a "Scenic and Preservation Easement" was placed on the George Spangler farm and property in perpetuity stipulating that only the Gettysburg Foundation will occupy the property unless it violates any of the clauses contained therein. The federal government paid the Foundation $750,000 and drafted the easement language, based on the specific historic buildings on the property in 2009. These buildings were required to be restored as closely as possible to their appearance in 1863 and maintained accordingly. In addition, all non-historic structures were to be removed. The easement is an important preservation tool that gives the National Park Service the power of rejection or approval on alterations such as digging on the property as well as allowing NPS to inspect the Foundation's care of the farm.

The Foundation board wanted to ensure the farm would not be sold at some future time and passed a resolution to that effect. The entire twenty-page document is a matter of public record.

Barbara J. Finfrock is a native of Indiana and holds a B.S. in English from Purdue and an M.A. in English from Old Dominion. She served on the Friends of Gettysburg

24 Ibid.; Busey and Busey, *Confederate Casualties at Gettysburg*, 956.

25 Fold3.

Board from 1995–2001, was Executive Vice Chair 1997–99, and was Chair of the Board 1999–2001. She was re-elected to the Board in 2002 and served as Vice Chair of Development. In 2003, Finfrock was elected to her second term as Chair of the Board. When the Friends of Gettysburg merged with the Museum Foundation in 2006, Finfrock became the Founding Vice Chair of the new Gettysburg Foundation. From 2020–2024 she has served as Co-Chair of the Gettysburg Foundation. She continues to serve on the Gettysburg Foundation Board of Directors as Immediate Past Chair and is chair of the Membership Committee.

Chapter 17

Soldier Stories: Northerners

"The days after a battle are a thousand times worse than the day of the battle."
— *5th New Hampshire Assistant Surgeon William Child*

ONE MAN, 8 WOUNDS
Corporal James Brownlee, 134th New York, Company G, Age 21

Most of what existed when three Northern regiments were vastly outnumbered, smothered, and slaughtered from three directions at John Kuhn's Brickyard on July 1, 1863, is gone now, making it far more difficult than elsewhere on the battlefield to imagine the horror that happened there. The kilns have disappeared, as have the barn and brickyard, replaced by houses, garages, parking lots, and businesses. Only the Kuhns' brick house remains, sitting precisely where it did on North Stratton Street during the battle, still clasping a Northern artillery shell in its south wall. Most of the rest of the site has been lost to modern development.

Today, there's a patch of grass similar in size to an average suburban yard near where the barn and kilns once stood. Three regimental monuments and a couple of signs occupy the grass and attempt to tell the story of what happened there, but it's difficult to picture amid so much development. What saves this area from being a complete historic wipeout is author, artist, and historian Mark Dunkelman's detailed and beautiful mural on the wall of a business at the edge of the grass and behind the monuments. Thanks to Dunkelman, we get an idea of the mayhem that day, the closeness of the fighting, and what the ground could have looked like. Thanks to Dunkelman, we get an idea of what 21-year-old Cpl. James Brownlee of the 134th New York saw as Confederates closed in and applied a vice to the Union troops. And thanks to Dunkelman, we get the best glimpse possible of how Brownlee could have been shot eight times in a matter of minutes at this location.

Not many people can survive being shot eight times, but Brownlee did. The native of Ireland was treated in a house before being transferred to Spangler after the battle. These were his wounds upon his arrival at the XI Corps hospital: Three buckshot traveled through his bladder. Urine freely escaped from these wounds at Spangler. Small pieces of bone discharged from the posterior wounds; one Minie ball hit his sternum and passed downward and outward, underneath the second, third, and fourth ribs, perforated the upper lobe of his right lung, and emerged between the fourth and fifth ribs; one ball lodged in his right thigh; another ball entered his left thigh and passed nearly through; he was hit superficially in the pelvis by a nearly spent ball, which he removed on the battlefield; he was struck in his knapsack by an 18-inch piece of railroad iron from a Confederate artillery piece and knocked down.

The five-foot-eight-inch, blue-eyed, dark-haired Brownlee was cared for by a Confederate surgeon before his arrival at Spangler. He was transferred from Spangler to Camp Letterman on August 6 and then to multiple hospitals after that until the end of the war, and it was the lung wound that troubled him the most for the rest of his life. The Confederate surgeon treated his sternum and lung wound with lint, and he breathed with difficulty whenever it was removed. He was unable to speak at Spangler. One doctor said, "The right lung is almost totally useless." Another said, "The right lung admits air freely. . . . When he stands erect his right shoulder falls considerably." Another said 4 ounces of pus discharged from his chest wound each day.

His pension application reveals his poor health after the war: Only a small portion of the upper part of the lung worked, the heart was displaced considerably to the right side, he leaned markedly to the right while walking, and he was incapacitated by any serious exertion.[1] One treating doctor observed, "In order to maintain a condition of normal health, it is of all things necessary to be supplied with a normal amount of Oxygen, which in this case was impossible. . . . It is shown that after two years residence in hospitals, he was discharged in a crippled, pulmonary condition, one lung being entirely incapacitated and the other, by overwork, became inelastic and dilated." He weighed a frightening 87 pounds upon his discharge in 1865, and he was advised by a surgeon to "go into the country and handle cattle and meat as a health giving occupation." Brownlee followed the advice, but it was reported in his pension application that "frequently the soldier was unable to walk any distance without resting at frequent intervals and that on numerous occasions he was able to follow his occupation of meat peddler with great difficulty—this especially was noticeable during damp cold weather

1 *The Medical and Surgical History of the War of the Rebellion (1861-65)*, Vol. II, Part 1, 488.

Cpl. James Brownlee

Haines & Wickes, Albany, NY

when the air was charged with moisture. On many such occasions the affiant has seen the soldier cling to the side of his meat wagon for several minutes."[2] Basically, "James Brownlee was shot to pieces at Gettysburg," a pension witness said.[3]

Coughing spells were prolonged, frequent, and crippling so Brownlee left his job as a butcher and went into the less-demanding work of clothing dealer. Through it all, and despite his dangerous and poor health, he married and raised a family. One son, Harris, became a doctor and treated his father. Physically weak he might have been, but his mental toughness and resolute attitude had clearly survived the Brickyard.

After sacrificing so much of his health for the United States, Brownlee died of a stroke at age 62 in 1904 in Schoharie County, New York, just west of Albany. Many doctors attributed his death to his Civil War wounds, but the Pension Bureau disagreed and denied his widow, Mary, a pension.[4]

"THE PHYSICAL PAIN IS NOT THE GREATEST PAIN"
Assistant Surgeon William Child, 5th New Hampshire, Age 29

The Granite Schoolhouse assistant surgeon wrote an emotional letter to his wife, Carrie, from Sharpsburg in September 1862. "The days after a battle are a thousand times worse than the day of the battle," he wrote,

> and the physical pain is not the greatest pain suffered. How awful it is—you have nor can have until you see it any idea of affairs after a battle. The dead appear sickening but they suffer no pain. But the poor wounded mutilated soldiers that yet have life and

2 James Brownlee Invalid Pension Claim 72303, NARA.

3 Ibid.

4 Mary Brownlee Widow Pension Claim 645033, NARA.

sensation make a most horrid picture. I pray God may stop such infernal work—though perhaps he has sent it upon us for our sins. Great indeed must have been our sins if such is our punishment.[5]

Those sentiments grew stronger after Gettysburg, the next great battle in which Child served, with the further devastation of the 5th New Hampshire and the death of his friend Col. Edward E. Cross.

On July 5, 1863, two days after watching his beloved colonel die on Spangler land, Dr. Child wrote home about his time at the Granite Schoolhouse hospital. He described helping with triage and early care on the battlefield on July 2, and the scene after the battle: "I have got through this fight unharmed but I never was under such terrific shelling. . . . I have been all over the field today. I will not attempt to describe the horrors of a battle field. It has been one of the severest of the war. Dead men and horses cover the field three miles long and one mile wide. The stench is awful."[6] Dr. Child worked for a month after the battle at the II Corps division hospitals.[7] He was promoted to regimental surgeon in 1864 and was division surgeon at the close of the war. He had seen much, but more was to come.

The Dartmouth Medical School graduate was in attendance at Ford's Theatre in Washington, D.C., and witnessed the assassination of President Abraham Lincoln on April 14, 1865. He wrote to wife Carrie: "My Dear Wife: Wild dreams and real facts are but brothers. This night I have seen the murder of the President of the United States. Early in the evening I went to Fords Theater. After a little time the President entered—was greeted with cheers. The play went on for about an hour. Just at the close of an interesting scene a sharp quick report of a pistol was heard and instantly a man jumped from the box in which was the President, to the stage—and rushing across the stage made his escape. This I saw and heard. I was in the theatre—and sat opposite the President's box. The assassin exclaimed as he leaped 'Sic Semper Tyrannis'—'Thus always to tyrants.'

"I never saw such a wild scene as followed! I have no words to describe it. . . . The city is now wild with excitement. The affair occurred only an hour since. Are we living in the days of the French Revolution? Will peace ever come again to our dear land? Are we to rush on to wild ruin? It seems all a dream—a wild dream. I cannot realize it though I know I saw only an hour since."[8]

---

5 Merrill C. Sawyer, Betty Sawyer, and Timothy C. Sawyer, trans., *Letters From a Civil War Surgeon: Dr. William Child of the Fifth New Hampshire Volunteers* (Solon, ME, 2001), 34.

6 Ibid., 138.

7 Granville Priest, *History of the New Hampshire Surgeons in the War of the Rebellion* (1906), 67.

8 Sawyer et al., *Letters From a Civil War Surgeon*, 342.

Dr. Child added the following in another letter one day later: "The President is dead. . . . It is supposed that an actor by the name Booth was the assassin. I could not sleep last night. The wild scene of last night will never be forgotten by me. I shall remember the fiendlike expression of the assassin's face."[9]

Dr. Child resumed his medical practice in his hometown of Bath after the war, was twice elected to New Hampshire's legislature, and served as anniversary chairman and president of the New Hampshire State Medical Society. He also served as medical director, Department of New Hampshire, Grand Army of the Republic. He died in 1918 at age 84.[10]

A LONG AND DIFFICULT LIFE
Private Orville O. Davenport, 157th New York, Company E, Age 22

The five-foot-six-and-a-half inch seminary student was in the middle of such terrible fire north of town on July 1 that he was hit six times: twice in the right leg, including one shot that broke a bone beneath the knee, twice in the back, including one ball that was never removed; and twice in the right forearm. Remarkably, and despite the fast-charging Confederates, the shot-up Davenport was taken to Spangler that day, where the typically understated XI Corps doctors officially recorded his wounds as in the mid-3rd right leg and right forearm, requiring a water dressing. Davenport was transferred from Spangler to a New York City hospital on July 22 and discharged from the army that December.[11]

He lived to age 82 despite the ravaging of his body at Gettysburg, but not easily. Those wounds remained with him every day for the rest of his life. He is listed as a farmer in each census after the war, but he described in his pension applications how he couldn't work much. He wrote in 1902: "I have carried one [ball] in my left side under pelvis bone ever since and it most kills me every day with pain. I have to be under the influence of morphine all the time so I can get about. . . . I would rather have lost my leg or arm than to suffer the severe, persistent pain." Then in 1919 when his request for an increase in pension was rejected, he wrote: "I do not know what it is to be without severe pain, all of the time. . . . The government has forgotten that at Gettysburgh we saved the Nation's

---

9 Ibid.

10 Child, *A History of the Fifth Regiment, New Hampshire Volunteers, in the American Civil War, 1861-1865*, 329.

11 Orville O. Davenport Invalid Pension Claim 29870, NARA; Davenport CMR, Carded Medical Records Volunteers, Mexican, and Civil Wars, 1846-1865, RG 94 Records of the Adjutant General's Office, Entry 534, 157 New York Butterworts, W. to Gartsee, J., NARA.

Capitol as well as several other citys. Had the Army of the Potomac failed to stop Lees Invasion, then and there all would have been lost."

Finally the bureau agreed to increase his pension. "I . . . want to express my sincere Gratitude to you," he responded, "as in these times of high prices, it will help to pay for Doctors Bills, and I have to call on one every little while, as some new pains attack me, as last month I had an attack of Rheumatism in my Broken leg, that Everlasting Pain in my side, was not enough to suffer, as soon as I get on my feet in the morning after a few hours fairly Comfortable in Bed, my Pain is more Severe and increases the more I move about. Then all of a sudden like a fit almost I groan and suffer for an hour or more." One imagines Davenport's melancholy as he concluded "I often wonder how old will be the last one of the G.A.R. as I have been one of them for many years. If there should be any Laws Passed I want you to remember that I am always Gratefull for anything you can do for me. Again I thank you, my eyes Blur so I can hardly see and at times I stagger about the room. My eyes & hearing are very bad."[17]

Davenport married wife Alida on Christmas Day, 1866. She died in 1907. The 1910 U.S. census and 1915 New York state census show Davenport's daughter Mary living with him, so she very likely was his caretaker until his death in 1923.[13]

THE YOUNGEST WOUNDED SOLDIER AT SPANGLER?
Private Cyrus Guffin, 134th New York, Company C, Age 16

Teenager Cyrus Guffin probably wanted to be a soldier like his big brother Otis. The elder Guffin served five months with the 7th New York Cavalry in 1861-62 before the unit was mustered out without seeing any fighting, so the then 20-year-old Otis re-upped in August 1862, this time joining the 134th New York Infantry. For a youngster like Cyrus, war brought excitement, honor, heroism, and a chance to fight on the side of good. Or, sometimes, you just wanted off the farm. So 16-year-old Cyrus wanted in.

The enlistment age for both armies in the Civil War was 18, but they each had boys far younger than that in the fighting. A boy who looked older could easily get himself in because of the lack of ID cards in the 1860s. So could someone with parental permission, and sometimes the potential young soldier would just lie and the armies would look the other way and welcome the eager kid because of the need for warm bodies.

12 Davenport pension claim, NARA.

13 https://bit.ly/42KPaCZ, accessed Feb. 17, 2024; Ancestry.com.

Cyrus Guffin was a good example of that. His muster roll and other army papers say he was 18 when he enlisted in 1862, but death records and federal and state census records clearly show he was 16 at his enlistment and he was still 16 when he arrived in Gettysburg with the 134th on July 1, 1863.

Cyrus was born in Carlisle, New York, just west of Albany. He was a five-foot-six-inch, blue-eyed farmer. Other records show him to be one of at least eight children. Both Cyrus and Otis were mustered in to the 134th New York as privates on September 22, 1862, but the elder Otis received a promotion to corporal that same day. His character and leadership must have been readily apparent, because Otis shot up the ranks to captain by the time he arrived at Gettysburg.[14]

Both Guffin boys were surviving the war unscathed until the 134th rushed from Cemetery Hill to the Brickyard with the 154th New York and 27th Pennsylvania and they were both hit. Cyrus was shot in the left leg and Otis in the left shoulder. Captain Perry E. McMaster of the 134th found Cyrus "in the door of a house in the town looking anxiously for an officer of the U.S.A." after the Confederates left downtown Gettysburg on July 4. "I thereupon picked up two damaged rifles removed the barrels, making two splendid crutches called a soldier and sent him hobbling as best he might to the Hospital." Once at Spangler, Cyrus was treated with water dressing.[15]

At age 16 Cyrus Guffin is the youngest soldier known to be treated at Spangler. If he was still at Spangler on July 9 as seems likely, then he turned 17 on George Spangler's farm. It's probable that Otis also eventually went to Spangler, but there's no record of it. Sergeant William Howe of the 134th saw the wounded Otis on the battlefield and later wrote that he "will probably die," but happily for their parents back home in New York both Otis and Cyrus survived.[16]

Cyrus was transferred from Spangler to hospitals in Harrisburg and York, served in the Veteran Reserve Corps, and later returned to York as commander of the Patapsco Guards militia unit. Interestingly, Otis also lied about his age, or was misunderstood when enlisting in the 7th New York Cavalry in 1861, being listed on government papers as 22 when in fact he was 19. He was accurately recorded as 20 the following year when joining the 134th. Otis was assigned to command Fort Mifflin near Philadelphia while still rehabbing his wound in 1864 and eventually returned to the 134th. Despite their muddled ages, this much is clear: Both Guffin

14 Cyrus Guffin, New York Civil War Muster Roll Abstract, Fold3.

15 Cyrus Guffin Invalid Pension Claim 141710, NARA. Cyrus is called both Guffin and Griffin throughout his pension file.

16 https://on.ny.gov/3OMSnw7, accessed Feb. 17, 2024.

boys displayed strong leadership skills that brought promotion after promotion as they provided service of great value to their nation.[17]

Cyrus married in 1869. He complained in later years "[m]y leg swells . . . and is numb. I have some trouble with my heart. My bowels are weak result of chronic diarrhea. I am troubled with bleeding, itching piles. I can do but little manual labor." A doctor said Guffin "can scarcely walk." [18] Cyrus Guffin died in 1898.[19]

YES, YOU REALLY NEED AN AMPUTATION
Private Reuben Hess, 153rd Pennsylvania, Company G, Age 30

A Minie ball crashed into Reuben Hess' left leg just above the knee in the XI Corps First Division's tough but eventually hopeless fight north of town on July 1. He was still lying there after the battle. Hess, five feet eight inches tall and 30 years old at Gettysburg, testified in 1899: "I was shot and taken prisoner on the first day of the fight at Gettysburg and lay four days in the hot sun. There are not many that could live after being shot and laying four days and nights in the hot sun and the blood slowly running away & now you can use your own judgment about that."[20]

Hess' boast about his survival was no bit of idle vanity, given the facts of Civil War medicine: The death rate doubled when an amputation was delayed more than 48 hours after a soldier was wounded because by that time blood poisoning, bone infection, or gangrene had often set in. And here was Hess arriving at Spangler on July 4 and still no amputation well after that 48-hour window. In fact, though he was now out of the fight and lying in a tent in a Spangler field, he was still fighting the idea of an amputation. His plan was to keep the leg.[21]

"The ball went straight through, carrying the bone away with it, or splitting the bone as it crashed through it," Pvt. Stryker A. Wallace of the 153rd Pennsylvania

---

17 George H. Warner, *Military Records of Schoharie County Veterans of Four Wars* (Albany, NY, 1891), 292; Otis Guffin, New York Civil War Muster Roll Abstract, Fold3.

18 Cyrus Guffin pension claim, NARA.

19 Because of the confusion often caused by Civil War cursive writing, the Guffins were called Griffin on many official documents and Cyrus was listed as Cyrus Griffin in the wounded list of *Too Much for Human Endurance.* Also, Otis signed a document later in the war stating he was the soldier known as Charles O. Griffin in the 7th New York Cavalry in 1861-62. And finally, Pvt. James Guffin of Company G of the 134th New York was treated with water dressing at Spangler for a flesh wound on the right side of his chest. James was not a sibling of Otis and Cyrus, but they all grew up in the same area of New York and very likely were related, meaning possible cousins Cyrus and James were treated at Spangler at the same time. James Guffin was killed at Kennesaw Mountain, GA, in June 1864; Otis Guffin, New York Civil War Muster Roll Abstract, Fold3; James Guffin, New York Civil War Muster Roll Abstract, Fold3.

20 Reuben Hess Invalid Pension Claim 26538, NARA.

21 National Museum of Civil War Medicine, Frederick, MD.

recalled after the war. "He was lying in a little tent opposite and apparently unconcerned, and without pain. When I found him I said, 'Well, you must go to the . . . operating table, to have your wound examined.' We had hoped the ball had gone around the bone, but it looked bad. The holes were opposite each other.

"He was afraid to go to the table for fear the surgeon would take off his leg, perhaps unnecessarily, so he wanted me to speak to the surgeon about it," Wallace said. "I cheerfully assented to do so. The doctor gave me the most hearty assurance that he would do no wrong to the patient. After placing the man under chloroform he ran his little finger into the wound and taking a pair of pincers from his vest pocket he pulled out a splintered bone several inches long, showing that the bone was badly fractured, and in fact carried clear away. I took a long piece of the bone and showed it to Mr. Hess to show him that the amputation of the limb was an absolute necessity. He seemed to be satisfied."[22]

The amputation took place in front of George Spangler's barn on July 5, along with July 4 one of the busiest and most crowded days at the hospital. One hundred XI Corps ambulances scoured the battlefield and brought in hundreds of men like Hess who had been wounded and left behind during the July 1 Confederate runover of the XI Corps. The Spangler amputation undoubtedly saved Hess' life and allowed him to return to his home north of Easton to his wife of four years Christiana and 1-year-old daughter Nettie. Hess was a laborer before the war, but he wore an artificial leg thereafter and it's not known if or how much he was able to work. It's possible that he and his family survived as best they could on his invalid pension, which started at $8 a month in 1863 then increased to $15 in 1866, $18 in 1872, $24 in 1874, $30 in 1883, $36 in 1886, and $46 in 1903.[23]

Though a Spangler surgeon saved Hess' life, the amputation brought unforgiving health difficulties later. Hess complained in 1881 that his stump was tender, congested, not fully healed, and opened frequently. Dr. B. F. Dilliard said in 1896: "I have been Mr. Reuben Hess' family physician for the last thirteen years. And during this period [he has had] various ailments which I considered were caused indirectly from the amputated stump. His present condition is such that he is confined to his house and has to depend a great deal on other people to assist him in dressing. And frequently he is confined to his bed and has to be nursed as a child."[24]

Dr. Dilliard followed up in 1899: "During the last three years he had frequent attacks of cerebral congestion in periods he is quite demented and helpless that it

22 Kiefer, *History of the One Hundred and Fifty-Third Regiment Pennsylvania Volunteers Infantry*, 242.

23 Hess pension claim, NARA.

24 Ibid.

requires a person to watch him and undress him. I made a physical examination yesterday and found considerable abrasions and atrophy of stump of left thigh and it requires large doses of anodynes to relieve him of pain. Also discovered that he has colitis [chronic digestive disease]."[25]

Hess amplified the description of his miseries. "The doctors all say that the laying on the battlefield so long and the amputation of my leg are the cause of my spells and sickness," he explained. "The spells that I get are bad and whenever I get them they last from 12 to 18 hours. . . . The blood rushes to my brain and I don't know nothing from 12 to 18 hours and I have to have somebody to take care of me and pay them." Dr. Dilliard said in 1900 that those spells were now lasting as long as two weeks, "during which time [Hess] is not responsible for his conduct; attempts to disrobe himself in public." Hess also developed chronic diarrhea.[26]

Hess' full-time caregiver and personal attendant starting in 1894 was John B. Parsons, his son-in-law and husband of Nettie, the 1-year-old daughter who was at home when Hess was at Spangler in 1863. Hess died at age 71 in 1904 and is buried with Christiana in East Bangor Cemetery in East Bangor, Pennsylvania.[27]

"PUT OUR TRUST IN THE LORD AND ALL SHALL BE WELL"
Private Henry A. Miller, 153rd Pennsylvania, Company B, Age 25

The Bethlehem bricklayer survived the rout at Chancellorsville unscathed in early May and did so again north of Gettysburg on July 1. But his luck ran out the following day on East Cemetery Hill. A gun shot hit Pvt. Henry Miller in the thigh, shattering the bone and assuring his death. Miller asked for a blanket after his wounding, but he was quickly loaded into an ambulance and taken to Spangler before one could be provided. He died at Spangler three days later.[28]

Miller was hopeful before Gettysburg as he neared the end of the 153rd Pennsylvania's 9-month enlistment. His older brother, Theodore, was with him in Company B, and he, too, was alive and well, as Henry reported to his parents in a letter dated May 25: "Health is a great blessing which we enjoy in this troublesome world. Let us lift our eyes to heaven and give God the praise. We are all well at present. We know not exactly when our regiment will get home," he added. "I hope and pray that the Lord will spare us to return. Let us put our trust in the Lord and all shall be well." Drawing a moral lesson from his experience, he closed with

25 Ibid.

26 Ibid.

27 Ibid.; U.S. Veterans Burial Cards, Pennsylvania, 1777–2012, Reuben Hess.

28 Kiefer, *History of the One Hundred and Fifty-Third Regiment Pennsylvania Volunteers Infantry*, 170.

the observation that "[t]his experience will teach many a man to lead a different life. . . . I would be very glad to get home and get to work. I am tired of this mode of life. Theodore and I unite in love to you all."[29]

Henry was buried in the Spanglers' orchard. "This afternoon I walked out to the hospital to see where he is buried and to ascertain the particulars about his death," a comrade in the 153rd wrote on July 7. "I found his grave in a field at a stone wall marked by a board on which was written: 'Henry A. Miller, Company B, 153rd Penna. Volunteers.' I wrote my name together with a few lines on the board with a pencil. I then went to Dr. [James] Armstrong and ascertained the following particulars. As nearly as the surgeon could inform me he was shot on the first day. . . . He was shot in the thigh, the ball having shattered the bone and flesh so that the wound was mortal. The surgeon gave me a pocketbook which contained twenty cents, also a letter found on his person after death."[30]

Henry was removed from near that Spangler stone wall not long after his death—likely by his parents or another family member—for re-burial elsewhere. Brother Theodore survived the war and was mustered out with the rest of the regiment in late July.

A FINGER AMPUTATION AT SPANGLER
Private Roland E. Perry, 75th Ohio, Company B, Age 19
By James P. Fielden Sr.

July 1 found Roland Perry posted on what is now called Barlow Knoll north of Gettysburg with the 75th Ohio. By July 1863 Perry was a seasoned combat veteran after enlisting nearly two years earlier at Athens, Ohio. He was the fourth son of Roland Sr. and Mary Perry, with his three older brothers already enlisted. Brothers John and Elijah were in the 75th with Roland, and they routinely sent money home to help support their parents, their farm, and two younger siblings under age 10.[31]

The men of the 75th held their ground as long as possible in the flank attack in May at Chancellorsville but were overwhelmed by superior numbers. Roland's brother Elijah was wounded in the right hand and finished out the war in the Veteran Reserve Corps. After Chancellorsville and two years of hard service, the 75th entered Gettysburg reduced from 984 men ready for duty to 292.[32]

29 Ibid., 168-169.

30 Ibid., 170.

31 1850 Census Canaan Twp., Athens, Ohio, Ancestry.com.

32 Elijah Perry Compiled Military Service Record, NARA; John W. Busey and David G. Martin, *Regimental Strengths and Losses at Gettysburg* (Baltimore, 1982), 82.

The 75th was ordered to "fix bayonets" and move forward to receive the assault as the Confederates approached the knoll. Afterward, Col. Andrew Harris admitted "It was a fearful advance and made at a dreadful cost of life. We could go no further, halted and opened fire, the enemy was close and still advancing. We checked them in our immediate front, but they continued to press on our flanks."[33]

The 75th suffered 69 percent casualties, Roland being one of them. The examiner recorded in Perry's pension application that he was "wounded by a gunshot through his left hand, entirely destroying the middle finger . . . was taken prisoner on the field and recaptured . . . when his wound was first dressed by a surgeon." Perry did not leave letters or diaries because he could neither read nor write, so we don't know where he was held for the three days between his wounding and rescue by Union forces after the Confederate retreat on July 4. He might have made it to the almshouse, where the 75th established a hospital, or perhaps as far as the German Reformed Church or public school in town, both of which were used to treat XI Corps wounded. What we do know is that he must have been in a great deal of pain and had received little or no medical care.[34]

The longer a wounded soldier went without care the greater the chance of infection. Perry likely went three days without care, implying that he had a strong constitution. In Perry's application for an invalid pension in 1869, the examining surgeon and former surgeon of the 75th Ohio Dr. Charles L. Wilson noted "in consequence of a gunshot fracture, the middle finger of the left hand was removed by an operation through the corresponding Metacarpal bone. As a result of the above there is some loss of strength and impaired usefulness of the left hand."[35]

Fortunately for Perry, hand injuries had a low fatality rate of 3.2 percent in the Civil War. The prevailing thought according to *The Medical and Surgical History of the War of the Rebellion* was "the advantage of one or two fingers, or the thumb and a finger is so great that much should be hazarded to save them. Sometimes a . . . finger powerless or rigidly contracted in the palm may interfere with prehension and be an encumbrance; but usually the most deformed digit is found preferable to none." Indeed, this was the case for Perry.[36]

Perry probably had his surgery under the forebay of the Spangler barn. The railroad connection from the East was re-established on July 7 and he was one of

33 James S. Pula, *Under the Crescent Moon with the XI Corps in the Civil War*, Vol. 2: *From the Defenses of Washington to Chancellorsville, 1862-1863* (El Dorado, CA, 2017), 53, 56; Perry pension claim, NARA; Perry CMSR, NARA.

34 Roland Perry Invalid Pension Claim 100168, NARA; Pula, *Under the Crescent Moon*, Vol. 2, 57; Coco, *A Vast Sea of Misery*, 13, 27, 29–30.

35 Perry pension claim, NARA.

36 *The Medical and Surgical History of the War of the Rebellion*, Part II, Vol. II, 1024.

the first soldiers to be evacuated from Gettysburg, arriving at Satterlee General Hospital in West Philadelphia on July 9. Corporal Aaron W. Lee of the 17th Connecticut arrived at Satterlee from Spangler at the same time as Perry and described the trip from Gettysburg in a letter to his father: "We left about dusk— was on the cars all night—got into Baltimore about nine o'clock the next day. The Citizens of Baltimore came near killing us with kindness. We left about noon—got into Wilmington [Delaware] about sunset. Here men, women and children came flocking around the cars with baskets full of all kinds of provisions . . . we [arrived] in Philadelphia about 10 o'clock the next day the 9th."[37]

Perry and his comrades enjoyed exemplary care at Satterlee. During its existence, Satterlee General Hospital boasted one of the best recovery rates of any hospital during the war, with only 1,100 deaths out of more than 50,000 men treated. Perry returned to the 75th in 1864, signing his re-enlistment papers with his "mark."[38]

The 75th was sent to Florida, and Perry was in and out of the hospital with various ailments. The 75th was converted into a mounted infantry regiment in Florida, meaning the men used horses to move around but still fought as an infantry unit. The 75th raided Gainesville in August 1864 and was nearly wiped out by local troops, with Perry's horse shot out from under him, falling on him, and breaking his hip. The captured men were moved by rail and steamboat.[39]

The captured soldiers from the 75th arrived at the notorious Andersonville Prison on August 22. By this time Andersonville was stretched beyond its capacity, so it must have been a shock for the men when they were turned loose in the stockade with little food, water, or shelter. In early September most of the prisoners at Andersonville were transferred to other prisons, the exceptions being those soldiers too debilitated to travel, including Perry. He apparently recovered sufficiently to be transferred to Camp Lawton in Millen, Georgia, on October 31, where he remained until November 22 when he was paroled in Savannah. The

37 *The War of the Rebellion: A Compilation of the Official Records of the Union and Confederate Armies*, Series I Volume XXVII, Part II (Washington, D.C., 1889), 25; www.seventeenthcvi.org/blog/letters/ corporal-aaron-w-lee-company-g/, accessed Sep. 28, 2022; carded medical records 75th Ohio, Box 2749 RG 94, Entry 534, NARA; Roland Perry CMSR; Hospital Register PA 217 Satterlee General Hospital RG 94 Entry 544, NARA.

38 https://bit.ly/48n9pYL, accessed Feb. 17, 2024; carded medical records, 75th Ohio, Box 2749, RG 94 Entry 534, NARA; Roland Perry CMSR; Ohio Roster of Soldiers, Volume VI, 220; 75th Infantry Regiment Ohio, Ancestry.com.

39 Ibid.; Roland Perry CMSR, NARA; carded medical records 75th Ohio, Box 2749, RG 94 Entry 534, NARA; William Marvel, *Andersonville: The Last Depot* (Chapel Hill, 1994), 188.

Union forces picked him up and moved him to the hospital at Camp Parole in Annapolis, Maryland, noting that he was suffering from scurvy.[40]

Perry was granted a 30-day furlough (his first furlough in more than three years) on December 22, presumably going home. Christmas 1864 must have been a joyous time at the Perry homestead as all of Roland's brothers had mustered out and headed home. Perry returned to Camp Parole in January and remained until mustering out on March 22, 1865, at Cincinnati, returning to where he started his Civil War service. While most soldiers returned home, Perry and two other soldiers from the 75th enlisted in the Navy during the spring of 1865. He served on three ships plying the Mississippi River including the *Red Rover*, a floating hospital ship that was docked in Illinois. He served until September 1865, when he mustered out and returned to the family farm.[41]

Perry married a Civil War widow with three children soon after the war. They settled in Vinton County, Ohio, south of Columbus. He applied for and was granted a partial invalid pension of $4 a month for his wounded left hand. He appealed to the pension office over the years for an increase based on the lingering effects of digestive disorders incurred during his imprisonment at Andersonville, but was denied. He was a widower by 1890 and remarried in 1892 to another widow, Phoebe Stryker. They had several children, two of whom lived to adulthood. Perry's health began to fail by the first decade of the twentieth century and the broken hip was becoming difficult to bear; he spent several extended stays in the Dayton Military Home. But he was unable to prove he had sustained a hip injury even though he provided detailed information of the events until he was X-rayed during his annual physical in 1924 and it was revealed that he indeed had a fractured hip that never healed properly. Roland died in Dayton a few months later on April 22, 1924, at the age of 80. Before he died he documented that his wife had cared for him, ensuring she would receive a widow's pension. The widow and his grandchild, also named Phoebe Perry, lived together for the next 16 years, surviving the great Depression on her widow's pension. The granddaughter in turn took care of her grandmother in her final illness, during which time she finally learned about her grandfather's experience at Gettysburg. She later became a nurse and a mother of two boys. She passed down the oral tradition about her grandfather to her sons, one of them the author of this story.[42]

---

40 Marvel, Andersonville, 199, 206–207, 219, 222; Roland Perry CMSR, NARA.

41 United States Naval Enlistment Rendezvous, 1855–1891, Publication No. M1953 Roll 31FHL Film Number: 2383580 Vol. 43 Page 253, NARA; Ancestry.com, Oct. 1, 2022; Perry CMSR, NARA; Perry pension file, NARA; Phoebe Perry Widow Pension Claim 952006, NARA.

42 1870 Census Eagle Twp., Vinton County, Ohio, Roll M593_1276; Ancestry.com; Perry pension claim, NARA; Phoebe Perry pension claim, NARA; *The Dayton Herald*, Apr. 22, 1924; Fielden family oral tradition.

Jim Fielden Sr. is a docent at the George Spangler farm and a descendant of Roland Perry of the 75th Ohio. He has been interested in history and archives from an early age. Jim is a lifelong resident of Ohio and graduate of Kent State University, earning a master's degree in library science. His research projects focus on the soldiers of the XI Corps at Gettysburg. Jim lives in Cleveland and works as an IT analyst.

A. J. RIDER'S ROLE IN SPANGLER HISTORY
Drummer Alfred J. Rider, 107th Ohio, Company A, Age 24

Musician A. J. Rider was assigned to fatigue duty—or general labor—at the XI Corps hospital on July 4, and because of that we know the details today of what happened to Confederate Brig. Gen. Lewis Armistead after his death at Spangler. In letters to Gettysburg historian John Bachelder, Rider described being on the crew that buried Armistead in the Confederate section of the Spangler cemetery and how he was instructed to exhume Armistead's body a month later for embalming then rebury him. He also recorded the names of the dead and turned in their effects. Without those Rider letters, this critical Armistead and XI Corps hospital history would be lost.[43]

What Rider left out of those letters, though, were his own health challenges during the month he worked at Spangler and the ensuing months at Camp Letterman. His application for an invalid pension fills in those gaps. He wrote:

> Marching on road to Gettysburg in 1863. . . . We were marching several days over turnpikes. When I got to Gettysburg I found my shoes were worn entirely out. The limestone cut feet terribly. My right foot was hurt terribly about upper front of right great toe. The limestone seemed to get into it & it caused my feet to swell & since then I have always been a sufferer with that toe. . . . I used to bathe it in hospital in cold water. At 11th Corps hospital I pulled the skin off the soles of my feet they were burned by the limestone dust of hikes cause of bunion.[44]

Wife Mary Ann visited Rider at Camp Letterman, where he was still suffering: "I staid 8 days with him at that time," she remembered. "He was still complaining of pains in his lower limbs and was then also complaining of something like catarrh (mucus) of the head. . . . He was also very lame in the right foot. It was swollen and about second joint of big toe there was a raw sore looking place. He told me that he wore his shoes out marching over the limestone pile and almost wore his feet out at

---

43 Alfred J. Rider Invalid Pension Claim 870410, NARA.

44 Rider pension file, NARA.

Drummer Alfred J. Rider

Bryan Baker

same time. His left foot was also sore but not near like the right."[45]

The five-foot-seven-inch Rider had black hair and what was described as black eyes. He was postmaster for the 107th Ohio and served in that role at Camp Letterman as well as hospital recorder after being assigned there after Spangler. He remained at Letterman until it closed in late November. Unknown to him, his regiment didn't know where he was so he was charged with desertion until 107th Ohio Col. Seraphim Meyer wrote on January 6, 1864, that "musician Rider has satisfactory vouchers with him showing by the Hospital Department at Gettysburg he was ordered to remain to do duty interring the dead & waiting on the wounded by order—detached in the service there until in December, 1863, when by order of Maj. Genl. Crouch, commanding Department of the Susquehanna, he received a furlough and before the expiration of that furlough he arrived at New York on his way to rejoin the Regt. & remained there no longer than it was necessary to obtain transportation to this Department, I respectfully recommend that he be restored to duty without trial."[46]

Rider returned to his role as musician in the 107th and served through the end of the war.

He went on to work as a harness maker in Navarre, Ohio, near Akron. Rider took charge of the regiment's Gettysburg monument committee and offered the keynote speech at the monument's dedication in 1887 on Barlow Knoll. Captain Augustus Vignos of the 107th, who lost an arm at Gettysburg and was a patient at Spangler and close friend with noted XI Corps hospital nurse Rebecca Lane Pennypacker Price, presided over the dedication ceremonies. The November 1 Gettysburg *Star and Sentinel* newspaper printed Rider's speech in full on the front page, explaining, "We gladly give space on our outside to the address of Comrade A J Rider, at the dedication of the 107th Ohio monument. We believe it will be of

45 Ibid.

46 Rider Compiled Military Service Record, NARA.

interest to the large body of veteran readers of the *Star and Sentinel*. . . . Comrade Rider fought here was detained for some time in the hospital and has a warm attachment for Gettysburg and her people."[47]

More evidence of the respect that Rider earned was his election to city clerk in Navarre in 1872 and justice of the peace in 1875. He also continued his work as a harness maker, fathered nine children, served as adjutant of Miller Post GAR, secretary of the National Temperance Union of Ohio, and he worked in Washington D.C. for a few years as federal inspector of mailbags.[48]

Rider continued to struggle with his health, though, as told by multiple witnesses in his pension file:

April 6, 1893: Nasal catarrh, deafness, rheumatism, heart, eyes & kidneys. Vertigo. Physically broken down. Large and painful bunion on right great toe. A real disability in standing and walking.

Rider's statement, on August 31, 1893: During my three years' service from August 1862 to July 1865 induces me to state that heart disease, rheumatism, catarrah, bunion and my other ailments are the results of continued exposure in the field, hard marching, wading waters, etc.

October 2, 1893: There is a visible decline in his health and ability to perform work. He's often confined to his bed and only by carefully guarding his health is he now able to do any work.

1894: Has constant discharge from the nose. Mucus accumulates in throat, causing constant hawking and expectoration. Breath very offensive. Sciatica and lumbago. Dyspepsia. Constipation. Frequent attacks of vertigo with severe pain in head. Diseased foot.[49]

Rider died on July 7, 1906, at age 67. He is buried in Unionlawn Cemetery in Navarre, where he served as a trustee for many years. But his legacy still resonates today in Navarre and Gettysburg, particularly at the George Spangler farm where visitors today can learn of his role in history. Wife Mary Ann died one month after her husband's death.[50]

---

47 Documents provided by Bryan Baker of Berryville, Arkansas, Rider's 2X great-grandson.

48 Family history provided by Baker.

49 Rider pension file, NARA.

50 Rider family history.

"I HOPE MOTHER WILL NOT WORRY HERSELF ABOUT ME"
First Sergeant Henry Seas, 82nd Ohio, Company D, Age 26

By Charles T. Joyce and Ron Kirkwood

First Sergeant Henry Seas wrote a thoughtful letter to his brother, David, on May 20, 1863, not quite three weeks after he survived when his 82nd Ohio and the XI Corps were run over by Stonewall Jackson at Chancellorsville. "This evening it is 18 months since I enlisted," he wrote. "Whether I will see the close of the next 18 months, God only knows. If I fall by the hand of death, I hope that I may not have lived in vain."[51]

Henry would not see the close of the next 18 months. He died on George Spangler's farm almost two months to the day after writing that letter.

Seas was born in September 1836 in what would become Germany. His family settled in Marion County, Ohio, a few miles north of Columbus, and he attended nearby Ohio Wesleyan University, later becoming a teacher. He mustered into the 82nd Ohio in November 1861. He was with the regiment on July 1, 1863, when it rushed through Gettysburg and into action near the almshouse between the Carlisle and Harrisburg roads as part of Col. Wladimir Krzyzanowski's XI Corps, Third Division, Second Brigade. It was in the madness of that XI Corps fight and retreat north of Gettysburg that Seas was struck in his upper leg. He probably was taken to a Confederate hospital until it was safe for a Union ambulance to pick him up after the battle.

Henry's next letter to brother David came from the XI Corps hospital at Spangler. "Dear Brother, we came here the 1st [July 1] and got into a fight the same day. I was wounded in the right leg, once in the thigh. The doctor thinks the leg will not have to be amputated as the bone is not broken. Our loss is heavy." Dr. Jacob Cantwell of the 82nd Ohio is one of the few surgeons known to have worked at Spangler through July, so he likely was in charge of the care of his 82nd comrade.[52]

Seas wrote home again from Spangler on July 10, and even though his condition had worsened he did not want his family to worry, a common practice among Civil War soldiers. Soldiers also often downplayed the severity of their wounds to other wounded men. "My leg was amputated yesterday (the 9th) just above the knee," he told his family. "I stood the operation very well, being under the influence of

---

51 *The Marion* (Ohio) *Star*, Apr. 4, 1961.

52 Ibid.

1st Sgt. Henry Seas

Charles T. Joyce

chloroform. I am well cared for and in a fair way to get along well. I hope mother will not worry herself about me."[53]

Henry died at the XI Corps hospital one week after writing that letter. He was buried in the Spanglers' orchard before someone—we don't know who, but perhaps it was David—traveled to Gettysburg, had his body exhumed and returned him home, where he is now buried in Pleasant Cemetery in Marion.

Seas' Company D comrade Sgt. Abraham Gable wrote to David Seas in August about the July 1 fight in Gettysburg. "Our boys saw him [Henry] fall, but could not do anything for him. At such a time like that every man had to look out for himself." Colonel James S. Robinson said at the dedication of the 82nd's Gettysburg monument in 1887 that his regiment "stubbornly contested every inch of ground."[54]

Despite, or perhaps because of, the death of his brother, David Seas was mustered into the 100-day 136th Ohio in May 1864 and survived to be mustered out that August. Henry's coat is in the possession of the Marion County Historical Society.

Charles T. Joyce is a lawyer, artist, and writer. For the past 20 years he's actively collected and researched images and artifacts of soldiers killed, wounded, or captured at the battle of Gettysburg. He currently serves as a senior editor for Military Images *magazine. Joyce lives in Media, PA.*

3 PLEAS TO COME TO A DEATHBED
Private Theodore A. Weaver, 153rd Pennsylvania, Company C, Age 18

Private Theodore Weaver was hit by four Confederate bullets on July 1, but he stayed in the fight because they were only flesh wounds. Not much later, though, he was sidelined from the war for good when he took a bullet in the spine. After

53 Ibid.

54 Ibid.; 2 James S. Robinson, "Robinson's Address at the Dedication of the 82nd Ohio Monument on September 14, 1887," Ohio Historical Society, GNMP VF6-OH82 PC.

lying on the battlefield, he was taken to the almshouse and then a house being used as a hospital. He was moved to the XI Corps hospital after the battle but things were so bad there and it was so overcrowded that his stretcher had to be placed outside in the mud. Seeing this, Company C comrades picked him up and moved him to a house elsewhere, where he was treated.[55]

The resident of Hellertown, just outside of Allentown, left the family farm in October 1862 and joined the army. He stood five feet eight-and-a-half inches with blue eyes and brown hair. His only treatment in his short time at Spangler was water dressing. Weaver was transferred from the Gettysburg house to the Cotton Factory Hospital on Front Street on the Susquehanna River in Harrisburg on July 16. Three letters written to Weaver's father, Samuel, and one written by his father in the Randy Hackenburg Collection at the U.S. Army Heritage and Education Center in Carlisle, Pennsylvania, take his story from there:[56]

> Cotton Factory Hospital
> Harrisburg, Pa.
>
> July 23rd, 1863
>
> Saml. S. Weaver
>
> Dear Sir,
>
> I think it my duty as chaplain of the above Hospital to inform you that your son is fast sinking & may not be alive in 48 hours.
>
> I am of opinion that under such circumstances you should be here with him in his dying moments at whatever cost or trouble as you can so well . . . to come & help to administer Christian comfort.
>
> I expect you will therefore hasten here at once on receipt of this. Do not delay a moment.
>
> In case he dies before you arrive we won't know what disposition to make of the body unless you telegraph to the surgeon . . . in charge.
>
> I rejoice to find that your son has been religiously brought up & is a professing Christian.
>
> Yours respectfully,
>
> W. H. D. Hatton
> Chaplain, U.S.A.
> Harrisburg, Pa.

---

55 Stocker, *We Fought Desperate*, 267, 286.

56 Carded Medical Record, RG 94, Records of the Adjutant General's Office, Entry 534, 153 Pennsylvania, Transhue, Jeremiah, to 155 Pennsylvania, Dawson, Brown H., NARA.

Cotton Factory Hospital
Harrisburg Penn.

July 23 1863

Dear Sir,

In the famous battle of Gettysburg, among the wounded was your son Theodore; the ball passed through the hip into the abdomen, inflicting a dangerous wound; he was admitted to this hospital where he still is. . . . I feel it my duty to inform you that his condition is very dangerous, though he may yet recover; he behaves nobly now, as he did, I doubt not, in battle but if you desire to be sure of seeing him, it would be better to come to the hospital as soon as convenient.

Sincerely yours,

Carleton A. Shurtless
Med. Cadet—U.S.A.

Harrisburg July 23, 1863

Dear sir,

It is with the greatest of pleasure that I embrace this opportunity of writing to you to tell you that I am getting better but I am very sorry to tell you that your son is worse and the Doctor says there is no hope of his getting well and says if you want to see him alive you must come immediately for he don't think that he will live long . . . if you want to see him then start right off . . . he has the very best attention paid to him he gets two clean shirts every day

yours truly,

Levi F. Walter (Private, Company F, 153rd Pennsylvania, shot in the knee)

Samuel Weaver wrote to his son on July 24 before receiving those three letters. He wrote:

Lower Saucon, July 24, 1863

Dear son,

I recd the letter which that Miss Ettler wrote for you understood that the bullet aint out yet our doctor Detweiler thinks your wound is very dangerous without having the bullet taken or an operation be made ask the doctor about the matter tell him to examin you perfectly & save your life, your Granfathers both talk to come out to Harrisburg visit you before long they bring you the news from home we are one more in the family a little sister to you other wise we are all well and was very glad to here of you but a great deal would please us to here that you wound getting fast better try & send us every week through somebody your getting along we feel very uneasy if we don't here of you every week if wish for something from home write & also let us know if you think the docters tend you Regular or no we are very busy hauling grain hartly have time enough to write you few lines

yours truly, Father

Samuel S. Weaver[57]

Young Theodore A. Weaver died at 4:30 p.m. on July 26, very possibly the day his father received the letters telling him to rush to Harrisburg.[58]

Northern Final Notes

Private Daniel Fischer, Company C, 27th Pennsylvania, was hit by a musket ball in the lower back. The ball traveled upward and lodged in his chest before being removed along with a piece of rib at Spangler on July 4. The 22-year-old Fischer was transferred from Spangler to Turner Lane Hospital in Philadelphia on July 11 and returned to the 27th Pennsylvania in August. The five-foot-eight-inch, blue-eyed Fischer was a shoemaker after the war and resettled in Nebraska, where he raised a family. Fischer was admitted to the Battle Mountain Sanitarium in Hot Springs, South Dakota, in 1915 at age 74 with "slight dilation of heart," right hernia, right ear deafness and "old gun shot wound, left side." Battle Mountain was part of a system of facilities called the National Home for Disabled Volunteer Soldiers, which provided care for Union soldiers after the war. He was discharged after six months and lived 11 more years.[59]

Private Eli J. Keeler, Company G, 17th Connecticut, was struck in the chest by a rail from a fence hit by a Confederate shell during the Northern retreat on July 1. XI Corps Assistant Medical Director Dr. Robert Hubbard of the 17th Connecticut treated the 32-year-old shoemaker from Ridgefield at Spangler and said the injury caused "progressive pulmonary disease." Keeler died in 1867 of lung disease caused by his 1863 wound.[60]

57 Randy Hackenburg Collection, Box 2, Theodore A. Weaver Letters—Civil War, U.S. Army Heritage and Education Center.

58 Carded Medical Record, NARA.

59 *The Medical and Surgical History of the War of the Rebellion* (1861-65), Vol. II, Part 1, 567; Ancestry.com; https://www.findagrave.com/memorial/12211745/daniel-fischer, accessed Feb. 17, 2024.

60 Amanda Keeler Widow Pension Claim 324722, NARA.

Private David Reed, Company C, 134th New York, had what Spangler doctors listed as a flesh wound that they treated with water dressing. In reality, he was hit by a piece of shell that tore away muscles and tendons and put him on his back for months. The five-foot-eight-and-a-half-inch, 20-year-old farmer from Broome, New York, west of Albany, went to Spangler after the battle, then to Satterlee Hospital in Philadelphia on July 9, then to Baltimore, then to Newark, and finally on April 30, 1864, at about the time he was discharged, back to Philadelphia. He developed gangrene somewhere along the way, destroying the entire calf of his leg, including the nerves and muscles. He wrote to his father in October 1863: "It will be some time before I can walk. I can not straighten my leg out to save my life. I have growed so poor that none of you would hardly know me if you should see me. I have laid so long in the bed that my hip bone is sore and the side of my foot is worn through on my lame leg. I have to lay just so or I cant take no comfort, but I am getting quite smart. I set up in the bed most all the time and begin to eat quite hardy. I fare tip top, get all I ask for and I am well waited on. I have road out [of] the ward twice in a big rocking chair with wheels to it." A doctor in 1866 observed that Reed's "general health is poor from the constant drain on the system. In my opinion he is permanently disabled." Reed married wife Catharine in 1868, but he continued to waste away and died at age 27 in 1870 of "wounds received in battle and chronic diarrhea."[61]

Private Isaac J. Sperry, Company G, 73rd Ohio, who was wounded on July 2 and taken to Spangler and died there on July 5, is the 4X great-grandfather of Screen Actors Guild and Emmy Award-winning actor Woody Harrelson. The former merchant Sperry was shot in the chest, possibly by a Confederate sharpshooter, as the 73rd lay near the intersection of the Emmitsburg and Taneytown roads and perilously close to the Confederate line. His lung wound was sealed on the battlefield, but as with most Civil War chest wounds the knowledge was not there to save him. At 37, Sperry was one of the oldest soldiers to die at Spangler. He left behind his wife of 13 years Huldah, 12-year-old daughter Ada Elizabeth, and 7-year-old daughter Allice May in Good Hope, Fayette County, Ohio. It is Ada Elizabeth's line that leads to her 3X great-grandson Woody Harrelson through Woody's mother, Diane Lou (Oswald) Harrelson. Woody graduated from high school in 1979 in Lebanon, Ohio, just 55 miles from where 4X great-grandpa Isaac lived in Good Hope when he joined the 73rd Ohio. Sperry was buried in the Spanglers' orchard and later removed to Soldiers' National Cemetery, where both

61 Reed Family Letters, (1862-1864), Collection Call Number: 14746, New York State Library, Albany; David Reed Invalid Pension Claim 31580 and Catharine Reed Widow Pension Claim 190701, NARA; Carded Medical Record, 134 New York, Patto, J. to Walsh, D., NARA; Fold3; Ancestry.com.

his first and last names are misspelled on his gravestone. He rests within a couple hundred yards of where he was mortally wounded.[62]

Spangler Farm Short Story

For five weeks in July and August 1863, Marilla Hovey of Dansville, New York, held the hands of soldiers at the XI Corps hospital as they died, spoke with them through their tears about their families to help take their mind off their physical and mental agony, prayed with them, and then wrote compassionate letters home after death. Word spread in Civil War medical circles of her caring work, character, and accomplishments, so Mrs. Hovey was among a select group of "accomplished ladies" chosen by noted Civil War nurse Annie Wittenmyer to open and superintend new special-diet kitchens in 1864.

The 40-something Mrs. Hovey was enlisted to set up and supervise U.S. government hospital kitchens that were charged with the monumental task of serving carefully prepared meals three times a day for up to 1,500 patients. These kitchens provided a variety of higher-quality meals as prescribed by the surgeons for patients with special needs caused by their disease or condition, thus improving their health and recovery.[63]

Wittenmyer chose Mrs. Hovey as one of the leaders of this new organization because she met her demanding requirements. "It will be readily seen that competent women were needed to take the management of this important work," Wittenmyer outlined.

They had not only to command a force of twenty or thirty men in these kitchens, and maintain discipline and good order, but they had, under hospital authority, the entire responsibility of supplying the proper preparation of food, on time and without the least delay or confusion. Their high position also demanded that they should be ladies of culture and social standing, who could command the respect and confidence of officers and surgeons in charge. It is greatly to the honor of the patriotic women of the North, that scores of accomplished ladies of high social position volunteered to fill these important places. Great care had to be taken in their selection, and none were accepted unless highly indorsed.[64]

---

62 Pvt. Isaac J. Sperry Widow Pension Claim 19739, Fold3.

63 Annie Wittenmyer, *Under the Guns: A Woman's Reminiscences of the Civil War* (Boston, 1895), 259.

64 Ibid., 217-218.

Wittenmyer's special-diet kitchens were eventually adopted by the surgeon general for the nation's hospital system, and she oversaw the establishment of more than 100 of them.[65]

Mrs. Hovey proved to be a woman of multiple talents, running these massive general hospital kitchens with the same adeptness and thoughtfulness that she displayed as she tended the wounded and dying at Spangler. She hired and superintended nurses and other workers in hospitals in Nashville, Memphis, and Louisville as well as at many smaller hospitals. Wittenmyer said Mrs. Hovey was "commended" by the surgeons "for her faithful and valuable services." She performed all of this work as a volunteer.[66]

65 Ibid., 264.

66 Wittenmyer statement in support of Marilla Hovey's pension application, date unknown, in family records provided by Mrs. Hovey's great-nephew, Rex Hovey.

Chapter 18

The Spanglers Move on
and Daniel Moves Away

Daniel "remembered the arms and legs being as high as the second story door [of the barn]."
— *Daniel's grandson Norman Spangler, a Kansas native*

It's probable that what happened to them and their farm in July and August of 1863 impacted all six Spanglers for the rest of their lives. Perhaps every single day. How could it not? They were engulfed by the sounds, violence, and terror of the Civil War. End to end, 24 hours a day, on that once peaceful and idyllic farm. They watched it happen and were, quite literally, right in the middle of it all.

They watched the Artillery Reserve arrive and its thousands of men and animals take over most of their property—consume the property, really. Hundreds of ambulances, wagons, and animals spanned their land. Thousands of infantrymen and artillerymen were held in reserve there. They had more wounded men on their property between the two hospitals there than the entire 2,400 population of Gettysburg at the time. They could hear the artillery of the entire Army of the Potomac coming and going and reloading on their property all night. And then there was the artillery on the hill that someday would be named Powers Hill that kicked off the Day 3 battle that was so overpoweringly loud that the Spanglers would have had to yell to hear each other in their bedroom a quarter-mile away.

Imagine their fear as they watched from the confinement of that upstairs bedroom as Confederate artillery arrived from the West and landed within feet of their barn and house, killing animals and wounding men. They really could actually watch the shells as they spiraled toward their farm, bringing destruction.

The Spanglers lost all their animals and most of their crops and their buildings were not just damaged or destroyed—they were fouled. After five weeks and two days of the XI Corps hospital, the Spanglers' house and barn were empty shells still

George and Elizabeth Spangler. *John S. Speights*

bearing the tragic human scars and stench of that hospital, still covered in blood and bodily fluids. They had to step over wounded and dying men and those body fluids to get out of their house. All six crammed into one bedroom in south-central Pennsylvania's high summer heat and humidity and no window screens. Flies are bad on a farm. They were probably indescribably, clinging-all-over-you bad in that bedroom on a farm with a hospital. And they probably had a chamber pot in their bedroom because their one outhouse was overrun by the hospital.

Yet they picked up and they moved on and they resumed their lives no matter what horrors were tucked away deep in their minds. George and Elizabeth gutted their house after the battle by expanding it, increasing its size by a third by 1864, according to Cumberland Township tax records at the Adams County Historical Society. They took a horrific situation and improved it, then went on to long and meaningful lives after buying and moving onto the smaller Musser farm next door in the 1870s. Each died at age 88, George in 1904 and Elizabeth in 1907.

A portion of the farm in the late 1800s while still owned by the Spanglers.

Gettysburg National Military Park

Oldest daughter Harriet left home in 1868 at age 26 when she married Samuel Schwartz and moved to a farm in neighboring Mount Joy Township. Many of her descendants today are active supporters of the farm where she grew up and are pictured in the next chapter.

No. 2 child Sabina followed her older sister out of the house in 1869 when she married neighbor William Patterson and moved to his family farm on the Taneytown Road. Sabina received a federal widow's pension in 1920 after William died; he had served in Company G of the 101st Pennsylvania Infantry at the end of the Civil War. The *Gettysburg Times* called her "an esteemed and pioneer resident of Gettysburg" after her death in 1924. She was survived by 10 grandchildren. As with Harriet, Sabina's many descendants have traveled from across the country to take in and honor their ancestors' farm.[1]

No. 4 child Beniah stayed home, in fact living in the very house in which he grew up, and in which he was exposed to the horrors of war. He ran the farm with hired help and returned it to its thriving ways until about 1890, when he moved into town and rented the property to working tenants.

We might never know why No. 3 child Daniel left home and moved halfway across the country to Kansas. His adulthood is the most mysterious of the six Spanglers. Did he leave because he was scarred by the terror that he and his family went through on that farm? Did he need to distance himself from that and the farm? Were there family difficulties? Or maybe, and probably most likely,

---

1 Sabina Patterson Widow Pension Claim 897493, NARA; *Gettysburg Times*, Sep. 25, 1924.

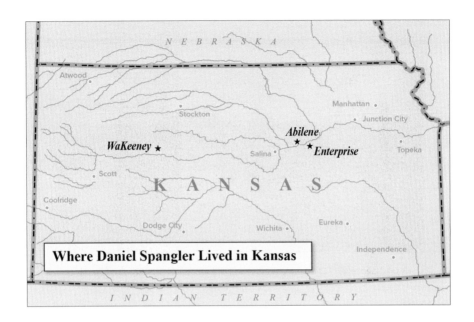

Where Daniel Spangler Lived in Kansas

Gettysburg and the East Coast were getting too crowded for him and he longed to explore and establish a life of his own on the frontier.

One record has him moving to the Midwest at age 21 while another says 27. Both say he attended college in Iowa for two years before going to Kansas, but it's not known which is accurate. If he left Gettysburg at age 21, that would have been in 1867 or 1868, and he is not shown in any Adams County records of that time or in the 1870 U.S. census. If it was 21, he would have been out there somewhere when lawman Wild Bill Hickok was battling rowdy, cattle-driving Texas cowboys in Abilene, Kansas.[2]

Spangler family lore also has Daniel helping hundreds of members of the Brethren in Christ Church from Lancaster, Lebanon, Dauphin, Cumberland, and Franklin counties in Pennsylvania move to Dickinson County, Kansas, outside of Abilene in the late 1870s. This group was also known as the River Brethren because many came from near the Susquehanna River in Lancaster County. These stories have Daniel moving families from Pennsylvania to Kansas in a wagon in two trips, even though it's on record that most of these travelers made the trip via train. It's possible, however, that Daniel helped the early River Brethren explorers who were scouting for land in Kansas to relocate to get there in that manner. Perhaps he was already there and helped them get settled or used his carpentry skills to help the River Brethren build settlements.

2 Dickinson County Cemetery Survey, Center Township, Mount Hope Cemetery (Abilene, KS, 1982), 358–359; Wilkie family history, 52.

Daniel lived for a while in a dugout in this hill south of WaKeeney, Kansas. *Calvin Spangler*

Daniel also does not show up in the 1875 Kansas census so his whereabouts are not known for more than 10 years of his life. Official records and newspaper reports pick up his trail in 1880, making it possible to track his movements thereafter. That 1880 census places him in a hotel on Broadway Street in Abilene and lists him as a carpenter. Then, after he vanished for so long, he turns up twice in the 1885 Kansas census, listed first as living with 21 other people probably in a hotel in Abilene and then as a laborer living on the farm of Henry A. Conant and family southwest of the village of Enterprise, likely indicating he either maintained dual residences or 1885 was the year Daniel moved to the quiet town on the Plains and the banks of the Smoky Hill River, and which would eventually become his long-term home.[3]

But first, the 40-year-old bachelor had one more itch for adventure. Following the Smoky Hill River 156 miles west in 1886 to just south of WaKeeney in Trego County finds a land of rolling prairie and scenic bluffs that was so little populated that it had only become a county seven years before Daniel arrived. Cheyenne Indian raids took place in the area eight years before he got there. Buffalo, elk, and antelope dominated the countryside 10 years before and the county's first church wasn't founded until 1878.[4]

3 Dickinson County Historical Society, Abilene, KS, courtesy of curator Andrew Pankratz.

4 www.legendsofkansas.com/trego-county-kansas/, accessed July 27, 2023.

Daniel and Effie Spangler on their wedding day.

Calvin Spangler

Into this wild, Daniel staked his claim to 180 acres of free land under the federal government's 1862 Homestead Act. That measure had enticed settlers to populate the prairie states and remove Native Americans. All he had to do was live on and work the land for five years, which he did, after which the land was awarded to him in 1891. Daniel's great-grandson Calvin Spangler has the deed on display in his home in Chapman, Kansas. Daniel built two dugouts in the side of a hill and lived in one and kept livestock in another. Dugouts were basically dirt houses with sod for a roof and were common in Kansas' early prairie days. This put Daniel even farther removed from the comfortable housing that his Adams County family members enjoyed back home.[5]

Daniel's former land is a few miles south of WaKeeney on U.S. Route 283. The land passed to Daniel's only surviving child George upon Daniel's death at age 91 in 1937. George lived outside of Enterprise and never used the property so he sold it to lifelong Trego County resident Mike McGinnis in 1976, who leases out part of the land today for cattle grazing. That land has had only three owners since 1891—Daniel Spangler, George Spangler, and Mike McGinnis. McGinnis can point out exactly where on his property the dugout once stood that housed the Pennsylvania immigrant Daniel.[6]

Daniel also claimed 180 nearby acres for free through the federal Timber Culture Act of 1873, which was designed "to encourage the Growth of Timber in the Western Prairies." The Timber Culture Act required settlers to plant trees on at least 10 of the 180 acres to be granted ownership, which he earned in 1903. Son George sold those 180 acres to the federal government in 1951 and they now are at the bottom of the Cedar Bluff Reservoir, which was formed from the Smoky Hill River.[7]

---

5 Trego County Historical Society, WaKeeney, KS; www.history.com/topics/american-civil-war/homestead-act, accessed July 27, 2023; conversation with Daniel's grandson, Norman Spangler, Apr. 2021.

6 Trego County Historical Society; conversations with Norman Spangler (Apr. 2021) and Mike McGinnis, July 2021.

7 Trego County Historical Society; Daniel filed a complaint against a neighbor in 1890 for not planting trees, *Western Kansas World*, May 17, 1890.

Daniel must have bounced between Trego County, Abilene, and Enterprise in those years. He taught school in western Kansas, according to grandson Norman Spangler and other family members, which is affirmed by a report in the March 23, 1888, *Wa-Keeney Tribune*: "D. E. Spangler's school in Dist. No. 36 closed on March 2 with a rousing big picnic. The scholars had a jolly good time."

Daniel met future wife Effie Wilkie in Abilene and they married in Enterprise in 1892, with the *Western Kansas World* reporting on January 26 that "Word reaches us that D. E. Spangler has taken a wife at Enterprise, Kansas." The wedding took place in the Enterprise home of R. L. Kirkpatrick where Daniel was living at the time, and the *Enterprise Eagle* newspaper called the marriage of the 46-year-old Daniel "quite a surprise as Dan was considered a confirmed bachelor but his many friends will wish him a thousand blessings." The *Western Kansas World* kept tabs on Daniel as he moved between his eastern and western Kansas homes, reporting on December 20, 1890, that "D. E. Spangler is at home again, after an absence of several months," and on November 5, 1892, "W. B. Cypher returned from Kansas City last Saturday morning. Mr. Cypher shipped several car loads of cattle and disposed of them at reasonably good figures. On his return he visited our old friend D. E. Spangler at Enterprise, Kansas, and found him prospering." It's not known where Daniel lived in his final years of residence in Trego County, but it's common sense that he had long since improved upon those early dugouts.

The J. B. Ehrsam Machine Co. hired Daniel in August 1890 and put his carpentry skills to use in making shipping crates for the company along the Smoky Hill River in Enterprise. Flour mill equipment was built in the vast factory, but the site is vacant land today and nothing remains of it in the once-bustling Enterprise. Daniel's wood plane has been passed down to great-grandson Calvin.[8]

Daniel and Effie rented or stayed with others south of Enterprise until they bought their first home on South Court Street in Enterprise in 1905 across the street from the Ehrsam factory. The house was built in 1900 and still stands today. Daniel expanded the home and built a barn either on this property or on property he owned on South Tell Street in Enterprise. With two 180-acre properties in western Kansas and two smaller ones in the eastern part of the state, Daniel followed in the entrepreneurial footsteps of his grandfather Abraham Spangler, who owned two large farms in Adams County, and father George, who bought land around his farm whenever it became available and eventually also owned two farms. Going into education also continued his family's tradition, as Abraham, George, and Beniah all served on the Cumberland Township School Board back home.[9]

8 Dickinson County Historical Society; conversation with Norman Spangler.

9 Dickinson County Historical Society.

Daniel lived a quiet life in the Enterprise area, though he often received newspaper accolades for his gardening skills and frequent mentions that he was doing carpentry and construction work for someone or selling a cow. Grandson Norman Spangler was told by his dad George that Grandpa Daniel rarely talked about what happened on the Gettysburg family farm in 1863, though Norman reported that Daniel "remembered the arms and legs being as high as the second story door [of the barn]. Now that's what my dad had always told me that his dad told him."[10]

Sabina's daughter Clara Patterson stayed with Effie and Uncle Daniel in Enterprise in 1906 when she moved to Kansas to work as a nurse. Clara grew up on the Taneytown Road and attended Granite Schoolhouse in the 1880s when her Uncle Beniah was on the school board there. She remained in Kansas, married, and died at age 91 in 1965 and is buried in Abilene.[11]

Daniel was a registered Republican and leader in the party during his time in western Kansas even though his father was a lifelong Democrat. His parents in Gettysburg, though, meant enough to him that he had copies of their circa 1863 photo reprinted by a professional photographer in Enterprise. Norman says Daniel never returned to Gettysburg after settling in Kansas and Norman's dad George never made the trip to his grandparents' ancestral home. Norman made the trip, though. He visited the farm of great-grandparents George and Elizabeth in 2023 with son Jeff (2X great-grandson of George and Elizabeth), daughter Susan (2X), and grandchildren Michaela (3X) and Griffin (3X).

We'll likely never know exactly why Daniel left home and settled a world away on the wild frontier of Kansas. We'll also probably never know why Daniel never returned to Gettysburg. But between 2021 and 2023 eight of Daniel's descendants traveled from Kansas, South Carolina, and Florida all the way to Gettysburg just to see the farm where he grew up and his childhood stomping grounds. More of his descendants have said they are making plans to do the same. So many of them remain anchored in Kansas because Daniel chose to relocate there from his historic Pennsylvania family farm. But there also is a deep fascination and family attraction that draws them to Gettysburg. Their connection to both Gettysburg and Kansas is strong.

10 Conversation with Norman Spangler.

11 *The Enterprise Journal*, Sep. 6, 1906.

One Final Note

Norman Spangler said grandfather Daniel found a rifle on the Gettysburg family farm after the battle. That rifle has been passed down to him and is still in his family's possession today. Also, a report from wife Effie Wilkie's family says Daniel shook hands with Abraham Lincoln after the president delivered the Gettysburg Address at the dedication of Soldiers' National Cemetery in November 1863. Beniah also is on record as having been present at the event so perhaps all six Spanglers were there.

Spangler Farm Short Story

George Spangler obviously took pride in his German heritage because he did a decidedly German thing by adding a second front door when he expanded his house in the mid-1860s. The Baltimore Pike house of George's father, Abraham, also had two front doors. George's design gave the Spanglers side-by-side front doors, which might not make sense to many but it's a German tradition that dates back 1,000 years.[12]

In this tradition, one door leads into a sitting area for formal occasions such as weddings and funerals. George served on many Gettysburg-area civic and church boards, so the Spanglers also could have used that room for entertaining the minister and other community leaders or for serving tea to area ladies. The other door was reserved for entry into a room for everyday living and eating. It was common with this two-door arrangement to have a porch much like is on the house today. The two doors were probably a source of pride for the Spanglers and a bit of a statement on how they were doing.[13]

Honoring the German tradition and the Spanglers, the Gettysburg Foundation kept both front doors when it modernized and expanded the house and turned the first floor into a conference room in 2019 even though the doors get little traffic and are mainly decorative today.

---

12 Landis Valley Village & Farm Museum; www.lovettsvillehistoricalsociety.org/index.php/the-german-american-zweiturhaus, accessed Aug. 3, 2022.

13 Ibid.

Chapter 19

The Spangler Descendants Today

Many descendants of all three surviving lines requested a gathering at the farm to meet one another, so the first Descendants Day took place in June 2022 with programs, living historians, barn experts, tours, and introductions.

Every person pictured in the three group photos printed in this chapter is descended from George and Elizabeth Spangler. George and Elizabeth are a part of them, as is the farm where the Spanglers spent 56 years of their married lives together. When descendants visit the Gettysburg Foundation's George Spangler farm today, they have come home.

I often wondered about Spangler direct descendants as I worked on the first book, but time and space constraints meant a search for them would have to wait. *Too Much for Human Endurance* was published in May 2019 and my Spangler genealogical search finally began in January 2021. But as much as I wanted to find these family members, inform them of their Spangler connection if they didn't know about it, and get to know them, my motives weren't altogether pure. What I really wanted, and held my fingers crossed for, was that one or more of them might be able to provide me with photos of George, Elizabeth, Harriet, Sabina, and Daniel (I already had a couple photos of Beniah.)

I also wondered if the Spanglers wrote letters to relatives as other Gettysburg-area residents had done that described what they endured during their 1863 ordeal. If so, were those letters passed down through the generations and saved in a dusty box in the back of a closet somewhere? How about a diary? Did one of the Spanglers leave behind details that still survive today? I had searched for all of the above for six years and found none of it. Could they exist with a descendant somewhere?

Thus, the search began. Sadly, youngest son Beniah has no living descendants today. His only child, Mary Elizabeth, also had only one child, Fred, who died at 2 weeks old. Mary Elizabeth's death in 1964 in Gettysburg ended Beniah's line. So

Daniel's descendants at the George Spangler farm in 2022, from left: Duncan Spangler, Calvin Spangler, and Maurice Spangler.

Barb Kirkwood

I moved on to the other three children. Using a variety of online genealogy sites, newspaper obituaries, and other sources, I soon developed a rough framework of all three lines traced until today. Then I contacted the family members I found to (1) tell them they were descendants in case they didn't know (and the vast majority didn't); (2) ask for their help in filling out their family line; and (3) ask if anything from George, Elizabeth, Harriet, Sabina, or Daniel had been passed down to them.

At this point progress slowed. In this age of spam phone calls, spam text messages, spam Facebook direct messages, and spam emails, many Spangler descendants initially didn't get back to me, just as I very likely wouldn't have gotten back to them in that situation. No doubt they wondered if this unknown person contacting them could be trusted. But I had at least one brave soul return my message in each child's line and that opened the door when he or she contacted fellow family members and the word then spread quickly about this farm and their ancestors. I found part of each of the three children's lines. The descendants did the rest for me. Word was out about their relationship to this farm and they were eager to get involved.

My brave hero in oldest daughter Harriet's line was George and Elizabeth's 4X great-grandson Jeremy Gantz. After figuring out he was a descendant, I found his work information online and contacted him through his work email. Jeremy lives and works in Vermont, but he grew up on Sachs Road south of Gettysburg not far from the former George Spangler farm where he used to hunt as a child, having no idea about his family connection to the historic land on which he was chasing deer. Jeremy's mother—3X great-granddaughter Tara Gantz Hixon—took it from there and Harriet's line opened up to me as she spread the word. Tara was then the first descendant after being contacted to visit her newly found family farm, excitedly arriving on a soaking wet and bitter cold Saturday in May 2021 with her mother Barbara Heffner (2X), sister Lori Heffner Baker (3X), and daughter Jessica Gantz Wilkinson (4X), who is Jeremy's sister.

A fun fact about Jessica and Jeremy is the amount of DNA they share with George and Elizabeth Spangler because each of their parents is a Spangler descendant. Mom Tara is descended from Harriet's son Ira while dad Donald Gantz is descended from Ira's sister Mary Ellen, making Tara and Donald third cousins. They found out about this surprise after their marriage. Tara likes to smile and say both Jessica and Jeremy turned out great despite both being descended from two of Harriet's kids, and she is absolutely right. They are smart and kind and have great jobs.

Donald, who died in 2006 at age 52, is a wonderful example of the commitment to community service exemplified by his ancestors Abraham and George Spangler. He was a life member, former fire chief, member, and secretary of the Relief Committee of the Barlow Fire Co.; member and vice president of the Gettysburg Fire Co.; member of the Fairfield Fire Co., the Adams County Fireman's Association, and Pennsylvania State Fireman's Association; instructor and member of the Training Committee for the Adams County Training Center; and a member of the Gettysburg Eagles. Gantz was the Barlow Fire Co. fire chief from 1990–1995. He was a Pennsylvania Certified Fire Instructor and was awarded the Medal of Valor from the Eastern Division of the International Association of Fire Chiefs. Additionally, Gantz was a member of St. James Lutheran Church in Gettysburg, just as George and Elizabeth Spangler were. It's where his 2X great-grandmother Harriet was baptized.[1]

2X great-granddaughter Carolyn Ketterman Hankey was my hero in Sabina's line with the critical assistance of her husband, Ron, another active community leader in the family and retired president of Adams County National Bank. I messaged one of the many boards on which Ron served and asked them to contact him for me, which they did. Ron told Carolyn, and she got back to me, though she now laughs and says she did so with hesitance and against her better judgment. Thanks to Ron and Carolyn, I now had much of Sabina's line.

---

1 www.findagrave.com/memorial/16880243/donald-alvey-gantz, accessed July 30, 2023.

Sabina's descendants at the farm on Descendants Day 2022. *Barb Kirkwood*

Carolyn's grandmother, Alice Patterson Ketterman, was George and Elizabeth's granddaughter and attended school in the middle of their farm at Granite Schoolhouse in the 1880s while also undoubtedly spending much time in her grandparents' historic house and farm buildings. Carolyn and her siblings grew up on what is now National Park Service land across from the modern-day Tommy's Pizza on Steinwehr Avenue, and even though they spent much time with Grandma Alice word never reached them about their connection to the farm and its importance. Many in those older generations, it seems, rarely talked about themselves and their childhood. Now fully engaged, Carolyn spread the word and 20 of Sabina's descendants plus family members gathered to celebrate their newly found heritage at the ancestral farm in June 2021. Not one of them had known about their Spangler connection.

I benefited from multiple heroes in Daniel's line, mainly in Kansas where he settled. George and Elizabeth's great-grandson Norman Spangler never met his grandfather Daniel, but Daniel's stories were passed down to him from Norman's father, George, so Norman and I had many phone conversations in which I learned a lot. 2X great-grandson Calvin Spangler shows impressive dedication to the farm, driving from Kansas to Gettysburg in June 2021 and June 2022, bringing wife Cathy on the first trip and son Duncan (3X) on the second. Calvin and Duncan also flew to Pennsylvania in 2023. The family has spent much time on the Spangler farm, where they are treated as honored guests. 3X great-grandson John Daley of Kansas contacted so many family members about the farm after learning of it that he got 16 of Daniel's descendants to join the George Spangler Farm Facebook Group in one weekend in 2021.

Many descendants of all three surviving lines requested a gathering at the farm to meet one another, so the first Descendants Day took place in June 2022 with programs, living historians, barn experts, tours, and introductions. The day was enjoyed by 63 direct descendants and a total crowd of more than 100. Five

Harriet's descendants at the farm. *Barb Kirkwood*

descendants of George Spangler's half brother, Henry, requested to attend and did. Descendants at the gathering ranged from 2X to 5X great-grandchildren and from seven months old to 90 years old. They traveled to Gettysburg for the event from California, Kansas, Illinois, Kentucky, South Carolina, Maryland, New York, Vermont, and all over Pennsylvania. Adams County was heavily represented, as many branches of the family had unknowingly stayed close to their Spangler roots. Hugs were common as descendants introduced themselves and many were surprised to learn that they are related to current or former classmates or one of their teachers. Clearly, George and Elizabeth's descendants have embraced their farm and heritage.

George, Elizabeth, Harriet, Sabina, and Daniel would be proud of their descendants. There are bankers, a pilot, teachers, professors, a Secret Service agent who has personally guarded a president, builders, a police chief, firemen, one psychologist, a butcher, graduates of prestigious Gettysburg College, engineers (including nuclear), business owners, active community volunteers, dedicated and loyal workers who have stayed in the same job for decades, and so much more, all descended from that special farm. A 3X great-granddaughter of Sabina became my Realtor in Pittsburgh. Descendant Sabina Stanger is named after her 3X great-grandmother, though her family didn't know about the farm at the time she was named. They just happened to see the name in their line and liked it. Sabina Stanger attended Descendants Day and received star attention. Spangler descendant Robert Thomas has generously donated thousands of dollars to the Gettysburg Foundation for upkeep of the farm from his Thomas Family Foundation.

As with most families, there have been tragedies in the generations between George and Elizabeth's era and today, including two publicly known suicides in Sabina's line. Many children have died from disease. Still, Harriet, Sabina, and Daniel's lines are solid and strong with many branches.

And what about my original goal that started all of this, of finding family photos and documents? I didn't unearth letters or a diary as I had hoped, but I still hit the mother lode when Calvin Spangler's older brother, Maurice Spangler of Kansas and now South Carolina, showed up at the 2022 descendants' gathering at the farm and handed me a photo of his 2X great-grandparents George and Elizabeth and asked calmly, "Is this what you're looking for?" And that is when the first hug of the day happened. Daniel's great-grandson, Dennis Rector, provided a photo of Daniel and wife Effie in their later years in Kansas. Calvin brought Daniel's carpentry plane to Gettysburg and photos that he took of the land that Daniel homesteaded in western Kansas. During his frequent trips to Gettysburg, Calvin often pays his respects at George and Elizabeth's grave in Evergreen Cemetery, where so many of his Spangler ancestors are buried. Conversations with Daniel's grandson, Norman Spangler, have recovered stories about the family and farm that otherwise might not have survived.

Blue collar or white collar, George and Elizabeth produced generations of impressive descendants who care about one another and the farm and now actively promote it. Now, they return to their roots often. They have helped me with my Spangler research more than they can know, and I am grateful to call them friends.

Spangler Farm Short Story

The modern-day George Spangler farm draws in descendants of the surgeons, patients, and workers at the 1863 XI Corps hospital as regular visitors and volunteers just as it draws family. The farm seems to beckon them to the place where their ancestor worked or suffered or both.

Rex Hovey of North Carolina is a living historian who portrays his great-uncle Dr. Bleecker Lansing Hovey every year at the farm. Dr. Hovey was a surgeon at the XI Corps hospital, and Rex uses the actual surgical kit used at the farm by his ancestor as part of his presentation. Spangler nurse Marilla Hovey is Rex's great-aunt.

Jim Fielden of Cleveland is a Gettysburg Foundation volunteer guide at the farm whose great-grandfather Pvt. Roland E. Perry of the 75th Ohio had a finger amputated at Spangler. Jim searched for years to find where Perry was treated, and he said he knew he had found the right hospital as soon as he walked onto the Spangler property. He could just feel it. Jim is so devoted to the farm that he drives

300 miles one way from Cleveland to Gettysburg several times a year to talk to and help visitors as a volunteer guide.

Descendants of hospital worker Alfred J. Rider of the 107th Ohio drove to Gettysburg all the way from their home in Arkansas to see where their ancestor worked. Rider was involved in the burial and exhumation of Confederate Brig. Gen. Lewis A. Armistead. Descendants of surgeon Jay Kling of the 55th Ohio traveled from Ohio to see the farm. Kling was involved in the treatment of Armistead. XI Corps hospital nurse Rebecca Lane Pennypacker Price is an ancestor of George Rapp, and he has visited the farm where she played such a critical role and has shown the author around her hometown of Phoenixville, including her grave. Brad Coe of Hallam, Pennsylvania, was so eager to see the farm after he found out that ancestor Pvt. Edward D. Coe of the 154th New York was treated there that he drove to Spangler to see it only to find it closed. Resisting a strong temptation to walk past the gate and the no-trespassing signs, Coe smartly refrained and returned when the farm was open for visitation.

Those named here are a small fraction of those who have come, or rather, been drawn. Now beautifully rebuilt to its 1863 glory and protected by the Gettysburg Foundation, this farm will continue to welcome eager Spangler and hospital descendants for generations to come. Their ancestors, after all, gave their duty, their service, their compassion, and often their blood to this place. Their ancestors played a vital role in the history of this farm.

Appendix 1

The Spangler Farm Vernal Pool

By Betsy Leppo, M.S., Invertebrate Zoologist

The first time I saw the George Spangler farm, I admired the red bank barn and stately gray stone house surrounded by lush green fields and woods. As I explored the property and heard the stories told by re-enactors and historians, the pastoral scene in front of me began to fade away, replaced by stark images of a farm turned field hospital, right behind the front lines of the battle of Gettysburg.

Just as the peaceful scene at the Spangler farm shrouds a dramatic moment from its past, nature cloaks its own secrets nearby. On a hot day in August, I walked with Ron Kirkwood through a sunny field to a patch of thick woods located about 1,000 feet northeast of the Spangler buildings. We picked our way through the woodland and soon encountered a small opening with lush vegetation. The opening in the tree canopy was centered over a low, flat, circular area defined by an earthen berm. The inside edge of the berm sloped gently into the basin, while the outside edge sloped more steeply away into the woods. There was no water visible at the surface, but water-loving plants were growing in the basin, such as ditch stonecrop and water plantain. Willow trees stood at the edge, stretching long limbs over the basin. We found a pocket of wet muck along the northern edge of the basin—the spring in its resting August state—with an odd-looking piece of drainage pipe jutting out of it. All of these signs were telling a story.

A map from 1863 shows a spring pool in this location at the time of the battle. In more recent history, previous farm owner Ken Andrew decided to deepen the spring and create a shallow pond, using excavated soils to build a raised berm to help hold the water in place. We guessed on our exploration of the pond that day

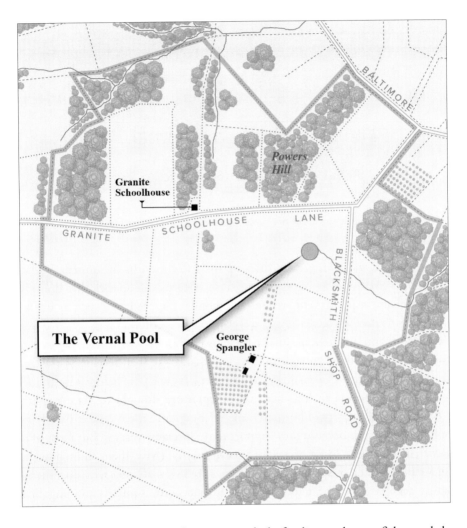

that someone probably wanted a watering hole for livestock or a fish pond, but Ron later talked to Mr. Andrew's son, Clarence, who grew up on the farm, who said his father and uncle used a bulldozer to build a pond around the spring 50 or 60 years ago to provide a better supply of water for the area in case of fire. The strange pipes we found were actually fiberglass containers used during World War II to drop supplies to soldiers from the air. Mr. Andrew found the containers at a junkyard on the Baltimore Pike and used them to create a barrier around the pond to keep people out for their own safety.

The pond never held water the way Mr. Andrew hoped it would, but what remains today is a kind of wetland that is far more extraordinary than a fish pond. What they inadvertently built is a vernal pool, a seasonal wetland that floods in

Left: The full vernal pool in February 2023. Right: Betsy Leppo's daughter, Amelia, sits in the dry vernal pool in August 2023. *Ron Kirkwood*

the fall, winter, and spring, then dries up for a few months in summer. The dry phase of a vernal pool is important because it keeps out species that dominate the food chain in permanent streams and ponds. Big predators such as fish and bullfrogs can't survive the dry phase, so vernal pools become a safety zone for frogs, salamanders, and invertebrates that have evolved strategies to survive the summer drought. Many of these animals produce aquatic larvae that develop in the pool, then transform into air-breathing juveniles that leave the pool before it dries. Little freshwater crustaceans such as fairy shrimp produce drought-resistant eggs that lie dormant in the dry pool bottom, only hatching once the waters return. Vernal pools are important because they support these specialist species. But most of the wildlife living in the forest around a vernal pool will visit them throughout the year for food, water, or shelter. Game cameras set at vernal pools have documented visitors such as deer, bear, bobcat, coyote, raccoons, squirrels, wading birds, songbirds, hawks, owls, and bats.

In my mind's eye I imagine what this basin looks like in the spring. The plants are flooded under a large dark pool of water that formed from snowmelt and rain. The water is several feet deep, full of frog and salamander eggs, tadpoles, aquatic insects, and tiny crustaceans. Birds wade along the edges, picking out nutritious morsels, while a deer steps in for a long drink. A light drizzle begins as night falls. A few spring peepers make tentative peeps, then more join in, and soon a deafening chorus reverberates through the woods. These tiny frogs are scarcely bigger than a paper clip but individually can peep as loud as a car alarm going off. I sit quietly by the water's edge, hoping to catch a glimpse of a large black salamander with canary yellow spots swimming through the leaves.

Ron and his wife, Barb, were lucky to experience the magic of this vernal pool in person one day in February. They heard a strange, loud, quacking sound coming from the woods and went to investigate. They thought they might see waterfowl, but instead they found wood frogs bobbing in the cold water. Wood frogs are unique because they are the only frog that can live north of the Arctic Circle. They spend the winter tucked into the leaves on the forest floor. They are astonishing creatures because they create their own cellular antifreeze before otherwise freezing solid and entering a state of suspended animation where all their organs shut down. In the spring, they thaw from the outside in, and their heart and brain reactivate.

Every year after the breeding season, wood frogs and spotted salamanders disperse into the woods. Sometimes they must travel long distances to find good feeding sites, suitable burrows or other shelters, and overwintering sites. Each spring they return to the pool where they were born to mate and lay eggs. It is not fully known how they relocate their birth pool, but it is essential that they do. A pool that successfully raised them will likely be able to raise their offspring as well. Vernal pool animals have their own deep ways of remembering and navigating their world. I admire their resiliency and how they can survive and thrive in a challenging environment. These are lessons that both the George Spangler farm and its vernal pool teach us very well.

Betsy Leppo grew up with parents who taught high school science in a home across the street from Gifford Pinchot State Park in York County and was thus destined to become a biologist. She started working with the Pennsylvania Natural Heritage Program (PNHP) as an intern in 1992 while attending Juniata College and became an assistant data manager in 1996. She completed her master's degree at Shippensburg University. Her thesis examined the environmental variables that shape the macroinvertebrate communities of vernal pools in the Central Appalachian ecoregion. This effort earned her a position as an invertebrate zoologist with the PNHP in 2006. Betsy works with landowners and partners across the state to survey for vernal pools and wildlife, plan and implement wetland restoration projects, build a geodatabase of vernal pool locations, and develop conservation recommendations and outreach materials for these special habitats. Many of these materials can be found on the PNHP Vernal Pool website at https://www.naturalheritage.state.pa.us/vernalpools.aspx.

Appendix 2

Updates to the Wounded and Dead Lists

The following updates are based on pension files, Volunteer Carded Medical Records, and Compiled Military Service Records at the National Archives and Records Administration in Washington, D.C., newspaper archives, adjutant general records, hospital and provost reports at Musselman Library, Special Collections, Gettysburg College, state and town historical societies, surgeons' reports, veterans' burial cards, and regimental reports.

More Wounded

The following men have been confirmed as having been treated at the XI Corps hospital at the George Spangler farm and can be added to the wounded list from *Too Much for Human Endurance*. A total of 1,446 wounded men are now verified as having been treated at the XI Corps hospital:

Middlebrook, James R., Pvt., 17th Connecticut, Co. D, hernia.
Morgan, Wilbur B., Pvt., 17th Connecticut, Co. F, left arm.
Parsons, Augustus, Pvt., 10th New York Cavalry, Co. M, sick.
Rannells, William, J., Capt., 75th Ohio, Co. D, left hip.
Rush, John, Pvt., 153rd Pennsylvania, Co. K, left arm and right shoulder.
Russell, George A., 2nd Lt., 75th Ohio, Co. B, right leg.
Scranton, Alonzo, Pvt., 17th Connecticut, Co. D, jaw.

More Dead

The following men have been confirmed as having died at the XI Corps hospital at the George Spangler farm. This takes the XI Corps hospital confirmed death total to 138. The number who likely died there is now at eight for a total count of 146.

* Aeigle, John, Pvt., 107th Ohio, Co. K.
* Anguish, Horace, Cpl., 157th New York, Co. I.
* Balmes, Joseph, Pvt., 26th Wisconsin, Co. C.
* Barry, Jeremiah, Pvt., 134th New York, Co. E.
* Beal, Joseph, Pvt., 33rd Massachusetts, Co. I.
* Beverly, Balts, Pvt., 107th Ohio, Co. C.
**** Costin Jr., John, Capt., 82nd Ohio, Co. F.
** Frey, Matthias, Sgt., 107th Ohio, Co. B.
* Gebauer, Carl (Charles), Cpl., 107th Ohio, Co. K.
* Goodspeed, James H., Cpl., 75th Ohio, Co. D.
* Greiner, George B., Cpl., 73rd Ohio, Co. G.
* Krenscher, Peter, Pvt., 26th Wisconsin, Co. C.
* Kuhn, Peter, Pvt., 26th Wisconsin, Co. G.
** Sanford, Lewis, Bugler, 73rd Ohio, Co. C.
* Schwister, Mathias, Pvt., 26th Wisconsin, Co. F.
*** Smith, Frederick, Pvt., 134th New York, Co. A.
* Stier, Christian, Pvt., 26th Wisconsin, Co. E.
*** Swales, Samuel, Cpl., 134th New York, Co. F.
* Thomas, John B., Cpl., 134th New York, Co. E.
# Wilcox, Alva E., Cpl., 17th Connecticut, Co. D.

* Buried in Soldiers' National Cemetery in Gettysburg.
** Buried in Evergreen Cemetery in Gettysburg.
*** Buried in Schenectady County, New York.
**** Buried in Mansfield, Ohio.
# Initially buried in Evergreen Cemetery. His body was later moved to New Haven County, Connecticut.

One Final Note

There are conflicting reports on where Maj. Henry Baetz of the 26th Wisconsin was hospitalized. The July 31, 1863, *Semi-Weekly Wisconsin* in Milwaukee ran a list that included Baetz among 28 men of the 26th who were still being treated at the XI Corps hospital on July 12. All of these men are confirmed Spangler patients except Baetz, a 32-year-old native of Germany. The following, however, is excerpted from Baetz's Invalid Pension Claim 1091297 at the National Archives and Records Administration in Washington, D.C., which places him elsewhere: "Received a gunshot wound in the right leg between the knee and ankle in the following manner: While the said 26th Wisconsin Regiment was deployed in line of battle and actively engaged with the enemy, the applicant's horse was shot under him, and becoming unmanageable and unruly he dismounted and was wounded in the act of dismounting. (He was treated) In a house at Gettysburg temporarily used as a hospital from July 1 to July 4th, when he was removed to the field hospital on or near Cemetery Hill, where he remained a day or two, being then conveyed to a neighboring farm owned by one Lightner, where he remained about 14 days, when he was sent to his home at Manitowoc, Wis., on sick leave of absence." In yet another conflicting report, Baetz's carded medical record at the National Archives says he was admitted to a Baltimore hospital on July 8, which of course would mean that he couldn't have spent 14 days at the Lightner home. Baetz didn't show up in the XI Corps hospital records used for *Too Much for Human Endurance*, so he stays off the list despite the newspaper's report. Baetz became a notary public after the war and lived to age 79, according to his pension.

Appendix 3

The Known Wounded at the First Division, II Corps Hospitals

Tragically, more than 40 percent of the Union army's dead in the Civil War are unidentified, according to the U.S. Department of Defense. For example, of the 17,000 men buried in the nation's largest Union cemetery at Vicksburg, almost 13,000 of those graves are marked as unknown. The numbers are grim at Gettysburg as well, with 979 of the 3,345 battle burials in Soldiers' National Cemetery classified as unknown.[1]

It is not only the unknown soldier who paid a price. The unknown man's family back home bore the extraordinary burdens of not knowing how their loved one died or where he was buried. All they knew was that he was dead. Thus was life for the families in the days before dog tags. The problem of identification of severely wounded soldiers was exacerbated in crowded field hospitals by the severity or placement of an injury, language barriers for so many recent immigrants in the Union army, surgeons drowning in a flood of wounded men causing imprecise records, or if a soldier was taken to a unit's hospital that wasn't his own and where he wasn't known.

The First Division of the II Corps had an additional record-keeping problem at Gettysburg because its hospital kept moving to get out of the line of fire. This division's surgeons initially set up an aid station at the William Patterson farm on the Taneytown Road on the morning of July 2, but they weren't there long before the battle forced them to set up Hospital Location No. 2 that afternoon

---

1 https://bit.ly/49HLrZj, accessed Feb. 17, 2024.

258 Soldier Stories From Gettysburg's George Spangler Farm

along Granite Schoolhouse Lane in a field between the school and Powers Hill in the middle of George Spangler's farm. That hospital was in full operation only until mid-afternoon July 3 when artillery from the Confederate cannonade prior to Pickett's Charge forced the surgeons to evacuate again, leaving behind only the wounded who couldn't be moved. Hospital Location No. 3 was merely a brief stop at McAllister's Mill, which was already occupied and thus unsuitable. Hospital Location No. 4 was well behind the line on the Jacob Schwartz farm, where all three II Corps division hospitals found safety at last in the woods and fields along Rock Creek.

A. C. Registers 96 and 97 at the National Archives and Records Administration in Washington, D.C., list 741 names of soldiers from both the North and South who were treated at one, some, or all of the stops of the First Division, II Corps hospital. These records do not identify hospital locations, but the majority of the men listed here were patients at Granite Schoolhouse and/or the Schwartz farm. These registers do not include the names of men from the division who were treated in homes or other hospitals.

Granite Schoolhouse surgeon and First Division Chief Operator Charles S. Wood of the 66th New York wrote in these registers after the battle: "There is probably sufficient names unavoidably omitted to make the number at least nine hundred. We were obliged to move the hospital . . . in order to get out of line of fire creating . . . confusion and rendering it impossible to present correct record. . . . [I] believe this to be as correct as circumstances under which we labored would permit."[2]

The names of 649 of the 741 men who were recorded as being treated at the First Division, II Corps hospital locations have been verified and spelling corrections made if necessary and listed here. The names of the remaining men in these historic and fragile registers are lost to history because they are either covered by tape or they could not be read or verified. As this so sadly indicates, a Civil War soldier can be unknown today even if a doctor attempted to write his name in a register.[3]

2 A. C. Register 96, 2nd Army Corps, Army of the Potomac, Sept. 1, 1862 to July 1863, List of Wounded of the 1st Division Hospital, II Corps at the Battle of Gettysburg PA the 3 Day of July 1863, NARA; A. C. Register 97 July 3, 1863–Feb. 6, 1864, NARA.

3 Names of men who are known to have been treated at one or more of the First Division, II Corps hospitals but were not listed in the registers at the National Archives have been added to this list.

One Final Note

The 140th Pennsylvania suffered by far the most recorded and verified wounded at the First Division, II Corps hospitals with 101 men. As with all regiments there were undoubtedly many more. The 145th Pennsylvania and 148th Pennsylvania each had 65 and the 28th Massachusetts followed at 33. The 64th New York and 2nd Delaware had 31 apiece. There were 94 confirmed Confederates recorded, topped by the 14th Virginia of Armistead's brigade at nine. Though Armistead was treated at the Spangler XI Corps hospital, his brigade had 23 known wounded men at the Jacob Schwartz hospital.

The Wounded

Adams, Albert, Pvt., D, 64th NY, left leg, flesh wound, simple dressing.[4]

Adams, Hugh, Pvt., H, 140th PA, both thighs, flesh wound, simple dressing.

Akam, Richard, Pvt., I, 145th PA, left leg, fracture, amputation.

Alexander, Edward S., Sgt., K, 140th PA, right hand, flesh wound, simple dressing.

Allen, Erastus, Pvt., I, 145th PA, abdomen.

Allingham, Robert, Pvt., A, 116th PA, right leg, gunshot, simple dressing.

Allison, James, Sgt., I, 1st RI Artillery, two fingers amputated.

Arnold, Dawson W., Pvt., G, 5th FL, left arm, fracture, amputation.

Arnold, Willis, Pvt., E, 24th GA, left leg, fracture, simple dressing.

Aubrey, Henry, Sgt., I, 145th PA, right thigh, flesh wound, simple dressing.

Austin, John W., Pvt., H, 18th VA, right arm, flesh wound, simple dressing.

Babcock, David, Pvt., F, 61st NY, body, contusion, simple dressing.

Babcock, Ithamar, Pvt., C, 145th PA, right side, contusion, simple dressing.

Baird, William, Pvt., K, 2nd DE, right arm, flesh wound, simple dressing.

Baker, DeWarren, Sgt., G, 61st NY, leg, flesh wound, simple dressing.

Banta, Daniel, 1st Lt., 66th NY, I, right arm, gunshot, simple dressing.

Barden, Alonzo, Pvt., D, 5th MI, shoulder, contusion, simple dressing.

Barnes, George D., Cpl., K, 9th VA, shoulder, flesh wound, simple dressing.

Barnes, Samuel, Pvt., H, 140th PA, right knee, flesh wound, amputation.

Barr, Bankhead, Cpl., G, 140th PA, left hip, contusion, simple dressing.

Barrett, John, Pvt., C, 28th MA, left hip, contusion, simple dressing.

Bathurst, Simeon, Cpl., F, 148th PA, left knee, flesh wound, simple dressing.

Battenhousen, Conrad, Pvt., I, 61st NY, left arm, flesh wound, simple dressing.

---

4 First Division, II Corps surgeons used the term "simple dressing" while XI Corps doctors used "water dressing," but it's the same thing—an application of an ointment to a wound covered with a wet cloth.

Beabout, Beden, Cpl., D, 140th PA, both legs, flesh wounds, simple dressing.

Beal, James H., Pvt., H, 140th PA, right hand, flesh wound, simple dressing.

Bean, Wilson, Pvt., B, 140th PA, calf, flesh wound, simple dressing.

Beeman, Warren, Sgt., F, 86th NY, left thigh, flesh wound, simple dressing.

Beirly, Joseph C., Pvt., A, 148th PA, calf, flesh wound, simple dressing.

Bell, Sample S., Pvt., D, 140th PA, breast, flesh wound, simple dressing.

Bennett, George M., Pvt., B, 140th PA, right leg, flesh wound, simple dressing.

Bermoy, John, Pvt., F, 148th PA, wrist and breast, flesh wound, simple dressing.

Best, Tilman, Pvt., F, 2nd FL, left thigh, contusion, simple dressing.

Bice, Peter, Pvt., B, 57th NY, face fracture, gunshot wound, simple dressing.

Biddle, Samuel, Cpl., C, 2nd DE, right thigh, flesh wound, simple dressing.

Birch, Abner, Pvt., D, 140th PA, back, flesh wound, simple dressing.

Birch, Robert, Pvt., D, 140th PA, forefingers, amputation, and flesh wound back.

Bird, Obadiah W., Pvt., G, 57th VA, left leg, flesh wound, simple dressing.

Birteil, Jerry, 2nd Lt., F, 145th PA, wrist, flesh wound, simple dressing.

Black, John, Pvt., I, 145th PA, left shoulder, gunshot, ball lodged under bone.

Black, John D., Adj., 145th PA, left cheek, flesh wound, simple dressing.

Blair, John, Pvt., C, 140th PA, knee and thigh, flesh wounds, simple dressing.

Blake, Edwin, Pvt., K, 19th ME, right lung, gunshot wound, simple dressing.

Bodwell, William L., Pvt., C, 27th CT, right lung, gunshot, simple dressing.

Bonewell, Benjamin A., Pvt., F, 140th PA, left hand, flesh wound, resection
    of carpal bone.

Bonnet, Casper, Pvt., C, 66th NY, left knee, gunshot, simple dressing.

Booth, Samuel, Pvt., H, 9th AL, right leg, flesh wound, simple dressing.

Boss, James P., Pvt., H, 8th VA, femur, fracture, amputation.

Bostler, Peter, Pvt., A, 2nd DE, left hip, flesh wound, simple dressing.

Bowen, John, Pvt., B, 28th MA, calf of leg, flesh wound, simple dressing.

Boyd, Jacob, Sgt., I, 2nd DE, forearm, amputated at upper third.

Boyer, Adam, Pvt., A, 148th PA, left knee, flesh wound, simple dressing.

Boyle, Thomas, Sgt., B, 69th NY, right shoulder, gunshot, simple dressing.

Bradshaw, Hartwell H., Pvt., G, 7th TN, knee joint, fracture, amputation.

Bradt, Garrett, Pvt., I, 61st NY, right leg, flesh wound, simple dressing.

Brady, Eugene, Sgt., D, 116th PA, left breast, contusion, simple dressing.

Braherty, John, Pvt., K, 2nd DE, left leg, flesh wound, simple dressing.

Brisbin, Brice D., Pvt., G, 148th PA, right side, flesh wound, simple dressing.

Brock, Peter, Cpl., K, 28th MA, left shoulder & lung, gunshot, simple dressing.

Brockway, William F., Sgt., A, 145th PA, left leg, flesh wound, simple dressing.

Brown, E. C., Pvt., C, 140th PA, anthrax.

Brown, Hiram L., Col., 145th PA, left arm, flesh wound, simple dressing.

Brown, Michael A., Pvt., B, 148th PA, forearm, gunshot, resection of 4 inches.

Brown, Oscar S., Sgt., F, 145th PA, knee joint, fracture, amputation.

Brown, William, Sgt., I, 145th PA, right thigh, flesh wound, simple dressing.

Brownlee, William A., Lt., H, 10th AL, left shoulder, fracture, simple dressing.

Brunton, William A., Pvt., H, 140th PA, right thigh, flesh wound, simple dressing.

Bryden, John, Pvt., D, 57th NY, right shoulder, flesh wound, simple dressing.

Buckley, John, Pvt., B, 1st NY Artillery, right thigh, flesh wound, simple dressing.

Burke, John, Pvt., K, 2nd DE, breast, flesh wound, simple dressing.

Burke, Patrick, Pvt., B, 69th NY, left breast, flesh wound, simple dressing.

Burke, Richard, Pvt., K, 61st NY, right leg, flesh wound, simple dressing.

Button, Marvin, Sgt., F, 61st NY, left arm, flesh wound, simple dressing.

Butts, Walter, Lt., F, 9th VA, left lung, gunshot fracture, simple dressing.

Buzzard John S., Pvt., I, 148th PA, right hand, amputated forefinger.

Caldwell, William, Pvt., G, 2nd DE, back, contusion, simple dressing.

Calfrient, Fritz, Pvt., I, 61st NY, right leg, flesh wound, simple dressing.

Calhoun, Edward A., Pvt., I, 61st NY, right shoulder, contusion, simple dressing.

Carey, Edward, Pvt., D, 28th MA, left thigh, flesh wound, simple dressing.

Carleton, Dalmar J., Pvt., H, 11th MA, left arm, shell wound, simple dressing.

Carley, Daniel, Sgt., I, 4th ME, left hand, flesh wound, simple dressing.

Carriher, Henry, Pvt., G, 145th PA, right arm, flesh wound, simple dressing.

Cashdollar, Samuel, Pvt., E, 140th PA, right lung, gunshot.

Caswell, John, Pvt., G, 28th MA, both thighs, flesh wound, simple dressing.

Chambers, James, 1st Lt., C, 73rd NY, right thigh, flesh wound, simple dressing.

Chambers, Martin, Pvt., I, 140th PA, left hip, flesh wound, simple dressing.

Charlesworth, Joseph, Sgt., C, 64th NY, head, flesh wound, simple dressing.

Chisholm, Isaac W., Pvt., K, 140th PA, left thigh, flesh wound, simple dressing.

Clapper, George, Pvt., I, 145th PA, face, flesh wound, simple dressing.

Clark, Henry W., Cpl., F, 27th CT, right side, contusion, simple dressing.

Clark, Thomas J., Pvt., D, 2nd DE, left shoulder, flesh wound, simple dressing.

Clever, Isaac, Pvt., C, 140th PA, back, contusion, simple dressing.

Cockin, Freeman, Pvt., H, 66th NY, forearm, gunshot fracture, amputation.

Coger, John, Sgt., F, 28th MA, forearm, fracture, amputation.

Cole, Franklin, Pvt., G, 61st NY, left leg, fracture, amputation.

Cole, Jacob, Pvt., A, 57th NY, leg and right arm, flesh wound, simple dressing.

Collins, William A., 2nd Lt., F, 61st NY, groin, shell, simple dressing.

Conaway, Thomas A., Pvt., B, 148th PA, forearm, flesh wound, simple dressing.

Condron, Patrick, Pvt., B, 88th NY, sick.

Conlin, William, Pvt., H, 140th PA, left thigh, gunshot, amputated
at upper third.

Cooper, John, Pvt., D, 140th PA, leg, flesh wound, simple dressing.

Cooper, Robert, Pvt., A, 145th PA, head, flesh wound, simple dressing.

Corbin, Joseph A., Pvt., K, 140th PA, right leg, flesh wound, simple dressing.

Corser, Norman D., Pvt., C, 5th NH, right side, flesh wound, simple dressing.

Cox, Daniel R., Pvt., I, 57th NY, left knee, flesh wound, simple dressing.

Coyle, Michael, Pvt., F, 28th MA, right side, shell wound, simple dressing.

Crandall, George, Pvt., B, 145th PA, left leg, flesh wound, simple dressing.

Crawford, Anderson M., Pvt., G, 145th PA, right ankle, flesh wound,
simple dressing.

Crawford, Thomas, Pvt., G, 145th PA, right ankle, flesh wound, simple dressing.

Crispin, Silas, Pvt., D, 140th PA, right foot, flesh wound, simple dressing.

Cronk, Chester, Pvt., D, 64th NY, right leg, flesh wound, simple dressing.

Cross, Edward E., Col., 5th NH, abdomen.

Crowningshield, Eben S., Pvt., B, 1st RI Artillery, breast, flesh wound,
simple dressing.

Curaw, Avery, Pvt., D, 145th PA, left leg, flesh wound, simple dressing.

Curley, Michael, Sgt., F, 2nd DE, left shoulder, flesh wound, simple dressing.

Curran, Dennis, Pvt., D, 28th MA, left knee, shell, simple dressing.

Curran, John, Pvt., B, 88th NY, debility.

Darby, John A., Sgt., A, 64th NY, right leg, flesh wound, simple dressing.

Davidson, James, Pvt., H, 145th PA, right arm, flesh wound, simple dressing.

Davidson William, Sgt., I, 148th PA, back, contusion, simple dressing.

Davidson, William G., Sgt., C, 2nd DE, fractured skull & side,
shrapnel, trephined.

Davis, Henry, Pvt., A, 57th NY, left forearm, flesh wound, simple dressing.

Davis, John H., Pvt., E, 38th VA, left thigh, flesh wound, simple dressing.

Delavan, Robert, Pvt., I, 2nd DE, lower jaw, flesh wound, simple dressing.

Denning, Hugh, Pvt., D, 116th PA, left hip, flesh wound, simple dressing.

Denoyer, Theodore, Pvt., B, 1st NY Artillery, scalp, flesh wound, simple dressing.

Devine, Peter, Pvt., I, 8th AL, right leg, flesh wound, simple dressing.

Dickie, John A., Pvt., C, 140th PA, right shoulder, flesh wound, simple dressing.

Dilley, Adam C., Pvt., B, 140th PA, right shoulder, flesh wound, simple dressing.

Dilly, Lewis, Pvt., D, 140th PA, elbow, groin, thigh, arm amputated.

Doak, William, Pvt., F, 140th PA, left ankle, flesh wound, simple dressing.

Dollan, Peter, Pvt., H, 61st NY, left arm, gunshot, simple dressing.

Dolph, William, Cpl., D, 53rd PA, fracture of humerus, gunshot, amputation.

Donnelly, John, Pvt., H, 28th MA, left hand, fracture, simple dressing.

Dorman, Isaac, Pvt., A, 145th PA, right shoulder, flesh wound, simple dressing.

Doty, Thomas, Pvt., D, 140th PA, left shoulder, flesh wound, simple dressing.

Doty, Wilson, Pvt., D, 140th PA, left thigh, contusion, simple dressing.

Dougherty, John, Pvt., I, 145th PA, head, fracture, simple dressing.

Dougherty, Joseph, Sgt., B, 69th NY, left leg, flesh wound, simple dressing.

Driscoll, Jeremiah, Cpl., E, 28th MA, left toe, flesh wound, simple dressing.

Dudley, Wentworth, Pvt., E, 64th NY, right thigh, flesh wound, simple dressing.

Duncan, Richard, Pvt., E, 14th VA, left hip, contusion, simple dressing.

Dunkle, Benjamin F., Pvt., G, 148th PA, right hand, flesh wound, simple dressing.

Dunn, John, Pvt., I, 2nd DE, right shoulder, flesh wound, simple dressing.

Dunning, Hugh, Pvt., D, 116th PA, left iliac region, gunshot, simple dressing.

Durbin, John, Pvt., I, 9th AL, left thigh, flesh wound, simple dressing.

Durst, John, Pvt., D, 148th PA, left ankle, contusion, simple dressing.

Dwyer, Edward, Pvt., C, 28th MA, left hip, contusion, simple dressing.

Eagan, Patrick, Pvt., B, 88th NY, left leg, flesh wound, simple dressing.

Earnest, Benjamin, Pvt., K, 140th PA, left foot, flesh wound, simple dressing.

Earnest, Joseph, Cpl., I, 148th PA, calf of leg, flesh wound, simple dressing.

Edwards, Henry, Pvt., F, 140th PA, right hip, flesh wound, simple dressing.

Edwards, Samuel, Pvt., B, 145th PA, left leg, flesh wound, simple dressing.

Egbert, Lewis F., Pvt., B, 140th PA, right thigh, flesh wound, simple dressing.

Eldridge, Lucius O., Sgt., D, 145th PA, hand, fracture, amputation.

Elliott, John, Capt., B, 7th TN, neck, flesh wound, simple dressing.

Erhard, Amos, Pvt., A, 148th PA, thigh, grape shot, simple dressing.

Evans, John, Pvt., B, 57th NY, left arm, flesh wound, simple dressing.

Fannerly, John W., Pvt., I, 140th PA, left heel, flesh wound, simple dressing.

Farmiloe, George H., Pvt., F, 28th MA, left forearm, flesh wound, simple dressing.

Farrar, William H., Pvt., F, 14th VA, left arm, flesh wound, simple dressing.

Farrington, Patrick, Sgt., G, 82nd NY, thigh, gunshot fracture, simple dressing.

Fassett, Ansel, Pvt., A, 4th U.S. Artillery, hip, laceration, simple dressing.

Ferdinand, Joseph, Pvt., F, 82nd NY, side of neck, shell, simple dressing.

Fergus, Samuel, Cpl., C, 140th PA, left thigh, flesh wound, simple dressing.

Ferringer, Daniel, Pvt., I, 148th PA, left hip, flesh wound, simple dressing.

Fink, Elijah C., Pvt., A, 28th VA, foot, flesh wound, simple dressing.

Fitzgerald, Patrick, Pvt., D, 19th MA, gluteal muscle, gunshot, simple dressing.

Fitzsimmons, Andrew, Pvt., K, 28th MA, left hand, flesh wound, simple dressing.

Fleisher, Henry, Pvt., G, 148th PA, right side, contusion, simple dressing.

Forbes, Frank M., Pvt., I, 145th PA, breast, flesh wound, simple dressing.

Ford, Gilbert A. W., Cpl., C, 27th CT, shoulder, flesh wound, simple dressing.

Forster, Trangott, Cpl., E, 52nd NY, left arm, flesh wound, simple dressing.

Fowler, Alonzo, Pvt., I, 148th PA, right hand, flesh wound, simple dressing.

Fowler, Edward B., Pvt., F, 27th CT, both legs, gunshot, amputation of left.

Fox, George, Cpl. H, 140th PA, right thigh, flesh wound, simple dressing.

Frank, Jacob, Pvt., K, 57th NY, hernia, contusion, simple dressing.

Franklin, Andrus, Pvt., B, 64th NY, left leg, flesh wound, simple dressing.

Frazier, William, Pvt., I, 140th PA, left leg, flesh wound, simple dressing.

Freeland, George, Pvt., A, 140th PA, back, contusion, simple dressing.

Freeman, David W., Pvt., C, 15th MA, right forearm, gunshot, simple dressing, ball extracted.

Freyling, Andrew, Pvt., E, 2nd DE, left foot, flesh wound, simple dressing.

Fridley, John H., Pvt., K, 28th VA, temple and leg, flesh wound, simple dressing.

Fry, Eben, Pvt., I, 52nd NC, right thigh, flesh wound, simple dressing.

Fuller, Charles, 2nd Lt., C, 61st NY, left leg & arm, gunshot, amputation thigh, resection humerus.

Garland, Frank, Lt., A, 61st NY, face & left lung, gunshot, simple dressing.

Garner, Calvin, Sgt., H, 14th VA, right leg, gunshot fracture, simple dressing.

Gerhards, Henry, 1st Sgt., E, 66th NY, right thigh, flesh wound, simple dressing.

Gibb, John, Pvt., H, 140th PA, thigh, flesh wound, simple dressing.

Gibbons, Henry, Pvt., F, 145th PA, left leg, flesh wound, simple dressing.

Gilbert, Charles, Pvt., H, 2nd FL, left forearm, gunshot, simple dressing.

Gilbert, Charles, Pvt., H, 28th MA, left elbow, flesh wound, simple dressing.

Gilbert, George, Pvt., G, 148th PA, left heel, flesh wound, simple dressing.

Gilbert, Manasses, Pvt., A, 148th PA, left shoulder, flesh wound, simple dressing.

Gilbert, Nehemiah, Pvt., C, 140th PA, left leg, flesh wound, simple dressing.

Gilhousen, Fred, Pvt., I, 148th PA, left leg, flesh wound, simple dressing.

Gill, Samuel, Pvt., C, 148th PA, left shoulder, flesh wound, simple dressing.

Gilliam, Rice A., Cpl., D, 18th VA, left thigh, flesh wound, simple dressing.

Gillin, Robert, Pvt., F, 140th PA, back, contusion, simple dressing.

Ginther, Joseph, Pvt., C, 116th PA, right foot, flesh wound, simple dressing.

Goad, Vincent, 1st Sgt., B, 14th VA, hips, flesh wound, simple dressing.

Goodrum, William, Pvt., A, 11th NC, left thigh, contusion, simple dressing.

Grady, Andrew, Sgt., D, 28th MA, shoulder, contusion, simple dressing.

Gray, George, Pvt., A, 140th PA, thigh, flesh wound, simple dressing.

Gray, John, Pvt., A, 140th PA, left foot, flesh wound, simple dressing.

Gray, Leonard S., Pvt., K, 145th PA, left leg, flesh wound, simple dressing.

Gray, Thomas, Sgt., C, 116th PA, abdomen, gunshot, simple dressing.

Grear, Thomas, Pvt., I, 2nd DE, right hand, flesh wound, simple dressing.

Green, John, Pvt., H, 148th PA, right side, flesh wound, simple dressing.

Green, Samuel R., Pvt., A, 5th NH, leg, gunshot fracture, amputation.

Griffin, John, Pvt., G, 27th CT, forefinger, flesh wound, simple dressing.

Griswold, George, Capt., I, 145th PA, right wrist, flesh wound, simple dressing.

Groft, George, Pvt., E, 148th PA, left knee, flesh wound, simple dressing.

Guiser, Matthias, Pvt., A, 148th PA, left leg, flesh wound, simple dressing.

Gunsalis, Samuel, Pvt., H, 148th PA, right hip, flesh wound, simple dressing.

Hacock, Richard, Sgt., H, 66th NY, left shoulder, contusion, simple dressing.

Hall, John, Pvt., H, 140th PA, flesh wound, simple dressing.

Hall, Thomas W., Pvt., C, 12th NC, left hand, gunshot, amputated finger.

Hamlin, James H, 1st Lt., I, 145th PA, foot, flesh wound, simple dressing.

Hammell, John S., Lt. Col., 66th NY, left arm, flesh wound, simple dressing.

Hancock, Winfield Scott, Maj. Gen., II Corps, thigh, gunshot.

Hannum, Stephen, Cpl., B, 2nd DE, left arm, shell, amputated at shoulder joint.

Hardenbrook, Cornell, 1st Lt., A, 66th NY, left shoulder, gunshot,
     simple dressing.

Hardin, Henry, Pvt., A, 2nd DE, right ankle, flesh wound, simple dressing.

Harpster, John, Sgt., G, 148th PA, right side, contusion, simple dressing.

Harrelson, Benjamin M., Pvt., D, 20th NC, left thigh, flesh wound,
     simple dressing.

Harrington, Dennis, Pvt., I, 28th MA, right arm, gunshot, simple dressing.

Harris, James L., Pvt., F, 56th VA, left leg, gunshot, amputation.

Hart, Dunning, Cpl., G, 140th PA, forearm, flesh wound, simple dressing.

Hassler, Frederick, Pvt., I, 52nd NY, left hip, flesh wound, simple dressing.

Hatch, M. W., Pvt., E, 4th ME, right arm, flesh wound, simple dressing.

Hathaway, William, Pvt., D, 116th PA, hip, contusion, simple dressing.

Havener, Christian C., Pvt., H, 148th PA, upper jaw, flesh wound,
     simple dressing.

Hayes, Charles E., Pvt., C, 2nd DE, right shoulder, flesh wound, simple dressing.

Hays, Grief, Pvt., E, 13th MS, both thighs, flesh wound, simple dressing.

Healy, Lewis S., Pvt., G, 64th NY, face, flesh wound, simple dressing.

Heathcock, Jackson, Pvt., C, 23rd NC, finger, gunshot fracture,
     amputated one finger.

Heim, Isaac, Cpl., I, 53rd PA, hand, flesh wound, simple dressing.

Helms, Aaron S., Pvt., F, 114th PA, scalp, contusion, simple dressing.

Helt, William A., Pvt., G, 140th PA, left knee, flesh wound, simple dressing.

Henderson, Charles H., Pvt., E, 27th CT, left forearm, flesh wound,
     simple dressing.

Henry, James, Pvt., F, 148th PA, sick.

Henry, John A., Pvt., H, 145th PA, right knee, flesh wound, simple dressing.

Herbig, Nicholas, Pvt., G, 64th NY, left thigh, flesh wound, simple dressing.

Herrick, William A., Pvt., B, 145th PA, left arm, flesh wound, simple dressing.

Hews, Richard, Pvt., I, 1st U.S. Artillery, back, contusion, simple dressing.

Higby, William, Cpl., E, 145th PA, left leg, flesh wound, simple dressing.

Hill, Edward, Pvt., 4th U.S. Artillery, left leg, solid shot, simple dressing.

Hilton, John C., Capt., K, 145th PA, right leg, flesh wound, simple dressing.

Hoffman, Edwin, Pvt., G, 145th PA, right leg, flesh wound, simple dressing.

Hoffman, Peter, Pvt., C, 26th WI, forearm, contusion, simple dressing.

Holland, Robert, 2nd Sgt., I, 28th VA, forearm, flesh wound, simple dressing.

Hopper, Barney, Pvt., F, 64th NY, right hip, flesh wound, simple dressing.

Horgan (aka Haynes), Owen, Pvt., C, 28th MA, scalp, flesh wound, simple dressing.

Horner, Henry, Pvt., E, 148th PA, right heel, flesh wound, simple dressing.

Hubbard, Alex, Cpl., C, 28th VA, right shoulder, flesh wound, simple dressing.

Hughes, James, Pvt., D, 140th PA, right leg, flesh wound, simple dressing.

Hulburt, Samuel, Pvt., I, 145th PA, right shoulder, contusion, simple dressing.

Hurley, Edmund M., Cpl., A, 4th U.S. Light Artillery, left side, flesh wound, simple dressing.

Hutchinson, William, Pvt., A, 116th PA, abdomen, flesh wound, simple dressing.

Ingraham, Simeon, Sgt., K, 64th NY, left hand, flesh wound, simple dressing.

Irey, Clark, Pvt., C, 140th PA, flesh wound, grape shot, simple dressing.

Isett, George W., Cpl., C, 53rd PA, right thigh, flesh wound, simple dressing.

Jenkins, David, Pvt., A, 11th NC, thigh, flesh wound, simple dressing.

Jenkins, Porter, Pvt., B, 145th PA, back, contusion, simple dressing.

Jobes, Hiram, Pvt., E, 145th PA, right shoulder, flesh wound, simple dressing.

Johnson, Andrew, Pvt., E, 140th PA, left shoulder, flesh wound, simple dressing.

Johnson, David, Pvt., F, 48th GA, back, shell, contusion, simple dressing.

Johnson, Henry M., Pvt., C, 14th VA, right thigh, flesh wound, simple dressing.

Jones, Andrew J., Capt., I, 11th VA, right foot, flesh wound, simple dressing.

Jones, John, Pvt., I, 11th VA, left knee, flesh wound, simple dressing.

Jones, Lewis, Pvt., I, 57th NY, scalp, contusion, simple dressing.

Jones, Nathan E., Pvt., I, 9th VA, left hip, flesh wound, simple dressing.

Jordan, John J., Pvt., C, 140th PA, left arm, flesh wound, simple dressing.

Kaanoy, Michael, Pvt., F, 57th NY, left knee, flesh wound, simple dressing.

Kane, James, Cpl., A, 88th NY, left foreleg, flesh wound, simple dressing.

Kaufman, Samuel, Pvt., I, 53rd PA, left foot, flesh wound, simple dressing.

Keating, William, Pvt., B, 88th NY, left cheek, flesh wound, simple dressing.

Keech, William, Capt., B, 61st NY, neck left side, gunshot, ball extracted.

Keenan, Levi, Pvt., E, 140th PA, right leg, gunshot, amputation.

Keeny, Daniel, Pvt., C, 140th PA, right hand, flesh wound, simple dressing.

Keinle, John, Pvt., G, 8th AL, left hip, flesh wound, simple dressing.

Kelly, George F., Pvt., D, 8th VA, right thigh, flesh wound, simple dressing.

Kelly, James, Pvt., G, 28th MA, right foot, contusion, simple dressing.

Kelly, Thomas, Pvt., G, 28th MA, left hand, simple dressing.

Kemmerer, Reuben, Pvt., I, 81st PA, right finger, flesh wound, simple dressing.

Kent, Daniel, Pvt., A, 145th PA, left leg, flesh wound, simple dressing.

Kerr, James P., Sgt., G, 140th PA, left foot, flesh wound, simple dressing.

Khyle, Joseph, Pvt., G, 53rd PA, left leg, fracture, operation not advisable.

Kincaid, James L., Capt., G, 52nd NC, left femur, gunshot fracture, amputation.

Kinsey, C. P., Cpl., G, 27th CT, general debility.

Knott, William W., Pvt., K, 55th NC, abdomen, gunshot, simple dressing.

Knuppenburg, Myron, Pvt., H, 64th NY, left leg, flesh wound, simple dressing.

Kreiss, William, Pvt., I, 52nd NY, thoracic wall (chest), flesh wound,
    simple dressing.

Kreps, David, Pvt., C, 148th PA, wrist, fracture, splints.

Kreps, William H., Pvt., B, 148th PA, face, flesh wound, simple dressing.

Kuhn, John A., Pvt., D, 145th PA, right arm, flesh wound, simple dressing.

Kunkle, John, Pvt., E, 148th PA, left knee, flesh wound, simple dressing.

Lancaster, William T., Pvt., F, 3rd VA, left hand, gunshot fracture,
    amputated two fingers.

Lattimer, John W., Pvt., G, 9th VA, left leg, fracture, simple dressing.

Leddy, Michael, Pvt., B, 69th NY, right arm, gunshot, simple dressing.

Leitzell, George W., Sgt., D, 148th PA, right heel, contusion, simple dressing.

Lenehan, Frank, Pvt., A, 88th NY, right hand, flesh wound, simple dressing.

Lewis, Henry, Sgt., B, 145th PA, arm, fracture, amputation.

Lewis, Horatio F., 1st Lt., D, 145th PA, left leg, fracture, amputation.

Lewis, John T., 2nd Lt., E, 14th VA, right little finger and hips, gunshot
    fracture, amputation.

Lewis, Richard B., 1st Sgt., E, 14th VA, hips, flesh wound, simple dressing.

Light, Charles M., Pvt., F, 38th VA, left shoulder, flesh wound, simple dressing.

Limbert, Frederick, Pvt., A, 148th PA, right foot, flesh wound, simple dressing.

Lincoln, Richard F., 2nd Lt., H, 64th NY, right thigh, flesh wound,
    simple dressing.

Linehan, Michael, Pvt., C, 88th NY, back, contusion, simple dressing.

Linnegar, Washington, Pvt., B, 145th PA, right leg, fracture, amputation.

Linton, David, Pvt., I, 1st U.S. Artillery, left leg, gunshot wound, water dressing.

Long, John, Pvt., A, 140th PA, left thigh, flesh wound, simple dressing.

Loyd, Lawrence, Cpl., I, 57th NY, left leg, flesh wound, simple dressing.

Luckhart, Thomas, Pvt., E, 148th PA, left knee, flesh wound, simple dressing.

Lynn, James H., Pvt., G, 140th PA, right groin, flesh wound, simple dressing.

Maguire, Patrick, Pvt., I, 28th MA, left arm, gunshot, simple dressing.

Mahan, James H., Pvt., C, 2nd DE, left shoulder, flesh wound, simple dressing.

Maher, James, Pvt., B, 88th NY, submaxillary, fracture, simple dressing.

Malin, Francis, Sgt., C, 116th PA, killed.

Mann, Horace, Cpl., I, 145th PA, right thigh, flesh wound, simple dressing.

Manning, John W., Sgt., F, 3rd GA Sharpshooters, left thigh, flesh wound, simple dressing.

Marsh, William F., Pvt., H, 56th VA, right thigh, flesh wound, simple dressing.

Marshall, James, Pvt., I, 81st PA, right foot, flesh wound, simple dressing.

Massie, John W., Pvt., I, 19th VA, left leg, fracture, amputation.

Masterson, Patrick, Pvt., K, 57th NY, left shoulder, flesh wound, simple dressing.

Mathews, Peter, 1st Sgt., E, 57th NY, ankle, flesh wound, simple dressing.

Mattern, John, Pvt., C, 148th PA, sick.

Matthews, Andrew J., Pvt., C, 28th VA, right leg, flesh wound, simple dressing.

Maxwell, William H., Pvt., F, 61st NY, left shoulder, flesh wound, simple dressing.

Mayne, Frank, Pvt., B, 57th NY, right elbow, flesh wound, simple dressing.

Mays, Robert, D., Pvt., G, 19th VA, both thighs, flesh wound, simple dressing.

McCarthy, James, Pvt., B, 88th NY, right leg, flesh wound, simple dressing.

McCarty, Denis, Pvt., I, 1st U.S. Artillery, right foot, gunshot wound, water dressing.

McClune, Thomas, Pvt., C, 140th PA, left wrist, contusion, simple dressing.

McCoy, Charles, Pvt., H, 140th PA, left thigh, flesh wound, simple dressing.

McCoy, John, Pvt., B, 2nd DE, left side, flesh wound, simple dressing.

McCullough, Andrew, Pvt., F, 140th PA, left hip, flesh wound, simple dressing.

McDevitt, Fenton, Cpl., H, 99th PA, tibia, gunshot fracture, amputation.

McElister, James, Pvt., A, 2nd DE, forehead, flesh wound, simple dressing.

McFadden, Daniel, Pvt., I, 57th NY, scalp, flesh wound, simple dressing.

McGee, Michael, Pvt., B, 88th NY, back, contusion, simple dressing.

McGee, William H., Pvt., B, 7th TN, left temple, flesh wound, simple dressing.

McGinley, Anthony, Pvt., D, 62nd PA, hips, shell wound, simple dressing.

McGlaughlin, John Thomas, Pvt., B, 13th AL, left tibia, fracture, amputation.

McGowan, Michael, Sgt., G, 28th MA, right hip, flesh wound, simple dressing.

McGowan, Patrick, Pvt., B, 1st NY Light Artillery, shoulder blade, laceration, simple dressing.

McGrath, Thomas, Pvt., D, 69th NY, right hip, gunshot, simple dressing.

McGuire, Francis, Pvt., B, 57th NY, right ankle, contusion, simple dressing.

McHenry, Michael, Pvt., I, 1st U.S. Artillery, head, contusion, simple dressing.

McIntosh, Thomas, Pvt., I, 57th NY, left hand, gunshot, amputated 3 fingers.

McKenna, Patrick, Pvt., B, 88th NY, sore leg.

McKethan, John G., Sgt., D, 23rd NC, left hip.

McKinley, David, Pvt., F, 145th PA, left leg, flesh wound, simple dressing.

McKinley, Samuel, Pvt., B, 140th PA, left arm, flesh wound, simple dressing.

McKinzie, Alonzo, Cpl., F, 140th PA, left arm, flesh wound, simple dressing.

McKoon, Chauncey, Cpl., B, 64th NY, right thigh, flesh wound, simple dressing.

McMahon, James, Pvt., F, 9th MA, left hand, contusion, simple dressing.

McManamy, John, Pvt., F, 140th PA, left thigh, flesh wound, simple dressing.

McMarin, John, Pvt., H, 13th MS, elbow joint, fracture, amputation.

McMellon, William H., Pvt., B, 57th VA, scalp, flesh wound, simple dressing.

McNary, Frank B., Pvt., C, 140th PA, right side, flesh wound, simple dressing.

McNeal, William, Pvt., C, 4th U.S. Artillery, abdomen, laceration,
     simple dressing.

Meenan, Michael, Sgt., E, 2nd DE, right arm, gunshot, amputation.

Meldoon, Robert, Pvt., K, 140th PA, heel & leg, flesh wound, simple dressing.

Merrill, Martin, Pvt., G, 27th CT, nose, flesh wound, simple dressing.

Messervey, James J., 1st Lt., C, 64th NY, left leg, flesh wound, simple dressing.

Metts, Henry A., Pvt., H, 24th VA, right arm, flesh wound, simple dressing.

Millam, James E., 1st Sgt., G, 53rd VA, arm, gunshot.

Miller, Andrew, Pvt., A, 57th NY, left hip, flesh wound, simple dressing.

Miller, Joseph L., 2nd Lt., PA Light Artillery C and F, knee joint, flesh
     wound, simple dressing.

Miller, Thomas, Cpl., H, 140th PA, hand, flesh wound, amputated fingers.

Miller, William DeWitt, Capt., aide-to-camp on Gen. Hancock's staff,
     abdomen, gunshot, simple dressing.

Millspaugh, Leander, Pvt., D, 64th NY, right arm, flesh wound, simple dressing.

Mingle, Elias, Sgt., A, 148th PA, right knee, flesh wound, simple dressing.

Mitchell, Samuel, Pvt., B, 88th NY, back, contusion, simple dressing.

Montgomery, Hugh, 1st Sgt., F, 61st NY, right arm, gunshot, simple dressing.

Moore, George D., Cpl., B, 140th PA, both legs and shoulder, flesh wounds,
     simple dressing.

Moore, Robert, Pvt., G, 2nd DE, hernia.

Moore, William, Cpl., F, 64th NY, right hip, flesh wound, simple dressing.

Moreland, Edward, Pvt., I, 1st U.S. Artillery, side, flesh wound, water dressing.

Morgan, Newell, Pvt., B, 64th NY, right hip, flesh wound, simple dressing.

Morris, Henry, Pvt., B, 82nd NY, foot, gunshot, simple dressing.

Morris, Orlando H., Col., 66th NY, right side, flesh wound, simple dressing.

Morris, Tallinghast, Pvt., C, 140th PA, both thighs, flesh wounds,
     simple dressing.

Morrison, Thomas, Capt., G, 61st NY, left side of neck, gunshot,
simple dressing.

Morse, W. A., Sgt., H, 27th CT, typhoid fever.

Mortimer, William S., Sgt., K, 148th PA, left thigh, flesh wound,
simple dressing.

Mower, John, Pvt., E, 145th PA, back, contusion, simple dressing.

Mullen, Robert, Pvt., K, 28th MA, face & neck, flesh wound, simple dressing.

Mullison, John, Pvt., I, 64th NY, head, flesh wound, simple dressing.

Murphy, G. R., Cpl., F, 13th MS.

Murphy, John, Pvt., G, 57th NY, right hand, gunshot, amputated two fingers.

Murphy, Patrick, Pvt., G, 69th PA, right hand, flesh wound, simple dressing.

Myers, Jacob W., Pvt., B, 28th VA, left lung, penetrating wound, simple dressing.

Nail, James M., 1st Lt., C, 42nd MS, right thigh, flesh wound, simple dressing.

Neely, Hugh L., Cpl., I, 1st U.S. Artillery, left ankle, flesh wound,
simple dressing.

Nevin, James, Pvt., B, 88th NY, left thigh, contusion, simple dressing.

Newell, Samuel T., Pvt., I, 1st U.S. Artillery, left thigh, flesh wound,
simple dressing.

Newman, Alvin, Pvt., C, 140th PA, humerus fracture, amputation.

Nichols, Charles, Pvt., D, 27th CT, biceps muscle, gunshot, simple dressing.

Nicholson, Thomas C., 1st Lt., I, 140th PA, back, contusion, simple dressing.

Nickerson, Colin, Pvt., K, 140th PA, breast, contusion, simple dressing.

Nims, Morgan A., Pvt., I, 145th PA, shoulder, flesh wound, simple dressing.

Nolan, Dennis, Pvt., I, 1st U.S. Artillery, forearm, flesh wound, simple dressing.

Nolan, James C., 1st Sgt., B, 140th PA, shoulder, flesh wound, simple dressing.

Noonan, John, Pvt., A, 88th NY, right shoulder, flesh wound, simple dressing.

Obermark, Francis, Cpl., B, 52nd NY, left foot, flesh wound, simple dressing.

O'Brien, Michael, Pvt., I, 1st U.S. Artillery, right leg, flesh wound,
simple dressing.

O'Dea, Patrick, Pvt., I, 1st U.S. Artillery, right foot, flesh wound,
simple dressing.

O'Flaherty, Patrick, Pvt., B, 28th MA, hip & lung, flesh wound, simple dressing.

Orr, James W., Pvt., I, 140th PA, groin, gunshot, simple dressing.

Osmon, George, Pvt., C, 148th PA, left hip, contusion, simple dressing.

Paine, Michael, Pvt., A, 28th MA, right side, flesh wound, simple dressing.

Parker, James H., Pvt., G, 2nd DE, back, flesh wound, simple dressing.

Parker, William, Pvt., F, 148th PA, right cheek, gunshot, simple dressing.

Parks, Marcus A., Lt. Col., 52nd NC, leg, gunshot, simple dressing.

Parmeter, S. L., Cpl., B, 145th PA, right shoulder, flesh wound, simple dressing.

Patch, Charles W., 2nd Lt., K, 2nd NH, abdomen, gunshot.

Patterson, Robert, Sgt., G, 148th PA, left arm, flesh wound, simple dressing.

Pearce, Josiah P., 1st Lt., D, 2nd DE., right thigh, gunshot, simple dressing.

Pearson, George W., Pvt., C, 2nd DE, left leg, fracture, simple dressing.

Pennington, John, Pvt., F, 148th PA, right arm, flesh wound, simple dressing.

Perkins, James, Pvt., E, 145th PA, right leg, flesh wound, simple dressing.

Perrin, James, Pvt., A, 14th VA, sick.

Perry, William, Pvt., F, 148th PA, left thigh, flesh wound, simple dressing.

Phelps, William, Cpl., F, 148th PA, body.

Phillips, John, Pvt., D, 27th CT, left leg, flesh wound, simple dressing.

Phillips, Phillip G., Pvt., I, 19th MS, right thigh, flesh wound, simple dressing.

Phillips, Wayne J., Pvt., G, 140th PA, right hand, flesh wound, simple dressing.

Pincus, Adolph, Cpl., C, 66th NY, shoulder, fracture, splints.

Pitts, William, Pvt., K, 42nd MS, right hip, contusion, simple dressing.

Platt, Legrand, Pvt., B, 86th NY, died July 6.

Plunkett, Timothy, Pvt., B, 88th NY, sides & arm, flesh wound, simple dressing.

Pollay, David, Pvt., E, 64th NY, neck, flesh wound, simple dressing.

Porter, John, Pvt., C, 5th U.S. Artillery, back, gunshot fracture, simple dressing.

Porter, William, Pvt., B, 116th PA, side, contusion, simple dressing.

Post, Jeremiah H., Sgt., H, 61st NY, left side, contusion, simple dressing.

Potter, James, Cpl., F, 148th PA, sick.

Presher, Horace, Sgt., H, 64th NY, left thigh, flesh wound, simple dressing.

Presnell, Stanton, Sgt., B, 52nd NC, right knee, flesh wound, simple dressing.

Primmer, Walter, Pvt., F, 64th NY, left leg, flesh wound, simple dressing.

Quail, Charles, Pvt., C, 140th PA, back, contusion, simple dressing.

Rambmeier, Frederick, Pvt., B, 52nd NY, right hip, flesh wound,
    simple dressing.

Ramsey, Calvin, Cpl., D, 140th PA, left leg, flesh wound, simple dressing.

Raugh, James J., Pvt., C, 53rd PA, left shoulder, gunshot, simple dressing.

Ray, James, Pvt., D, 64th NY, right thigh, flesh wound, simple dressing.

Ray, James, Cpl., C, 148th PA, shoulder, flesh wound, simple dressing.

Reed, Reuben, Pvt., G, 148th PA, right thigh, flesh wound, simple dressing.

Reese, John, Pvt., I, 53rd PA, right thigh, flesh wound, simple dressing.

Reeser, Jacob, Pvt., D, 148th PA, right arm, flesh wound, simple dressing.

Reggles, Andrew, Pvt., A, 64th NY, left leg, flesh wound, simple dressing.

Reilly, Thomas, Pvt., A, 88th NY, right knee, flesh wound, simple dressing.

Remig, William, Capt., I, 81st PA, left arm, fracture, amputation.

Reynolds, James, Capt., B, 61st OH, right arm, gunshot, simple dressing.

Reynolds, John W., Capt., 145th PA, head, flesh wound, simple dressing.

Richardson, Cyrus J., Pvt., F, 145th PA, left thigh, flesh wound, simple dressing.

Richey, Martin, Pvt., D, 10th AL, left chest, flesh wound, simple dressing.

Riddle, Robert, Sgt., F, 140th PA, back, contusion, simple dressing.

Riley, Terrence, Pvt., E, 28th MA, left arm, flesh wound, simple dressing.

Robb, George, Pvt., B, 1st NY Artillery, scalp, flesh wound, simple dressing.

Rogers, Augustus, Pvt., B, 1st NY Artillery, right leg, fracture, amputated.

Rohletha, Herman, Pvt., H, 57th NY, left knee, laceration, simple dressing.

Roy, Eugene, Pvt., C, 5th MI, left arm & leg, gunshot, simple dressing.

Royer, George, Pvt., I, 145th PA, right leg, flesh wound, simple dressing.

Royer, Jonas, Pvt., D, 145th PA, left leg, flesh wound, simple dressing.

Rudiger, John, Cpl., A, 66th New York, right leg, gunshot, amputation.

Ryan, Patrick, Pvt., C, 66th NY, left third finger, fracture, simple dressing.

Saders, Philo W., Cpl., K, 64th NY, right thigh, flesh wound, simple dressing.

Sattler, Alexander, Sgt., H, 52nd NY, left foot, flesh wound, simple dressing.

Savage, Joseph, Sgt. Maj., 64th NY, right arm, gunshot fracture, amputation.

Saville, Francis, Pvt., I, 2nd DE, abdomen, penetrating wound, simple dressing.

Sawdy, Alexander, Cpl., D, 145th PA, thigh, flesh wound, simple dressing.

Sayer, James P., Cpl., C, 140th PA, arms and legs, flesh wounds, simple dressing.

Schmidt, William, Pvt., A, 4th U.S. Artillery, left shoulder, flesh wound, simple dressing.

Schneider, George, Pvt., F, 57th NY, ankle, flesh wound, simple dressing.

Scott, David, 1st Sgt., I, 140th PA, face and right side, gunshot, simple dressing.

Scott, Henry, Pvt., A, 140th PA, left hip, contusion, simple dressing.

Scott, Joseph, Pvt., D, 145th PA, left arm, flesh wound, simple dressing.

Scoville, John M., Pvt., B, 1st NY Artillery, side & arm, flesh wound, simple dressing.

Searson, Edwin, Pvt., B, 148th PA, left cheek, flesh wound, simple dressing.

Secor, Eugene, Sgt., H, 61st NY, left leg, gunshot, amputation.

Secor, Gabriel, Pvt., I, 61st NY, elbow, flesh wound, simple dressing.

Shallenberger, William S., Adj., 140th PA, left leg, shell, simple dressing.

Shapleigh, George R., Sgt., D, 5th NH, right arm, gunshot, simple dressing.

Sherman, Stephen R., Pvt., B, 1st NY Artillery, left arm, flesh wound, simple dressing.

Shields, Arthur, 1st Sgt., H, 140th PA, right thigh, flesh wound, simple dressing.

Shields, John, Capt., E, 53rd PA, right arm, gunshot, simple dressing.

Shifflett, Octavius, Sgt., H, 57th VA, right arm, flesh wound, simple dressing.

Shipley, Presley H., Pvt., C, 140th PA, shoulder and leg, flesh wounds, simple dressing.

Shippey, Leroy, Pvt., C, 64th NY, left hand, flesh wound, simple dressing.

Shirk, Reuben, Cpl., F, 148th PA, both thighs, flesh wound, simple dressing.

Shuey, Daniel, Pvt., C, 148th PA, ear, flesh wound, simple dressing.

Shultes, William A., Pvt., I, 61st NY, left breast, flesh wound, simple dressing.

Shultz, William, Pvt., H, 148th PA.

Siemers, Henry, Pvt., B, 39th NY, right leg, shell, amputated.

Sifford, William A., Pvt., G, 52nd NC, tibia, partial fracture, simple dressing.

Silverthorn, A., Pvt., D, 145th PA, right side, contusion, simple dressing.

Simmon, Andrew, Pvt., K, 2nd FL, left hand, gunshot, simple dressing.

Simmons, Edmund, Pvt., E, 32nd MA, left fingers, gunshot fracture, amputation of fingers.

Simmons, Thomas N., Cpl., C, 14th TN, right leg, gunshot, amputation.

Simpler, Benjamin B., Sgt., E, 1st DE, left arm, gunshot, amputation at middle third.

Simpson, William, Pvt., D, 145th PA, right thigh, flesh wound, simple dressing.

Sisson, Eli, Pvt., B, 145th PA, left arm, flesh wound, simple dressing.

Skeet, John, Pvt., I, 1st U.S. Artillery, right leg, flesh wound, simple dressing.

Skelton, Alex, Pvt., A, 53rd VA, left thigh, flesh wound, simple dressing.

Skinner, George L., Pvt., B, 145th PA, left side, flesh wound, simple dressing.

Slaven, John, Pvt., I, 61st NY, right thigh, flesh wound, simple dressing.

Slinker, Joseph, Sgt., D, 116th PA, shoulder joint, gunshot, amputation of arm.

Smith, Benjamin, Pvt., A, 64th NY, right groin, flesh wound, simple dressing.

Smith, Davis, Pvt., I, 57th NY, spine, fracture, simple dressing.

Smith, Henry E., 1st Sgt., F, 14th VA, left arm, flesh wound, simple dressing.

Smith, Joseph, Pvt., K, 116th PA, left foot, gunshot, simple dressing.

Smith, Owen, Pvt., C, 2nd FL, left foot, spent ball, simple dressing.

Smith, Owen, Pvt., C, 28th MA, left foot, contusion, simple dressing.

Smith, Robert G., Pvt., B, 140th PA, right groin, flesh wound, simple dressing.

Snyder, Charles, Pvt., H, 61st NY, right leg, flesh wound, simple dressing.

Snyder, Richard, Pvt., I, 148th PA, left knee, flesh wound, simple dressing.

Speedy, Joseph, Pvt., E, 148th PA, calf, flesh wound, simple dressing.

Speer, John, Pvt., G, 140th PA, right hand, contusion, simple dressing.

Speer, Robert, Cpl., G, 140th PA, both thighs, contusion, simple dressing.

Speice, Henry, Sgt., I, 53rd PA, right thigh, flesh wound, simple dressing.

Spencer, James A., Pvt., C, 145th PA, left shoulder, flesh wound, simple dressing.

Sprague, Charles, Pvt., A, 4th U.S. Artillery, arm, fracture, amputation.

Sprouce, Henry, Pvt., F, 19th VA, right leg, flesh wound, simple dressing.

Sprowls, Jesse, Pvt., A, 140th PA, right leg, flesh wound, simple dressing.

Stahlman, John, Pvt., I, 148th PA, left leg, flesh wound, simple dressing.

Stallman, Lewis, Pvt., I, 145th PA, right hand, flesh wound, simple dressing.

Stannis, William H., Cpl., G, 27th CT, left shoulder, contusion, simple dressing.

Stanton, Michael, Pvt., A, 88th NY, fever.

States, Oscar, Pvt., B, 1st NY Artillery, left elbow, flesh wound, simple dressing.

Stedwell, John, Pvt., F, 145th PA, left leg, flesh wound, simple dressing.

Steffey, George W., Pvt., F, 148th PA, left hip, shell wound, simple dressing.

Stewart, John W., Pvt., G, 19th VA, right thigh, flesh wound, simple dressing.

Stewart, Robert L., Pvt., G, 140th PA, leg, shell fragment.

Stockwell, James, Pvt., C, 140th PA, left hand, flesh wound, simple dressing.

Stokes, Patrick, Sgt., F, 28th MA, stomach, flesh wound, simple dressing.

Stricker, David L., Lt. Col., 2nd DE, gluteal muscle, gunshot, simple dressing.

Sullivan, Dennis, Pvt., I, 8th AL, lumbar region, flesh wound, simple dressing.

Sullivan, Dennis, Pvt., I, 28th MA, arm & right hand, gunshot, simple dressing.

Sullivan, William, Pvt., C, 28th MA, both ankles, gunshot wound,
    simple dressing.

Swank, George T., 1st Sgt., D, 27th CT, thigh, flesh wound, simple dressing.

Swart, Andrew J., Pvt., D, 140th PA, right leg, flesh wound, simple dressing.

Swearingen, William H., Pvt., F, 140th PA, right arm, flesh wound,
    simple dressing.

Sweet, Benjamin F., Pvt., A, 145th PA, right hip, flesh wound, simple dressing.

Sweetwood, Isaac, Pvt., H, 148th PA, right breast, flesh wound, simple dressing.

Tanzy, James, Pvt., I, 57th NY, left leg, flesh wound, simple dressing.

Tate, Hugh A., Pvt., D, 11th NC, right leg, gunshot fracture, amputation.

Taylor, Abraham S., Pvt., B, 2nd DE, left shoulder, flesh wound, simple dressing.

Taylor, Alvin, Pvt., F, 140th PA, left thigh, flesh wound, simple dressing.

Taylor, George W., Sgt., G, 27th CT, chronic diarrhea.

Taylor, Roland, Pvt., G, 5th NH, knee joint, gunshot fracture, amputation.

Tenner, Richard, Pvt., D, 27th CT, shoulder, flesh wound, simple dressing.

Tevnen, Mark, Sgt., A, 88th NY, calf of leg, flesh wound, simple dressing.

Thayer, J. D., Cpl., C, 4th U.S. Artillery, nose, flesh wound, simple dressing.

Thompson, James, Pvt., G, 148th PA, stomach, contusion, simple dressing.

Thorn, Robert F., Cpl., B, 1st NY Artillery, ankles, contusion, simple dressing.

Tickle, Andrew, Pvt., K, 47th NC, chest & back, contusion, simple dressing.

Timberlake, Frank A., 1st Lt., B, 7th TN, side, flesh wound, simple dressing.

Toppin, Johnson, Pvt., K, 140th PA, left shoulder, flesh wound, simple dressing.

Tormey, John, Pvt., I, 1st U.S. Artillery, left side, gunshot wound, water dressing.

Tosh, Josiah, Pvt., B, 53rd VA, right hip, flesh wound, simple dressing.

Trainor, Bernard, Pvt., A, 69th NY, left shoulder, flesh wound, simple dressing.

Triscut, Charles, Pvt., E, 145th PA, hip & face, flesh wound, simple dressing.

Troy, Norval, Pvt., A, 140th PA, flesh wound, simple dressing.

Truckenmiller, Zechariah, Pvt., C, 148th PA, sick.

Turner, George, Pvt., A, 116th PA, wrist, gunshot, flesh wound, simple dressing.

Turner, William H., Pvt., B, 140th PA, right knee, flesh wound, simple dressing.

Twitchell, Henry C., Cpl., B, 145th PA, thigh, flesh wound, simple dressing.

Union Man (unknown), died July 6.

Vale, Herman, Pvt., F, 61st NY, elbow, fracture, amputation.

Van Camp, Sanders, Pvt., A, 145th PA, wrist & breast, flesh wound, simple dressing.

Vance, Isaac N., 1st Lt., C, 140th PA, left arm, amputated.

VanDyke, James, 1st Sgt., D, 140th PA, back, contusion, simple dressing.

VanHazen, William L., Pvt., I, 61st NY, elbow, flesh wound, simple dressing.

Van Valin, Oliver W., Cpl., B, 148th PA, left foot, flesh wound, simple dressing.

Vath, Charles, Pvt., B, 140th PA, hernia.

Virtue, Robert, Pvt., K, 140th PA, left lung, penetrating, simple dressing.

Vreeland, Michael, 1st Lt., I, 4th MI, right lung, gunshot, simple dressing.

Wadding, Robert M., Pvt., I, 148th PA, left leg, flesh wound, simple dressing.

Wagner, Michael, Pvt., I, 72nd PA, right cheek, contusion, simple dressing.

Walch, Tenny L., Pvt., F, 64th NY, right thigh, flesh wound, simple dressing.

Walker, Alex F., Sgt., H, 2nd FL, chest, flesh wound, simple dressing.

Walker, Benjamin J., Pvt., H, 53rd VA, humerus, gunshot, amputation.

Wallace, Corodon, Pvt., B, 1st NY Artillery, left ankle, flesh wound, simple dressing.

Waller, John R., Pvt., I, 52nd NC, left thigh, gunshot, amputation.

Walsh, Simeon, Pvt., G, 28th MA, left groin, flesh wound, simple dressing.

Ware, Edwin S., Sgt., I, 19th VA, right leg, fracture, amputation.

Ware, George W., Pvt., K, 13th NC, left knee, fracture, amputation.

Warner, Morris, Pvt., K, 13th MS, left knee, gunshot, simple dressing.

Watch, Seymore, Cpl., G, 2nd FL, left groin, gunshot, simple dressing.

Watkins, Benjamin F., Pvt., B, 148th PA, back, contusion, simple dressing.

Watson, Robert, Pvt., C, 28th MA, left hand, flesh wound, simple dressing.

Way, Mariton O., Sgt., B, 145th PA, wrist, flesh wound, simple dressing.

Wayehoff, Daniel, Sgt., A, 140th PA, thigh, flesh wound, simple dressing.

Weil, Siegmund, Sgt., B, 52nd NY, died July 6.

Weiser, Charles W., Pvt., A, 148th PA, calf, flesh wound, simple dressing.

Wells, James K., Pvt., E, 148th PA, left arm and back, flesh wound, simple dressing.

Welsh, Edward, Pvt., B, 2nd DE, right forefinger, flesh wound, simple dressing.

Wert, Charles, Pvt., I, 81st PA, calf, flesh wound, simple dressing.

Wertz, Abraham, Pvt., C, 148th PA, right thigh, flesh wound, simple dressing.

Whalen, Martin, Cpl., D, 66th NY, left thigh, flesh wound, simple dressing.

Whitcraft, Mark, Cpl., C, 2nd DE, calf, flesh wound, simple dressing.

White, Henry P., Pvt., G, 57th VA, left leg and elbow joint, gunshot wounds, resection.

White, John, Cpl., A, 28th MA, left arm, shell wound, simple dressing.

White, Joseph, Pvt., I, 148th PA, back, contusion, simple dressing.

Whittey, Lewis, Pvt., E, 14th GA, right hip, flesh wound, simple dressing.

Willard, Ebon, Pvt., B, 64th NY, right knee, flesh wound, simple dressing.

Williams, Alex L. P., Cpl., 56th VA, both thighs, flesh wound, simple dressing.

Williams, Charles, Pvt., E, 56th VA, thigh, gunshot.

Williams, James A., Pvt., E, 56th VA, hip, gunshot.

Williams, Thomas A., Pvt., E, 56th VA, right hip, flesh wound, simple dressing.

Williams, Tyre G., Pvt., I, 33rd NC, left leg, fracture, amputation.

Williams, William H., Sgt., D, 13th MS, right thigh, fracture, amputation.

Williams, William H., Pvt., D, 140th PA, right shoulder, flesh wound, simple dressing.

Wilson, David, Pvt., D, 116th PA, left foot, gunshot.

Wilson, John, 1st Sgt., G, 140th PA, both arms, flesh wound, simple dressing.

Wise, Samuel, Pvt., C, 140th PA, right hand, flesh wound, simple dressing.

Wood, Daniel F., Sgt., K, 64th NY, right wrist, flesh wound, simple dressing.

Woodruff, George A., Lt., I, 1st U.S. Artillery, intestines.

Yale, Merritt, Pvt., G, 27th CT, chronic diarrhea.

Yale, Thomas G., Pvt., D, 27th CT, left thigh, gunshot, simple dressing.

Yoders, Jacob, Pvt., D, 140th PA, left arm, flesh wound, simple dressing.

Youker, Jefferson, Pvt., C, 140th PA, both thighs, flesh wounds, simple dressing.

Zeiders, James, Sgt., I, 53rd PA, right thigh, flesh wound, simple dressing.

Zibble, Thomas, Cpl., F, 64th NY, hand, flesh wound, simple dressing.

Zook, Samuel K., Brig. Gen., 3rd Brigade, 1st Division, II Corps, abdomen, died July 3.

Appendix 4

The Eliakim Sherrill Collection

Fifty— year-old Colonel Eliakim Sherrill of the 126th New York died in the Spanglers' house on July 4 after being wounded in the bowels the day before while defending Ziegler's Grove during Pickett's Charge. He had been in command of the Third Brigade, Third Division, II Corps. The beloved colonel was honored with a turnout of thousands for his funeral and ceremonies in Geneva, New York, and he is honored still today with his image on the 126th's monument on the Gettysburg battlefield. In addition, Gettysburg Foundation Interim President & CEO and former VSP Technologies Chief Operating Officer David Malgee honors Sherrill every day with an impressive collection of Sherrill's military belongings in Malgee's Gettysburg-area home.

Here is just a portion of Malgee's collection of Sherrill's military paraphernalia:

Gold bullion tassels from a flag captured at Harper's Ferry.
Frock coat (with his name inside the pocket) and vest and pants.
Headquarters flag (Stars and Stripes).
Binoculars and case, suspected to have been used at Gettysburg.
Weather-beaten shoulder boards believed to have been removed from his
 Gettysburg uniform and returned to his widow.
Two pairs of gloves (dress and winter).
Camp towel.
Writing slate and sponge eraser, probably hung on his tent pole for messages.
Campaign hat with restored U.S. emblem.
Spurs, believed to have been worn at Gettysburg.

Col. Eliakim Sherrill, 126th New York

Library of Congress

Malgee's wife, Sherri, is the 2X great-granddaughter of Pvt. Adrian Contant of the 111th New York, who fought at Gettysburg and was in the same brigade as Sherrill, and the Malgees grew up an hour from Geneva where Sherrill lived. "The collection is my direct contact with a genuine Gettysburg hero," Malgee said. "The Sherrill collection is a perfect example of history coming alive when a soldier's personal items can be seen, touched, and even smelled." The emotional connection is real for Malgee, who "get[s] chills thinking about Sherrill dying in the Spangler house among

Gettysburg Foundation Interim President & CEO David Malgee stands amid his museum-like collection of memorabilia in his home. *Sherri Malgee*

These materials were found on the former George Spangler farm in the 1900s and now reside in the collection of David Malgee. *David Malgee*

11th Corps soldiers and not his 2nd Corps friends. Every time I am on the property I think about his life and death and the family he left behind. I am so thankful to the Gettysburg Foundation for restoring the Spangler property."

Malgee's collection is so impressive that he's been asked to join the faculty of the Civil War Institute at Gettysburg College and show artifacts from it, tell the stories behind the soldiers with whom the artifacts are associated, and talk about material culture and its impact on Civil War memory. Malgee also has written a book about Sherrill that's tentatively scheduled for publication in fall 2024. The Malgees have lived in the Gettysburg area since 2011. He is vice chair of the Gettysburg Foundation Board of Directors.

"I pray God I may never see another such a battlefield."

— *XI Corps hospital worker Sgt. William Howe, Company F, 134th New York*[1]

Bibliography

Newspapers

Adams County News (Gettysburg)
Baltimore Sun
Baton Rouge Tri-Weekly Gazette and Comet
Bradford (PA) *Evening Star and Daily Record*
Bridgeport (CT) *Times and Evening Farmer*
Brooklyn Daily Eagle
Brooklyn Standard Union
Buffalo (NY) *Commercial*
Buffalo (NY) *Courier*
Coos (NH) *Republican*
Dayton (OH) *Herald*
Enterprise (KS) *Journal*
Galion (OH) *Inquirer*
Gettysburg Compiler
Gettysburg Star and Sentinel
Gettysburg Times
Grand Junction (CO) *Daily Sentinel*
Greensboro (NC) *Daily News*
Louisiana Democrat (Alexandria)
Marion (OH) *Star*
Meadville (PA) *Evening Republican*
New York Herald
New York Sun
New York Times

New York Times Union
New York Tribune
Norwalk (OH) *Reflector*
Philadelphia Inquirer
Philadelphia Times
Schenectady (NY) *Evening Star and Times*
Shasta (CA) *Courier*
Summit County Beacon (Akron, OH)
The Caucasian (Alexandria, LA)
Toledo (OH) *Blade*
Vermont Journal
Washington (D.C.) *Evening Star*
Western Kansas World (WaKeeney)

Government Documents

A. C. Register 96, 2nd Army Corps, Army of the Potomac, Sept. 1, 1862 to July 1863, List of Wounded of the 1st Division Hospital, II Corps at the Battle of Gettysburg PA the 3 Day of July 1863.

A. C. Register 97 July 3, 1863–Feb. 6, 1864.

"Annual Reports for 1874 Made to the Sixty-First General Assembly of the State of Ohio." Columbus, 1875.

Bachelder, John. Maps of the Battlefield of Gettysburg. Library of Congress. 1863 and 1876.

Cultural Landscape Report for Gettysburg National Military Park Record of Treatment. Vol. 1. Boston: National Park Service, 2018.

Ladd, Audrey J. and David L. Ladd. *The Bachelder Papers: Gettysburg in Their Own Words*. Vols. 1 and 3. Dayton, OH: Morningside Press, 1994.

Map of the Railroads of the State of New York. Library of Congress. 1863.

Oversight Hearing on Gettysburg National Military Park General Management Plan and Proposed Visitors Center, Feb. 11, 1999. Washington, D.C.: U.S. Government Printing Office, 1999.

Pennsylvania Register 554 (*Register of the Sick and Wounded*). Washington D.C.: U.S. Surgeon General's Office.

The Medical and Surgical History of the Civil War. Vol. XI. Wilmington, NC: Broadfoot Publishing Company, 1991.

The Medical and Surgical History of the War of the Rebellion 1861-1865. Washington, D.C.: Government Printing Office, 1870-1875 and 1883.

United States Sanitary Commission. "Report on the Operations of the Sanitary Commission During and After the Battles at Gettysburg" in *Documents of the US Sanitary Commission*. Vol. 2, nos. 61-95. New York: 1866.

United States Surgeon General's Office. *The Medical and Surgical History of the War of the Rebellion (1861-65)*. Washington, D.C.: Government Printing Office, 1875.

United States War Department. *War of the Rebellion: Official Records of the Union and Confederate Armies*. Washington, D.C.: Government Printing Office, 1880-1901.

Autobiographies, Biographies, Published Personal Papers

Brinton, Daniel G. "From Chancellorsville to Gettysburg, a Doctor's Diary." *The Pennsylvania Magazine of History and Biography*. Harrisburg, PA: University of Pennsylvania Press, 1965.

Corby, William, C.S.C. (Congregation of Holy Cross). *Memoirs of Chaplain Life: Three Years With the Irish Brigade in the Army of the Potomac*. New York: Fordham University Press, 1992.

"Diary of William R. Kiefer, Drummer Co. F 153rd PA Vols. 1862-63." Easton (PA) Area Public Library.

"Diary of Rev. Philip W. Melick, Chaplain, 153rd PA Vols. 1862-63." Easton (PA) Area Public Library.

"Diary of Francis Stofflet, Private Co. D 153rd PA. Vols. 1862-63." Easton (PA) Area Public Library.

Dunkelman, Mark, and Margaret Smith, trans. "Civil War Letters From Emory Sweetland, Little Valley, Cattaraugus County, New York, to His Wife Mary Jane (Holdridge) 1862-1865."

East, Charles, ed. *Sarah Morgan: The Civil War Diary of a Southern Woman*. New York: Simon & Schuster, 1991.

Fields, Annie. *Life and Letters of Harriet Beecher Stowe*. Boston: Houghton Mifflin, 1897.

Hedrick, David T., and Gordon Barry Davis Jr., eds. *I'm Surrounded by Methodists: Diary of John H. W. Stuckenberg Chaplain of the 145th Pennsylvania Volunteer Infantry*. Gettysburg: Thomas Publications, 1995.

Holland, I. C. Family history provided by the Kingdom of Callaway Historical Society. Fulton, MO.

Holland, Thomas C. Journal provided by Kingdom of Callaway Historical Society. Fulton, MO, and the Gary Altheiser family.

Howard, Oliver O. *Autobiography of Oliver Otis Howard*. Vol. 1. New York: The Baker and Taylor Company, 1907.

Hunt, Henry J. *Battles and Leaders of the Civil War*. Vol. 3. New York: The Century Company, 1884.

Meade, George Gordon. *With Meade at Gettysburg*. Philadelphia: The John C. Winston Company, 1930.

Presidents, Soldiers, Statesmen. Vol. 2. New York, Toledo, and Chicago: H. H. Hardesty & Co., 1899.

Sawyer, Merrill C., Betty Sawyer, and Timothy C. Sawyer, trans. *Letters From a Civil War Surgeon: Dr. William Child of the Fifth New Hampshire Volunteers*. Solon, ME: Polar Bear & Company, 2001.

Schantz, F. J. F. "Recollections of Visitations at Gettysburg After the Great Battle in July, 1863." *Reflections on the Battle of Gettysburg*, Vol. 13, No. 6. Lebanon County, PA, Historical Society: 1890.

Smith, Jane, diary, Gettysburg National Military Park.

Stowe, Charles Edward and Harriet Beecher Stowe. *Life of Harriet Beecher Stowe: Compiled From Her Letters and Journals.* New York: Houghton, Mifflin and Company, 1889.

Strickland, Chuck and Peggy Strickland. *The Road to Red House.* Punta Gorda, FL: BookLocker. com Inc., 2007.

Warner, George H. *Military Records of Schoharie County Veterans of Four Wars.* Albany, NY: Weed, Parsons & Company, 1891.

Campaigns and Battles

Baumgartner, Richard A. *Buckeye Blood: Ohio at Gettysburg.* Huntington, WV: Blue Acorn Press, 2003.

Bigelow, John. *The Peach Orchard Gettysburg.* Minneapolis: Kimball-Storer Company, 1910.

Busey, John W., and David G. Martin. *Regimental Strengths and Losses at Gettysburg.* Baltimore: Gateway Press Inc., 1982.

Busey, John W., and Travis W. Busey. *Confederate Casualties at Gettysburg, a Comprehensive Record.* Jefferson, NC: McFarland & Company, 2017.

Busey, Travis W., and John W. Busey. *Union Casualties at Gettysburg: A Comprehensive Record.* Jefferson, NC: McFarland & Company, 2011.

Coco, Gregory A. *A Vast Sea of Misery: A History and Guide to the Union and Confederate Field Hospitals at Gettysburg July 1–November 20, 1863.* Gettysburg: Thomas Publications, 1988.

Gallagher, Gary W., ed. *The Second Day at Gettysburg: Essays on Confederate and Union Leadership.* Kent, OH: The Kent State University Press, 1993.

Jacobs, Michael. *Notes on the Rebel Invasion of Maryland and Pennsylvania and the Battle of Gettysburg.* Philadelphia: J. B. Lippincott & Co., 1864.

Pfanz, Harry W. *Gettysburg: The Second Day.* Chapel Hill, NC: University of North Carolina Press, 1987.

Reed, Merl E., ed. "The Gettysburg Campaign—A Louisiana Lieutenant's Eye-Witness Account." In *Pennsylvania History: A Journal of Mid-Atlantic Studies.* University Park, PA: Penn State University Press, 1963.

Reid, Whitelaw. *Two Witnesses at Gettysburg: The Personal Accounts of Whitelaw Reid and A. J. L. Fremantle.* Malden, MA: Wiley-Blackwell, 2009.

Smith, Jacob. *Camps and Campaigns of the 107th Regiment Ohio Volunteer Infantry, From August, 1862, to July, 1865.* Navarre, OH: Indian River Graphics, 2000.

Unit Histories

Ames, Nelson. *Captain Nelson Ames' Battery G*. Marshalltown, IA: Marshall Printing Company, 1900.

Baker, Levi W. *History of the Ninth Massachusetts Battery*. South Framingham, MA: Lakeview Press, 1888.

Brown, J. Willard. *The Signal Corps, USA, in the War of the Rebellion*. Boston: U.S. Veteran Signal Corps Association, 1896.

Child, William, M.D., *A History of the Fifth Regiment New Hampshire Volunteers, in the American Civil War, 1861-1865*. Bristol, NH: 1893.

Clark, Walter, ed. *Histories of the Several Regiments and Battalions From North Carolina in the Great War 1861-'65*. Goldsboro, NC: Nash Brothers, 1901.

Cowles, Luther E., ed. *History of the Fifth Massachusetts Battery*. Boston, 1902.

Divine, John E. *8th Virginia Infantry*. Lynchburg, VA: H. E. Howard Inc., 1984.

Dunkelman, Mark. *Brothers One and All*. Baton Rouge, LA: Louisiana State University Press, 2004.

Frederick, Gilbert. *The Story of a Regiment: A Record of the Military Services of the Fifty-Seventh New York State Volunteer Infantry in the War of the Rebellion*. Chicago: The Fifty-Seventh Veteran Association, 1895.

History of the Fifth Massachusetts Battery. Boston: Luther E. Cowles, 1902.

Ivanoff, Carolyn. *We Fought at Gettysburg; Firsthand Accounts by the Survivors of the 17th Connecticut Volunteer Infantry*. Gettysburg, PA: Gettysburg Publishing, 2023.

Kiefer, William R. *History of the One Hundred and Fifty-Third Regiment Pennsylvania Volunteers Infantry: Which Was Recruited in Northampton County, Pa., 1862-1863*. Easton, PA: 1909.

Kirkwood, Ronald D. *"Too Much for Human Endurance": The George Spangler Farm Hospitals and the Battle of Gettysburg*. El Dorado Hills, CA: Savas Beatie, 2019.

Livermore, Thomas L. *Days and Events 1860-1866*. Boston and New York: Houghton Mifflin Company, 1920.

Morhous, Henry C. *Reminiscences of the 123d Regiment, N.Y.S.V.* Greenwich, NY: People's Journal Book and Job Office, 1879.

Muffly, Joseph Wendel, ed. *The Story of Our Regiment: A History of the 148th Pennsylvania Vols*. Des Moines, IA: The Kenyon Printing & Manufacturing Company, 1904.

Mulholland, St. Clair A. *The 116th Pennsylvania Volunteers in the War of the Rebellion 1861-1865*. Philadelphia: F. McManus Jr. & Company, 1903.

Osborn, Hartwell, et al. *Trials and Triumphs: The Record of the 55th Ohio Volunteer Infantry*. Chicago, IL: A. C. McClurg & Co., 1904.

Powelson, Benjamin Franklin. *History of Company K of the 140th Pennsylvania Volunteers*. Steubenville, OH: Carnahan Printing Company, 1906.

Priest, Granville. *History of the New Hampshire Surgeons in the War of the Rebellion*. New Hampshire Association of Military Surgeons. Concord, NH: Ira C. Evans Co., 1906.

Pula, James S. *Under the Crescent Moon with the XI Corps in the Civil War*. Vol. 2 of *From the Defenses of Washington to Chancellorsville, 1862-1863*. El Dorado Hills, CA: Savas Beatie, 2017.

Salmon, Verel R. *Common Men in the War for the Common Man: History of the 145th Pennsylvania Volunteers*. Bloomington, IN: Xlibris Corp., 2013.

Sawyer, Franklin. *A Military History of the 8th Regiment Ohio Vol. Inf'y*. Cleveland: Fairbanks & Company, 1881.

Stewart, Robert Laird. *A History of the One Hundred and Fortieth Regiment Pennsylvania Volunteers*. Philadelphia: 140th Regimental Association, 1912.

Stocker, Jeffrey D. *We Fought Desperate: A History of the 153rd Pennsylvania Volunteer Infantry Regiment*, 2004.

Underwood, Adin Ballou. *The Three Years' Service of the Thirty-Third Mass. Infantry Regiment, 1862-1865*. Boston: A. Williams & Company, 1881.

Other Publications

Ball, Edward. *Life of a Klansman: A Family History in White Supremacy*. New York: Farrar, Straus and Giroux, 2020.

Baughman, A. J. *History of Seneca County Ohio*. Chicago and New York: Lewis Publishing Company, 1911.

Crary, Catherine S. *Dear Belle: Letters from a Cadet & Officer to his Sweetheart, 1858-1865*. Middletown, CT: Wesleyan University Press, 1965.

Diagnostic and Statistical Manual of Mental Disorders-II. Washington, D.C.: American Psychiatric Association, 1968.

Dickinson County Cemetery Survey, Center Township, Mount Hope Cemetery. Abilene, KS: 1982.

Edson, Obed. *History of Chautauqua County, New York*. Boston, MA: W. A. Fergusson & Company, 1894.

Encyclopedia of Biography of Illinois, Vol. 3. Chicago: The Century Publishing and Engraving Company, 1902.

Fauci, Anthony, et al, *Harrison's Principles of Internal Medicine*. New York: McGraw Hill Medical, 2008.

Faust, Drew Gilpin. *This Republic of Suffering: Death and the American Civil War*. New York: Vintage Books, 2008.

Flannery, Michael A. *Civil War Pharmacy: A History*. Carbondale, IL: Southern Illinois University Press, 2017.

Heller, William J. *History of Northampton County Pennsylvania and The Grand Valley of the Lehigh*, Vol. 2. Boston, New York, and Chicago: The American Historical Society, 1920.

Marvel, William. *Andersonville: The Last Depot.* Chapel Hill, NC: The University of North Carolina Press, 1994.

Merenoff, Barry N. *The Mechanical Advantage: Reference Books for the Pulley & Hay Carrier Collector-Hay Carrier Systems.* New Haven, MI: The Mechanical Advantage, 2003.

Morris, Roy Jr., *The Better Angel: Walt Whitman in the Civil War.* New York: Oxford University Press, 2000.

Nicholson, John P. *Pennsylvania at Gettysburg: Ceremonies at the Dedication of the Monuments Erected by the Commonwealth of Pennsylvania*, Vol. 2. Harrisburg, PA: 1914.

Ross, Peter. *A History of Long Island, From Its Earliest Settlement to the Present Time*, Vol. 2. New York and Chicago: The Lewis Publishing Company, 1902.

Smart, James G., ed. *A Radical View: The "Agate" Dispatches of Whitelaw Reid 1861-1865*, Vol. 2. Memphis, TN: Memphis State University Press, 1976.

Warner, George H., *Military Records of Schoharie County Veterans of Four Wars.* Albany, NY: 1891.

Wittenmyer, Annie. *Under the Guns: A Woman's Reminiscences of the Civil War.* Boston: E. B. Stillings & Co., 1895.

Articles

A. F. C. "Horrors of Battle." An interview with National Lightner. *Washington, D.C. Evening Star*, 1893.

Croop, Donald W. "The Valiant Men of Battery M." Wilson Historical Society, Wilson, NY.

Hale, Maj. Charles A. "With Colonel Cross in the Gettysburg Campaign." Gettysburg National Military Park.

Holland, Thomas C. "With Armistead at Gettysburg." *Confederate Veteran Magazine* 29, 1921.

Lange, Katie. "Dog Tag History: How the Tradition & Nickname Started." U.S. Department of Defense.

"Re-burial of Union Dead in the National Cemetery." Adams County Historical Society.

"The Innovative Career of Surgeon Benjamin Howard." National Museum of Civil War Medicine.

Warren, Leander H. "Recollections of the Battle of Gettysburg." Adams County Historical Society.

Websites

www.ancestry.com
www.answers.com
www.archive.org
www.archives.sbu.edu
www.battlefields.org
www.civildiscourse-historyblog.com
www.civilwardata.com
www.civilwarhome.com

www.civilwarmed.org

www.defense.gov

www.dmna.ny.gov

www.ehistory.osu.edu

www.familydoctor.org

www.findagrave.com

www.fleaglass.com

www.fold3.com

www.gilderlehrman.org

www.haytrolleyheaven.com

www.history.com

www.hopkinsmedicine.org

www.in2013dollars.com

www.legendsofkansas.com

www.loc.gov

www.lovettsvillehistoricalsociety.org

www.naturalheritage.state.pa.us

www.newspapers.com

www.nih.gov

www.nps.gov

www.npshistory.com

www.ny.gov

www.nytimes.com

www.owlwebdev.com

www.seventeenthcvi.org

www.vermontcivilwar.org

www.vintagekansascity.com

www.webmd.com

www.wikipedia.com

www.wordpress.com

Index

Acknowledgments

Guides at the George Spangler farm thank and honor the Gettysburg Foundation in every presentation and tour of the farm so it's only right that the first thank-you in a book about this farm should also be to the Foundation, the property's owner. Foundation leadership—including current Immediate Past Chair Barbara Finfrock—had the vision in 2008 to pay almost $2 million to save the farm from development and preserve it for visitation and future generations. Her successors have maintained that vision by spending millions more to return the historic and critically important farm in the battle of Gettysburg to its 1863 glory. Gettysburg Foundation, we thank you and honor you for your foresight and allowing us to visit this property today.

This book contains subjects about which I have little knowledge, so experts in the field stepped in and bailed me out. Because of that, I will always be grateful for the expertise provided by Licensed Battlefield Guides Dr. Richard Schroeder and Nurse Anesthetist Fran Feyock (Armistead's death); Dr. Ryan Neff (hernias); Dr. Jon Willen (resections); Dr. G. Terry Sharrar (diarrhea); psychotherapist Michele Montenegro (Capt. Samuel M. Sprole); Historic Gettysburg Adams County Board of Directors member and retired Army Col. Greg Kaufmann (the Spanglers' hay fork); Barbara Finfrock (the easement on the farm); and invertebrate zoologist Betsy Leppo (the farm's vernal pool). Feyock also edited and offered insight on a chapter that I sent to him when I wanted to make sure I got it right. Likewise, widely respected Gettysburg experts and authors Carol Reardon, Wayne Motts, and Britt Isenberg studied the book before publication and offered ideas for improvements. I'm grateful to have such expertise. Reardon, Isenberg, and Spangler guide Howard Burrell wrote advance praise for the back cover and Motts shared his vast knowledge on Capt. Sprole and helped me write that chapter.

Burrell and another Spangler guide, James P. Fielden, were my editors as I prepared the book to send to publisher Savas Beatie. Both have intimate knowledge of the farm so they made subtle suggestions of what would be good to cover, corrected errors, studied Powers Hill with me, and provided photos. Visitors to the farm are in excellent hands with Jim and Howard and every guide out there as well as their lively and respected boss: farm coordinator Paul Semanek. The guides have a passion for the farm and sharing its story. Gettysburg Foundation Vice President of Facilities Brian Shaffer oversees the property and—just as he did with the first book—answered my questions in detail. Even more Foundation help came from Interim President & CEO David Malgee, who owns a museum-like collection of Civil War-era artifacts from Col. Eliakim Sherrill and the battle itself.

John D. Hoptak of the National Park Service found materials for me in the Park Service's archives and then was patient and supportive with my frequent questions, never failing to answer. Hoptak replaced the well-known and highly respected John Heiser in the archives and continues to maintain Heiser's high standards, a monumental feat indeed. Christopher Gwinn and Troy Harman are NPS legends with their knowledge of the battle of Gettysburg and they, too, always seemed ready to help when asked, as was the retired Heiser when I needed to call on him in his post-NPS career. Also exceedingly helpful was NPS volunteer Tom Greaney, who assists Hoptak in the archives.

Sometimes you get fortunate when the research of others clears the path for you, such as was most definitely the case with this book with authors Mark Dunkelman (154th New York), Carolyn Ivanoff (17th Connecticut), Jeff Stocker (153rd Pennsylvania), and Chuck and Peggy Strickland (Sgt. Francis Strickland, 154th New York). Their years of high-quality work, research, and dedication appear throughout this book, and readers and I are most fortunate beneficiaries of their knowledge and dedication.

Critical help came from most corners of the modern, beautiful, and expansive new Adams County Historical Society building, including from Andrew Dalton, Tim Smith, Abbie Hoffman, Rodger Rex, and Roger Heller. Terry Reimer at the National Museum of Civil War Medicine in Frederick, Maryland, was her usual friendly, knowledgeable, and helpful self, as was curator Andrew Pankratz at the Dickinson County Heritage Center in Abilene, Kansas, and Marjean Deines of the Trego County Historical Society in WaKeeney, Kansas, both of whom spent hours helping me figure out Daniel Spangler's travels throughout Kansas. Daniel's former farm in western Kansas has been owned by only three people since Daniel was granted it in the late 1800s—Daniel, his son, George, and current owner Mike

McGinnis. Son George told Mike all about the property and Daniel when Mike purchased it, and Mike took the time to talk to me and then show George and Elizabeth's 2X great-grandson Calvin Spangler around it, including where Daniel lived in a dugout in the side of a hill. As mentioned earlier in the book, Calvin's uncle Norman Spangler—George and Elizabeth's great-grandson—provided many stories of Daniel's time in Kansas.

Clarence Andrew grew up on the former Spangler farm and was involved in the sale of his family's farm to the Gettysburg Foundation and he has been a reliable source of information and guidance as we seek to further understand the history of the property that he lived on for decades. Andrew owns a farm today on Blacksmith Shop Road, the northern tip of which borders today's George Spangler farm. Ron and Mike Shealer and their sister Susan Hartman grew up at the base of Powers Hill and they were exceedingly thoughtful in leading me and Susan's daughter, Allison Hartman, on a tour that included all sides and the top and base of that hill. They greatly expanded my knowledge of the land.

Former Harrisburg *Patriot-News* co-worker Derek Wachter once again did the maps for this book, and I'm sure they will receive just as much praise as the first book's maps did. Derek's maps are essential to the telling of the full story of this farm. Witness tree expert Greg Gober spent a Sunday afternoon walking the 80-acre farm with me and my wife, Barb, and found four trees that he estimated are close, but not quite, witness trees and one swamp white oak that most definitely is at 180 to 200 years old. Then retired Pennsylvania forester Bruce Kile visited the farm with me and without knowing anything about another tree expert's thoughts he, too, estimated the swamp white oak's age at 180 to 200 years.

Other critical and greatly appreciated help came from Gettysburg legend Dean Shultz, whose knowledge of the area is probably close to unmatched; Confederate soldier descendant Robert Russell "Rusty" Cloninger Jr.; Shari Gollnitz of the McClurg Museum/Chautauqua County Historical Society in Westfield, New York; Kingdom of Callaway Historical Society in Fulton, Missouri; attorney and historian Charles T. Joyce of *Military Images* magazine for the photo and scholarship on 1st Sgt. Henry Seas of the 82nd Ohio; Karin J. Bohleke, director of the Fashion Archives and Museum of Shippensburg University; Gettysburg photography guru William A. Frassanito; Robert H. Lowing of Lancaster, Pennsylvania, on his 2X great-grandfather Chaplain Henry Dyer Lowing of the 154th New York; Bob Mcilhenny of Historic Gettysburg Adams County; Gettysburg College Research and Instruction Librarian Clinton Baugess; Diana Lakomiak and Chuck Hollabaugh of The Museum Bookstore at the Gettysburg National Military Park Museum and Visitor Center; Jim Schmick of the Civil War and More bookstore in Mechanicsburg, Pennsylvania, and his deep knowledge of the Harrisburg area;

Research Librarian Walter Dembowski, Trumbull Library in Connecticut; the Blue & Gray Hospital Association; and the countless and far-flung Civil War round tables and historical societies that have so kindly invited me to share the Spangler story with them.

Savas Beatie Media Specialist Sarah Closson plays a kind of Tetris in her position every day at work to balance the demands and needs of dozens of authors while at the same time arranging speaking engagements for them and handling so many other duties. And just like the best Tetris players, she makes everything fit in just the right place. Savas Beatie authors are fortunate to have her on their side. Savas Beatie Managing Director Ted Savas took a chance several years ago accepting a book on a farm that he had never heard of and is now so invested in and appreciative of Spangler that he not only is printing Book 2 but also writing the Foreword for it. He is the perfect person to write that Foreword. Veronica Kane and I both live in the Pittsburgh area, so I was pleased that she was the one who brought this book to life with her outstanding design of each page. She also surprised me by working magic and getting in a few poor-quality photos that I didn't think would make it. Copy editor David Snyder is a wordsmith with a knack for smooth sentence structure, and he bailed me out many times with those skills. Happily, David is a Pittsburgh-area native, so including myself, Pittsburgh folks were the most integral in the production of every aspect of this book. Also, marketing specialist Sarah Keeney was instrumental in the design of the book's cover.

Finally, I have been married to the lovely Barbara Jean Mann of South Haven, Michigan, for 47 years as of this writing, the last eight of which she has patiently put up with me as I almost single-mindedly focused on the George Spangler farm. We have developed the term "book brain" for when I reset into this mode of tunnel vision and she carries on and handles just about everything else in our lives while I research and write. Barb has grown her own strong love and appreciation for the farm and its descendants, and for that plus her kindness, love, patience, and 47 years of marriage, I dedicate this book to her. For better or worse for Barb, I'll be around a lot more now with the completion of Spangler Book No. 2.

About the Author

Ronald D. Kirkwood is retired after a 40-year career as an editor and writer in newspapers and magazines, including *USA TODAY*, the *Baltimore Sun*, *Harrisburg* (PA) *Patriot-News*, *York* (PA) *Daily Record*, and *Midland* (MI) *Daily News*. Ron edited national magazines for *USA TODAY Sports* and was NFL editor for *USA TODAY Sports Weekly*. He won state, regional, and national awards and managed the copy desk in Harrisburg when the newspaper won a Pulitzer Prize in 2012. Ron has been a Gettysburg Foundation docent at the George Spangler Farm Civil War Field Hospital Site since it opened in 2013. He is a native of Dowagiac/Sister Lakes, MI, and a graduate of Central Michigan University, where he has returned as guest speaker for journalism classes as part of the school's Hearst Visiting Professionals series. Ron and his wife of almost 50 years, Barbara, live in the deer-filled countryside near Murrysville, PA, just outside of Pittsburgh.